Also by Walt Odets

*In the Shadow of the Epidemic:*
*Being HIV-Negative in the Age of AIDS*

# Out of the Shadows

# Out of the Shadows

## Reimagining Gay Men's Lives

## Walt Odets

Farrar, Straus and Giroux   New York

Farrar, Straus and Giroux
120 Broadway, New York 10271

Printed in the United States of America
First edition, 2019

Library of Congress Cataloging-in-Publication Data
Names: Odets, Walt, author.
Title: Out of the shadows : reimagining gay men's lives / Walt Odets.
Description: First edition. | New York : Farrar, Straus and Giroux, [2019] |
    Includes bibliographical references and index.
Identifiers: LCCN 2018050164 | ISBN 9780374285852 (hardcover)
Subjects: LCSH: Gay men—United States. | Gay men—Identity.
Classification: LCC HQ76.2.U5 O326 2019 | DDC 306.76/620973—dc23
LC record available at https://lccn.loc.gov/2018050164

Designed by Jonathan D. Lippincott

www.fsgbooks.com
www.twitter.com/fsgbooks • www.facebook.com/fsgbooks

1   3   5   7   9   10   8   6   4   2

For the hundreds of gay men I have worked with over the past thirty years, for the hundreds of thousands of gay men who have fought to be themselves against all odds, for Matthias, and for Robb and for his parents, Charlotte and Arthur, who supported him in being himself.

# Contents

*Acknowledgments*   xi
*A Word to the Reader*   xiii

Introduction   3

1. Are Gay Men Homosexuals?   19
   What Is a Homosexual?
   The Story of Larry
   A Study from Indiana
   The Significance of Words
   The Story of Stuart
   The Developmental Gender Split: The Story of Felix
   Sexual Expression of the Gay Sensibility
   It Is Not the Cow That Makes the Frycook

2. Stigma and Shame   60
   The Story of Gabriel Fernandez
   The Consequences of Stigmatization
   The Story of Ronald Reagan
   What Is Shame?
   The Story of Peter
   Sex and Shame

3. Our Tripartite Communities Today   75
   Three Groups of Men Defined
       The Older Group: The Story of Luis
       The Middle Group: The Stories of Franklin and Richard
       The Younger Group: The Story of Jason

Young Men and the Legacy of the Condom Code
PrEP and the Legacy of the Condom Code

4. The Significance of Early-Life Experience   118
Erik Erikson and the Story of Quentin
The Eight Ages of Man
    1. Basic Trust vs. Basic Mistrust
    2. Autonomy vs. Shame and Doubt
    3. Initiative vs. Guilt
    4. Industry vs. Inferiority
    5. Identity vs. Role Confusion
    6. Intimacy vs. Isolation
    7. Generativity vs. Stagnation
    8. Ego Integrity vs. Despair
A Word for the Young

5. Some Obstructions to Self-Discovery and Self-Realization:
Diagnosis, Isolation, and Grief   146
Diagnosis: The Story of Paul
Isolation: The Story of Sean
Complicated Grief and Guilt: The Story of Harry
The Aftermath of Harry's Aftermath
What *About* Harry's Drinking?

6. Emerging from Trauma, Loss, and Isolation   186
What Is Trauma?
How Trauma and Loss Interact: The Story of Aaron
Our Great Unmentionable
The Four Stages of Recovery: The Story of Ralph
    Stage One: Emerging from Isolation
    Stage Two: Safety
    Stage Three: Grieving and Talking Through
    Stage Four: Working Through and the Story of Bill

7. Gay Men's Relationships   217
The Hope
The Hopelessness: The Story of Michael

The Fear: The Story of Amado
The Fantasy: The Story of Brice
Ways That Gay Relationships Work
Sex
Sexual Interest and the Story of Lester and Bill
Attraction and the Loss of Attraction
A Songbook for Young Men

8. The Life and Times of Matthias Johnston    257

An Afterword for Young Men's Futures    299

*Notes*    303
*Index*    333

# Acknowledgments

During the research and writing of this book, I was fortunate in having extraordinary assistance, feedback, and support from many friends and colleagues: Donald Abrams, James and Debra Allan, Robert Aude, John Badanes, Ella Baff, Jon Robin Baitz, Jerry Ballew, Elaine Baskin, Marianne Baskin, Andre Bishop, Connie Booth, Francesca Bowyer, Daniel and Beverly Brown, David Buchanan, Richard Burd, Joy Carlin, Peggy DeCoursey, Daniel DiVittorio, John Ewing, Gary Feldman, George Getzel, John Glusman, Judy Goldberg, Justin Hecht, Michael Hickcox, David Hollander, Travis Salway Hottes, Philip Keddy, Brett Kennedy, Ken Krechmer, John Lahr, George Lane, Rob Levy, Larry Long, Craig Mole, John Nienow, Ondine Norman, Todd Pearson, Beth Philips, Hillary Reinis, Andrew Ross, Sepha Schiffman, Jack Shallow, Brad Smith, Leslie Sobelson, Keith and Rosmarie Waldrop, Dianne Woods, and Stephen Zollman. I express my deepest appreciation to all.

I would also like to express my gratitude to Gillian MacKenzie and Jonathan Galassi. Both have been extraordinarily generous with their insight, guidance, and support, and they are responsible for bringing the book to its final form and to publication.

# A Word to the Reader

I have written *Out of the Shadows* for a number of audiences, most obviously gay men of all ages who have grown up in America. Among these men, I think particularly of those who have survived the early AIDS epidemic, both contracting and avoiding HIV; men, young and old, raised in stigmatizing families and communities; and young gay men who are now coming out into the challenges of slowly shifting social values in some parts of America, the current "late" HIV epidemic, and socially incoherent gay communities that publicly voice a highly assimilationist political agenda that excludes too many, an agenda that many younger men thoughtfully—or only intuitively—reject.

In addition to my most obvious audiences, I believe that straight men and women have been and will be engaged by the discussion. Despite our differences, gay lives are about nothing more or less than human thoughts, feelings, and needs, mostly shared and familiar to all. In early readings of this book, most women have experienced a strong identification with the stories of gay men, in part because of the stigmatization and marginalization the two groups share. On purely psychological matters, several discussions have also been meaningful for female readers, including my examinations of the developmental roots of conventional gender differences, the socially constructed "male" identity that has so long baffled women, and the idea of a "gay sensibility" as a blend of conventionally female and male sensibilities. Although I am not writing specifically to women—this is, after all, a book about gay men—my admiration for the insight and compassion women contribute to our lives cannot be overstated: the so-called feminine sensibility is everything that makes loving, intimate relationships possible, gay or straight.

Finally, I write for fellow psychotherapists, gay and straight, who work with gay men. Gay men engage in psychotherapy at about three times the rate of heterosexual men, and for good reason. The complexity of growing up gay in a heterosexist society; distorting developmental influences, including the early and late HIV epidemics; and ongoing marginalization in adult life all often conspire to make therapy a useful endeavor. The more difficult journey gay men travel also provides benefits, for it nurtures a capacity for emotional introspection that is personally valuable and productive in therapy. To be truly helpful, the therapist must understand the issues clearly and without historically rooted misconceptions and prejudice: too much of how we have traditionally thought about gay developmental experience and "being gay" is still evident in current psychological theory and practice. I hope my examination of gay developmental issues, and my reconstruction of what it means to be gay, will be useful to both psychotherapists and those they work with.

Because the general reader may find some of the more purely psychological material technical, I have placed much of it in clearly indicated endnotes to maintain the accessibility and flow of the main text. I hope all psychotherapists and other readers with an interest in psychodynamic, developmental, and narrative psychology will read this material. My use of notes is not intended to suggest that the discussions placed there are merely peripheral or of secondary importance.

Within these covers, I tell my personal story and the stories of twenty-three other men. All are derived from personal memories, from my experience with three decades of therapy with hundreds of gay men, from friends, and from the approximately forty interviews I conducted during the planning and writing of the book. Unless otherwise identified, all the stories, including the personal ones, are constructed in a manner that conceals identities and ensures privacy. The individuals depicted are generally composites of two or more men, and the stories are told with fictional details and events to further disguise identity. Confidentiality for therapy patients is particularly important, and the stories of those in therapy are never drawn from a single individual, but from a number of men who shared similar issues and life experience. All identifying information has been changed by fictionalizing names, specific family backgrounds, ages, occupations, dates, and locations.

Berkeley, 2018

# Out of the Shadows

# Introduction

Many years ago, Will came to see me for therapy to help him come out as gay. He was a retired dentist, and he wasn't nineteen, or twenty-nine, or even forty-nine. "Why now?" was my obvious first question, and his answer was succinct: "I was waiting for my wife to die," and she had. Will told me he had loved, but had never been in love with, her, that they had been "best friends" for five decades. Now, he wanted to talk about the life he had neglected, for he had never had an experience with another man. "Before I die, I would like to *be in love*, and I know—I have known forever—that could only happen with a man." Will was sweet, gentle, and likable, but he had a touch of the unfocused, empty stare of a person who was starving and had suffered. He *was* starving, starving emotionally, and even as he energetically outlined new possibilities for his life, I could feel his hopelessness hanging in the air between us. As I listened to his story, I hoped I was not mirroring back that hopelessness, but I was certainly feeling it. And I was feeling helpless, for I had seen many men reconstruct their lives for the better, but had never seen that transformation begin at the age of seventy-four. How could I help a man who had put nearly his entire life—put *himself*—on hold for almost a lifetime?

Then I thought, if Will had only five or ten years left to find a new life and live as Will, the effort would be worth it. He was intelligent, he had access to his feelings, and he was certainly motivated, and for now, I would simply sit and listen. The central task would be to help him find some self-acceptance, by allowing him to be himself and be heard. He had not yet forgiven himself for being gay, and he had not forgiven himself for having lived as if he were *not* gay. "I was a coward, and I lived like one. I sometimes hate myself for that," he said at our first meeting. Born in 1923 into a religious Arkansas family, being gay seemed impossible, too frightening to even consider. Instead, he decided on a life with Emily, his best high school friend, whom he loved and respected. Emily had always known that Will was complex, and that he lived in some kind of perpetual sadness. But they had never even broached the idea of his being gay, and she never understood what his sadness was about. Will was loving and kind, and he was funny, and Emily simply accepted him. It was as if they had decided on a life together, but on opposite banks of a shared river they both cherished. With Emily now gone, Will badly needed to reveal himself to someone, which for now would be me. As I looked at him sitting in the chair, I tried to think hopefully that he might find a boyfriend and have some years of the life he should always have had.

The terrible outcome was that two months into our work Will was diagnosed with pancreatic cancer, and four months later he died in the ICU at Sutter Hospital. He asked me to visit him there, which I did several times. We sat mostly in silence, but my presence was clearly meaningful to him, for I had become his internal companion, the first who knew Will as *Will*. On my last visit—which would be the last fifteen minutes of his life—he asked me to hold his hand. As his breathing changed, I realized he was dying and gripped his hand more firmly. With his other hand, he waved a goodbye and smiled faintly, and I thought I heard him say, "Thank you," so quietly that I wasn't sure. I smiled back. It was the first time I had seen him without the unfocused stare and hopeless look. I thought this was probably the most important moment in his life, probably the only moment in which he'd been himself, the only moment of repair in a seventy-four-year life of almost unbearable, unfulfilled longing. When he stopped breathing, I stared at his body and then felt enough grief that I started tearing. It was mostly not about his death, or the loss of someone I was close to, for I barely knew him. It was grief about the emotional life he had led, a life I knew about mostly secondhand. Having then practiced as a psychotherapist for only a decade, I had already witnessed unrealized lives in too many men, young and old, out and closeted. These lives had germinated in an early-life experience that left them with too much self-doubt or, at worst, self-loathing.

It would be a huge exaggeration to say that, today, it's easy to be gay in America. It is still not easy, unless one comes from the relatively rare insightful family, or one of a handful of educated, socially progressive enclaves. Today, young gay men often *come out* more readily than Will did—they know from the Internet that there are others like them—but simply coming out is a poor predictor of the quality of the internal life that follows. There are still many men, young and old, who remain closeted, and a majority who are out but still struggle with the legacy of early-life stigma and a deficit of self-acceptance. When people ask me what this book is about, my answer starts with "gay men," of course. If people are interested, I usually rattle off the eight or ten central issues in more or less chapter order. But there is a much more succinct answer: the entire book is about the life of Matthias Johnston, one of three men I have deeply loved—the others are Hank and Robb—beginning with our days in college. I tell this story in the closing chapter because it is a story about four men finding self-acceptance. True self-acceptance is readily recognizable: it is largely free of needless explanation, apology, and pandering, and free of reactive, unrealistic self-confidence and compensatory false pride. Self-acceptance allows realistic self-confidence, which is significantly unhinged in adulthood from the expectations and approval of others. In the end, authentic self-acceptance—or the lack of it—is almost the entirety of what defines a life. Without true self-acceptance, there is no true self-confidence or self-realization. Without self-realization, lives feel squeezed, purposeless, and truncated, cut short long before physical death finally ends them entirely. During the AIDS epidemic, I sat with dozens of men as they were close to death, and I heard a single line more often than any other: "I should have taken more risks." *No one* ever said that he'd taken too many.

The operative force in Will's unrealized life is still familiar today: the trauma of his early childhood, in which being gay was an unforgivable transgression in the eyes of his family and Little Rock society. His not-atypical family and the culture of Little Rock—the culture of most of the United States—had launched him on a trajectory aimed at a future that was not authentically his, a future that insisted on his living a shadowed life. As a psychologist—not a community organizer, lob-byist, or legal advocate—I wrote the chapters that follow in the hope of helping gay men find better, more authentic trajectories. I try to reconstruct how we think about gays lives by considering everything from the misleading idea of "the homosexual," to the potential richness and diversity of gay men's relationships. Between these two lie a variety of other topics, including the historical role of stigma and shame in gay lives; the significance of youth and of aging in today's gay communities; how we develop in childhood as gay men, and how that experience informs adult lives; the obstructions that sustain the effects of trauma and foil self-discovery, self-acceptance, and self-realization; and how we find paths of emergence from developmental and later-life trauma. My discussion of all these topics is intended to help lives be less reac-tive and more expressive of internal agency. I believe it is time that we act out of who *we* are, not who they are or whom they would want us to be to bestow their approval. We—particularly the still-young among us—must construct our own paths through life, paths that lead us out from under the smothering shadows of childhood and adolescent stigmatization.

I did not live through the childhood and adolescent trauma of be-ing gay that Will and many others are subjected to. I was lucky to have had a relatively accepting and supportive family—one living in a pro-gressive enclave in Manhattan. But I lived through a different kind of trauma: at the age of seven I lost my mother to an untreatable pneu-monia, and at sixteen my father to cancer, and my only sibling was a brain-damaged sister for whom I was given too much responsibility. But early-life traumas such as Will's and mine have something impor-tant in common: they engage and are engaged by later-life trauma in a destructive synergy. The early AIDS epidemic—from 1981 to 1996—engaged both my trauma of loss and the early-life trauma that a majority of gay men had experienced and still experience today. If being a gay child made one "sick, dirty, and a danger to others," how did that resonate with the American public's ignorant and hostile treat-ment of those living with HIV? Even without HIV in one's own body, how about being part of a community that had, in the homophobic public mind, become defined by "promiscuity," infectiousness, and ugly deaths? For too many gay men, the heroic battle against AIDS became another shaming experience. The inescapable trauma of the epidemic merged with earlier developmental trauma and propelled shame forward with destructive force. For me, the epidemic engaged my early-life trauma, the trauma of loss. Just after the film release of a wonderful love story, *Out of Africa*, my later-life safari began on a Friday, the evening of December 20, 1985.

That evening, I had given a talk in Berkeley. Afterward, walking to my car, someone I recognized from the audience skipped up alongside me, tugged at my sleeve, and said, "You and I—we're going to be friends."

*"Really?"* I was a bit incredulous.

He was young, wearing a threadbare army jacket and a knapsack that looked like the dilapidated remains of an arduous journey, and the idea that we would be serious friends seemed implausible. But he had unusual poise, and his face was both interesting and beautiful. Even the hand that tugged at my sleeve was beautiful, and his bright, penetrating dark brown eyes were insistent. He had certainty written all over his face. *"Really,"* he replied. "We're going to be friends."

I asked him out for tea so we could talk. While driving to a neighborhood café on Telegraph Avenue, he suddenly said, "It's Friday." I looked over at him, and he was pointing to a newsstand at the curb and asked me to pull over. Leaping from the car, he collected a pile of newspapers from one of the boxes, returned to his seat, slammed the door shut, and looked triumphant. He had a stack of twenty or so copies of *The Watchtower*, the Jehovah's Witnesses' illustrated magazine.

"Don't tell me you read that? And an entire stack of them?"

"No, I'm going to take it to recycling in the morning. Everyone has a responsibility to keep garbage off the streets."

Refastening his seat belt and leaning back in the seat, he then briefly told me about his adolescence, during which his born-again-Christian, much-older sister had hounded him for years with humiliation and threats of hell for being gay. This person with a stack of papers on his lap was Robb. He didn't like being called *Robert* because it sounded too prim; *Robbie* was too cute; and *Rob* implied he was somehow mixed up in a felony crime. So he called himself Robb—pronounced *Rob*—and that's what I called him. That night, I found out that the jacket and knapsack had accompanied his father, Arthur, in the Ardennes Forest during the Second World War. I was taken with Robb, his jacket and his knapsack, and I would have called him anything he wanted. After a three-hour tea and conversation, I dropped him off at his apartment, and before he got out of the car, we kissed for a short while. He opened the car door and stumbled backward, disoriented.

"Are you okay?" I asked. "Surely you've kissed someone before."

"Yes," he mumbled. "But not like that."

A month later, we were lovers. In the intervening weeks, I had told him about Matthias and Hank, our relationships, and the time I routinely spent with them in New York. But Robb, unfazed, seemed only delighted with the prospect of meeting them. He was assertively independent—in both thought and action—in a way that I admired and respected. He was also smart, funny, and beautiful, and he was optimistic and had the energy to put it all to use. He had graduated from Rutgers two years earlier and was planning on going to graduate school and becoming a child psychologist. I knew he would forge himself a wonderful life, and I wanted to see it flower and be part of it. He and I were surely birds of a feather, and I was irrevocably in love with him. Much later, a close friend said to me, "You love Robb the way you love your dog—unreservedly." *Yes,* I thought, *that's exactly it.*

In 1986, one year after our first meeting, twenty-nine thousand AIDS cases had been reported in the United States, and twenty-five thousand of those men had already died. It was in the summer of that year that Robb and I found out he had HIV and I did not. That was a horrible discovery, and a horrible divergence of paths that seemed impossible. The situation led me to write a whole, very painful book about being HIV-negative and the relations between positive and negative men.[1] I rarely slept well after we found out about Robb's HIV status, and he never again talked about graduate school or working with children. He never again talked about anything in the future. Sitting one night in a restaurant watching him eat, I told him I wanted to completely remove HIV from his body and take it into my own. "If I could take your HIV from you and make you okay, I'd do it in a second." He glanced at me and said, "You're crazy," and he kept on eating. I remember it; it was paella.

While I was immersed in my feelings about Robb, something else was happening in my life. Outside the house, the epidemic was proceeding relentlessly, and I had numerous therapy patients newly diagnosed with HIV, falling ill, or dying. By the end of 1989, ninety thousand had died, and during that year I had four people, all members of a therapy group for HIV-positive physicians, die in a single week. One man in the group, a retired physician named Charlie, said he was straight, but he wore pink socks, and none of the younger men believed him. He was one of the four that week; the three others were all under forty.

I was seeing another physician in individual therapy, Jim, a pediatric oncologist in his late thirties. He was hanging on tenaciously to his precarious life and arrived twice a week, carried up the stairs to my office by his attendant, Frank, who was an enormous man, an RN who looked like an African-American sumo wrestler in XXL blue scrubs. He would set Jim in a chair in my office, with a shoulder bag on the floor beside him. Two intravenous lines emerged from the flap of the bag, pumping medications into Jim's arm and chest. The electric pumps would quietly hum and stop, hum and stop, throughout the session, and the rhythm was nearly hypnotic. Jim talked mostly about little things, such as trips to the aquarium, where he and Frank would sit and watch fish. Jim also talked about problems with his medical care, and he occasionally voiced shame about his life as a gay man and the humiliation he felt about having HIV. He was also frequently silent, sometimes dozing. I would simply sit with Jim during the silent times, which seemed important to him. I thought he somehow felt safe in my office, and he confirmed that when I asked him. I could not save his life, and with so much emotion to untangle, nothing *could* be untangled. There was no time to do that. His complex threads of grief, fear, shame, anger, and regret had woven themselves into an apparently impenetrable mass. As with Will, I was disturbed by my feeling that I had so little to offer.

On a Tuesday afternoon and about halfway through our hour, Jim had been dozing for a long while and was unresponsive when I spoke. I waited a bit, and then finally walked over to his chair and realized he was dead. After a stunned moment, I went to the waiting room where Frank was sitting alone, reading *The New Yorker*, which looked tiny in his giant hands. "Frank, I think Jim just died." Frank looked at me and slowly stood up. "Well, I'm not surprised," he said quietly, and he walked into my office and felt for a pulse. "I'll take him home and call the coroner from there." Frank switched off the pumps and carried the body down the office stairs. With Jim in his sumo arms, Frank turned at the bottom of the staircase and looked up at me. "Thank you for everything you've done. I know you meant the world to him. And I know this is where he would have wanted to die." Frank turned and left the building, and I never saw Jim or Frank again. I remember at that moment feeling empty, useless, and very frightened. Twenty minutes later, I was sitting in the office with another man who was fighting HIV.

With those days at work weighing heavily on me, I devised an extremely marginal coping scheme, the only one I could think of. Whenever someone died, I put a new flower in a small vase I had on my dining table. When the flower died, my mourning for that person was supposed to be over, but it didn't work. When loss follows loss with such rapidity, grief simply accumulates. I never discussed any of this with Robb, who had his own problem to live with, and his own friends dying. He had no idea what the flowers represented. "The flowers are nice," he once said to me, "but why do you get them one at a time?" "A whim," I said, and suddenly I had a memory of my mother telling me at the age of five or six that flower arrangements should always have odd numbers, because even numbers "make people sad." "*One*," I now reassured myself, "is an odd number." I had the unconscious idea that in pleasing my mother with the odd-numbered arrangement, she and everyone else would come back. When I was seven, my father told me she had died the day before, and I didn't know what that meant. "That means," he said, "Mommy won't be here anymore." His explanation instantly sucked me into a silent, chilly, bottomless hole that I would never forget, and the epidemic was pulling me back in all over again. I needed help getting out: Robb, at the very least, *had* to survive, for his blossoming life and for mine.

On an atypically hot Berkeley summer night about a year after his diagnosis, I was sitting up in bed, Robb sleeping motionless beside me. The recurring thought that woke me on most of these sleepless nights was *There must be something I can do for him, and I haven't done it yet.* It brought up an instant of panic, which I quelled by trying to imagine what I would do if he died. I never thought *when*, which was the only plausible idea, given what had been going on all around us: people had been falling like leaves in autumn, but not gently, violently, and on the ground lay a carpet three feet deep. If I thought of Robb dying, my body temperature would drop and my teeth would chatter, as if I had fallen back into the miserable hole I'd discovered at seven. So I didn't think about his actually dying. Sometimes in life, bold-faced denial is the only possible approach, and I had become expert. But even in that denial, I had developed a habit of listening in the dark to make sure he was breathing.

After a few hours of my barren rumination, the sleeping Robb, still facing away from me, suddenly spoke.

"You know, *you're* the one with the big problem."

The words hovered ominously in the darkened room. I had been stunned at his being awake—perhaps, unconsciously, at his being alive—and stunned by what he'd said.

"Why am *I* the one with the big problem?"

He rolled over to face me. "Because you're the one who's going to be left behind." And then he turned away and returned to sleep.

While I was still digesting his warning, Robb suddenly spoke again, this time without looking at me, almost as if he were talking to himself. "In ten years I'll be dead. By then, the only gay people left will be those whose lives were ruined by watching the rest of us die."

Since finding out that he had HIV, Robb had acquired a disturbing knack for dropping bombs and returning to sleep. I knew he did this because the bombs were too painful to talk through. Now deeper in rumination, I suddenly understood something for the first time. In this one bed lay the entire future of gay communities. Half of us—at *least* half—would die, and the rest of us would lead ruined lives. My childhood trauma had been fully resurrected, but until this moment, I had denied it. I had simply taken for granted that at the instant Robb died, I, too, would cease to exist. I didn't *want* the future Robb predicted; I could barely outlive the present. None of us could outlive a future such as that. No one would want to.

The next morning, awake and in the light of day, Robb sat at the kitchen table eating a blueberry muffin. I was staring at his profile and thinking that it made me happy just to look at him. He suddenly turned to me, the muffin suspended between his plate and his mouth, and he said something he had not said in the dark the night before: "I was sitting in the backyard yesterday afternoon, and I realized that nothing in the world is as important to me as you are." After a moment of silence, I started crying, and then he did. Seeing Robb cry felt unbearable, and it reminded me there was so much—almost *everything*—I could do nothing about.

Robb died on Monday, November 30, 1992, four days after Thanksgiving and 2,537 days after we first met. By Christmas of that year, 194,476 men had died of AIDS. Robb was two months and seventeen days short of his thirtieth birthday, which followed mine by thirteen days. "An unlucky number to separate us," he had said as we blew out the candles on our joint 1988 cake. He had died much too young, mostly unrealized, which seemed horrible, impossible. A week after his death I still existed, in the nightmare future of loss that my childhood had predicted and Robb had described in the dark, and I was disoriented, without even the focus to feel morose. During our seven years together, our beings—our minds, hearts, and bodies—had somehow constructed and shared a complex physical matrix that felt like a fact of the world. For me, Robb had *defined* the world. Without him, that world vanished, as if someone had quietly switched off the sun, and everything had faded gracefully away.

I canceled all my therapy appointments for the week. Walking down the street to get out of the house, I found that almost everyone looked like Robb, including people who looked nothing like him. The buildings I shuffled past looked like a film-studio back lot, with facades of cardboard and peculiarly bright paint, but uninhabitable. Then I suddenly imagined Robb existing in everything—the trees, the substance of the sky and the clouds, and the dogs on their way to the park, and I thought to myself, *He is finally safe.* I started weeping, and a passing woman asked if I was okay, a question I could not answer. After five or six such lost and unsteady days, I called my own therapist, Justin, whom I had not seen in several years.

"Robb died" is all I said. It was the first time I had uttered that phrase. I wanted to burst.

"Oh my God, *how awful!* How are you *doing?*" Justin asked incredulously, as if he, too, could not believe that Robb no longer existed.

"I'm wobbling terribly" is the only other thing I said, except "Yes" when he offered an appointment time for that afternoon.

As I sat in his office, the first thing I said to Justin was "I knew that if Robb died, there would be a huge hole in the world, but I didn't count on the world disappearing. I can't perceive it." I spent seven months talking to Justin because I needed to endlessly repeat every detail of the story of Robb's death, and how I was feeling during every minute of it. I told him how Robb had become confused and said that he wanted to phone me while I was standing next to his bed. I described how he looked before his death and what he had last said to me and I to him: "I asked him if he wanted some orange juice, and he said yes." I described how he looked after his death, which was pale and cold, and not at peace. I related removing his urinary catheter and dressing him in a fresh T-shirt and sweatpants before two men from the Neptune Society wrapped what was left of Robb in a white sheet and carried him from the house at 10:22 that Monday evening.

"How do you know so exactly what time it was?" Justin asked.

"Because I looked at my watch. Because I knew from that moment on, I would never see him again."

"Perhaps also because you were feeling out of control, and having that information would give you some control back. Or maybe you were feeling that you wanted to set your watch back."

Both sounded right, but I didn't respond. I was thinking such things as *You also looked at your watch because you wanted to see something that was reliable, something that—unlike human lives you loved and needed—could be trusted. In an hour, your watch will show one hour later.* I had also, I thought, wanted to make a mental record of the time *my* life ended. On Monday at 10:22, my life would have ended after forty-five years, nine months, twenty-six days, and twenty-one hours. Seven years of it was with Robb, give or take a month. I also calculated in my head that I had spent fifteen years of that forty-five-year life asleep, which seemed like a terrible waste.

Then I said to Justin, "I would often sit in bed and stare at the back of Robb's head while he was sleeping."

"What were you feeling when you did that?"

"I was feeling like I had an angel in my bed. I've never felt so at peace with life. Did I tell you—yes, I must have—how we met, that he skipped up behind me and tugged on my sleeve?"

"Yes, you did, but tell me again."

While I was seeing Justin, I had a simple dream in which Robb and I were sitting at a desk and I was showing him how to fill a new fountain pen with Pelikan Royal Blue ink. I thought he'd need it in graduate school. That was the whole dream. "A normalization dream," Justin said, meaning that I was trying to restore a normal life with Robb. Then, over several months I had another dream four times. It was very intense, a dream that, on awakening, I could almost not distinguish from waking consciousness. In the dream, I was always sitting in the same chair in the bedroom listening to music, and Robb appeared, standing five or six feet in front of me. Startled—and intensely happy—I started to get out of the chair to embrace him.

He held up his palm to stop me. "I'm not here like that," he said. "*You can't actually touch me.*" I was confused and then grief stricken, and he saw it on my face. "I just wanted to make sure you're all right."

"I'm *not* all right," I shouted back, sobbing, and then the dream ended. The first time I had the dream, I woke up sobbing. The next three times, I did not shout back at him, and I awoke feeling joyful that I'd been in the same room with him. Justin did not need to interpret this dream, its meaning was obvious.

It would take me several years to feel I had truly survived, and that I wanted to. And it would take years more to figure out how to *really* live in my new future. In 1995, three years after Robb's death, I was still wobbling from the loss, and 319,845 men had already died of AIDS, which had become the leading killer of Americans aged twenty-five to forty-four. But just one year later, things began to shift: In 1996, the International AIDS Conference was held in Vancouver, and the news was startling. With the introduction of HAART (highly active antiretroviral therapy) multidrug cocktails, HIV-positive men who seemed headed for suffering and certain death began remaining alive and improving. Suddenly it seemed possible that positive and negative gay men might survive together. If this miracle was true—and it took a long while to gain authentic confidence—we found ourselves with new, unexpected futures to think about.

What would those futures offer, and how would we actually find them? We would certainly need to address the emotional trauma the fifteen-year epidemic had wrought for millions of surviving men, and we would have to go back further, to the decade of gay liberation that the epidemic had disrupted and completely stalled. And we would need to do more than that. We would need to think about the long-standing stigma and trauma that young gay lives have been subjected to, for by itself the end of the epidemic and a restoration of gay libera-tion would address none of that. Emergence from the dark shadows of early-life trauma had to be about more than surviving; it had to al-low living better, more vital, and more authentic lives than American families and society had offered us. Gay men gained great strength through suffering in the epidemic and the herculean effort to simply survive, and we now needed that strength as much as ever. We needed to reconstruct how we think about our lives and how we live them. We needed to live *our* lives rather than the compromised, reactive lives that have for too long been a legacy for too many men.

That Robb never had the opportunity to fully realize his life will always remain one of my most painful memories. But for those who have survived, the potential for gay lives in America today seems in-creasingly hopeful. Older men *have* significantly outlived the future Robb conjured in the dark, and today we have a new generation of young men who entirely escaped any direct experience of the monstrous plague. What older and young men have not yet adequately outlived is early-life developmental trauma wrought by families, communities, and the larger society, and the interaction of that trauma with later-life experience. To outlive these influences, at least three issues must be acknowledged and explored. But all three have been persistently denied or ignored by a majority of gay men, and by today's gay community political agendas. For unexplored emotional pain, denial can be a very destructive defense: it is often indiscriminate and global and risks deadening *all* of our feelings, including those that allow us to live fully, to sometimes live happily, to love, and to love intimately. Denial may steady a life, but it can also crush it.

The first of the three issues is the ongoing psychological aftermath of an uncontrolled, deeply stigmatizing fifteen-year plague that resulted in a third of a million deaths in our relatively small, long-stigmatized gay communities.[2] Many of the surviving men—today, over the age of forty-five or fifty—are, in the strictest sense of the idea, survivors of trauma. At the very least, they are survivors of extraordinary, accumulated loss, which is itself a trauma. In our denial, too many of these gay men have been left to lead isolated, lonely, marginalized lives. Tens of thousands of these now-sequestered men demonstrated intelligence, tenacity, and courage while living, working, and surviving during the epidemic. They are heroes. It is their contributions that have allowed gay communities in America to survive in any recognizable form.

The second issue requiring acknowledgment and attention is that today we have a *current* HIV epidemic. It is remarkable that this needs to be pointed out, but denial is a muscled, reality-distorting defense against anxiety and pain. Because of the differences wrought by HAART regimens, I will call the current epidemic—roughly after 1996—the late epidemic. The statistics about it surprise and shock almost everyone I have spoken to, gay men included. In the United States today, approximately six hundred thousand gay men are living with HIV.[3] We have forty thousand *new* infections a year, the majority among gay men. Approximately 2.4 percent of all gay men newly contract HIV every year.[4] Gay-identified men, who account for 7 or 8 percent of the U.S. male population, account for 78 percent of new infections among men.[5] Finally, the Centers for Disease Control and Prevention (CDC) estimates that 50 percent of all eighteen-year-old gay men will be HIV-positive by age fifty; for African-American gay men, the 50 percent mark will be reached by age thirty-five.[6] These few figures are surely enough to establish the undeniable reality of the late epidemic, which has been significantly tempered—but not *cured*—by contemporary pharmaceuticals.

The third issue that demands serious attention is the still-ongoing childhood and adolescent trauma that gay people are subjected to, and the often-lifelong emotional legacy it bestows. This legacy still shadows a majority of gay men of all ages and, like the emotional aftermath of the late epidemic, is an issue that must be addressed. I know well that any discussion of gay men's developmental trauma or emotional lives can feel pathologizing to members of stigmatized communities that hope, today, to quell feelings of internalized stigma—self-stigma—through marriage and the attainment of other legal rights and privileges.

There is no better indicator of internalized stigma than gay people's current focus on the idea that they were "born gay" and thus have no culpability for *being* gay. Few assert that they are gay simply because they *want* to be. Even if biology were purely responsible for the fact of being gay, our childhood and adolescent lives would obviously influence how we experience that fact: people are routinely stigmatized for biological differences and "abnormalities." I do not know why anyone is gay, and I very much doubt that being gay has a neat causal explanation in either nature or nurture. Gay people should give thought to why the *why* feels important. As far as we know, being gay is simply one expression of natural human diversity, for which explanations and justifications are owed to no one. Despite a slowly improving trend in American society, destructive families and societal stigma are still playing a major role in how young gay men experience themselves. We need to address this problem by finding ways to discover, to live as, and to accept ourselves, regardless of how we got that way. Only through self-discovery and self-acceptance can we most fully realize our lives.

As a gay man and a psychotherapist working with many gay men, I experience the diversity and richness of gay life as a compelling opportunity. In the twenty-first century, our lives are an obvious, simple human right, no questions asked. While the diversity-phobic, conventionalizing forces in American society so often work to deny and thwart gay lives, I am forever admiring of how many gay men—in so many different ways—have persevered in living the lives they wanted. I know a hundred stories. One is of a twenty-three-year-old raised in a culturally isolated, religious, and severely disapproving South Carolina family who spent five months working his way across the country doing odd jobs. He wanted to live in San Francisco, to continue his music studies, and to learn about life with other gay men. Another is the story of a forty-four-year-old who grew up and lived in Northern California and had a successful career as a public defender in a large city near his socially conservative hometown. Only at the age of forty-two did he acknowledge to himself that he was gay, and that he needed to move to a gay community, regardless of the familial and financial consequences. These are simple stories, but ones of courage, of heroes. Early in life these men, and countless others, were forced to live under gloomy, often-crushing shadows that they should never have had to en-dure. Such lives can be explored and reconstructed.

Being gay in an adverse society is a sometimes-daunting, sometimes-lifelong task. But millions have found ways to have lives that authentically express who they are: the realization of gay lives is all around us. I hope for such self-realization to take root and flourish for as many men as possible. Crawling out from under the trauma of destructive early-life experience and the two epidemics, and into a new century of slowly shifting social values, provides us an opportunity to explore our possibilities, rather than live with limitations imposed by others. The time is ripe.

# 1

# Are Gay Men Homosexuals?

What is your line?
It is not the cow that makes the frycook.
—Keith Waldrop, *The Not Forever*[1]

## WHAT IS A HOMOSEXUAL?

There are two different perspectives on what makes a man "a homosexual." The first—the heterosexual perspective—is that homosexuals are "men who have sex with men." The gay man's perspective, briefly put, is that he is "attracted to other men." The difference between the two descriptions is important: the heterosexual identifies a single, objective behavior, the gay man an entire internal life of feeling. While the straight man may feel support, indifference, fear, or contempt for the idea of "the homosexual," the gay man has more complex feelings, in part because the term has historically been used to stigmatize. "Are you a homosexual?" is easily, often correctly, experienced as the opening salvo of an attack. The majority of gay-identified men do have at least a marginally conscious sense that being gay is about more than sexual attraction or sex; but many gay men *have* been swayed by the heterosexual definition and have accepted the narrow, behaviorally defined identity. In today's gay assimilationist politics, gay men often explain themselves to heterosexuals with the idea that they are "attracted to men, but otherwise just like you." In that assertion, the gay man is accepting the heterosexual perspective on who he is: the gender of his sexual partner defines him as gay and is his only distinguishing difference. From a psychological perspective, this is simply not the whole truth, and the claim often does a serious disservice to gay lives.

For gay men, sexual attraction to other men is only one expression of something more fundamental, something that might be called a gay sensibility. As I am using the term, *gay sensibility* describes both the man's internal experience of himself, and his characteristic external expression of self to others. Together, the two constitute "a sensibility," and a gay sensibility is often different from that of heterosexual men. Sexual attraction is not the cause of gay sensibility, although it may influence and inform it; nor is the simple idea of the homosexual an adequate characterization of that sensibility. The question I am raising—whether or not gay men *are* homosexuals and should be characterized as such—is not at all intended to dismiss the importance of gay sexual lives. Sexuality is of central importance in all human life, whether acknowledged or not. What it means to "be gay" has for too long been defined by others, and too much of that imposed definition has been incorporated into gay self-experience. Being gay offers important opportunities that can only be realized if gay people can free themselves of societal and internalized stigma, much of which stems from the conventional idea of the homosexual. Freed from this narrow characterization, gay people have lives that are, in some ways, like heterosexual lives and, in other ways, appreciably different. Lives that express such complexity are often better, fuller, more authentic lives.

Gay people—with the historical focus largely on men—have been designated homosexuals in the psychological literature since the late nineteenth century, when the previously little-used term appeared in the German psychiatric text *Psychopathia Sexualis*.[2] In addition to *homosexuality*, the author, Richard von Krafft-Ebing, cataloged other psychosexual phenomena, including *bestiality, exhibitionism, pedophilia*, and *sadism*. The company homosexuals kept in this tome of "perversions" was a good indicator of where the understanding of gay lives was headed in the developing psychiatric literature, the popular mind, and, too often, the gay mind. But the significance of *Psychopathia Sexualis* went disturbingly beyond the classification of same-sex behavior as a pathological perversion. Before this treatise, homosexual sex had been only a behavior, a single anomaly in an otherwise "normal" human being. With *Psychopathia*, homosexual behavior became something that could identify and characterize an entire person. Not only was the behavior pathological, the entire man was: the man with a discreet cancer had become "a cancer." The newly assigned identity was readily incorporated into the self-experience of gay men, giving rise to a self-perpetuating psychosocial dynamic of imposed social stigma and reactive, internalized shame that, in turn, bolstered the stigma. Gay men were being identified as homosexuals, and that is what they started to feel like.

What the new psychosocial dynamic persistently ignored was the complex sensibility—the experience of self, others, and the world— that lay behind and gave expression to the sexual behavior. The psychological lives of gay people would be lost to psychiatry, which embarked on a campaign to explore gay lives with the intent of revealing the psychopathology that was presumably the root of the "problem." In his seminal history of the American homophile movement, John D'Emilio discusses the role that the nineteenth- and twentieth-century "medicalization" of homosexuality played in the new homosexual identity:

> Ironically, the medical model promoted the articulation of a gay identity and made it easier for many lesbians and homosexuals to come out. In elaborating upon their theories, doctors helped create the phenomenon that most of them wished to eliminate. They transformed an evil impulse that the morally upright strove to resist into the primary constituent of one's nature, inescapable because it permeated one's being. . . . Medical theories made homosexuality not a deed that one avoided but a condition that described who one was.[3]

While the attention of psychiatry beneficially "promoted the articulation of a gay identity," this narrow, stigmatized, and polarizing identity would prove to be immensely destructive. The earlier perception of the "evil impulse" left the person's identity as a human being otherwise relatively intact; but the new approach would shrink the entire identity into the evil impulse itself. As D'Emilio points out, psychiatry usefully, if inadvertently, accomplished an important affirmation for gay individuals: they had *something* in common with other people, gay people. Psychiatry thus brought being homosexual out of the one-man closet into a new group closet. This group closet was equipped with a newfangled light—the light of psychiatric diagnosis and "insight"—that turned on automatically whenever the closet door was opened, and scrutinized and pathologized the very homosexual identity that psychiatry itself had created.

Unavoidably, the new group closet did something else: it polarized the homosexual identity for gay people themselves. A person does not have the self-experience of being distinctive and an outsider until he encounters a group from which he is different and excluded. Being a member of the new group closet clearly excluded one from most of society, a society that left no doubt about the differences. "Gay communities" were thus born, populated by deviants who, by definition, had one thing in common—socially disapproved sexual interests. Where homosexual behavior is *not* disapproved, it is much less likely to be experienced as an identity, and if it is, the identity is much broader. When I recently asked a gay Dutch public health official what it meant to "be gay in the Netherlands," he responded, "I'm not sure what the question is. If you mean, do we live in our own parts of town as you do in the U.S., the answer is no. The whole issue doesn't mean as much in the Netherlands, we don't really have gay and straight people the way you do. It's more like we have *people*, and *all* people are different."

Today, a majority of American gay men still very much live in the group closet defined by the homosexual identity. A gay friend recently told me that he had asked his mother why she never inquired about how he and his partner were getting on. "Why would I?" she responded. "I never ask your brother about what he and his wife are doing in bed." While we have become accustomed to the social construction of the homosexual, from a psychological perspective it is peculiar that we would classify and characterize a group of people entirely by their sexual behavior. As essential as sexuality is in human life, sexual behavior does not constitute a complete relationship to another or a complete life, and sexual practices are not close to a complete description of anyone. The origins of this odd practice lie partly in the different so-cial roles that gay men play—in particular, that they do not breed—and in the fact that sex is a concrete, observable behavior. The other part of gay men—the complex, rich *internal* sensibility—is not usu-ally observable by others, and many gay men have become necessarily expert at limiting any external expressions of their internal lives, even to other gay men.

Walking in San Francisco's Castro or New York's Chelsea, I am often struck by how many men on the street appear to be uncomfort-able making eye contact or offering a passing hello. They look slightly furtive or inauthentically aloof. Some of this behavior is probably a product of the male adolescent's learned caution about revealing *any* interest in another boy, and being discovered as gay. But the homo-sexual identity is characterized by sex, and the furtive or apparently aloof gay man is sometimes also avoiding any response that suggests acceptance of a feared or unwanted sexual invitation. Having found their first experience of social currency in their sexual desirability, too many men are left feeling that the only interest another man might have in them is sexual. Over the years, one thousand gay men have said to me, "The only thing other men are interested in is sex, and that's not what I want, it's not enough." To this, I usually respond, "But the other nine hundred and ninety-nine gay men I have spoken with have said the same thing. I think that many others *share* your feelings." The Castro and Chelsea are too often not social communities, but neighborhoods of people wandering the streets, all looking for some-thing they are convinced is unattainable because of who gay men are. The wanderer knows only his own internal sensibility, not that of others, who are homosexuals, pure and simple.

The homosexual identity is not only problematic because it is nar-rowly defined by sex; it is made even worse when the sex is consid-ered deviant. As D'Emilio points out, the term *homosexual* has always been used to express religious, social, or medical disapproval: homo-sexual behavior has been a sin, a crime, or a sickness.[4] Even as many gay men may be unconscious of such feelings *about themselves*, some have feelings—not usually ideas—that other gay men are sinful, crim-inal, or sick, none of which makes them desirably obtainable. One solu-tion for such gay men is the not-uncommon interest in "straight-acting," straight-identified men, who are, for other reasons, also usually unobtainable. There is something else I have heard a thousand times from gay men: "I am never interested in men who are interested in me, and those I *am* interested in never return the feeling." What this peculiar, completely implausible predicament suggests is that the obstruction lies not in who other gay men actually *are*, but in what he, the seeker of relationships, feels about himself. The psychological mechanism is *projection*: when a man shows interest in another man, the interested man becomes a deviant homosexual in the eyes of his object, and this works bidirectionally. Both men feel some—probably unconscious—sense of their own homosexual undesirability and project the feeling onto each other. In such a mutually projective scheme, anyone who shows interest is disqualified.[5]

## THE STORY OF LARRY

Larry and I first met for therapy in 2014, and he clearly expressed the problematic nature of the homosexual identity and the role of stigmatization in codifying it. Larry was a twenty-eight-year-old African-American who, by his own description, grew up in Ohio in "a seriously Catholic family." At the age of twenty-three he moved to San Francisco, where he worked as an electrical engineer. Larry had come to me to talk about "having relationships," in which, he said, he had "been a complete failure." When Larry was twelve, his mother had found him in sexual play with another boy, and the event became the family's preoccupation.

> "After my mother discovered me, everything changed. It was then that I realized I didn't want to be an astronaut, I wanted to be a homosexual."
>
> "A homosexual *instead* of an astronaut? It's difficult to imagine them as conflicting options."
>
> "*Homosexuality* became everything—it's all that my parents talked about, that's the word they used, and it was all I thought about when I thought about my future. I wasn't even black anymore, just gay. They told me a hundred times

that if I didn't change, I was going to hell. Not going to hell was all that mattered to them. I would think to myself, 'I am a homosexual,' and everything seemed to start from there. So being an astronaut, well, that wasn't even on the table anymore."

"Being a homosexual seems like a very narrow way to think about yourself and your future. You *did* become an engineer. Was that okay—perhaps the question is, is it okay to think of yourself that way, as primarily a homosexual?"

"No, not really—because being a homosexual is a hopeless thing to be as far as I know."

"Because?"

"Because—you know all the things. Homosexuals don't have relationships, their families reject them, and they die lonely. And being black and gay is even worse, much worse. You belong nowhere."

"Do you still feel that hopeless? Do you believe that gay people don't have relationships? And what about being black and gay?"

"I *know* they have relationships—I don't know how *good* they are, but I know they do—but that's not what I feel. I *do* feel it's hopeless. And I don't belong with black people or gay people. I don't know if you understand that. For gay men, there's a lot of racism, and I'm pretty much *a thing*, which some guys are into and some are not. As far as my life has gone, being gay has been about having sex with guys who are into black men. I've never really had anything beyond that."

At the age of twelve, Larry had engaged in a single activity—physical play with his friend—and it had become his entire identity. Overnight, he had become "a homosexual," and in elaborating on this label, the family strengthened that identity with polarizing rejection: Larry was the only one in the family who would end up in hell. Neither Larry nor his parents had been able to give any attention to the internal life—the person—that motivated the natural physical exploration of two young adolescents. My thirty-year working experience has made clear that gay men with the most oppositional and hostile families are likely to hold the strongest, deepest, and narrowest identities as gay men. As with Larry's experience, sexual behavior becomes, if not the entire sense of self, a too significant part of it. On his own, Larry would almost certainly not have created so narrow an identity. A perceptive and thoughtful man, he had successful interests in many areas. He was not only an engineer, but an accomplished furniture maker and a budding pilot. But in his deepest feelings, he remained "a homosexual" and felt hopeless about himself and the possibility of relationships. This fundamentally gregarious and empathetic man was emotionally isolated and lonely, which was the very life his parents warned him about. American society had successfully created another homosexual, a man who experienced himself as a sexual "thing," and not much else.

## A STUDY FROM INDIANA

The extent to which *homosexual* still defines being gay in America is revealed not only in Larry's story, but in a useful study conducted by members of the Department of Sociology at Indiana University.[6] The psychological insight offered by the study lies in the authors' distinction between "formal rights" and "informal privileges" for couples. The formal rights polled in this study excluded gay marriage—the 2015 Supreme Court decision had not yet been handed down—but included other formal rights such as legal partnerships, insurance benefits, and hospital visitation. Informal privileges included telling others of the nature of their relationship, as well as holding hands, kissing on the cheek, and "French-kissing" in public. The last three items are known as public displays of affection, or PDA. The 1,073 subjects polled were approximately half heterosexual males and females, and half gay- and lesbian-identified people.[7]

Given the recent rise in public support for gay marriage, it is not surprising that the Indiana study concludes, "Overall, heterosexuals are as willing to grant formal rights to the same-sex couple as they are to the heterosexual couple."[8] However, the responses from heterosexuals are very different on the matter of informal privileges, particularly public displays of affection:

Beginning with heterosexual males' attitudes, we find clear evidence of sexual prejudice across *all* the informal privilege items. Heterosexual males are significantly less approving of informal privileges for both the lesbian couple and the gay couple than for the heterosexual couple . . . but they are significantly less approving of the gay couple than of the lesbian couple.[9]

The heterosexual females polled for the study were similarly less supportive of informal privileges, including displays of affection, though they were *"not* significantly less approving of the gay couple compared to the lesbian couple, with the exception of kissing on the cheek."[10] In addition to the 505 heterosexuals, the study polled approximately the same number of lesbians and gay men. The two same-sex groups were more willing to grant displays of affection to heterosexuals than to themselves; and the gay men were significantly less approving of gay men kissing on the cheek and French-kissing than were the lesbians.[11]

In addition to this study data, the same authors have collected data on whether heterosexuals perceive gay and lesbian couples as "being in love." The short answer, particularly for the gay male couples, is that they do not.[12] Study respondents were asked to read exactly the same short story about a romantically involved couple, with only the names changed to indicate whether the couple was heterosexual, lesbian, or gay. In a brief online summary of the study, the lead author, Long Doan, notes:

> The findings suggest that people seem to think of loving relationships in a hierarchy, with heterosexual couples being the most "in love," followed by lesbian couples and then gay couples. Additionally, how "in love" a participant understood the couple to be led them to decide how many informal or formal rights they may deserve as a couple, from holding hands in public to having the right to marry.[13]

The study authors provide insightful discussion of the meanings of both studies, but in the following paragraphs I draw on my own, more psychologically focused interpretations. Data on the display of affection, marriage, and love suggest that heterosexuals do not readily perceive gay men as having emotional lives or relationships similar to their own: kissing on the cheek or being in love implies an internal sensibility that flies in the face of the behaviorally based homosexual identity. Gay men are homosexuals, and empathy for them is thus low. As the authors state it, "First and foremost, we find that gay couples are at a disadvantage regarding love: They are deemed as less loving than both heterosexuals and lesbian couples. . . . Gay relationships, but not lesbian relationships, are seen as more physical and sexual in nature than heterosexual relationships."[14] Steeped in the idea of the homosexual, heterosexuals do not perceive gay male relationships as emotionally significant, "real" relationships. Even gay men's sexual relationships are not quite real; they are physical acts that lack the emotional, human significance that heterosexuals claim for their own sexual lives.[15]

Such ideas and feelings have been internalized by too many gay men. Among them is an intelligent, sexually active twenty-six-year-old with whom I recently spoke. I asked Bernie how he *felt* about sex, and his response was succinct and to the point:

"It's a behavior, isn't it?"
"Well, it's a behavior that is often motivated by feelings, and sometimes brings up feelings," I responded.
"For me it's a behavior."
"Have you ever been in love with someone?"
"No. Why are you asking that?"
"Because the feeling of loving or being in love with someone sometimes motivates sex, and sex sometimes brings up the feeling of love."
"Not for me," Bernie concluded.

Bernie had clearly internalized the homosexual identity that obscures the sensibility behind sexual behavior. The obscuration has been so complete that a majority of heterosexuals—and, apparently, many gay men—do not approve of a peck on the cheek in public. Bernie's experience of gay sex is certainly not universal among gay men, but it is not uncommon.

The Indiana study authors suggest that the attachment to conventional male-gender stereotypes may contribute to heterosexual disapproval of gay male displays of affection. This is no doubt true. But heterosexual men can openly express and receive affection with women, and thus the "male-gender stereotype" that gay men violate is not a male stereotype, but a *heterosexual* male stereotype: in displaying affection for each other, gay men reveal mutually shared emotional intimacy between two men. Such intimacy is integral to the gay sensibility, but it violates the narrow behavioral definition of the homosexual, and a large majority of heterosexuals do not want to see that definition challenged. The gay sensibility can feel emotionally threatening and socially disruptive to those who are trying to sustain heterosexual identities and heterosexually constructed lives. The enemy of those identities and lives must be contained, and that is accomplished with narrow, stigmatizing labels.[16]

If the idea of "the homosexual" is much too narrow and destructive, what is the inclusive and expansive alternative? It is the idea that men sometimes live with an internal sensibility that allows them to form significant emotional attachments to other men. A gay man is a man who is inclined to fall in love with other men. Free of imposed developmental distortions and stigma, gay men would do this quite effortlessly, very much as heterosexuals do. In psychology, the term used to describe such "attachment of emotional energy" is *cathexis*. Because of its history—it was first used in an English translation in place of Freud's original German word, *Besetzung*—the term *cathexis* is understood and used somewhat variably.[17] For purposes of my discussion, cathexis is the natural human channeling and attachment of emotion to other people. When someone likes or loves, he is cathected; when he "falls in love," he is deeply cathected. "Being gay" is nothing more or less than relatively consistent same-gender cathexis. Sexual interaction between men is not the defining issue in being gay because sexual desires are directed by and *follow from* cathexis.[18] While sex may, in turn, direct or deepen cathexis—or, in bad sexual experiences, weaken it—the particular form of sexual expression is not the defining issue.

That many gay men are capable of sex without significant emotional cathexis has given rise to the idea that gay men are "promiscuous."

This observation—one of the key planks in the campaign to keep gay men homosexuals—tells us little about being gay. The issue has come to the fore because the campaign is focused on sex, and because gay men are typically more forthcoming about their sexual lives than heterosexual men, many of whom envy the sexual freedom gay men experience. Gay men have the same capacity for purely libidinous, uncathected sex that a majority of human males have; but gay men are unfettered by the traditional, socially promoted sensibilities and sexual expectations of women. Gay men are, in fact, often seeking cathexis in seemingly purely libidinal pursuits, for many are attempting to overcome a developmental experience that inhibits—often prohibits—the expression of cathexis. Those restrictions leave purely libidinal sex as the only path of connection to other men. As the Indiana study suggests, same-gender sexual behavior does not threaten heterosexuals so much as the possibility that the sex has meaning— that it reveals cathexis.

Heterosexual society has a significant investment in keeping gay sex apparently promiscuous and emotionally empty. Gay men must learn to reject this influence, and to experience themselves not as homosexuals, but as naturally *homocathected*, entitled to that cathexis, and entitled to its expression. When gay men deeply understand this distinction, they have a very different experience of themselves. There might also be another, secondary benefit in the triumph of homocathexis over homosexuality. Judging by the Indiana study on love, the larger society might experience gay men differently if it did not define gay men entirely in sexual terms. In the words of the study authors, "Perceptions of love are related to willingness to grant social recognition to romantic couples of all types."[19]

## THE SIGNIFICANCE OF WORDS

There is a humanly important difference between homosexuality and homocathexis, but the common use of language continues to obscure it. In 1989—eight years into the early epidemic—*The New York Times* first deemed it appropriate to use the term *gay* rather than *homosexual*. According to the national media watchdog for LGBTQ people, the

Gay & Lesbian Alliance Against Defamation (GLAAD), "style rules" regarding homosexuals have changed significantly over the past twenty-five years:

> The Associated Press and *The New York Times both* restrict usage of the term "homosexual"—a word whose clinical history and pejorative connotations are routinely exploited by anti-gay extremists to suggest that lesbians and gay men are somehow diseased or psychologically and emotionally disordered. Editors at the AP and *New York Times* also have instituted rules against the use of inaccurate terminology such as "sexual preference" and "gay lifestyle."[20]

GLAAD had a significant hand in bringing about useful changes, but the new language still offers little clarification of the differences between homosexual and homocathected. GLAAD, the *Times*, and the AP all still define *gay* as describing "people who are attracted to the same sex," which is most readily understood as "people who are *sexually* attracted to the same sex," which means *homosexual*.[21]

The now politically correct term *gay* has a complex history, but it is thought by some to have originated in early twentieth-century America, where it was used among homosexual men themselves.[22] It was almost certainly first used as code for "homosexual" and was certainly not an assertion of pride, or a public assertion of any kind. That it originated with gay people speaks in its favor, as does the implication by omission that sexual behavior is not gay people's one and only defining characteristic. For these reasons, *gay* is today widely experienced as less prejudicial than the original *homosexual*, even as it is a meaningless designator that clarifies little about gay lives. Today, the term feels like "discreet," perhaps euphemistic, code that is intelligible only because of its now-familiar usage. Much as we might like it to be true, joy, merriment, and carefree lightheartedness are not the defining characteristics of many lives, gay or straight.

While *gay* is now in wide use in English, French, Dutch, Danish, Japanese, Swedish, and Catalan, it still means "homosexual." Merriam-Webster, the *Oxford English Dictionary*, and Dictionary.com all now provide the single word *homosexual* as the first definition of *gay*. For the *Oxford English Dictionary*, the *second* definition is the "informal or derisive" use of the term to describe something as "foolish, stupid or unimpressive: 'he thinks the obsession with celebrity is totally gay.'"[23] At this point in the history of the term, *gay* is well established and, in itself, innocuous; but the term it references—*homosexual*—needs correction among the professions that seek a "scientific" word. The first definition of *gay* should rightly be "homocathected."

## THE STORY OF STUART

The labeling of gay men as homosexuals—and the narrow understanding it provides—has had many deleterious consequences. Frightened and tortured adolescent lives, desiccated adult lives, and suicides at all ages are at the top of the long list. For the majority of gay men who are relatively fortunate survivors, perhaps the worst consequence is that so many have never had confidence in the possibility of being in love. "Did you ever fall in love with another boy as a teenager?" I asked Stuart, a thirty-five-year-old man who, in 2012, was just coming out. He responded hesitantly at first:

> No . . . but, now that you're asking, starting at the age of twelve or so, I did have a friend, David, and we were very connected. . . . I really couldn't stand not being with him, and when we were together, I'd stare at him, which I was self-conscious about, but he never seemed to mind. I couldn't stop thinking about him when one of us went on vacation with our families. Once during my family's vacation, I can remember lying in bed in the dark, trying to visualize his face. I felt desolate. I missed him too much, though I don't think I said it that way to myself at the time. I don't think I understood why I had so much pain, terrible pain about just not being with him. I would never have told anyone about my feelings—I never have until right now—but maybe that's being in love. I don't know what being in love *is*, but maybe that's it.

As a sixteen-year-old, Stuart had been aware that other boys were starting to fall for girls, but it had never consciously occurred to him that he and David had fallen for each other. Stuart and David never had a sexual interaction, even in their high school years, during which they "remained together." Stuart had become "vaguely aware" of sexual feelings for other boys, but he dismissed them and never acted on them with anyone.

"Sex with David never entered my mind. I think I feared it would risk our friendship, that he might have rejected me."

"But your fear suggests that sex with David *had* entered your mind, if only unconsciously. And I'm virtually certain that you *were* in love with him. You know more about being in love than you think you do."

"I never put two and two together. Boys didn't fall in love with other boys. I knew there were gay men who were couples, but to me that sounded more like having a buddy you go biking with. Maybe you had sex with other men. But you weren't *in love*. I don't know what David was feeling when we were kids. We were like glue on glue for six years until we both went away to college. I don't think I told you, but several months ago I found out on Facebook that David is gay, too. He has a boyfriend, and they live in Atlanta. When I read that, I felt incredibly jealous. And sad. I haven't contacted him. But I think reading that is why I decided I had to come out."

Stuart's incomprehension about his relationship with David is a common experience for young gay men. After a year of working together with me, Stuart—now out and more sexually active, but still largely unconvinced that men fell in love and had "that kind of relationship"—left therapy. A year later, in 2015, I received an e-mail from him asking that we start up again. In the note, he told me that he had met Geoff in 2014, and that a few months ago they had made plans to live together. The note continued:

I came to understand that Geoff and I were a couple of dreamers who, until we met, had pretty much given up on finding the kind of love we came to share. Until I met him, I never really realized that I had always had a dream, much less given up on it, but with Geoff, all this came clear. I had fallen in love with him, which completely surprised me despite everything you'd said that I had not understood or allowed with David. I realized that all around us, we have been told, as much by gay culture as anything else, that this love existed rarely, if at all, and not between men. It was very difficult for me to let go of all this, even after my work with you. I look back on my life, at half of my life, and I feel anger and grief about it for the first time. What happened to Geoff and me feels like something that existed in some other kind of time and space, in some other dimension, and I'm wondering now if it was real. I hope I can talk to you about all this. Geoff died two weeks ago of a cerebral aneurysm, and I am completely lost, I'm reeling.

As I write in 2015, Stuart and I are working together in the aftermath of Geoff's death. Even with the loss of Geoff, Stuart recognizes that he was fortunate to have had an experience of the "other dimension." In their short time together, Stuart had not only discovered Geoff, Stuart had discovered within himself a capacity that he had not known he had, a capacity to love and be in love that he had doubted in all gay men. As adults, many gay men find themselves bewildered by gay relationships, often having ongoing sexual encounters that, in the longer term, become unsatisfying. Such sexual experiences, however, are only rarely meaningless and casual. They are almost always a search for emotional connection to another man, but one often conducted without the developmental experience that would facilitate and support the process. Many gay men have difficulty integrating sex into relationships, and relationships into sex, because the homosexual idea does not permit it. In his time with Geoff, Stuart had surmounted the limitations of "being a homosexual" and had found a personal liberation that left him feeling whole and authentic, if also bereft. He was clearly the happier for it, even in his grief. "What you said to me about love being *my* capacity is very important to me, I cherish it," Stuart said to me. "I hope I still have it, and that Geoff's dying will not make me afraid again."

"Once we discover it, we have it for life," I responded. "You *have* it."

## THE DEVELOPMENTAL GENDER SPLIT:
## THE STORY OF FELIX

The internal sensibilities of gay men are often perceptibly different from those of resolutely heterosexual men. In the nineteenth century—before the "discovery" of the total homosexual—same-sex behavior was sometimes described in the psychiatric literature as a "gender inversion," an idea that hints at something real, but misconceptualizes the issue. Gay sensibility and the sexual connections it fosters suggest neither an inversion nor a "third gender," but a variable *integration* of what we think of as normative female and male character and sensibility. This integration is the purely internal correlate of what the queer movement calls gender bending. It is emotional gender *blending*, often without external, physical expression. Many years ago, I knew a male-identified, effeminate HIV-prevention specialist, Frank, who, on our first meeting, appeared at a conference in a flowered hat, an army fatigue jacket, a pleated green velvet skirt, and hiking boots. From head to toe, he was obviously well bent, and internally, he was well blended. His complex, integrative internal sensibility made him unusually astute in recognizing and articulating the psychology of HIV-prevention issues for gay men; and for him, the fashion statement was an important expression of self. Although some gay men are obviously effeminate—a term too often used derisively to mean "unmanly"—many are not, even as they hold some mix of feminine and masculine sensibility behind a largely conventional male presentation.

The phenomenon known as gaydar—the ability to sense if someone is gay—is significantly reliant on one's capacity to read another's internal sensibility. If—the gender of sexual partners aside—all gay men were just like everyone else, gaydar would be useless. But gay men and many women are particularly adept in its use; straight men generally less so. For gay men, effective gaydar is partly a necessary skill for living in a hostile society, and partly a normal human—particularly female—capacity to sense shared sensibility. Sometimes it takes one to know one. Gaydar is a form of empathy, and it allows two men to click, often with nothing more than brief eye contact.[24] Heterosexuals also have gaydar, but the efficacy is more variable, partly because they often place too much weight on the obvious, visible expressed sensibility. Gay sensibility is more readily perceived and appreciated by women because they share some of the gay man's internal sensibility, and because gay men often lack the conventional male posturing and sexual interest apparent in straight men. If, defensively, gay men *do* posture, it is more likely with heterosexual men than with women.[25]

Some heterosexual men are able to read the sensibility of gay men and appreciate it; many are not. Those who are—through some combination of developmental outcomes and their experience with women—often admire the emotional insight of gay men, their comfortable discourse with women, and their freedom from the familiar, constricted male identities that are preoccupied with the denial of vulnerability and focused on the avoidance of humiliation. These accepting heterosexual men are relatively comfortable and secure in their own identities. Those who are threatened by gay men are sometimes aggressively homophobic. For much of the twentieth century, "homosexual panic" was a widely used—and often successful—legal defense for a man who had assaulted or murdered a gay man. The defendant claimed *diminished capacity*—the legal term for a defense of temporarily impaired mental capacity—because his own "pathological" homosexual feelings had been induced by the gay man. It was, the legal defense posited, the gay man who caused the homosexual feelings in the straight man—a ridiculous construction. The process is actually one of projection: I am not the fag, *he* is.[26]

If the gay sensibility is distinctive in its integration of conventional male and female traits, how and why does such integration take place? My partial answer lies in a description of the developmental gender split, in which young female and male children reach a developmental fork. Most children take one of two different paths, significantly in response to broad social expectation and parental pressure. Girls more or less take the "feminine path," boys more or less the other, and gay men sometimes more or less integrate the two. This developmental integration is not an explanation of "why people are gay," it is a description of an observable process that is seen in the young lives of some gay men, some gay women, and, indeed, in some male and female heterosexuals. As evidenced in observed adult character and sensibility, an integrated result is much more common in gay men than in heterosexual men.

While the child's particular handling of the gender split is significantly influenced by often-biased societal expectation and parental pressure, it is almost certainly also influenced by biological differences. Such biological influences are elusive and complex, and how they influence the development of character and sensibility is, today, only a matter of speculation. During the childhood negotiation of the developmental gender split, biological differences may not at all *directly* influence the integration of gender sensibilities. They may influence the child's capacity to read and internalize social expectation; his capacity to willingly defy those expectations; his self-confidence; his resilience and tolerance for perceived disapproval; or his capacity to identify with a more complex sense of self. Plausible explanations are legion, but it is implausible that most developmental results have single causes.

All humans, gay and straight, male and female, begin life in utero as females. Most progress to an in utero *biological* sex split and, after birth, have a clear biological—or, when the physiology is ambiguous, an assigned—sex.[27] In postpartum life, both sexes are completely helpless and dependent for a very long time. We cannot roll off of our back until the age of five or six months, cannot place food in our mouth until several months after that, and it may be two years before we develop urinary-bladder control. Compared to the offspring of other species, human infants are extraordinarily vulnerable and dependent. Even as we grow and the particular vulnerabilities and dependencies change, many of us remain both vulnerable and dependent for twenty or more years. Those feelings of vulnerability and dependence from infancy and childhood—and the feelings that they provoke, including humiliation, shame, and resentment—remain with us throughout life, whether consciously experienced or not. As fully grown adults, dribbling food down our chins, loss of bladder or bowel control, tripping on the sidewalk, or incompetence in the smallest task can easily provoke feelings of humiliation and shame. The feelings behind the humiliation and shame—vulnerability, dependence, and a loss of autonomy—constitute the core conflict in virtually all adult relationships. Like the infant and the child, we want to be nurtured and loved, and we want to be left alone: we push personal boundaries back and forth, in the hope of finding the impossible, perfect balance between intimacy and autonomy. This struggle is largely an adult reenactment of early developmental experience that is never outgrown, forgotten, or resolved.

The developmental gender split usually begins at the age of two or three and is fully in play by the age of four or five. The conventional construction of gender sensibility dictates that girls and boys handle universal feelings of vulnerability and dependency in different ways. Girls are expected to maintain conscious connections to those feelings: they are allowed, even encouraged, to sustain a sense of vulnerability, to show emotional sensitivity, and to be expressive of their emotional lives; and they are often encouraged to remain dependent on men. In contrast, boys are expected to separate themselves from feelings of vulnerability and dependency, initially with the suppression of "inappropriate behavior," and, ultimately, an internal denial or repression of the feelings themselves. For boys, the objective is a false, socially constructed male sensibility of physical and emotional invulnerability and needlessness. Boys are told that "only sissies cry," a kind of training that deliberately shames to enforce compliance. In internalizing the shaming, a boy becomes progressively less conscious of the internal life that allows emotional introspection, empathy for others, and adult intimacy.

Both of the socially constructed gender sensibilities are unnatural and humanly impoverishing, but both also serve some conventional social objectives. In more polarized developmental outcomes, adult women's partially infantile identities allow men to care for them and help men feel "manly" and in control. This manliness, in turn, allows women to sustain the sense of dependency and feel "feminine." Roles and responsibilities are assigned to both the helpless and the strong, resulting in a more predictable social order. The "womanly woman" and the "man's man" are a mutually supportive, if ill-conceived and unstable, team that destructively stunts the authentic lives of both parties. In its most polarized outcome, the gender split results in histrionic, helpless, and dependent women who are perpetually preoccupied with the fear of never finding, or of losing, the men they need. Men become posturing, intellectualizing, and emotionally empty and are preoccupied with the avoidance of any expression of vulnerability or need that might arouse feelings of humiliation.[28] In such polarized social constructions, women remain in an infantile state of helplessness, men in fear of returning to it. Women are teeming with emotional needs, men are emotionally needless and unavailable. Women live in their emotional lives, men in their intellects and the external world. Women are expressive, men contained. Women are reparative, men destructive. Women are passive and inactive, men assertive and controlling. Women get depressed, men get angry. Women talk, men take defensive action. Women are on the bottom, men on top. Women receive, men insert.

Fortunately, such narrow, polarized outcomes do not describe all Americans, particularly today's younger, educated, urban adults. But to some degree, the polarized characterizations I have offered provide insight into the subjective emotional experience—the sensibility—of many women and men. Some biological differences between the two sexes also certainly contribute to differences in gender roles. Throughout life, the primitive emotional response to body size and physical strength remains a powerful influence for people born as infants and raised in a world of giants. Some differences in brain structure and the sex-specific balance of hormones are also characteristic. But even with a complex combination of biological influences, the differences between genders would be far more subtle without the conventional social construction of gender and the developmental split it spawns. Women and men are simply not *that* different, which the women's movement and an expanding sense of women's potential in Western societies has made obvious in recent decades. Posturing males have a lot to learn from women—how to be *human*, among them—and so do gay men, whose own liberation movement has, not coincidentally, paralleled the women's movement. The expanded lives of women have been of great benefit to gay men, allowing many to be much more accepting and appreciative of the conventionally feminine components of a gay sensibility.

Many people, gay and straight, are able to accomplish some integration of traditionally feminine and masculine sensibilities. But for gay boys—who live with a substantial, secret difference from other boys—an integrative developmental experience is often problematic. Families and peers—who are living out their own developmental legacies and uncertain or precarious identities—often feel threatened by a boy's complex gender sensibility. The gay boy is thus often forced to conceal the overt expression of any internal feminine sensibility, and the boy who does not is too often the object of emotional and physical abuse. This conflict between internal and external life—internal sensibilities and the extent to which they can be expressed—allows two possible solutions. In the first, the boy may develop doubt about his internal sensibilities because they are disapproved and cannot be safely expressed. Naturally seeking a sense of integrity, and caught between a hostile world and his unexpressible internal life, he sacrifices his internal life through conscious denial and unconscious repression. Such a boy has created an injurious internal rift, and a life in the world that is substantially inauthentic. In the second solution, the boy endures the rejection and abuse and consciously sustains his internal sensibility. While the rejection and abuse are destructive, the experience of being openly different often fosters a more resolute sense of self. The boy who is able to traverse this path has maintained his integrity and authenticity, at the cost of emotional hurt. In a more intelligent, secure, and comprehending world, both solutions would be unnecessary. In *that* world, people would just more or less be themselves.


A childhood and adolescent path through the developmental gender split is well described by Felix. His is a helpful story for gay men of all ages, but particularly for younger men whose personal trajectories are not yet cemented. Felix and I worked in therapy for about three years in the mid-2000s. He was then in his early thirties. Felix had grown up in Wisconsin, the youngest of three children, with two older sisters, and nonreligious, fundamentally supportive, and caring parents. Felix's father was a water-resource analyst for the State of Wisconsin, his mother a school counselor with a master's degree in psychology. In my perception, Felix was a remarkably well-integrated, comfortably gay man who had had the good fortune to negotiate the gender split against only modest odds, and he had emerged with a well-defined gay sensibility. During our work together, Felix was in graduate school earning a doctorate in clinical psychology. Between sessions, he reflected on what we had discussed and often sent me letters executed in fountain-pen ink and refined script. The following section is a compilation of portions of twenty-nine of those letters. (Felix, who is today working as a psychologist in his own private practice, has given me permission to use this material.) I have changed many details to protect his privacy.

If there is a central issue from my childhood that we have to talk more about, it is the feeling of disappointing my father, a feeling I have never surmounted. I'm still tangled up in it. It was *who I was* that was a disappointment to him—something I was first aware of at the age of four or five—and there was never anything I could do about it. Even at that age, I can remember being self-conscious about how I walked, which was more like my oldest sister, Sally, than another boy. She walked with a certain grace, other boys charged, and I know that my father noticed this—I would see him looking at me—though he never said anything.

He was always dragging me off to go fishing with him, and when I was nine—I remember it very, very well—he took me on one of these excursions. I had tried for years, but I hated it, I was no good at it, and though I'd go on the boat with him, I had started to refuse to fish. I thought the whole thing was disgusting and cruel, and I really wanted no part of it. On this particular day there were a bunch of other people on the boat, including another kid about my age, and he was really into fishing. My father started talking to him and showing him how to do things, and he spent the whole day with him, and I just sat there watching them. And I remember thinking, "Well, that's who my father wants me to be. And I will never be that, I can never be that." That's when I gave up on my father—on our relationship. Before that day, I think I sort of admired him. I wanted to emulate him, even though I was afraid of him. But from that day on, it changed. We talked less, and I know he never understood why. He never asked me to go fishing again.

That one fishing trip changed everything. That wasn't the moment I gave up on *myself*, though I think I was teetering on that edge. I knew that I had to give up on one of us because we were too different, and I sort of made the decision to give up on him and learn how to become myself. You know the thing [Erik] Erikson said, about wanting to be the person that the people we love want us to be. *I couldn't do that.* I decided that day I would figure out how to be myself, and I did have support for that from Sally and, to some extent, my mom. I'd done my last fishing trip, and then my poor father had to do it alone. The same for baseball. Since I had refused to play catch with him, he bought a machine that threw balls that he would catch and dump in a basket. I would see him out in the driveway with that machine, which I called Felix Junior, and my mother called it "Dad's baseball machine." I felt sorry for him, but I stuck to my plan—it wasn't a plan, it was a feeling—to be myself. I can remember a day when my father said to me, "Do you have *any* interest in coming out and playing some ball with me?" And I said, "No, I can't, Mom and I are making blueberry muffins, which will take a long time." I remember the look on his face. It was pathetic, and there was nothing to do about it and I didn't want to.

Later that afternoon, he was still out in the driveway with the machine, and I went up to my room to practice the violin, which I was very involved with by that time. I opened the window to my room—which faced out on the driveway—so my father could hear me play, and I practiced for a couple of hours. I was aware of deliberately opening the window, but at the time I didn't know why I'd done it, particularly because the ball machine made quite a bit of noise. Now I think I was hoping my father would appreciate the playing and love me, but at the time, it was more like a *fuck you, this is who I am. You play baseball and I play violin.* In those days, all the way through high school, I never felt more myself than when I was playing. I don't think I've mentioned this to you, but there were Brahms and Schubert pieces that made me cry.

This feeling about *being myself*: I was much older before I really knew what that meant or why it was so important. When I was younger, I was aware that I was different, that certain things about me were girly, and I was always going back and forth about trying to hide them. It was clear that girly meant weak, though in many ways I didn't feel weak. It was more

like a sense of not knowing who I was, of having to keep thinking that through and putting it together, though it seemed so
automatic for other boys. I had no idea who other boys were—
it was to me an alien world that I didn't know anything about.
I'd watch them walk and talk and be completely mystified by
what was in their heads. Even if I hadn't figured out the girly
thing and who I was, I wasn't going to be *no one* and slink
around.

I went through a period around the age of eleven or twelve
thinking maybe I *was* a girl, and I'd stare at myself in the mirror to see if that was possible, and to see if my face looked
like a girl's or not. I felt vulnerable like a girl around other boys.
I spent much more time with girls than boys, and I thought
about it a lot and decided that, no, I had a dick and I was a
boy. I was just a certain kind of boy, or would become one. I
was a boy who had some girly traits, and I'd just have to figure out how to make that work. Being a boy *or* a girl wasn't
the answer. I remember sitting with a girlfriend during recess
at school and her so-called boyfriend came over—we were
about twelve or thirteen at this point—and sat with us. And I
looked at the two of them and thought, "I'm not like either one
of them." And I was aware that I was more attracted to him
than her, and I remember trying to visualize how he'd look
with his clothes off. He was wearing shorts and I remember I
was looking at his legs, and trying not to be conspicuous.

My parents and I went to the movies one night, and in
one scene I started to cry—I can't remember about what—
and my mother put her arm around me and my father looked
over at us and didn't say anything. That was too emotional for
him, I'm sure. As I had gotten older, I had started to fear crying in front of other people, I'd gotten more self-conscious
about it, and I still am to some extent. As a kid, I thought the
whole thing about crying was about not being a wimp, and being ridiculed or laughed at. It was really, I think, about not
being a *gay* wimp, but I didn't quite know that until I was older.
When I did get older, that became what I was afraid people
would discover, that I was gay. The feeling of being different,

which I had had most of my childhood, was becoming the feeling of being gay. Somehow I knew that in not being myself—in not showing myself to other people—I was sort of stunting myself. I could *feel* that—it was like something squeezing me. My mother once talked to me about this, when I was maybe twelve or so, because I think she knew I was struggling, and this was right after she saw me staring in the mirror, which was definitely about a struggle. She said something like "Felix, you just have to be yourself, and some people will like you and some won't, which is true for everyone." So I tried to be comfortable being myself, and sometimes it worked.

I was very aware around the age of thirteen or fourteen of feeling a physical attraction to other boys, particularly handsome athletic ones, and this made it clearer to me who I was, which in some ways made it easier to be myself. It's as if in discovering I was gay, I had discovered what all of the difference was about—or if it wasn't *all* of the difference, at least I had something to *call* it, something to hang it on. I still had no idea what other boys were about, and I had to be very careful in the gym not to get a hard-on. I would bite my lower lip so that the pain would prevent it—so that's not really being yourself, but, you know, there were limits. If I just looked at another boy of a certain type, I could get a hard-on, and it became very awkward. It was particularly the legs for some reason. Once in the locker room, another kid saw me with a hard-on while I was trying to get dressed, and he shouted at the top of his lungs, "Hey, Felix has a boner!" I felt completely humiliated that I'd been discovered, and turned completely red, but it turned out that none of the other guys connected this to sexual attraction, they thought it was great that I had a boner. This was just more confirmation that I had no idea who they were. I was an outsider; they were collecting baseball cards, and I was studying the scores to Brahms quartets. At the same time, they were the ones giving me the hard-on, so it was all very confusing. I don't think even now I understand the whole thing. It wasn't at all that I wanted to *be* them, because I didn't want to be anything like them. I just *wanted* them. I guess this is something that straight women feel about men.

Around this time I started to spend time with David, who lived down the road, and we were in school together. I had always known him, but not paid much attention, but we started having sex together in the woods pretty regularly. He was *very* girly, much more than I was, and I think I had always avoided him because of that. It turned out I liked him, and we had fun together. Then I began to realize that he was getting very emotional about me—today I'd say he was falling in love with me—and I didn't know what to do with that. It frightened me, and I broke it off, and David wasn't in school for a week. Now, I'd like to apologize to him for what I did, but then I couldn't help it, it was just too scary. When I asked my mom about him a while ago, she told me that he had died and didn't say how, but I think I can guess. She is still terrified of AIDS, and when I first told her I was gay, that was the only thing that bothered her. Her first response was something like "Honey, that's wonderful, but you know you have to be very, very careful about AIDS." And then she said, "Don't tell your father until I've had time to talk to him." I said, "Don't worry, I won't." I was afraid to tell him.

After David, I met a few other gay kids, and I started to realize that I was sexually attractive, which gave me the first feeling of any kind of social power *as myself* that I'd ever had. But I found out something else around this time, which is that a lot of these gay kids were very uncomfortable with anything that seemed too feminine to them, so I'd be careful about that. They could be very feminine in sex, but not otherwise. I had one guy from school I had sex with for about a year—Steve, and he was three years ahead of me, and he graduated and went away to college—and the sex with him was wonderful, like a revelation to me. We would fuck each other, and I think we both had the experience that being fucked was the most wonderful thing in the world. It was like the violin, which was about letting the music in, of letting myself be taken over and getting transported somewhere else. With music, you ride on a wave of melody, harmony, and rhythm, and the sex with Steve was something like that. Getting fucked was about letting someone else in, and it was a big discovery for me, maybe the major one in my life if you can believe that. I can't imagine life without that experience. If I had never had it, it would have been a huge loss, a deprivation that would have made me a much shallower person. Women would know what I mean, most straight men definitely wouldn't. They'd probably be horrified and run out the door.

This being able to bring feelings out, to bring them to my own consciousness and to relationships, is something I think I'm pretty good at now, but not good enough. Maybe that's something we just work on for all of our lives.

Felix had had an unusually introspective, well-supported developmental experience, free of overt disapproval or hostility from his family and, to a great extent, from peers. The decision that he made after his last fishing trip at the age of nine was pivotal. Even as he felt like a disappointment to his father, he decided that he would have to try to be himself, and he managed to more or less stay the course. Felix's mother was actively supportive, and that was undoubtedly a significant influence in his growing capacity for self-acceptance. His sensibilities as a child and his current adult sensibilities were an integration of conventionally female and male qualities. Sally and his mother were models that he drew on, and I would describe Felix as a man with a distinctively gay character and sensibility. Although he is not particularly feminine in presentation, his freedom from masculine posturing and emotional constriction intuitively suggests femininity. I believe that almost any gay man would readily recognize Felix as gay. He has a lively internal life that he comfortably expresses, a quality of emotional receptivity, and a sense of human vulnerability that are all elements of a gay sensibility. With unusual alacrity and determination, Felix had threaded his way through the complex developmental challenge of the gender split, and he had emerged whole.

Felix is now the first violin in a local string quartet. "The violin is *me*," he had once said to me. "It is the thing in the world that I am

closest to, the thing that along with sex most allows me to be myself."
Felix occasionally sends me an e-mail, and in one a few years ago he
related a story. Felix's father had given him a new, apparently extraordinary violin for his fortieth birthday, carrying it on a plane from Wisconsin to personally deliver it. When Felix's father arrived at the San
Francisco airport and presented the instrument, Felix began crying,
and then so did his father. "We embraced," Felix said in his note, "and
standing there in the airport with him, I realized how much I love him.
I guess I always have."

## SEXUAL EXPRESSION OF THE GAY SENSIBILITY

As I have defined the term, *emotional sensibility* can be thought of as
the interaction of three variably related components. All human beings
have an internal unconscious emotional life; to varying degrees, all
have an internal *conscious* emotional life; and all have some external
expression of the two components of the internal life. Emotional sensibility thus describes the totality of how we internally experience
and variably express unconscious and conscious feelings, and our experience in the developmental gender split significantly informs the
balance of that totality. The split dictates that women be more emotionally conscious than men, and that women be more thoughtfully
emotionally expressive of their relatively integrated internal lives. The
split encourages men to repress unconscious feeling, and to limit the
expression of conscious feeling. The result is often poor self-insight and
the destructive expression of unconscious feelings, particularly anger
and aggression. It is remarkable that such differences allow women
and men to spend lives together.

Both subjectively and interpersonally, the issue probably most affecting the quality of a life is the degree of coherence among the three
components of emotional sensibility. There are two kinds of coherence, one internal, the other a bridge between the internal and the external. The first, the internal one, is the coherence of unconscious and
conscious feelings; the second, the coherence of those feelings with
how the person presents and expresses himself in the world. Both
kinds of coherence foster a sense of wholeness, authenticity, and

well-being. Incoherence in either or both is a form of inauthenticity that can leave one fragmented and fragile, both in self-experience and the experience of others. For most of us, the effort to be and remain both internally and externally coherent is a lifelong struggle. For all but the profoundly unconscious or sociopathic among us, it is a natural human struggle.

For gay men growing up and living in an adverse world, the effort to live coherently can be a struggle, because the internal life of unconscious and conscious feelings is significantly what makes the gay man "different." Many men keep some feelings unconscious, and to the extent that they *are* conscious, they can be difficult to express to disapproving others. Fortunately, the natural struggle against internal and external incoherence often fosters a capacity for introspection that is relatively unusual among males. Gay men are thus often more emotionally conscious and internally coherent than their heterosexual peers. An important early step in finding internal coherence is what gay men commonly describe as "coming out to myself." The next step is simply being *out*, which is reflected in a growing coherence between the now more coherent internal life and the expression of that life to others. If an internal life of incoherence is a kind of private closet that does not allow us to know ourselves, the incoherence between the internal life and expressed sensibility is the social closet that does not allow others to know us. The two closets exacerbate each other: the private closet demands a social closet, and the social closet encourages a private one. Both closets are destructive in lives that might otherwise be lived with more wholeness, authenticity, and human connection.

Gay men's necessarily developed capacity for introspection reveals an emotional transparency that is usually perceptible to others. Such transparency in a man violates the expectations of the conventional gender split and is often perceived as undesirable vulnerability or weakness. American culture would have us believe that vulnerability is unsuitable in men. One of the strengths of the gay sensibility is that it allows a conscious experience of vulnerability, which nurtures authentic resilience. The deficit of that capacity in many conventionally acculturated males is one of the most treacherous vulnerabilities in human life. At its worst, it leaves a man stranded between two extreme possibilities: unassailable strength and a feeling of humiliating help-lessness. This is the vulnerability that leaves so many men brittle, de-structive, emotionally inaccessible, and incapable of intimacy.

How vulnerability is handled internally defines the divide between traditionally feminine and masculine sensibilities. The divide begins forming in the early developmental gender split and continues grow-ing at least through adolescence and the later teenage years. Jed, whom I first saw for psychotherapy in 2009, described to me his personal struggle with a developmental experience that had destructively di-vided him, and the implications of that division for intimacy:

> I have been working for years to get over that bullshit,
> authoritative radio announcer's voice that I use, that voice I
> learned to put on as a teenager so I wouldn't get beaten up.
> I am still very aware of how I walk and talk, aware that people
> are watching me, and at forty, it's all fake. I don't even know
> who I am anymore, I don't know how to walk in a natural
> way. A guy I recently met at a party said to me, "I really like
> you," and I had the reaction I always have. My first thought
> was to run, because what he liked was the radio announcer.
> If I got to know him, he would discover me, and he'd be
> really disappointed. That's why I have never really had a
> relationship. *Who* would be having it? Who would I be?

Jed's inauthentic expressed sensibility was a self-protective postur-ing that left him fragmented. In his internal life he was emotionally complex and insightful, he was gentle and funny. He was a gay man, and he wanted to love and be loved—none of which was revealed to others by "the radio announcer." His internal and expressed sensibili-ties were incoherent, and the incoherence left him feeling that he did not know who he was—or that he was no one. Over time in our work together, Jed came to recognize that he *was* his internal life, including the many unconscious feelings that he was slowly able to make con-scious. He had to learn to express that increasingly coherent internal life to others. He would have to work for an expressed sensibility that somehow blended the forbidden off-the-air-feminine and masculine sensibilities that he lived with internally. To feel whole and real, he needed to be more honestly himself in the world. He was someone whom many would be happy to discover, not someone who needed to be hidden from view, and he began to accept that.

Authentic lives are significantly nonreactive: they are primarily rooted in an internal center rather than in others' norms and expectations. Predominantly inauthentic lives are reactive and are decentered by external influences. In their most polarized forms among gay men, both feminine and masculine expressed sensibilities suggest some reactivity. The man is not seeking himself; he is reactively embracing or rejecting the person that others expect him to be. "Straight-looking, straight-acting" and highly effeminate gay men are sometimes examples of such reactivity. The man who strives to present himself as largely masculine or feminine must support the effort by keeping aspects of his internal sensibility unconscious. In that unconsciousness, he hides himself, not only from others, but from himself. Reactive lives are understandably a hallmark of all stigmatized minorities. While stigmatization provokes reactivity and makes an internally centered life more difficult, a remarkable number of gay people have managed to live relatively centered lives and live them well. This is a notable triumph in the face of persistent adversity. In a better world—a considered, comfortably secure, and eclectic world—such lives would be natural.

Even as homosexuality is not the whole story of who gay men are, sex in gay lives, as in all human lives, is usually an important experience. In addition to providing a sometimes-intimate connection to others, sex can be a means of self-discovery: the altered, disinhibited consciousness of sexual arousal often allows us to experience normally unconscious feelings that are self-revealing. For most gay boys, adolescence is turmoil, but sexual experiences and a developing internal sensibility mutually influence each other, sometimes for the better, sometimes not. As adults, that early-formed association often continues to inform the nature of our sexual lives. If a self-accepted early feminine sensibility and supportive sexual experiences incline us to adult sex as a tender and affectionate emotional "conversation," an exaggeratedly masculine early sensibility encourages Erik Erikson's idea of "genital combat." Genital combat is a sparring exchange that prohibits any vulnerable emotion, and if not full combat, it is a very male "sport sex" focused on the physical act. Almost inevitably, finding our sexual lives is distorted in one way or another by the destructive social idiocy that attempts to prohibit the natural adolescent exploration of feelings, relationships, and sex, particularly for gay people. The prohibition almost never works, but the humanly limiting consequences of the effort are all around us.

Most adult sexual lives would find value in both making love and engaging in sport, and the complete absence of either is likely a loss. While the loss of emotionally focused sex sometimes expresses simple inexperience, it can also suggest discomfort with one's internal sensibility, and expression of that sensibility to oneself or others in the revealing act of sex. A surprising number of gay men I have known and worked with over the past three decades grew up entirely on sport sex, almost certainly reinforced by both the requisite adolescent segregation of sex from relationships, and the narrow, coarse model of most pornography. These men have never thought about the possibility of sex as an emotional conversation and often have little sense of what that idea even means. This is notable in a group that stands out among men as introspective and emotionally transparent. What many of these men *do* sense is that the sex they are having is, by itself, ultimately unsatisfying and inadequate, even as they continue to seek something better in more sport sex with other men who, themselves, know nothing but sport sex.

What these men have in common—the blind leading the blind in sexual matters—is a developmentally truncated postadolescent, teenage experience that is not of their own making. Adult heterosexual men—at least those who are paying attention—do have one advantage over many gay men: they have encountered the emotional and sexual sensibilities of women. In fact, many gay men *have* had sex with women, and there is often a significant difference between the sexual sensibilities of gay men who have and those who have not. Members of the Sport Sex Club have something to learn from some other gay men, and this need not be only from men who have had sex with women. A gay man who, like Felix, has found his own blended internal sensibility and learned to express it sexually may have much to impart to those who are interested and open.

For gay men, one uniquely gay sexual experience can support the exploration of unconscious and conscious feminine sensibilities and allow sharing those sensibilities with others. This is *receptive* anal sex, which, as Felix put it, is "the most wonderful thing in the world." While receptive anal sex can be enacted as sport sex—and often is—it holds much more potential. This physical act can pleasurably express a receptive emotional state of trusting vulnerability and intimacy, feelings more usually understood and valued by women. A man lets another man *inside*, both physically and emotionally, in a way that straight men rarely do. Felix described the lack of receptive anal sex as "a huge loss, a deprivation that would have made me a much shallower person," and he is not alone in such feelings. Even as having sport sex and making love are both ways of connecting to others, they share relatively little emotional territory.

Being in love and making love are among our most vulnerable experiences, and there is little doubt about why so many men, gay and straight, find love and tenderness daunting. A constant diet of sport sex that insists on dominance and invulnerability—or sometimes-masochistic submission—is often a fallback position for those who are afraid of gentler feelings. *All* men have at least an unconscious component of feminine sensibility, formed in infancy and childhood. Pure sport sex keeps that sensibility unconscious, where it cannot contribute to a sense of wholeness and, for gay men particularly, authenticity. While still in graduate school, Felix once said to me during a therapy session, "I know this is going to set psychoanalysis back a hundred years, but until I got fucked, I didn't know what it meant to be a real person. It was the first time I felt I was whole. It was an experience I wouldn't give back for anything." It is not clear whether the physical act of sex instinctually informs the emotion, or the conscious and unconscious emotion interpret the act and give it its meaning. I believe it works both ways, simultaneously. Human sex is magic.

Many assume that the readily observable expressed sensibilities of a gay man—physical carriage, speech, dress, or interests—are a reasonably good predictor of his "position" in sex. Car buffs are assumed tops, interior designers bottoms. In actuality, gay men's sexual lives—which are only one aspect of expressed sensibility—correlate quite variably with other aspects of expressed sensibility because the coherence between our internal and external lives is so variable. Sex is a relatively private event that can allow expression of internally felt emotion that may be little expressed in other aspects of life. The ability to experience and share feelings that we do not normally consciously experience or express is one important reason that sex is so powerful in our peculiarly self-conscious human lives. Males are physically capable of both insertion and receptivity, which in sex between two men offers a rich range of physical possibilities, each of which can express some aspect of the emotional sensibility: the sexual act is often a physical metaphor for a feeling. In a sexually altered state of consciousness, we exist not in our everyday cortical lives, but in our emotional lives, and we are, for the moment, more expressively open and thus more connected both to ourselves and to others.

If sex—particularly communicative sex—can open us up and provide desired connection, why are so many frightened of sex, and why is it so difficult to talk about? One answer is implicit in the question: many are afraid of fully knowing themselves, and of revealing what they do know to others. The sexual expression of unconscious or conscious internal sensibility works against the very effort to keep the sensibility unconscious or private. Even as we are aware that almost everyone engages in sexual acts, emotionally expressive sex can feel as unmentionable as the unconscious—or the conscious, but private—sensibility that is expressed in the sex. When we limit or hide our sexual lives, we are concealing not the physical acts, but the feelings we fear or feel shame about.

The sexual act that I have cited as most characteristic of the gay sensibility—the anal-receptive or "feminine" position—remains an often-contentious issue, even among gay men. Many are self-professed "pure bottoms" or "exclusive tops," although every gay man has experienced ardent bottoms on the top, and self-professed tops on the bottom. Many gay men hold an unspoken, often-unconscious contempt for bottoms, just as straight men often hold contempt for women—not to mention womanly men. The feelings are not so much about the behavior itself, but about the feminine sensibility expressed in the bottom position. In "bottom men," the exclusive top sees parts of himself— unfamiliar, alien-feeling parts—that he cannot accept or express, an idea that supports the common insight among gay men that the exclusive top is often attempting to prove, to himself and others, that he is not a bottom. Sometimes those with exclusive bottom or top identities are accurately expressing their entire conscious internal sensibilities; but often, they are also containing aspects of their unconscious sensibilities that might, if recognized and allowed expression, nurture a broader, more authentic experience. The complexity of internal sensibility and its sexual expression is seen in another experience that most gay men also know: there are masculine ways to be on the bottom, the "assertive bottom," and feminine ways to be on top, the "affectionate top." Such positions, even when they are exclusive, are often expressions of more complex, more integrated sensibilities. With exploration comes discovery.

Despite the number of relatively exclusive bottoms and tops in gay communities—roles that, not coincidentally, partly mimic heterosexual life—a third possibility more obviously expresses a blended gay sensibility. In the parlance of gay communities, this is the man who is "versatile." As the term suggests, the versatile man is both bottom and top—receptive and insertive—depending on the partner, the dynamics of the relationship, or the sensibility of the moment. Different people, different relationships, and different moods motivate the expression of different aspects of the internal sensibility. Some of this versatility seems instinctual, in which I include unconscious memory of the infantile and childhood experience of growing up with parental giants. Many men are more likely to be on the bottom with partners who are physically stronger, taller, older, or more self-assured and accomplished than they are. With a slighter, shorter, younger, or less-accomplished partner, the same man may be on top. Some men are attracted to stronger, taller men precisely because of the more feminine sensibility they engage, while others are avoidant because that feeling is uncomfortable. A young man who described himself as "typically a bottom" once told me that he was sexually interested in men "who are a bit taller than I am, but if they get much taller than that, I get uncomfortable. I'm not into men who are shorter than me. Men about my height are possible, depending on the rest of them." This man was not merely sorting out his "physical attractions," he was describing how differences in others engaged his emotional sensibilities. Some engaged a valued part of his feminine sensibility, some intimidated it, and some left him unengaged. Although women as a group tend to be more flexible and eclectic in choosing partners, this young man's feelings mirror those of many heterosexual women.

Gay men often describe themselves as having a physical "type," which is often asserted as an almost-axiomatic, unchangeable fact. But in pursuing a particular type, a man is not merely sorting men for their aesthetic appeal, he is responding to how different physical types engage his internal sensibilities. Those sensibilities—often including unconscious components—are neither axiomatic nor unchangeable; they are dynamic and open to change for the man who is able to explore them. Internal sensibility is far richer and more complex than anything that could be defined by physical types, and being gay is an opportunity to explore the potential. As an older friend once told me, "I've always thought that I had a type, but the truth is that if Rumpelstiltskin crawled out from under the carpet, I might well find myself enchanted. That's the way it has always *actually* worked for me." Another friend, Morris, told me that after dinner, he and his partner, Billy, sometimes arm wrestled to see "which one of us gets to be on the bottom that night." The winner would be on the bottom. I knew both Morris and Billy, and they both expressed the kind of developmental outcome—and integrated sensibility—that Felix expressed. They felt authentic and comfortable in both their feminine and masculine aspects, and they also manifested both in their nonsexual lives. They were *emotionally* versatile, and they expressed that sexually and otherwise. Their relationship worked without the polarization of emotional and sexual roles that is common in heterosexual and some gay relationships.

If the *natural* differences in the unconscious and conscious internal sensibilities of women and men were substantial, we would not need to insist on the socially constructed differences in expressed sensibility that we almost universally rely on. Carriage, manner of speech, dress, and ornamentation are all socially dictated trifles that, in themselves, are inconsequential. Apparently, anxiety about gender sensibility as expressed in trifles is long-standing: Deuteronomy 22:5 of the Christian Bible states, "A woman shall not wear a man's garment, nor shall a man put on a woman's cloak, for whoever does these things is an abomination to the Lord your God."[29] It is no accident that today's more acknowledged gender-integrated sensibilities are coincident with unisex clothing, the rise of the metrosexual, and the gender queer movement, where women's cloaks are often seen on men. Most of us take the idea of gender and gender identification much too seriously, and in doing so, we impoverish ourselves by splitting off aspects of the natural human experience that are rightly ours. Morris offered me one more piece of information about arm wrestling with Billy: if either lost the wrestling match three times in a row, that third time he was on the bottom anyway. The two-time loser, third-time winner, was usually Morris.

> I'm not as strong as Billy, so this keeps things fair and square. But, since it's pretty much a one-in-three deal—unless Billy has had too much wine with dinner—I've learned a lot about topping, and I like it. It's also me. When I met Billy, I was more a bottom, and Billy told me he was pretty much an exclusive top. When he said that, I thought, *Yeah right, then what's the point of being gay?* It took about a month for us to straighten *that* out. When I fucked him lovingly, I could see a beautiful, sweet, gentle woman in his face, and I loved him for that side of himself. I *fell* in love with him partly for that, and he fell in love with me. I had given him something he had never had, and he had given me more than I ever expected.

## IT IS NOT THE COW THAT MAKES THE FRYCOOK

Through the conflation of biological sex and sensibility, a society establishes a template for "gender-appropriate" internal and external sensibilities that contradicts human nature. In the social plan, vaginas get one internal life and a wardrobe to match, penises something else. As I have described it—and both Felix and Morris have expressed it—the gay sensibility constructs gender more humanly, by integrating elements of conventionally feminine and masculine sensibilities into the life of a single person, who is most often of one biological sex. While all people have this integrative potential—and many, gay and straight, exercise it to varying degrees—as a group, gay people most visibly assert it. The gay sensibility blurs the conventional social construction of gender, and I am certain that the stigma surrounding gay people—and any people of apparently ambiguous gender—is much less about sexual behavior than about the threat gay people appear to pose to the conventional construction of gender identity. Relatively few heterosexuals would be as enchanted as Morris by Billy's emotional transformation during sex into "a beautiful, sweet, gentle woman." They would be threatened, just as they are inversely often threatened by assertive, self-sufficient, and competent women.

In insisting that biological sex and sensibility be aligned in dictated, unnatural ways, society has emotionally impoverished a great many people; and it has posed a dilemma for LGBTQ people who accept the authority of the societal construction, an acceptance usually tied tightly to early parental expectations. A majority of gay-identified men are biologically male and have a male self-identity, regardless of the mix of feminine and masculine sensibilities. The mix of feminine sensibilities does not change the biological sex and only rarely changes the internal gender identity. As a child, Felix thought briefly about being a woman and abandoned the idea because he had a penis; and Billy never thought he might be a woman, and Morris never experienced him as one. Morris experienced Billy as a man with an emotional complexity that Morris valued and loved. As young adult men, all three significantly surmounted their restrictive developmental experiences and accepted what they really felt and who they really were. The experience for all three was expansive.

The root of the dilemma that social constructions of sex, gender, and sensibility broadly pose for gay people is simple: gay people are often not like heterosexuals. Unfortunately, the social constructions they face go beyond the simple conflation of biological sex and sensibility. In the societal model, observed biological sex, gender self-identity, internal sensibility, and expressed sensibility must all be aligned. As children and young adults, we easily internalize this model, and any discontinuity between the four components becomes a painful internal struggle that is worsened by societal stigma and rejection. Although society has created the conflict by imposing a simplistic, inhuman model, it is left to LGBTQ people to deal with the problem: it is

LGBTQ people who are left feeling deviant and "misaligned." We have the choice of either rejecting the social construction in a pursuit of wholeness and authenticity, or bringing ourselves into alignment.

Today, the public voice of American gay communities—which is usually the voice of older men who were born in an era of almost-universal social intolerance—has largely accepted the conventional social construction of sex and sensibility. This voice is attempting the realignment of negative gay self-experience through the assimilation of gay lives into mainstream society. Some older and many younger men reject this effort, but the public voice insists on one primary tenet: the biological sex of sexual partners aside—the little "homosexual" piece—gay people are "just like everyone else." It is *for this reason*—not because human diversity must be accepted and respected—that LGBTQ people should be accorded the legal rights, protections, and respect that everyone else (presumably) receives. While this may be a politically expedient strategy for gay spokespeople, it shifts the burden of self-acceptance and self-realization back onto the LGBTQ individual. The strategy asserts the right of LGBTQ people to have sexual relations with those of the same sex, but not to live with complex internal and expressed sensibilities that are misaligned with the conventional four-part formula. In gay marriage, both men become "husbands," and except for the fact that the other party to the marriage is also a husband, both men, like all married men, become "marrieds" who presumably embody every socially desirable trait that such identities are meant to imply. This community agenda largely abandons the needs of gay people who would insist on their own more complex sensibilities and forms of life, leaving them to face the penalizing sanctions that other nonhusbands—and nonwives—must also unfairly endure. For many gay men, today's community agenda is not support, but abandonment. It appears to offer not a new life out of the closet, but life in a new closet, an emotional closet that is, like the gay closet of lore, a destructive space in which to live.

From an early age, Felix largely followed his own construction of gender and sensibility. But Felix's inborn capacities, and his favorable family and social support, were relatively unusual. For the male-identified gay man who feels that he must accept—or who cannot understand how not to accept—the conventional social construction

of biological sex, gender identity, and sensibility, there are no easy solutions. Such a man can attempt to bring his sensibilities into conformity with his biological sex and gender identity, at the cost of
authenticity and wholeness. He can attempt to bring his gender into
conformity with his sensibilities, at the cost of abandoning his male
self-identity, or, more radically, by also forfeiting his biological sex. As
a last resort, the man who accepts the validity of conventional alignment can realign nothing and live with a sense of incoherence, failure, rejection, and, too often, self-loathing. All of these problematic
solutions take conventional ideas about sex, gender, and sensibility too
seriously, and all can result in lives that are compromised and incapable of authentic human connection and intimacy.

Fortunately, all three solutions and their human consequences are
unnecessary if we are able to sidestep the narrow conventional construction of gender and sensibility and live, inside and outside, more or
less as ourselves. A gay friend who had grown up in a gay-adverse
family once said to me, "I realized a long time ago that I had only one
really important thing to do in life. If I accomplished nothing else, I
would figure out how to be myself." Being ourselves is almost always
a struggle, sometimes a discouragingly difficult, but never impossible,
one. In its inevitable mix of happy and unhappy consequences, the
struggle offers a real, fully human life. For those who doubt the possibility, allow me to repeat the words of a poet: *It is not the cow that
makes the frycook.*[30]

# 2

# Stigma and Shame

Benzine removes stains. Take off your overcoat.
Take off—pull off—gloves, hat, boots.
Love deprives men of their reason.
—Keith Waldrop, *The Not Forever*[1]

Although we often forget or deny it, gay men have been hounded by stigma for centuries; and both the traumatizing stigma itself and the internalized shame it propagates are the prime obstruction to gay men's self-realization. Still today in America, simply for being gay, young men are disavowed and disowned by families, and men of all ages are socially ostracized, forced from housing, fired from jobs, refused medical care, legislated against, harassed, beaten, raped, and murdered. The only other minority group members in the United States that have been so brutally treated over such an extended time are African-Americans, though, today, gay men are twice as likely to be the object of hate crimes as African-Americans.[2] While gay men can more readily conceal themselves than can most African-Americans, gay men in public must remain alert and cautious. From an early age, gay boys learn that heterosexual men can be dangerous. The simplest gesture (a particular gait, a lilt in the voice) or display of affection (holding hands, sustained eye contact, or simply walking down the street a few inches too close to another man) can garner emotional or physical assault. For personal safety, most gay men become intuitively adept at avoiding such natural, human behavior in all but the known-to-be-tolerant social environment. There have been thousands of stories about the physical brutalization of gay men, some widely publicized, some not. One less-publicized story is that of Gabriel Fernandez.

## THE STORY OF GABRIEL FERNANDEZ

In 2013, Gabriel, an eight-year-old Southern California boy, was beaten to death by his thirty-year-old mother, Pearl, and her thirty-four-year-old boyfriend, Isauro. At the grand jury hearing, Deputy District Attorney Jonathan Hatami said, "For eight straight months, [Gabriel] was abused, beaten, and tortured more severely than many prisoners of war."[3] Gabriel's two slightly older, unassaulted brothers testified that he was starved and made to live in a locked cabinet.[4] The *Los Angeles Times* story from which this information is taken is of interest for a disturbing reason. Although the story noted in passing that Gabriel's mother and her boyfriend "called Gabriel gay, punished him when he played with dolls and forced him to wear girls' clothes to school," the article offered little content on the antigay sentiment that motivated the crime, but focused on the failure of the child welfare system. "In the wake of Gabriel's death, the Board of Supervisors convened a special commission to study the county's response to child welfare issues," the article reported. "They ordered a reorganization that includes setting up a 'child welfare czar' to better coordinate communication between departments charged with protecting children and responding to reports of abuse."

Even though California is one of thirty-two states that classify "sexual orientation" as one target of hate crimes,[5] Gabriel's case was never investigated and prosecuted as such a crime. Hate crimes carry higher automatic penalties, but authorities are often reluctant to properly classify them, sometimes because of their own prejudice, and sometimes because of the additional complexity of the investigation and prosecution. When I asked seven gay male friends about the broad issue of hate crimes against gay people, four spontaneously mentioned Gabriel Fernandez. When I asked seven heterosexual friends the same question, not a single person mentioned the tragedy, and only one recalled it after I prompted him with specifics. "But wasn't it a child abuse case?"

he asked. "You said the boy was only eight years old." It seemed not to occur to my well-intentioned friend that an eight-year-old can "be gay." But adult gay people were all once eight, and as adults they feel implicated and threatened by any stigmatization of other gay people. They pay attention to such stories. Whether the Fernandez case should be considered primarily child abuse or a hate crime is not the point—it was both. The point is that many gay men experienced Gabriel's murder as a hate crime, and as pertinent to their own lives. This horrible death of a child, the heterosexual public's interpretation of the event, and the media handling of the story are all troubling products of the unhealthy, ongoing social history of gay men in America.

The troubled and troubling feelings that appear to have motivated the murder of Gabriel Fernandez are widespread in America. According to the Offices of the United States Attorneys within the U.S. Department of Justice, "Some studies have indicated that assaults motivated by hatred are more violent, and more likely to result in serious injury to the victim, than other types of assaults. That is particularly so with respect to victims in the lesbian, gay, bisexual, and transgender (LGBT) community."[6] The article continues with a discussion of the Matthew Shepard and James Byrd, Jr., Hate Crimes Prevention Act, which had recently been signed into law by President Barack Obama:

> [The new law] for the first time recognized certain violent acts directed at individuals because of their actual or perceived sexual orientation as federal hate crimes. The Shepard Byrd Act provides investigators and prosecutors with important new tools to deploy against hate crimes. Before the passage of the Shepard Byrd Hate Crimes Prevention Act in October 2009, there was no single federal hate crime statute.[7]

The law is named for two victims. In 1998, Matthew Shepard, a twenty-one-year-old gay college student, was beaten, tortured, and left to die, tied to a fence near Laramie, Wyoming. In the same year, James Byrd, Jr., a forty-nine-year-old African-American, was murdered by two white supremacists and a third man in Jasper, Texas. They dragged Byrd, chained behind a truck, down an asphalt road.[8]

## THE CONSEQUENCES OF STIGMATIZATION

Some of the stigma gay men are subjected to is expressed violently, some not. In an extensive survey published in 2014, the Henry J. Kaiser Family Foundation asked gay men to identify the "most important issue facing gay and bisexual men today."[9] At 43 percent, "discrimination, stigma or lack of acceptance" was the number one response.[10] The report summary states:

> Discrimination and stigma (whether HIV-related or not) is the most frequently-named issue when asked about the most important issues facing gay and bisexual men today. When it comes to their own experiences, many report having faced various forms of stigma and discrimination as a result of their sexual orientation, including being rejected by a friend or family member (32 percent), being threatened or physically attacked (26 percent), experiencing unfair treatment from an employer (15 percent), poor treatment from a medical professional (15 percent), and discrimination in trying to find housing (7 percent).[11]

Both the mental health and medical consequences of such stigma are immense, and the effects were compounded when the stigmatized community was immersed in the stress of an extended, destructive epidemic. Stigma itself is a serious, enduring stressor. In a report from the Centers for Disease Control and Prevention, "stigma and discrimination" are identified as the source of troubling consequences. Young adult gay men are 8.4 times as likely as young heterosexual men to have attempted suicide, and 5.9 times as likely to report high levels of depression. They are also 3.4 times as likely to use illegal drugs and to engage in "risky" sex.[12] Suicide and depression are among the obvious, expected results of stigmatization. But it is important that the CDC also identifies drug use and higher-risk sex among the *consequences* of stigma. While drug use and sexual behavior are often used as justification for stigmatizing gay men, the stigma itself is significantly driving the behavior. People who are taught not to value themselves do not exercise self-care, and high-risk behavior is one way we play

out the self-devaluation and shame that stigma creates. Sustained societal stigma—which is internalized as *self-stigma*—almost invariably
results in elevated shame, anxiety, and depression, and behaviors that
express such feelings. This observation is too often alarming to gay
men because it feels pathologizing, blaming, and, itself, stigmatizing.
It feels like a characterization and indictment of gay life and an "ad-
mission of weakness." In truth, it is an indictment of the stigmatizing
society that has initiated the entire destructive chain. How could the
stigma gay men have been subjected to not produce some differences?
These differences are not weaknesses, they are appropriate and
understandable human responses. When we experience *problematic*
differences, they are usually addressable, which is the focus of several
of the following chapters.

In 2014, for a perspective outside that of psychotherapy, I spoke
with Gary Feldman, a San Francisco primary-care physician. He has
a large, long-standing practice with populations of both gay men and
heterosexuals and is particularly articulate in discussing his perceptions of gay men:

> The number of people I see who are depressed and on
> antidepressants is huge. If you're talking about the group
> of gay men that had been sick [with HIV-related illness],
> I'd guess that seventy-five percent are on some type of
> psychotropic medication. In those who haven't been sick
> [but are HIV-positive], definitely less, forty or fifty percent,
> but they've been able to carry on life with a certain normality.
> Negative [HIV-negative] men, it's still high, just for being
> gay. Maybe twenty percent on antidepressants, anxiolytics
> [antianxiety medication], or sleepers, medications to
> help make life easier. There's also a high incidence of
> psychotherapy in all three groups, higher than the straight
> population. There's a greater acceptance of the value of
> talking about your internal state and the feeling that you're
> not supposed to live in psychic pain.
>    I think if you take gay men in general, this is a
> population that's going to be more accepting of the idea of
> depression, of the idea of a psychological state that affects

their wellness. They're more internal, their internal worlds are more dominant in their being because of dealing with their differences in society. Men are different than they used to be, but in general [heterosexual] men have little internal space that they live in, they have no idea what anxiety is. A gay man is likely to bring up depression, anxiety, and substances much more often than straight men, maybe fifty percent higher to throw out a number. Straight men feel their masculinity is impaired by talking about such things, while for gay men masculinity has a different tone, is more complicated. Straight men accept their situations, gay men are looking for help for the most part.[13]

Primary-care physicians with this level of psychological insight are relatively rare, and gay men in San Francisco are fortunate to have such care available. Unfortunately, outside of large cities, gay men are much less likely to find a primary-care physician to whom they can even acknowledge being gay.[14] A large body of qualitative and statistical literature supports Feldman's observations and estimates about the psychological issues affecting gay men.[15] But again, it must be asserted that the problems that arise in being gay are not the results of *being gay*, they are the results of how being gay is treated by the larger society. It is not *we*, but *they*, who are accountable.

## THE STORY OF RONALD REAGAN

Ronald Reagan has a lot to account for: the early AIDS epidemic unleashed more stigmatization of gay men than any other event in the history of gay life in America, and Ronald Reagan presided as president over the first seven years of that slaughter. Three years into the epidemic, we had already seen 7,239 reported AIDS cases and 5,596 deaths.[16] In that year, Larry Speakes, the acting White House press secretary, held a telling press briefing on December 11, 1984. A reporter, Lester Kinsolving, who had for two years raised questions about the epidemic and been consistently rebuffed by Speakes, tried again.

The press secretary and other journalists were apparently amused by his persistence:

SPEAKES: Lester's beginning to circle now. He's moving in front. [Laughter] Go ahead.

REPORTER: Since the Centers for Disease Control in Atlanta—[laughter]—reports—

SPEAKES: This is going to be an AIDS question.

REPORTER: —that an estimated—

SPEAKES: You were close.

REPORTER: Well, look, could I ask the question, Larry?

SPEAKES: You were close.

REPORTER: An estimated three hundred thousand people have been exposed to AIDS, which can be transmitted through saliva. Will the president, as commander in chief, take steps to protect armed forces food and medical services from AIDS patients or those who run the risk of spreading AIDS in the same manner that they forbid typhoid fever people from being involved in the health or food services?

SPEAKES: I don't know.

REPORTER: Could you—is the president concerned about this subject, Larry—

SPEAKES: I haven't heard him express—

REPORTER: —that seems to have evoked so much jocular—

SPEAKES: —concern.

REPORTER: —reaction here? You know—

SPEAKES: It isn't only the jocks, Lester. . . .

REPORTER: No, but, I mean, is he going to do anything, Larry?

SPEAKES: Lester, I have not heard him express anything on it. Sorry.

REPORTER: You mean he has no—expressed no opinion about this epidemic?

SPEAKES: No, but I must confess I haven't asked him about it. [Laughter]

REPORTER: Would you ask him, Larry?

SPEAKES: Have you been checked [for HIV]? [Laughter][17]

Although HIV was discovered in 1983, Speaks was apparently unaware that in late 1984 we did not yet have a badly needed lab test available for HIV. The ELISA HIV antibody test would become widely available the following year.

Two years after this press briefing—five and a half years into the epidemic—we had accumulated 28,712 reported AIDS cases, 24,559 deaths, and the almost-certain probability of hundreds of thousands of existing infections that had not yet manifested as clinical AIDS.[18] The president of the United States had still not publicly uttered a single word on the subject.

In 1985, Harvey V. Fineberg, dean of the Harvard School of Public Health, said publicly, "Bisexual men and prostitutes who are drug addicts are spreading the virus to the general population."[19]

Dr. Fineberg warned that "the college coed and her boyfriend, who experimented two years previously with a prostitute," from whom the man may have contracted the infection, may both be carrying and spreading the virus. Everyone who has multiple sexual contacts in a city such as New York, where there is a high incidence of AIDS, he said, "is now at some small and growing risk of contracting AIDS."[20]

The New York Times article that reported Fineberg's presentation did not clarify the meaning of "general population," and it did not question why gay men, African-Americans, and intravenous drug users (IVDUs) were not considered part of it. The article was headlined "Panel Disagrees over AIDS Risk for Public." The Times apparently did not consider gay men, African-Americans, and IVDUs part of the American "public."

In late October 1986, the National Academy of Sciences, the most prestigious science organization in the United States, released a report. Dr. David Baltimore of the Massachusetts Institute of Technology, cochairman of the report committee, said at a news conference in Washington that the academy was "quite honestly frightened by the AIDS virus's potential to spread. This is a national health crisis . . . of a magnitude that requires presidential leadership to bring together all elements of society to deal with the problem."[21] By the end of his presidency in 1989, Reagan had done nothing of substance, and the United States had suffered 89,343 deaths.[22] The death rate was still rapidly rising, and more than three hundred thousand would be dead before the epidemic came under better control seven years later. Stigma had triumphed, and the death toll of young gay men was the fruit of its labor.


## WHAT IS SHAME?

A few years ago, I answered a knock at my front door to find a well-dressed, gentle-looking elderly African-American couple, both holding copies of *The Watchtower*. Before they could say anything, I smiled and said, "I'm gay, so I'm probably not your audience."

The gentle, grandmotherly woman responded immediately, "You should be ashamed."

"I'm not ashamed," I said. "I'm happy being who I am. *You* should give some thought to what you just said."

Even as I asserted myself, I was aware that I was disturbed by being a disappointment to another human being. I thought to myself, *You want everyone to like you, even as that is a hopeless expectation.* With my seven decades of life experience, and all the thought I've given to what it means to be gay, this otherwise-gentle, elderly grandmother had induced a bit of shame in me, shame about not being more universally likable. Shame is probably the most fundamental, pervasive, and destructive consequence of stigmatization. Society projects its own fear, hatred, and self-hatred onto others through stigmatizing treatment, and the stigmatized individual converts that stigmatization into self-stigma and shame. We begin feeling like the person we are treated as, we've bought the message. Shame among gay men is thus a product of the internalization of social stigma.

Shame underlies most of the mental health issues—depression, anxiety, suicide, and substance use—previously identified as more prevalent in gay men. Shame is expressed in not wanting to be seen by others because we feel we are someone we do not want others to see. Shame breeds self-doubt and fosters an impaired sense of self-worth and competence that encourages unnecessarily limited lives.

Self-doubt sometimes leads to a perfectionism or, more problematically, to an effort to regain a feeling of competence and control through compulsive and sometimes self-destructive behavior. Shame creates rage at the stigmatizing society, but the rage is easily turned on the self as self-neglect or self-abuse. Shame leads to secrecy, which further heightens shame and leads to still more secrecy. Shame produces reactive, compensatory defiance that is sometimes self-injurious. Shame suppresses self-expression because one is hiding the self in shame. Shame results in the inability to love because one experiences oneself as unlovable. All of these expressions of shame are among the costly consequences not of personal failure, but of social stigmatization. Unfortunately, shame is often deeply unconscious and remains unrecognized and unaddressed.

## THE STORY OF PETER

Peter is gay and first came to see me in 2006 at the age of forty-two. He was disappointed in his life and his lack of accomplishment and thought he was "a little depressed," a feeling that had started in his teens. He was clearly intelligent and seemed a potentially accomplished pianist and composer. He was supporting himself giving private piano lessons and doing part-time teaching in the music department at a community college. He lived with Jason, a former partner—"We're roommates now, but very good friends"—and did little dating. Peter had been "out as gay since the age of seventeen" and was sexually experienced. He went two or three times a month to the baths for sex and wondered if he was a "sex addict." He advised me that some friends felt he was, and thought he should be in a 12-step group for the problem. The three-year relationship with Jason before they became roommates was Peter's only extended intimate relationship.

Peter was an unusually attractive, physically fit man and initially presented himself as self-assured, relaxed, and open. But exploring his lack of career development and of "success with relationships" made it clear that he had a significant lack of reasonable self-confidence. Much of his apparent self-assurance was compensatory and tenuous. His self-doubt and his self-assured masking posture were so seamless for

Peter that it took a long time for him to recognize and acknowledge the problem. Indeed, Peter's apparent self-assurance was so credible that it took me several months to begin to understand his life experience.

Although Peter described himself as "completely out, and proud of being gay," details of his life did not support this. He had come out to himself and selected friends at seventeen, but he did not discuss being gay with his parents until he was in his late twenties. His mother, in particular, responded badly to the news, and much later, when he told her about Jason, she told Peter, "I do not want to hear the sordid details of your life in San Francisco." With his parents, Peter had never again brought up the subject of being gay or anything that implied it. "They just don't want to talk about it," Peter first said to me, "which I understand, and that's fine." When Peter occasionally attended family events in Colorado, Jason was never welcome. Peter had complied with this restriction by leaving Jason at home, which had caused considerable conflict with Jason, who was hurt and resentful.

Well into our work together, I thought Peter might finally be ready to discuss his feelings about sex.

"What about your sexual life at the baths?" I asked. "You've seemed reluctant to actually talk about it."

"I don't know what there is to talk about. It's fine."

"Well, for one thing, you've told me that friends have said it was an 'addiction,' and that you thought that might be true." I paused. "So I'm wondering what that means and why you would think that. I'm also thinking of your mother mentioning your 'sordid life in San Francisco' and imagining that sex had something to do with her choice of words."

"Well, it's important to me, so I wouldn't generally call it an addiction. But it's true—and this is where I think about the idea of addiction—I find it *compelling*. I sometimes *crave* it, and that sounds like addiction to me."

"Well, people quite naturally 'crave' sex—I think you're describing the feeling of sexual desire, or being horny—and that in itself surely wouldn't define addiction."

"It wouldn't?"

"Touching and being touched, doing intimate physical things with other people, having those kinds of connections to other people—these are all important, natural, and instinctual aspects of human life. Everyone needs that, whether they acknowledge it or not."

To my simple response, Peter suddenly teared up and was silent. After a few minutes, he continued, "I've never heard someone talk about sex that way. They talk about it as if we were out humping rocks, as if it meant nothing. The baths are the only place I feel like people think I have something to offer them. This is the only place I feel like *a person*. Just now, as I was thinking about what you said, I realized that I'm very lonely."

As we continued the discussion over the next several sessions, it became increasingly clear that sex was more than just the only connection to others that Peter had been able to find. It was also the only time when he felt that he honestly expressed *himself*. Not even in his music composition did he feel as authentic. Peter mentioned intense, intimate moments with other men at the baths, and those moments meant a great deal to him: "They are my most *alive* moments."

As Peter began having these important insights about his life at the baths, he was also becoming conscious of feeling shame about his sexual behavior. And he recognized that he also felt shame about having shame—"Gay men should be proud," he said—and he thus denied his shame. He said to me, laughing, "Very often when I'm at the baths, walking around in a towel, I have one thought: 'I'm so glad my mother can't see me now.'" Peter had long been aware of having this thought, but had never allowed himself to consider its meaning. The thought was an expression of shame, but with his sense of shame suppressed, being sexually attractive allowed him the feeling of "being a desirable person." But this feeling was short-lived, and his experience of desirability was never internalized or extrapolated. It never became part of how he experienced himself; it was an experience in the moment. And it never extended to any aspect of himself other than his body and sexual desirability. For Peter, sex at the baths had been simultaneously a temporary liberation from shame and a source of it.[23]

Over time, Peter realized that he had begun feeling shame during very early life. From before he was an adolescent, Peter had memories of his parents—particularly his mother—discouraging behavior they thought feminine, which included his interest in music. He was shamed by them, as well as by peers in school. During high school, Peter kissed another boy who called him a fag and "warned others" about Peter. (This boy, Peter told me, now lives as a gay man in West Hollywood.) The self-doubt that grew out of Peter's shame had also started early and would truncate his entire life. He was hiding from the world. When I first described to Peter the interaction between shame and self-doubt, he responded instantly, "The first thing my mother said when I came out to them was 'You should be ashamed of yourself.' I remember the look on her face, and I'll never forget it. She looked like she hated me, and it made me feel like a nobody, a mouse." Peter's self-doubt was affecting his career as a musician and a composer as well as his sense of potential in personal relationships. After much discussion, Peter recognized that he approached both issues in a disempowered and passive way. He felt largely unworthy of success in either area—although he sometimes also had an arrogance about music and about his attractiveness—and he pursued neither with the kind of *reasonably* confident approach that might lead to better results.

Shame usually works out of conscious reach, which makes it much more destructive. As Peter became more consciously aware of how shame informed his feelings, his sense of self, and his behavior, he was slowly able to change that behavior and improve his results. By the time we stopped meeting after four years of work, Peter was composing regularly and, at last, felt that he was writing the music that *he* wanted to write. "I hear myself in my music for the first time in my life—*my* feelings." He had had one new piano concerto performed and had another performance in preparation. He was also dating a man—a violinist, by no coincidence—and said to me, "I have no idea if it will go anywhere, but I'm enjoying it. I like him a lot. And I actually feel that I have something to offer him—other than my dick."

Peter's intelligence, resilience, and capacity for insight served him well. In my experience, gay men have done admirably with lives that have usually been forced to navigate an obstacle course of destructive social influences. That so many have persevered in simply living as gay

men is remarkable and moving. But shame still often lurks unconsciously behind the most successful of gay lives, and Peter's life is a
good illustration of how subtle its presence and influences can be. We
are never completely free of shame acquired in childhood, adolescence,
and early adult life, and the mere assertion of "gay pride" does not undo
it; it hides it. The ability to consciously recognize shame when it attempts
to play itself out can transform our lives. In recognizing shame, we
can decide to interrupt its inclinations and play things out differently.
In doing that, we sometimes get better results, and our shame and
self-doubt slowly diminish.

## SEX AND SHAME

America has always been steeped in a profound erotophobia—at least
in the *telling*—and all gay men, including today's young gay men, live
with that heritage. Too much of our shame is shame about sex. But
gay men, young and old, also live today with another legacy, that of
the early AIDS epidemic. For older men it is often the trauma of the
events, but for younger men it is something else. Younger men sometimes hold a notion that men of an earlier generation were "irrespon-
sibly promiscuous" in the years of Gay Liberation preceding the onset
of the epidemic, and that they caused a slaughter that has stigmatized
young men's lives and sexuality. In fact, the stigmatization of gay lives
and sexuality long preceded the epidemic, and young men often mis-
understand the Gay Liberation years. In those years, men were simply expressing new freedom from a society that had distorted their
adolescent and early-adult experience by prohibiting relationships and
encouraging surreptitious, shamefully experienced sex. The Gay Liberation movement, in its reactive, adolescent fervor, demanded bringing all that had been prohibited into the street, insisting that it not be
conducted in secrecy and shame. If such behavior was promiscuous
by the conventional, erotophobic standards of American society, it was
also completely understandable and long overdue. Older men have not
caused the stigmatization of the highly sexual lives of today's younger
men; they have cut the path that young men today follow.

The AIDS epidemic was not the first time that human sexuality inadvertently wrote a disturbing chapter in human history. Despite our denial, sexual feelings and behavior have felled dynasties, downed civilizations—and almost terminated a U.S. presidency, that of Bill Clinton. The obvious truth is that sex in human life is fundamental, essential, and compelling. Sex is an important source of vitality and pleasure, and a necessary form of emotional communication between human beings. It is some kind of magic, and just as baffling. Nevertheless, because of the epidemic, *reasoned* sex became a standard that gay men were expected—and expected themselves—to meet. Nancy Reagan said, "Just say no" to drugs, but she might as well have included sex. For anyone who has observed human life, reasoned sex is a ridiculous standard. "Reasoned sex is like jumbo shrimp," a friend once said to me. Sex is not conducted out of good sense or reason, and it never will be. By its very nature it is irrational, and both the importance and the irrationality of sex are beyond negotiation. Societal stigma, self-stigma, and shame are often about sex because these issues are rooted in feelings that many human beings find self-revealing and frightening. The only way out of this perceived conflict is to use our rational minds to come to some acceptance of human life as it is. Our choice is simple: we can be ourselves, or we can be ourselves pretending to be something else.

Stigmatization of diverse minority groups is a heritage in America, a country of immigrants built on the Constitution and the Bill of Rights. For gay men struggling with shame about their identities and sexual lives, let it be clear that no heritage of stigma and shame can change who we are. And no fear and repression will effectively deny that we are all partly irrational, very sexual beings. Our sexual lives are a mysterious blessing from nature, our roses and scrub brush, our sunlight and thunderclouds. Sex is ecstasy and disappointment, and everything in between. We should not forget that, and no one will.

# 3

# Our Tripartite Communities Today

Rain beats at the window, while from the other side precise daylight, gray under a comprehensive cloud but brighter than I would have expected for such a gray day, filters through.
                                    —Keith Waldrop, *The Not Forever*[1]

For gay men alive in America today, three pivotally defining years are 1969, 1981, and 1996, even if some of us are too young to know it. In 1969, the Stonewall riots opened the possibility of a new future for gay people by confronting stigma, demanding freedom for gay lives, and insisting on, if not acceptance, at least recognition that gay people were going to live their lives openly. We would have a mere twelve years living out this new future, until 1981, when HIV first hinted at its presence. The dream of Stonewall would quickly be eclipsed by an unexpected nightmare that hurtled through gay communities, leaving in its wake devastating death, desolation, fear, and shame, as well as a legacy of incredible courage and heroic action in confrontation of a society that was largely ignoring our plight. In 1996, new and substantially effective HIV medication regimens—highly active anti-retroviral therapy, widely known as HAART—would finally become available, and they would allow gay communities to slowly return to something resembling everyday, noncombat lives.

Now, a half century after Stonewall and almost a quarter of a century after HAART became available, our communities are no longer united by a radical, in-your-face liberation movement or a struggle for biological survival. Without liberation or plague to unite us, today's gay communities—still living in a highly stigmatizing American society—are surprisingly divided on what it means to be gay and live a gay life. Some push to return to liberation, insisting on distinctively gay lives. Others push for the acceptance of gay lives through social assimilation. Some experience these differences of purpose as problematically divisive, others as an expression of welcome diversity. However the differences are understood, this new postepidemic era has offered us the possibility of finding and living lives as ourselves, both as individuals and as communities that do, after all, have some common interests. Out of incoherence came a universe, but a complex one.

The early and late epidemics have been hugely influential in all American gay lives, and the totality of the two epidemics has created a psychologically complex community of men. Men have different historical relationships to the two epidemics, and their emotional and social lives reflect those differences. The demarcation of these groups is largely defined by age and by one's relationship to gay communities at the time of each of three events. The first occurred in 1981, when we became cognizant of an epidemic in progress; the second in 1985, when we were first able to test for HIV, and each man could know with some certainty if he was positive or negative; the third in 1996, the year of the introduction of HAART and the possibility that HIV-positive men might survive. For individual men—rather than whole communities—another obviously pivotal event is the discovery that one has contracted HIV. In this ongoing event in the United States, approximately twenty-six thousand more gay men contract HIV every year.[2]

## THREE GROUPS OF MEN DEFINED

We live today in tripartite communities, with significant psychological and social differences that define each group. The first of these—I will call them *older-group* men—includes those who were out and active in gay communities before the introduction of HAART in 1996. Older-group men experienced the early epidemic firsthand and were directly exposed to levels of death, loss, and trauma not usually experienced by younger men. Older-group men are divided between those who personally experienced the early epidemic before 1985—when we were first able to test for HIV—and those who entered gay communities later. Those who were active in gay communities between 1981 and 1985 were exposed to significant additional trauma simply for living with four years of uncertainty about their own HIV status: they lived in fear of the onset of clinical symptoms that were commonly fatal within days. Men who became active in gay communities after 1985 largely avoided this trauma.

The second group—*middle-group* men—is populated by those who were out and active in gay communities after 1996. While they had no direct, personal contact with the early epidemic, they were old enough to have absorbed, secondhand, the frightening association between gay men, AIDS, and horrible, disfiguring deaths. As young children and adolescents, they learned that association from widespread public media, parents, and teachers. They were thus primed from childhood with significant anxiety about being gay and having gay sex. This early exposure was a significant developmental force for middle-group men, and today they often feel psychologically like survivors of childhood and adolescent trauma.

The third group—*younger-group* men—includes those who were too young to have had exposure to the early epidemic or, during childhood, to the association between gay men and AIDS in the pre-HAART era. Today's young men have never known HIV as almost inevitably fatal and never experienced the trauma and loss that older- and some middle-group men could not escape. This younger group—born into a less-ominous prognosis for sexually transmitted infections—has some social, sexual, and psychological commonality with gay men living in the pre-epidemic, Gay Liberation years between 1969 and 1981. Like members of those earlier communities, young men today exercise a great deal of sexual freedom, but within a milieu that is significantly defined by new technology, not all of which is for the better. And lest we forget, like those of the liberation era, a majority of young men today are still raised in rejecting or overtly stigmatizing families and communities. The consequences are often profound.

Who falls into which of the three groups is not hard-and-fast and varies with the specifics of any individual's social and psychological development. The developmental markers include at what age a child first had a sense of being gay or "different" in a way he associated with a gay identity; at what age a man was first sexually active; at what age he first came out as gay and became socially connected to other gay men; and at what age a child was first cognizant of media coverage of the pre-HAART epidemic. Although individuals vary widely on all of these specifics, I have made some credible, if debatable, assumptions about social, psychological, and sexual development to approximate the age ranges of our three groups.[3] Based on these assumptions, older-group men were born in 1971 or earlier. Middle-group men were born between 1972 and 1988. Younger-group men were born in 1988 or later. These age designations are approximations, with overlap at the margins between groups.

Despite the divisions that my tripartite model delineates, our three groups of men share a great deal, both socially and psychologically. One common shared experience is shame about the early and late epidemics, which is largely rooted in shame about sex. It is not often explicitly stated, but the HIV epidemic among gay men has been almost completely vectored by the practice of receptive anal intercourse—RAI in the language of public health and epidemiology. Gay men have known this anecdotally since the early years of the epidemic, and methodically collected epidemiological data indisputably supports the idea. While not universally practiced by gay men, RAI is the most distinctive—nonheterosexual—sexual behavior that gay men engage in, and the behavior that heterosexual men most fear and stigmatize. For many gay men, RAI is also the most intimate form of sexual communication and, for many of them, has the same importance that vaginal sex has for heterosexuals. Because of the stigma directed at RAI, it is also the sexual act that gay men experience the most shame about and most shame each other about.

RAI is by no means the only source of shame and shaming within gay communities. For gay men who are also members of ethnic or racial minorities, shame and shaming are often even more complicated, entrenched, and destructive. As illustrated later in this chapter, many younger-group men hold essentially racist feelings about HIV, treating infection as something that happens only to "certain kinds of people." Partly because of the association with RAI, many HIV-positive men in all three groups feel shame about having HIV, and negative men *do* often shame those who have it. Many gay men in all three groups, both positive and negative, experience shame about the very fact of the HIV epidemic—as if it confirmed the justice in broadly stigmatizing gay lives—and attempt to shame those who would call attention to it.

Minority groups of all kinds internalize societal shaming, feel shame about themselves and about others like them, and respond with intragroup shaming. This destructive chain is characteristic of stigmatized minorities, and I routinely see evidence of it in my work with gay men. "Call me old-fashioned, or whatever you like," an older gay man once said to me, "but I find effeminate men pretty much repulsive." A twenty-seven-year-old recently told me, "Whenever I come across an [HIV-]positive guy on Grindr [a smartphone hookup app], I just block him." Both men experienced broad societal prejudice about these characteristics in others, disavowed the characteristics in themselves, and were repulsed by other gay men who had them. They protected themselves by projecting what they feared for themselves onto others.

In 1985, when laboratory tests were first available and every man could determine his HIV status, "positive" and "negative" gay men were born. HIV status importantly bifurcates each of the three primary groups of older, middle, and younger men. Positive men—who often have their own sources of shame about HIV—find the problem exacerbated when negative men treat them with active, sometimes overtly hostile, avoidance and rejection. As a result of both the internal and external stigma, positive men too easily experience themselves as "damaged" or "contaminated" undesirables within their own communities. In turn, positive men sometimes express contempt for negative men not only for the prejudice with which negative men treat positive men—a not-unfounded reaction—but because negative men live in constraining fear and remain negative through the inhibition of emotionally expressive, sexual gay lives. While many positive and negative gay men are versatile—both tops and bottoms—the positive-negative tension can sometimes feel like a correlate to the sometimes-polarizing conflict between bottoms and tops.[4]

### The Older Group: The Story of Luis

Born in 1971 or before, older-group men share three determining life experiences. They are, by my definition, the only men of the three groups who had direct exposure to the pre-HAART epidemic. Most grew up in a more problematic social environment than many younger- and middle-group men. And in 2018, older-group men—in their middle forties or older—are often experienced in gay communities as *old*. These three issues—loss and trauma in the epidemic, problematic early developmental experience, and aging—conspire to isolate older-group men in contemporary gay communities. Trauma typically leaves survivors isolated, and this has clearly been true in the aftermath of the early epidemic. In the American society that these older survivors grew up in, gay teenagers more often lived ostracized, secretive, isolated lives than teenagers do today, and these older men experienced themselves as outsiders by nature. The fortunate ones finally found a gay community, and in those days it was often a community with coherence and purpose—driven first by a pre-Stonewall, homophile counterculture, then by Stonewall liberation, and later by the compelling emergency of the early epidemic. Today, gay communities have little such coherence. Unfortunately, older communities lost many to AIDS, along with much of the potential social support for survivors.[5]

Despite the perception of many younger men, older men continue to have sexual lives and, thus, concerns about HIV. Adults fifty and older account for approximately 10 percent of new infections in the United States.[6] Even with the huge number of deaths before 1996, people fifty-five and over still account for 19 percent of long-standing infections.[7] Older men are also more likely than younger men to receive an HIV diagnosis later in the course of illness.[8] In 2010, 53 percent of HIV-related deaths were in people aged fifty or older.[9] A later diagnosis and the consequent delay in initiating treatment have medical consequences with poorer prognoses; and symptoms of HIV and HIV treatment itself interact with many medical problems that older people experience. One of the reasons for the apparent inattention to HIV in older men lies in the mistaking of HIV-related symptomatology for other effects of aging. Older men may also have greater reluctance to discuss their sexual lives with their physicians; and their

physicians—who are often younger than patients in this age group—
are often reluctant to ask or simply assume that older men are sexually
inactive.

In addition to inadequate health care, the inattention to the
sexual lives of older people has another consequence. A 1994 study
from the University of California, San Francisco—which may still
have relevance—suggested that people over the age of fifty who had a
known risk for HIV "were one-sixth as likely as those in their 20's to
use condoms and one-fifth as likely to be tested."[10] Older people
themselves often do not think of themselves as "sexually active" and
thus part of a "risk group," and one could easily imagine their primary-
care physicians holding similar assumptions.

The secrecy around older men's sexual lives is troubling. There exists a widespread feeling that there is something unseemly about
older people having sex, despite many older people being sexually more
skilled, more sensitive, and more connected than inexperienced younger
people. Perhaps some of the feeling of unseemliness is rooted in the
childhood and adolescent inability to imagine parents having sex
because the child or adolescent is, himself, so uncomfortable with
the subject and so narrowly conceives of his parents: it would be like
discovering that God and the president both masturbate. Or perhaps
it is—the more realistic—deterioration of the older body. Regardless
of the source, many of us live with the unproductive notion that sex
among older people is not important or is nonexistent, and if it does
exist, it should at least be invisible. In fact, sex is an important form
of communication and a source of pleasure and vitality for people of
all ages. Older people must not allow others to relegate them to asexuality, social invisibility, constricted lives, and isolation. Older people
must be active and not wait for—or seek—the recognition, acceptance,
and approval of younger people.

Luis is a fifty-eight-year-old Latino American who describes a
great deal about older-group gay men today. Luis and I first started
meeting for therapy in 2013. He had discovered that he was HIV-
positive in 1988, at age twenty-eight, living in San Francisco. At the
time, he was a law student at the University of California, Berkeley,
but despite the diagnosis, he decided to finish school and attempt a
career as an immigration attorney, working largely with Mexican

clients living in the United States. His father had immigrated to the United States from Mexico in the early 1950s and met Luis's mother a few years later. She was born in Colorado, of immigrant Mexican parents. Luis's father had retired after many years of working in his own construction company; Luis's mother had retired after teaching secondary school for most of the years after her three children were born. Both parents were alive and well in Colorado.

When I first saw him in 2013, Luis had a law office in Oakland—and told me that he "buried" himself in his work—but he continued to live across the bay in San Francisco. He had never been ill and described himself as being "in good health, considering the usual things for someone my age." His partner of eleven years, Cary, had died from pancreatic cancer six years prior to our first meeting. Cary had been HIV-negative. Initially, Luis wanted to talk about his social isolation, and after a short while he did.

> "I first came in because of something that happened about a month before I met you, and I want to talk about it now. I was at a friend's party—a very rare thing in my life—and I met a guy about my age, and there was something that really clicked. He was—well, you could look at his face and know that you had something in common, that he was a person with whom you'd have some kind of mutual understanding. I could tell that almost before he started talking."
>
> "And what were you perceiving?" I asked.
>
> "I don't know exactly. He was very direct—honest-looking—he seemed solid. I wanted to say that he looked like he'd been around the block—the *epidemic* block—and made it home. I feel like it was the same block I've been around, and that we'd seen the same things. It was a feeling. And he had a little bit of sadness on his face that I recognized, or maybe it was seriousness. He seemed alone, too, like me. Whatever it was exactly, it told me that we would understand each other."
>
> "So you did talk?"
>
> "We talked for a couple of hours. Not a word about the epidemic, but that's not what I was after. We talked about a lot of other things."

"Did you find that your first perceptions of him were true? What's his name?"

"Mark. They were completely true. It was one of those odd things, like I'd known him all my life, and that we were getting back together after a little hiatus. I have a couple of really close friends from school in New York and Boston who are like that—you don't see them for a year, and after talking for one minute, you feel like you last saw them a half hour ago. I don't have friends like that here anymore, they're all gone. With Mark, I kept thinking, 'I must have met this guy before,' but I don't think I had. But . . .'"

"You started to say something."

"I don't remember what I was going to say."

"Well, you were saying how familiar he felt, how good the connection was, but I sensed that there was something bothering you about Mark."

"Oh, no, it wasn't about Mark. It was that I never followed up. We exchanged numbers and I've never called him." Luis was silent, staring across the room at the bookshelves.

"Why?"

"Why what? *Oh*—because I can't imagine why he'd be interested in me—just as a friend. Forget anything else. I'm not interested in sex with him anyway. I've been pretty lonely since Cary died, and I'm just after a friend I can talk to."

"You still haven't said why you couldn't be friends."

"One is being Latino, which guys are into or not, though that's more a sexual thing, which wasn't going on here. The other is that I'm pretty sure he's negative. So my being positive alone—I mean with no idea of sex—is something that a lot of people avoid. I mean, *look at me*." Luis pointed to his collapsed cheeks, which showed a substantial loss of normal, subcutaneous fat, an HIV-related condition known as lipodystrophy.[11] "I look awful."

"I know a lot of positive and negative men who are friends these days, older men especially. I don't know Mark, but I could imagine his being accepting of you as a friend, and maybe sexually. Did you have the sense that he had a sexual interest in you?"

Luis looked puzzled. "No, I didn't get a sexual vibe from him. But why are you asking that?"

"Because some negative men will avoid positive men sexually, and some won't. And some positive men will avoid negative men. I doubt this is all news to you. I was wondering if you're avoiding his possible sexual interest in you."

"No, of course I know that—even Cary and I had a problem with it. I think it's just the whole idea of a positive man—he's *contaminated*, radioactive. Sex or no sex, for another guy my age, I think he just takes one look at me and the whole epidemic comes rushing back."

"That all seems *possible*, but why don't you actually *ask* Mark? Why don't you try calling him and get together and talk about it? Does that feel like it would offer too much of a possibility of rejection?"

"Yes, actually it does." Luis seemed to think for a few minutes. "I've been through *a lot* of that, twenty-five years to be exact. And I guess I just don't want to risk it anymore."

"But right now, as we're sitting here talking, you're feeling all the rejection and—"

*"And I don't want more."*

"I do understand that. But you're cutting off the possibility of having a different experience. Without calling Mark, we know the outcome—you're going to sit with the rejection that you already feel anyway. If you call him, you might not have to. I certainly don't know, but I don't think you do either."

"He hasn't called *me*."

"I know that, but I don't know *why* he hasn't. It *is* possible that he thinks you're not interested in him, and that's why he hasn't called. Maybe you two are in a standoff."

Luis and I sat together silently for another ten minutes, until the end of the hour. As he walked toward the door, he turned to me. "I'm going to call him. If he tells me to fuck off, I'm going to blame you." Luis laughed, and just before he closed the door, he put his head back in and said, "Thank you."

During our appointment the following week, Luis gave me a report. He had called Mark, and they had had dinner on Saturday. When Luis called, Mark said that he thought Luis might not be interested in him because Mark was HIV-negative. Mark's speculation about why Luis might avoid a negative man was not empty. Sometimes positive men do avoid negative men, and one important reason is that positive men can be uncomfortable having to disclose their HIV status—particularly when the relationship is potentially sexual—and risk rejection. Other reasons are that a positive man may be more self-conscious about having HIV—and about the visible consequences of HIV—with men who are not positive; or the positive man may fear that negative men will be judgmental or blaming about the positive man's HIV status. Positive men often anticipate being more readily accepted and better understood by other positive men, and this is sometimes true. Some negative men—particularly those who have been involved with positive men—are perceptive and sensitive about such feelings, as Mark was.

During their dinner, Luis had found out a great deal about Mark. He was sixty-one and had had two partners die of AIDS, one in 1984, the other a decade later. He told Luis that during the early years of the epidemic he had thought that he was himself positive. Mark had been alone for the past eight years and, like Luis, was grateful to have a friend to talk to. Their conversation left Luis feeling even more strongly that the two had much in common, both historically and currently. Both men had had partners die, and both had lost numerous friends to HIV. Both had little remaining social support, other than families who lived at a considerable distance— Mark's in New Orleans. And both men—one positive, the other negative—had survived the early epidemic. Luis had told Mark of *his* apprehension about their different HIV statuses, and Mark had responded, "Now we're on the same side of that fence—the one that used to divide us. I had that with both my partners. You and I, we've both survived." Luis spoke to me about his experience of what Mark had said:

"What used to separate us—our HIV statuses—seems to
have disappeared, at least in some ways. The fact is, we *are*
both still alive—which Mark had not expected either—and
we're both wondering how we got here. It wasn't until our
dinner that I was aware of how baffled I am about being
alive. I don't think I completely accept it after all these
years. And it's such a relief to be able to talk to someone
who understands that. I want to learn to use that."

"Use *what?*" I asked.

"Just *being alive.* Even if I'm bewildered about it, it's
true, and at my age it's going to be over one way or another.
In the meantime I want to use it. Mark and I talked a lot
about that. It's as if we've both been sitting around wondering
if it's true, and it is. We're *here.* I told Mark that my fifty-
ninth birthday was coming up, which puts me right on the
cusp of sixty, and I was wondering whether to cry or have a
party, and he completely understood what I meant. He said,
'Have a party. I hope you'll invite me.'"

"And—being HIV-negative—how is it that Mark is so
surprised by being alive? How is it that you share this feeling
of surprise?"

"I don't know exactly. He thought for four years that he
was positive, but that's a long time ago. . . . Yes, I do know.
He had his two partners die, he had all these other people,
too. You're connected to people you're close to, and you
expect to be like them. You *want* to be like them. I've had
exactly the same experience he's had. I had all these people
die, and I was left behind. Mark and I were both left
behind, and HIV or not, you don't understand why you're
still here. It's just baffling. . . ." Luis was suddenly silent.

"What?"

Luis teared up, but sat silently, then slowly began
speaking. "This is the first time I've thought this . . . but
I'm wondering if I deserve it."

"Deserve what?"

"Being alive. Being so lucky. You'd look at me and say,
'What's so lucky about *this?*'" Luis pointed to the lipodystrophy

in his cheeks again. "But it's *lucky*, like a miracle. And I should use it rather than sit around and wonder about it. I think Mark and I both realized that, all in one dinner."

"I guess that's one of the better dinners you've ever had."

"The best. The very best. Except for the night I met Cary."

Luis's relationship with Mark continued and had, after four or five months, also become sexual. "It's not hot sex. But it's good, and I appreciate it," Luis told me. The two had made friends with another couple of similar age and life experience. One member of the new couple was HIV-positive, the other negative, and they had been together for twenty-six years. Luis and Mark had created a new, small community of friends, rooted, but not living, in a common history. As my discussions with Luis continued, we realized that he and Mark had both partly avoided new friends because the two could not readily relate to those who had not shared their historical experience; and those who did share it often feared that talking about it would only be retraumatizing. They would simply remind one another of things they wanted to forget. Both Luis and Mark had independently been afraid of becoming permanently mired in an ongoing, debilitating, depressive reliving of the epidemic. Instead, they found a balance in a present-day life that was also informed by a common history shared with others with whom they mutually bore witness. Luis and Mark recognized that they would not "get over" their historical experience, but they *could* construct new lives that accounted for it without being consumed by it. They were not living in their histories, but they were acknowledging them, and recognizing that they were a significant part of the bond the two felt for each other. This understanding, and the new social support it allowed, was a valuable change in Luis's life. He was living with more resilience and less protective rigidity, and he experienced this change in a vitality that he had not felt since before Cary's death. Luis worked less, too.[12]

### The Middle Group: The Stories of Franklin and Richard

The middle group of men, as I have defined it, includes those born between 1972 and 1988. These men are too young to have had direct experience of life in the early epidemic, but old enough that they had childhood exposure to information about it. They have experienced relatively little death and loss from AIDS personally, but many did experience significant trauma when they were exposed to "the fate of gay men" through media. A now-middle-aged man told me a personal story:

> When I was about ten—which would make it around 1990—I had no idea about being gay, no conscious idea at all. I'm not even sure I knew what *gay* or *homosexual* meant exactly, though I'd heard the words. One night I walked into the living room while my parents were watching TV. On the screen there was an image of a completely emaciated man lying in a hospital bed, and I instantly said to myself, "That is my future." I don't know where that came from. It made such an impression on me that I could draw you an image of what was on the screen, where my parents were sitting, and what lights were on in the room. I remember my father looking over at my mother and saying, "That's one sorry-looking bastard." The whole thing terrified me because I knew that it was somehow about me.

This kind of experience among middle-group men has several consequences. They were the first gay men with no adult life or sexual experience before AIDS. For them, the gay identity seamlessly included fatal infection and disease. HIV was an integral, seemingly normal part of being gay—in the language of psychology, a *syntonic* element of self-experience. From the beginning of memory, AIDS characterized gay life and sex between men, and being gay was dangerous and doubly shameful. Sex was a lethal business. This early-life experience understandably inhibited the coming out of many middle-group men—some still have not come out—and many resisted any internal or external identification with a group that was now so clearly a multifaceted pariah in American society.

When middle-group men did come out, many were extremely cautious about relationships and sex, and many had anxiety-bound, truncated sexual lives. Many middle-group men blamed older gay men for creating the epidemic and simultaneously resented and envied the sexual freedom that older men had "before they ruined everything." Having had no sexual experience before HIV and the rise of the Condom Code—which dictated a condom for every instance of sex[13]— middle-group men have *voiced* an absolutely rigid adherence to condom use. But since 1996, middle-group men have had the highest rates of new infections in gay communities. Because they were human beings, the condom—code or no code—was often forgotten or dismissed in the altered consciousness of sexual arousal. Middle-group men would feel deep shame about this behavior, and they would conceal it from others. In truth, condoms suggested more than just the assurance of safety promoted by AIDS prevention educators. Condoms were also a lurking reminder of the potential lethality of sex, and a significant physical and emotional barrier between two men who were trying to connect. In the subdued light of the bedroom and the elevated intimacy of sex, condoms spoke of safety, but whispered a more complex message of danger, distrust, and separation.

Franklin is a thirty-nine-year-old from Nebraska, now living in San Francisco. In 1996—the first year of HAART—he had not yet come out to himself and had not had any sexual experience. Franklin's story is representative of the lives of many middle-group men whom I have interviewed or worked with in therapy.

> I came out to myself at twenty-five, a few years after I moved to San Francisco in 2000. I'd known it but not accepted it. I can't imagine how I would have done this without the Internet. I used to buy gay movies online, mostly about coming out, and they were so intense, sometimes I'd have to stop them and continue the next day. I never got through all of them—it only took three or four. I can remember exactly where I was standing in my apartment, and I said out loud to myself, "I am gay." This was in 2002, and it was the first time I'd said that.
>
> As a teenager, I never had sex, I was too afraid, but I had a girlfriend who kept asking me why I looked at guys, and I said I was interested in what they were wearing. Right before coming out, I had sex with a girl—not very successfully—no erection. Because of the Internet, I could connect with gay

men, and it was a year after I came out that I first did
something with a guy. He was a guy who liked to find guys
who weren't experienced and have sex with them once, and
you'd never see him again. I'd always been inclined to
relationships, but this experience was very intense and
wonderful. I was sort of glowing the entire next day. Then I
met another guy, and he was my boyfriend for two years. It
was a way to dial down the intensity and also to learn the
ropes.

I certainly didn't know anything about HAART in '96.
HAART didn't change anything for me. Even after I came
out, I didn't know anyone who was sick, or maybe I would
hear socially that a person was positive, but I didn't personally
know any of them—except my family's priest, who died of it
when I was ten. He had a wife and kids and they suddenly
moved away, and my mother talked about his having AIDS.
And I had read a lot, and the press was full of it from the time
I was a kid. It was in the newspapers and television news,
protests against the Reagan administration and things like
that. It was a big deterrent to my coming out, even though
now gay doesn't equal HIV, it's just a part. Before—when
I was a kid—the only coverage about gay people was about
AIDS. Except for things like Elton John on MTV, it was all
about AIDS. My family went to church on the weekends—an
Episcopalian thing—and I was aware that a lot of Christian
people didn't look favorably on gay people. It was a bad thing.
And AIDS was a bad thing, and I suppose this all got mixed
up together. So I thought Elton John was a bad thing, and
I was trying to reconcile his being a decent person with his
doing this bad thing. I knew that this all somehow related to
me, though I wasn't quite sure how, and I thought it was a
phase I could grow out of. That was the fantasy I told
myself. I thought of being gay as being sick and being an
outcast.

When I did first come out, I thought I knew how HIV
was transmitted, and I was *very* aware of not wanting it. I
had no interest in penetrative sex because of that, at least

not initially. I'd never even kissed a guy, so penetrative sex would have been a big leap. In that first two-year relationship I had, we started having intercourse, and I was always insistent on condoms. I didn't have intercourse without a condom until my current boyfriend, in 2012 or so. It was unthinkable before that, and no matter how small the possibility, there was a possibility. I'd seek out people online who were like me, who were worried about HIV. I had great anxiety about it. It was a third rail, a place you wouldn't go. As a result, I didn't have much sex. Online, if a guy said he had HIV—they'd put it in their descriptions like hair color or height—I would drop them if it was about dating or hooking up. It scared me too much.

You hear now [in 2014] about young men in their twenties and thirties feeling impervious, that they won't get it, but that was something people my age never felt. For me, normal sex meant condoms or not having intercourse. For intercourse, for sure I used a condom, not using it was never an option. When I first did that a few years ago, I had a lot of anxiety. It was my partner's request. It was like driving without a seat belt, which I would never do, like I was doing something wrong. For my partner, it's an intimacy thing, being closer by not using condoms, and I've heard that a lot. I'm mostly insertive, and any benefit I get from not using one is offset by the risk, and I get anxious. It was Magic Johnson who made me think that as a top you were quite at risk, because he said he had a lot of sex with a lot of women, and I don't know if that's true, but that's what a lot of us took to be true. Everything was condoms. I had read *a lot* about it over the years. When I first came out to my mother when I was twenty-eight, the very first thing she said was "Do you have safe sex?" I know why she asked that, because it's the first thing that would go through your mind about being gay. She asked me if I wanted her to tell my father, and I said yes. He has never, to this day, said anything to me, and I've never asked him how he feels about my being gay. I'm not close to him, and as a kid I hated him. He was verbally abusive, and it wasn't a loving household.

I never thought he was proud of me. He doesn't like difficult conversations.

I feel quite certain that the epidemic changed my life. Much of the effect was subtle and tangential. Without a doubt, it helped create my identity as a gay man and what it means to be gay, because HIV and being gay were highly associated in the world and in my mind, all the way from childhood. Thoughts like that go on and on. I feel sheepish saying all this because it's nothing compared to the impact it had on people who lived in San Francisco—or anywhere— earlier on and had friends die. I know my life is nothing in comparison. I know that some people now think of HIV as a chronic manageable disease, but I think of it as instant death. I still think of death, I think of not using condoms as playing Russian roulette.[14]

Franklin was meticulous about avoiding HIV, but he voiced a nearly universal feeling among men in his age group: he never felt reasonably confident that he could have a gay life without contracting HIV, and this doubt had stayed with him. Anxiety learned in childhood is not easily surmounted and often shadows us for the remainder of our lives. Franklin took one of the two courses available to men confronted by such fear. He limited his sexual life, he adhered zealously to the use of condoms until recently, and he avoided men he knew or conjectured were HIV-positive. The result has been that he remained uninfected, but he has, in his own description, paid some significant emotional costs. He has experienced less connection to others, less intimacy, less pleasure in sex, and less freedom and spontaneity than he would have liked. His life has been constricted by diligence.

Another course Franklin might have taken, but did not, was that taken by Richard, a thirty-four-year-old who came to see me in 2010 because he had recently tested positive for HIV. Long before he actually contracted it, he had substantially abandoned hope of *not* contracting it, because having HIV felt inextricably bound to being gay. "Risky sex" was what gay men did, and Richard had known that "fact" from the age of twelve. Among middle-group men, this abandonment of hope is expressed in relatively high rates of potential exposure, low rates of HIV testing, and the highest rates of new infections.[15] The hopelessness is either consciously accepted and acted out or repressed and denied and acted out less consciously, often impulsively. When repressed and denied, at least one of two related psychological actions is probably operative: *breakthrough* or *counterphobic* processes. The two may result in similar behavior, and both may be facilitated by the use of disinhibiting substances that are also used to self-medicate mood and anxiety. Alcohol, along with methamphetamine and other stimulants, is commonly used to allow oneself to act out breakthrough or counterphobic behavior. The substances rarely cause the behavior, they usually *facilitate* it. The purposeful psychological process behind the behavior is the primary motivator: constrained and frightened men do not have sex because they drink, they drink to facilitate sex, whether they are conscious of the true causal relationship or not. If a man asserts that he did something because he was drunk, the obvious question is why did he get drunk.

Breakthrough behavior is the sporadic, impulsive release of emotional tension through the acting out of normally forbidden or self-forbidden behavior. Bridling under external or internal constraints, we suddenly release pent-up feelings, and the behavioral impulse has "broken through." A life characterized by breakthrough behavior is tensely strung between unreasonable or impossible constraint on one end, and impulsive, sometimes-destructive release on the other. Both ends of this polarized life are potentially destructive, but there is a more constructive middle ground: to think through the validity of our constraint and make decisions to take reasonable risks for things we value. The exploration of that middle ground requires *conscious* consideration of both the constraints and the benefits.

Initially, Richard described a relatively simple breakthrough experience to me, but with suggestions that something more was going on:

"I don't really know what happened, because I'm normally very cautious. I know about HIV—I have forever—and it's not been a big deal in my life, but I sure didn't want to get it. But every now and then, I felt like I couldn't stand it, and I'd find someone on Grindr,[16] go to his place, and fuck my brains out. The night I got infected—I don't know, I was a bit drunk, but not really *drunk*—I was lonely, exhausted. and tired of all of it."

"All of what?" I asked.

"The tiptoeing around, all the tension. Every once in a while, I just had to get *out*. I really regret this one night, but I don't know if I could have done it differently. I was just at a point where I couldn't go on the way I'd been living."

As Richard and I worked together over five months, it became clear that he had spent a childhood and adolescence tiptoeing around in fear, including fear about being gay and about HIV. His current break-through behavior was very much modeled on how he lived during that time, as an intimidated, frightened, occasionally acting-out ado-lescent. Both of his parents had grown up in midwestern farming fam-ilies, and a puritanical, midwestern ethos was very much a part of Richard's childhood:

"The primary thing with my dad was to never have feelings about anything, especially because I was a boy. It was the don't-be-a-sissy warning. My mom . . ." Richard stopped.

"Your mom—what?"

"I was going to say that she did whatever he told her to do. And she expected me to do that, too. Once I turned on a light in the living room, and she said, 'Oh, don't do that, you know it's going to upset your father. *Don't upset your father.*' And I turned it off."

"So it sounds like you really had no support from anyone to have your own life or to be yourself."

"Definitely not. My mom was very frightened of him, and she made me more frightened of him. If you didn't do exactly what he wanted, my dad's favorite thing to say to me was 'Can't you think about anyone but yourself?' It was a way to make me feel ashamed of being selfish. And I did, I felt ashamed for wanting anything."

"Did you have friends, or perhaps relatives, aunts, or uncles, who were supportive?"

"No one. My grandfather lived with us, and he was senile, he hardly ever talked. He just drooled food on himself, and it was one of my jobs to clean him up. My mom would try to relate to me, but it was always for her, it was always like she was taking something from me and not giving me anything back. She had no one either. She was married to my father, and her father was just drooling."

"Right now I'm imagining that you experienced *a lot* of loneliness. And I'm wondering about your adolescence and about dealing with feelings in general, and feelings about being gay—which would certainly have been something for yourself."

"I was buried in sci-fi books. I spent most of my time at home, when my dad wasn't making me do something, just lying on my bed reading."

"And your social life, your emotional life?"

"I didn't know what those things were. I couldn't tell anyone I was gay. I didn't want to be gay, I didn't want to be sick."

"Sick?"

"Sick like a faggot. And sick, you know, with AIDS, which I knew about. Sick for being selfish. When I told my parents on the phone four years ago that I was gay, my father said, 'You've driven a stake through your mother's heart. Can't you ever think about anyone but yourself?' And I haven't talked to them since."

"I know that your family was giving you very little, but I imagine that you must also feel some loneliness from the break with them?"

"And I'll tell you what I started doing when I was maybe fifteen or so, which I've never told anyone. I would ride my bike to a truck stop on Route 70 near our house and go into the parking area for the big rigs and find a trucker I liked and tell him I'd suck him off or ask him to fuck me. And most of them agreed, almost all of them. They had those double cabs with beds in the back, and we'd do one or the other, and then I'd leave. I did that at least fifty times, maybe a hundred."

"This sounds like what you were doing when you contracted HIV. I imagine that your completely constrained life, your loneliness, and your need for companionship had become unbearable. You needed to do something about it."

"I *did*, in the only way I knew how."

"And going to the truck stop, were you not fearful about HIV, which you just said you knew all about as a kid?"

"I was afraid, but . . ."

"But what?"

"But I didn't want to be afraid, I couldn't stand it anymore. I was afraid of everything, and it was squeezing me to death. I had to try to get out of it."

"Richard, *that* is what you said to me in slightly different words about the night you got HIV. You were doing two things as a teenager, and you're still working on them. You were trying to break out of the isolating constraints you lived with, and you were trying to confront the things you feared, including being gay, disappointing your parents, and HIV. There are ways to deal with these problems more thoughtfully—I should say, more *consciously*—and that's what we need to try to talk about. Your life now need not be written by your parents and your fear of them. *You* need to write your own life now."

Compared to the breakthrough process, the counterphobic process is a somewhat more complexly motivated adaptive strategy, but not unrelated. Counterphobia might be described as a fear-centric iteration of a breakthrough process: we break though not simply to relieve tension and obtain the things we need, but to engage in the behavior we most fear. Through exposure and "practice," we hope to learn to either repress and tolerate the fear or, even better, to master the situation and make it less fearful.

The pervasive fear that Richard had lived with since childhood suggested not only breakthrough behavior but also some elements of a counterphobic process. Even in his first rendition of what had happened the night he contracted HIV, Richard suggested some counter-phobic elements by describing himself as "normally very cautious" and "tiptoeing around." In my experience, some of the most cautious men—including many working in AIDS prevention—are among the most fearful and the most likely to sporadically take high HIV risks. When Richard first came to see me, he was not fully conscious of the amount of fear he felt about sex and HIV, in part because it was so entangled with other long-standing fears. He first said, "[HIV has] not been a big deal in my life"—but later on he talked about his father, and about not wanting to be "sick." As we talked over the months, Richard became much more conscious of his fear.

If breakthrough processes are about sporadically and impulsively breaking out of imposed or self-imposed constraints, counterphobic processes are about confronting fear in the hope of resolving it. Counterphobic behavior is not just about blowing off steam, nor is it simple thrill seeking; and counterphobic behavior is often more consistent—less sporadic and impulsive—than simple breakthrough behavior.[17] Breakthrough behavior without an underlying counterphobic component is seen in men of all ages—particularly highly libidinal young men—who quite naturally respond sporadically to any excessive sexual constraint they live with because of apprehensions about HIV. Fear and apprehension—both of which we often repress into unconsciousness, for obvious reasons—are usually more constructively addressed when we allow ourselves to consciously consider them. Like shame, unconscious—and thus unconsidered—fear and apprehension are much more likely to play themselves out harmfully.

### The Younger Group: The Story of Jason

I have defined our younger-group men as those born in 1988 or later. In 2018, mostly in their twenties, they are finding gay communities, just entering adulthood, and trying to plan for and make sense of adult lives. This is a daunting time in life, and the denial of inexperience, uncertainty, and vulnerability is probably the primary adaptive tool that young people bring to the task. Without denial, becoming an "adult" would otherwise often feel impossible, and all the more so when one is gay. This developmental adaptation is one important source of the common observation that young people "act as if they were invulnerable."

And the same observation has often been made about younger-group men's handling of HIV.

In the pursuit of clarifying self-experience and finding self-acceptance, younger-group men have three potential advantages over older men. First, some of these men have had the benefit of greater acceptance from families and local communities. Second, unlike middle-group men, younger-group men did not experience a traumatic childhood in which the death sentence of HIV became inextricably bound up in a gay identity. Third, *like* middle-group men, younger-group men did not suffer the direct loss and trauma of living through the early epidemic. If younger-group men have seen an older man bearing the medical consequences of long-term HIV infection, they often do not distinguish it from old age. The vast majority of younger-group men have no experience of HIV-related deaths. Only about 8 percent of men between the ages of eighteen and thirty-four have known someone who died of AIDS. Over the age of thirty-five, that figure jumps sixfold to 47 percent.[18]

Unlike middle-group men, who experience HIV as *syntonic*, as a familiar component of being gay, younger-group men experience HIV as *dystonic*—unexpected and foreign to their lives. Because it is dystonic, young men typically shun HIV, and men under the age of thirty-five are much more likely than middle- and older-group men to express discomfort about relationships or sex with someone who is HIV-positive. Seventy-nine percent of young men are "very or somewhat uncomfortable" with a long-term sexual relationship with an HIV-positive man; 89 percent feel similarly about casual sex with such a man. What about a *nonsexual friendship* with a positive man? Fully *40 percent* in this group describe themselves as very or somewhat uncomfortable with that possibility.[19] Younger men are—consciously—both unfamiliar with HIV and, by self-report, highly avoidant of it. In contrast to this stated avoidance of HIV, 58 percent of HIV-negative younger-group men also reported unprotected anal intercourse in the twelve months prior to a CDC survey.[20] HIV testing levels are also low in this group and, as a result, so is proper early treatment of infection. The CDC reports that 24 percent of otherwise healthy twenty-five-to-twenty-nine-year-olds progress from first diagnosis of HIV infection to clinical AIDS within twelve months.[21]

The contrast between young men's stated avoidance of HIV and their behavior is not perplexing. Precisely because they experience HIV as dystonic—as foreign to their lives—young men give it relatively little thought. When a man is emotionally or sexually attracted to another man, he experiences the other man syntonically—as nonalien and like himself. The *assumption*—what else could it be on first meeting?—of a syntonic experience is one of the important elements of initial attraction. For an HIV-negative man, this would suggest that the other man is also HIV-negative; the same often occurs for positive men, who make an assumption that another is positive. In the early stages of romance, we often describe one man's experience of another as "blinded by love." We perceive another as we *want* him to be in new romances and in novel, one-off sexual encounters. The "syntonic assumption" has been a problem in HIV prevention for men of all ages since the beginning of the epidemic, and it is all the more powerful and obfuscating for a generation that has never identified with HIV and has never seen someone apparently healthy one day and dead two days later.

Bewildered and angry older gay men readily stigmatize younger men for their handling of sex and HIV. But it is simplistic—and unproductive—to take the above-cited statistics and issues and attribute them to nothing more than carelessness, ignorance, stupidity, or prejudice. Younger-group men grew up in a society that declared in 1996 that the epidemic was over, when the *oldest* men in this group were eight years of age. When these men entered gay life, they found themselves in communities preoccupied with "gays in the military" and marriage equality, with HIV a fringe issue relegated to a small back burner: if young men have been inattentive or in denial about HIV, there is little doubt about why. Historically, these young men were handed a very different relationship to HIV than older men had, and there is little reason to expect them to experience HIV as older men do. For younger men, HIV is not part and parcel of being gay, and not something they expect to be part of their lives. In addition to allowing for their different historical relationship to HIV, we must also remind ourselves that younger-group men are appropriately characterized by youth. They live with the difficulty of finding meaningful adult lives and the challenging discovery of irrational human sexuality and relationships, and they navigate all of this with a characteristic, developmentally adaptive denial of vulnerability. Younger-group men deserve much more than dismissive ridiculing of their behavior. We live now with HIV *endemic* in America's gay communities, and young men deserve attention, support, and mentoring from comprehending communities that actively demonstrate concern for their health and well-being.

Jason grew up in Arizona and attended the University of Arizona at Tucson, receiving a B.A. in philosophy. After graduating in 2011, Jason—a handsome African-American—moved to San Francisco, having decided that he wanted to live in a large gay community, and that he wanted to be a chef and someday have his own restaurant. When I interviewed him in 2014,[22] he was twenty-seven and a full-time student at Le Cordon Bleu College of Culinary Arts in San Francisco. His parents were helping him with part of his tuition and living expenses, and he was also working part-time as a sous-chef for a San Francisco restaurant. Jason was HIV-negative.

> I moved here for the [culinary] school, and because I wanted
> to finally be part of a gay community, which I never really
> had in Arizona. My family paid for my college expenses and
> was very supportive of my being gay, which is unusual for a
> black family. Other black families I've known treat their gay
> kids like Uncle Tom, like they've violated the solidarity of
> African-Americans because being gay is a white thing. I
> think that's crap, and my parents don't go for it either. While
> in my senior year of high school, I came out to them at
> dinner with great trepidation, and my mother said, "Jason,
> eat your zucchini. Your father and I have known this for
> several years, and we want you to be happy. We love you."
> My father said, "Ditto what your mother said," and then we
> pretty much went on with dinner. I was flabbergasted. Later,
> my mother talked to me about dating and sex, and things
> like that, which was very embarrassing. But family isn't
> enough, and I knew that in San Francisco there were
> thousands of gay men I could meet. And because I knew
> San Francisco was very liberal, I didn't think being black

would be a deal. Arizona is provincial, and there's a lot of
sexism and racism if you just walk off campus.

As it turns out, I've been very lonely here—it's not the
panacea I thought it would be, on any score. There *is* no
community, it's just a lot of gay men crammed into a small
town—smaller than I thought—and everyone's out doing his
own thing. You can go to bars, but it's a big dick hunt, and
half the people are drunk or high. Mostly people hook up
online, and if you stand on the corner of Castro and Eigh-
teenth and look on Grindr, there are three hundred guys
within fifty feet of you, all looking for hookups. That can be
fun, and I sometimes do it, but it's not a life. After being
here for three years, I've had a hard time making real friends.
I have two guys I hang out with a lot when I have free time,
and we're pretty tight, but they're not what I'd call *good*
friends. One of them, Noah, is positive, and he's only a year
older than I am, and that's a deal in itself. What the three
of us share is this sense of not having a community, but
somehow *we're* not one either. None of us much uses [drugs],
and of the three of us, I'm the only one who hooks up pretty
regularly.

There are two big things I really didn't count on about
the so-called community here. The first is that being black,
you're a commodity and people are either into your commodity
or they're not. In school, I was more just another gay guy
because there weren't that many gay guys to choose from.
Here, there's no in-between, and practically nothing else
matters, and I don't like that, I resent it. You look on Grindr
and a guy says, "Looking for black dude, 20–30, ddf ub2."[23] So
that leads me to the second thing, which is HIV. It's always
been around, so it's no big deal like it was for you older guys.
When I was in school [in Arizona], no one ever said a word
about AIDS. I never heard a single person mention it, and I've
never used a condom for fucking. I've never met someone who
did. Here, it hardly ever comes up—almost never except
in the "ddf" kind of way, or someone will ask if you're
"clean." Some guys use condoms, but it's the minority in my

experience here, just every now and then. And you can never tell who's telling the truth. I also think there's a kind of—well, it's almost a racist thing. It's that HIV is something normal people don't get. Well, I'm not in the normal group as far as a lot of white guys are concerned, and I think maybe I get questioned more than a white guy would. You get the feeling that white guys don't think white guys—normal people—get infected.

I started talking about Noah, who's white. He's in pretty bad shape really—I don't mean physically—because when you get HIV, that's pretty much the end of your social life, especially sex. Guys that we both know—I'll be someplace with Noah, and they act like he isn't there, they completely ignore him and talk to me. It's embarrassing, and I feel bad for him. I'd bet that he hasn't had sex since he got it. I see this all the time when I'm out with him, and it pisses me off. It's made me a lot more worried about getting it because I don't want a life like that. Once when I asked him about people ignoring him, he said, "It's like turning forty—no one's interested in you." People are sometimes really hostile to him—say things to him directly—and tell him he was stupid and got what he deserved, and that kind of thing, and you know they're doing the same things he used to do. He closed his Grindr account because when he would tell people he was positive, he'd get all kinds of crap. It's that racist thing, and I think a lot of these guys think they wouldn't be interested in anyone who was the type who would get HIV and therefore they won't get it. I used to have sex with much older guys—you know, in their forties or so—but I've stopped because I know a lot of them have HIV and I don't trust them to be honest. I think getting HIV is probably the worst thing that could happen to me. I'm not worried about getting sick because I know that doesn't happen anymore, but I'd definitely never have a boyfriend for the rest of my life.

Jason's experience in the gay mecca of San Francisco does not suggest that all is well in gay communities, or that individual gay lives in America have been suddenly transformed by a small handful of recent—and, with Donald Trump as president, potentially tenuous—political and judicial victories. In my conversation with him, Jason raised at least three distinct issues of concern: the ongoing late epidemic and how young men experience and handle it; the social incoherence of gay communities and the role technology plays in that problem; and the stigmatization that young men sometimes direct at one another. I have heard expressions of similar feelings from many young men.

For·older gay men with direct, personal experience of the early epidemic, the lack of young men's concern for the medical consequences of HIV often seems inexplicable; but for a majority of younger men, HIV concerns are more about potential stigma than medical issues. Stigma alone can make contracting HIV a life-changing trauma for a young gay man, who is suddenly ostracized from a community in which he had sought companionship and refuge from a still-stigmatizing larger society. Young men's relative lack of concern with medical issues is understandable: they have grown up in a highly pharmaceuticalized culture in which people routinely use prescription medications for chronic, manageable medical issues. And it is true that if diagnosed and treated early enough, HIV infection hardly resembles what older men once lived through. The San Francisco physician Gary Feldman put HIV in a contemporary context:

> With the meds we have now, HIV is in some ways easier than diabetes. Checking your blood sugar and controlling your diet is harder. Guys [with HIV] who have never been sick, they take a pill when they brush their teeth, and they're done and they get on with their lives. That person puts very little effort into their day compared to someone with diabetes.[24]

HIV infection today is not, however, without its medical consequences—and expense—whether young men are aware of them or not. But the consequences are not the ones so many older men have seen and personally experienced, and we cannot expect younger men to have the perspective of older men, or to behave as older men feel they ought to. Young men are naturally sexual, and today young gay men often have very active sexual lives that echo those of the

Gay Liberation years. Any intervention aimed at ameliorating the consequences of the late epidemic must be built on an acceptance of that fact.

Several influences are behind the second issue that Jason raises, social incoherence in gay communities and its consequential isolation and loneliness for gay men. As discussed in chapter 1, gay communities today are fundamentally incoherent, significantly divided between the championing of diversity and a push for assimilation into the larger society. Young men generally have little say in the matter: gay politics and "community organizing" are generally conducted by middle-aged and older men, with their own needs in mind, and the young are left to follow or fend for themselves. In many men, we witness the fruit of the typical gay adolescent experience, which does not support authentic—gay—socialization. It usually obstructs or prohibits it, and the consequences are readily evident in later life. I will more fully discuss the problem of isolation, its early-life developmental roots, and its exacerbation by contemporary technology in chapters 4 and 5.

Jason's third issue—the stigmatizing treatment that young gay men often direct at one another—is the consequence of many influences, including early-life experience, unvoiced apprehension about the late epidemic, and social incoherence. Such treatment of others has significant roots in a craving for acceptance of oneself, a need that is, for obvious reasons, often a part of gay lives. Feeling unacceptable, we reject others who appear unacceptable, in hopes of thus turning the tables and vindicating ourselves.

Young people must be understood as young people: they are attempting to discover themselves, and erratic trajectories and unresolved lives are a natural part of that exploration. The young learn largely from their own experience—rather than from the often-questionable wisdom of elders—and working with young men in therapy, I see how they go about building adult lives: each man does it as if it had never before been done. My most useful role is not to inform them with solutions, but to help them with *self*-discovery. For young men, discovery is the game—be it an exploration of the solar system or another man's body, both of which are paths to discovery of the world and oneself. When we are young, we rightly assemble the materials to build a bridge to the moon. When we get older, we often use those materials to build a shack, which is a questionable kind of progress.[25] The old among us must allow the young to be young. They will be anyway.

## YOUNG MEN AND THE LEGACY OF THE CONDOM CODE

As members of communities with a new, assertive public voice, gay men entered the early epidemic riding the crest of an important liberation movement. But privately they also carried a centuries-old legacy of stigma and shame about sex and sexuality. The epidemic would catapult this legacy violently forward, and today that same legacy is borne by young gay men two generations later. Even as contemporary young men are highly sexual, the legacy is still doing its nasty work behind the scenes: the shaming of young men for their sexual behavior—and for HIV infection when it does occur—is now rampant. But this time around we have a new twist. Stigmatization of sex and sexuality is probably more commonly perpetrated by gay men themselves than by the larger society. The longtime AIDS activist Peter Staley wrote a 2014 piece on this subject, in which he enumerates ways that "gay-on-gay shaming" is expressed:

> Here are salvos from a new battle: Calling a young, HIV-negative gay man a "Truvada whore" simply for choosing a prevention option [pre-exposure prophylaxis] with a higher efficacy rate than condoms. Becoming indignant when someone says AIDS is still a gay problem.[26] . . . Putting "I'm clean, ub2" in your online profile. Joining digital stonings via online comment sections when a 20-something dares to come out as HIV-positive. . . . These are just some of the examples of the new HIV war, with its gay-on-gay shaming.[27]

Psychologically, this gay-on-gay stigmatization is comprehensible. Despite engaging in behavior that risks HIV infection, many men repress their feelings of endangerment by denying their own vulnerability. They protect the denial by stigmatizing others who acknowledge taking risks or who have HIV. The problem is not me, it is *them*—the kind of "HIV racism" Jason referred to. This is precisely the psychological mechanism of most societal stigmatization—self-dissociation and projection onto others. We unconsciously identify things about ourselves that we are most uncomfortable with, attribute those things to others, define them as a group, and reject, shame, and disempower the group and, by default, all its members. This is a description of the entire history of gay stigmatization, but it has now become a widely implemented behavior within our own communities.

Older gay men who participate in the stigmatization and shaming of younger gay men are sometimes motivated by feelings different from those of younger men who stigmatize each other. Older men often envy younger men their youth, sexual desirability, and apparent freedom. Older men often envy the relatively easy medical course that young men encounter if they do contract HIV. And older men also sometimes feel that the apparently casual approach young men bring to HIV dishonors what older men experienced in the early epidemic. Young men, the feeling goes, do not bear witness with a gravity and respect that supports and comforts older survivors of trauma: young men should feel more horror about HIV, and their lack of such feelings raises doubt about what older survivors of the early epidemic now experience in the psychological aftermath. But it is unreasonable to expect younger men to bear witness to something they never lived and know little about in any detail. Born seven years after the end of the Great Depression, I have little truly comprehending empathy for the survivors of that event, and unlike my father, I do not store canvas bags of nickels, dimes, and quarters in the bedroom closet, just in case.

Another important influence contributes to both the extension of the current late epidemic and to sanctioned gay-on-gay shaming: our often misconceived and misleading HIV-prevention education, which has too easily—if unintentionally—perpetuated the legacy of centuries-old stigma. While HIV-prevention work has gained insight and improved since the days of the early epidemic, too much of it still plays a destructive role in how young gay men experience sex, sexuality, themselves, and the reality of the late epidemic.[28]

The fundamental link in prevention work's chain to the old legacy of stigma is the unconsidered assumption or feeling—or, sometimes, the explicit idea—that sex between young gay men is a dispensable behavior that lacks the meaning and human importance of hetero-sexual sex. Gay men have thus been expected to abstain from sex or certain forms of sex, or to conduct it in inviolably restrictive ways that would never be expected of heterosexual couples: frottage—the rubbing together of bodies—has actually been proposed as an alter-native to oral or penetrative sex. Although most heterosexual sex is not conducted in the pursuit of pregnancy, it would be unimaginable to instruct heterosexuals to abstain from vaginal sex, or to inviolably conduct it with condoms for a lifetime. To force compliance with exactly this expectation for gay men, prevention education has tradi-tionally not informed men of even the correct and complete facts about how and how frequently HIV transmission occurs.[29] With purely instructional "education," men are told what to do and are left with unexamined generalizations that posit an inflexible, impossibly monolithic task for avoiding HIV. The Condom Code is such a task, and until recently it has—along with HIV testing—been the core strategy of most prevention education. Historically, the Condom Code dictated the universal use of condoms in "sex," every time for a lifetime, with no distinctions for the kind of sex involved or the HIV status of the two partners. *Any* sex without a condom was labeled "unsafe sex."[30]

In both the early and the late epidemics, the Condom Code and other purely instructional approaches have been destructive for two obvious reasons. First, they do not allow men to make considerations that reflect their own lives and values and thus develop personally viable approaches to avoiding HIV infection in the long term. Second, impossible expectations sometimes breed hopelessness, which leads men to abandon *any* efforts to avoid HIV. The Condom Code's indis-criminate expectation of condoms for oral sex—which widely contin-ued for fifteen years in the United States—was a significant reason that many men distrusted the entire message and abandoned the code entirely. As one informed, clearheaded man put it to me, "If you could get it from giving a blow job, *everyone* would have it." But even with-out the inclusion of oral sex, the code remains monolithic and impos-sible, if only for the *every time for a lifetime* clause. Because the code has been a long-standing tenet in gay communities, when a young man today *does* contract HIV, he experiences it as a personal failure because he did not adhere to a "community standard" that few men could or do adhere to. He is shamed for his "failure" and for his HIV.[31]

Particularly within long-stigmatized communities, the attempt to coerce and shame people into compliant behavior is destructive. A widely used public health approach for HIV prevention in America, *social marketing*,[32] is largely based on coercion and shaming, although advocates present it in different, euphemistic language. Coercion is called "influence" or "persuasion," and shaming is cloaked in the idea that those who do not comply are failing to achieve "desirable status" by complying with "prosocial ideas and behaviors." Social marketing is very much what the name suggests: it is marketing. You convince everyone in the neighborhood that he wants, needs, and can afford a Cadillac by parking a Coupe de Ville in Mr. Big's driveway and talking it up with neighbors. Neighbors who do not buy feel inadequacy and shame. A 1996 paper in the *Journal of Health Communication* explains the use of social marketing in San Francisco HIV prevention:

> Social marketing is a process of designing, implementing, and controlling programs to increase the acceptability of a prosocial idea among population segments of consumers. . . . A social marketing perspective conceptualizes target audience members as consumers and seeks to establish "brand" loyalty, perceptions of desirable status associated with the social product, and a network of product support.[33]

The facile idea of using commercial marketing techniques to sell a Condom Code has at least three obvious problems. Most men, gay and straight alike, are much more enamored of Cadillacs than condoms; car ownership is less psychologically complex than the tactical use of condoms in the heated, altered consciousness of sexual arousal; and if you don't have a Cadillac, the entire neighborhood knows, but no one knows who is not using condoms in private sex. Social marketing may have sold a lot of Cadillacs by shaming people who own Chevrolets, and it may have done some good for some gay men, but it has also done a lot of harm by inducing still more shame in a historically coerced and shamed population.

The Condom Code is an impossible standard for real lives, and the frequent consequence of its social marketing is that men are left with the belief that there is a community standard, which does not, in fact, behaviorally exist. It is a community standard in word only. For two men in the private maelstrom of sexual arousal, the "prosocial" idea easily flies out the window with the Levi's and T-shirts. These men then feel shame about their behavior because they have been led to believe that the community standard actually exists, and that they are virtually alone in violating it. When asked, they profess adherence to prosocial behavior. These men are not "change agents" or "consumers," they are deliberately confused and shamed men, possibly exposing themselves to unnecessary risk.

While studies show—through *self-reported* data[34]—some short-term prevention efficacy for social marketing, its value is highly questionable over any extended time, much less a lifetime. Social marketing exacerbates shame, both when its instructional standard is ignored in private with no ill result, and when a seroconversion does occur. HIV prevention conducted through social marketing is one of the significant sources of today's gay-on-gay shaming among young men. Shaming does not enhance self-care, it dispirits the effort, and it encourages the shaming of others, who are in turn dispirited. Shaming has no place in any kind of education, especially in education for gay men who have been raised in shame and long been shamed for the very sexual behavior that education most hopes to change. Receptive anal sex—which is largely responsible for vectoring HIV—has been a perpetual focal point for shame. Every AIDS educator should know that and consider its significance.

Physical intimacy is essential and desirable in human life. Any useful prevention strategy must be respectful of and proceed from that premise. The confusion, denial, unnecessary risk, and shame that much of our prevention effort has created among young men is illustrated by a conversation I had in 2012 with Lyndon, an intelligent and thoughtful twenty-six-year-old. He had come to see me about "relationship problems" with his lover, Tim, and the following discussion took place during our second meeting. I had asked Lyndon, very broadly, about his "experience with HIV."

"I haven't had any friends die, if that's what you mean. I don't even know anyone who's positive, though I have friends who have friends who are."

"So I gather that you're HIV-negative?" I said.

"Yeah."

"Do you think you can avoid getting HIV for the rest of your life?"

"What do you mean?"

"Does it seem possible to *never* get HIV?"

"Well, I'm in a relationship now . . . as you know."

"Do you have some kind of protected sex together?"

"We have safer sex."

"Does that mean that you use condoms for anal sex?"

"Well, no, I mean, we have an arrangement. . . ."

"What is that?"

"We both got tested and we're negative."

"And together you have unprotected sex?"

"Well, yes . . . ," Lyndon responded cautiously.

"And do you have an understanding about having sex outside the relationship?"

"Well, for my part, I don't have sex except with Tim. I used to live in New York and did the whole coming-out thing and all of that, and sort of got it over with. But Tim is younger than I am, twenty-two. When we got together, he was nineteen, and he's never done the coming-out thing, and you know, I wonder if he can do it, if he can just have sex with me or he needs to . . . But we have a rule, which is that if anything happens, you know, if anything should happen that might make a problem, then the person has to tell the other one right away."

"And what is 'anything that might make a problem'? What does that mean?"

"Well, I'd do it. I *think* I would."

"You would tell Tim what?"

"Tell him there might be a problem."

"You're not telling me what *the problem* is."

"Well, you know, maybe he did something that might make a problem."

"Lyndon, you've been talking around it, and it's obviously difficult for you to think about, which I understand. I'm

taking 'the problem' to be that you or Tim did something
that might have exposed one of you to HIV."

"Yes, that's what I meant. You know, the rule is that
you're *supposed* to tell right away—regardless of the
consequences."

"You don't sound very confident when you say it
that way."

"I was surprised by your question. No one has ever
asked me these kinds of questions. We don't tell our friends
what we do, even though I'm pretty sure most of them do
the same thing. They'd say, 'Are you *kidding?* You mean you
guys have *unsafe* sex?' As a matter of fact, we'd never be
having a conversation about all of this in the first place. No
one talks about it. No one has ever asked me these kinds
of questions—and I've never really had to think about it
before."

"And why would your friends react that way—if they are
doing the same thing you do?"

"Because condoms are what you're supposed to do.
There aren't that many people who would admit to not using
condoms."

*"Admit?"*

"Yeah, I know, it sounds like I'm confessing a crime. Well,
it feels that way, it *is* practically considered a crime. It's not
the kind of thing you'd tell other people about."

"I don't think of it as a crime, it's just natural sex—but
perhaps with some risk, which is why I asked about it. Have
you *asked* Tim if he wants or has sex outside the relationship?
Have the two of you talked about this?"

"No, we never have."

The purely instructional Condom Code had obviously clarified
little for Lyndon and Tim, but the homemade "arrangement" that Lyndon reluctantly revealed to me does have a name in the world of HIV
education. *Negotiated safety*[35] is a concept first introduced in 1993 as
a long-term approach to HIV prevention, and it has shown efficacy in
longitudinal studies of gay couples. But it is little promoted by American

AIDS educators and rarely even mentioned as an option. Some educators characterize negotiated safety as the promotion of "unsafe sex" simply because it describes sex without condoms. In truth, safe—or, more correctly, *safer* sex—is any approach to sexual relations that lowers the probability of an uninfected man becoming infected with HIV. Regardless of its characterization by educators, negotiated safety *is* widely used by gay men and has usually been the standard prevention approach for heterosexual couples. Knowledgeably and thoughtfully implemented, negotiated safety is among our better responses to the ongoing late epidemic among young men. It is a *risk-reduction* strategy.[36]

A 2014 Kaiser Family Foundation study[37] provides additional insight into the failures of traditional American prevention work and other influences that fuel the late epidemic in which young men live. The study asked gay men how much information about HIV they had received in the past year from a variety of sources. These included the Internet but also LGBT-targeted media; HIV/AIDS organizations; gay/LGBT community organizations; doctors and other health professionals; mainstream media; and friends and family. Thirteen percent of men reported receiving "a lot of information" from the Internet in the past year. Ten percent reported receiving a lot of information from doctors and other health professionals. Combined, LGBT-targeted media and community organizations had provided a lot of information for 7 percent of gay men. Friends and family had provided information to 2 percent. Forty-three percent reported receiving "no information at all" from doctors and health professionals. Fifty-seven percent had received no information at all from friends and family. The study concludes, "Despite a general sense that LGBT organizations are doing enough to address the problem of HIV/AIDS in the U.S., few gay and bisexual men say that they've personally gotten a lot of information about the disease from these organizations—or any other source—in the past year."[38] Clearly, focus, open discussion, and support are lacking for gay men who might want to consider the issue.

The 2014 Kaiser study also reports figures on condom use, which reveal the disparity between a promoted community standard and actual behavior.[39] Only 39 percent of gay men self-report "consistent condom use," and 24 percent say they "never" use them. Because of "social-desirability bias" in self-reported statistics,[40] the first figure is probably lower than reported, the second higher. This means that fewer than 39 percent consistently use condoms, and more than 24 percent never use them. James Krellenstein, a twenty-three-year-old gay New York medical researcher and AIDS activist, provided an interesting, informed young man's perspective on that question:

> Sex without condoms is more enjoyable biophysically. The end of the penis has the highest density of nerve endings in the world, and you put a plastic bag on it. Barebacking is fetishized *because* it's stigmatized, feels more intimate and liberated because you're taking a risk. You are willing to take that risk to be with this person. And when you're in the throes of sex, it just happens. Passions run high. People slip up even when they want to use condoms all the time. Sometimes you don't want to think about safety and biology, and apathy grows. "I just want to have sex."[41]

With HAART, young gay men in America are unlikely to have anything like the experience of older men living through the terrifying early epidemic. But we must acknowledge, address, and end the late epidemic in gay communities if young men are to fulfill their human potential. That objective is feasible, and even today—with much more "in the pipeline"—we have one suggestion of what might allow that: PrEP, the controversial oral pre-exposure prophylaxis.

## PrEP AND THE LEGACY OF THE CONDOM CODE

If centuries-old stigma catapulted American gay men into the shame wrought by the Condom Code, the legacy of the Condom Code has catapulted too many young men into shame about PrEP. Given the conflict PrEP has generated in gay communities, it is clear that the "PrEP battle" is a nearly perfect reflection of the perpetual gay struggle against stigma, a struggle between self-acceptance and life-crushing shame and self-rejection. Since 1981, the natural sexual expression of intimacy between men has held dangers, dangers that have repeatedly been invoked to stigmatize gay lives: fags get AIDS, and they're getting what they deserve. PrEP *could* beneficially contribute to gay lives.

Two years after PrEP was introduced in 2012—but still rarely prescribed and used—2.5 percent of U.S. gay men were newly contracting HIV every year, with a disproportionate share among young African-Americans. Against these unacceptable numbers, PrEP offers a significant countermeasure; and it offers an important emotional opportunity. For many middle-group and young men who have had no significant sexual experience before HIV, PrEP has allowed sexual relations without fear and anxiety for the first time in their lives. As an HIV-negative forty-one-year-old man recently put it to me, "PrEP has finally let me understand what sex can be. For me, it has always been an exercise in worry and fear. Now, it's a very, very different experience, one I had never known about or hoped for." With PrEP, many HIV-negative men are less fearful of contracting HIV, and many positive men less fearful of transmitting it. This is a very important shift in the relations of gay men and their feelings about sexual life: pre-exposure prophylaxis is helping to disentangle sexual pleasure and intimacy from fear and shame, correcting an entanglement that, for gay men, has destructively endured for almost four decades. Fortunately, PrEP use among urban young gay men has been rapidly rising.

In 2012, PrEP was approved by the U.S. Food and Drug Administration (FDA) as a once-a-day pill marketed under the trade name Truvada. In a pioneering, U.S.-based, multiyear trial called iPrEx, Truvada demonstrated unprecedented efficacy in preventing HIV infection; additional studies in both the United States and Western Europe have supported the iPrEx results. In practice, nothing else—including the problematic condom—has been as effective.[42] The addition of PrEP to other prevention measures may well offer the first possibility of extinguishing the ongoing late HIV epidemic.[43] Extinction does not require *eliminating* new infections; it requires that the statistical probability of contracting HIV begin a sustained, descending trend. An epidemic in such a trend will eventually self-extinguish. In the years before the introduction of PrEP, the trend had plateaued, and since the 1980s, we have even seen reversals with climbing rates.

With all the opportunities PrEP appears to offer, what is the PrEP battle within gay communities about? The question has already been answered: it is about the legacies of long-term stigma and the Condom

Code, which encourage fear and shame within oneself to be turned on others. The code, effective or not, has so indoctrinated itself in gay lives that young men—who were all born after the code was founded—take it for granted as a hallowed institution. Some men, both young and old, have claimed that PrEP makes sex "too easy," and that people use it to allow "irresponsible behavior." Some young men have called others who use PrEP "whores" and "sluts." The president of Los Angeles's AIDS Healthcare Foundation, Michael Weinstein, has declared PrEP advocacy a "war *against* HIV prevention" because it supplements—and, he fears, will displace—the woefully restrictive, problematic, and inadequate condom.

The message in much of the anti-PrEP position is that sex should not be easy, and people should not be free to have sex without fear and anxiety. "Good gay citizenship" is expressed only in strict adherence to the Condom Code, and any sex without condoms is "unsafe" sex. The implied message is, if you are going to insist on having sex, the least you can do is fumble with a condom and worry about contracting a potentially lethal virus if you fail to use it in the heat of an intimate moment, or it falls off or breaks. A possible alternative—a pill taken in the morning, in the heat of nothing more than your coffee and toast—lets you off the hook much too easily.

The controversy about *this* pill is clearly reminiscent of that about *the* Pill—the oral contraceptive Enovid—which so stigmatized women when it was introduced in 1960. Against pregnancy, Enovid provided the same very high 91 percent efficacy that Truvada provides against HIV,[44] but women were called whores and sluts for using the Pill, and many felt shame about it. It took five years for the Supreme Court to rule that, for married couples only, use of the Pill was protected as a right to privacy under the Constitution. But twenty-six states continued to prohibit Enovid for unmarried women, and it would be another seven years before the court finally legalized oral contraceptives for all citizens. In the early years of a new century, are gay men really going to reenact this despicable history of stigma and shaming? Against themselves?

There are generational divides in any family or community, for there is some truth in the idea that, with different histories and futures, one generation simply does not fully understand another. But I believe that

generational divides in gay communities today are unusually wide—
and unusually entangled in shame. I have long been surprised at the
extent to which older gay men withhold authentic friendship, support,
and mentoring from younger men. Both older and younger men readily
assume that the other is hostile, disinterested, or interested only in
sexual pursuit. Older men feel that younger men are disinterested
because of the older man's lack of cultural currency, and—sex or no
sex—their physical aging, about which older gay men can feel a great
deal of shame. Younger men often believe that older men are disinterested in them for their lack of experience, maturity, and accomplishment, and for their presumably careless sexual behavior, about which
older men *have* been stigmatizing.

Each group thus fears the rejection of the other for a variety of
reasons. But much of this fear is unfounded, and both groups have
much to learn from and offer to the other. My work as a psychotherapist is, in part, such an exchange, and young men are often eager to
talk to me, and learn *with*—not from—someone older. In turn, I learn
a great deal that I never knew or have forgotten, and I value the vitality, spontaneity, and novel insight that young people often express: the
young are less encumbered by assumptions gained through too much
experience. Such valuable intergenerational exchanges need not exist
only in formal relationships, and their potential in other forms should
not be overlooked.

Historical experience is also always a component of generational
divides, but gay communities have an important dividing historical
issue. In our tripartite community, gay men of different ages have had
very different—life-forming—experiences with the early and, now, late
epidemics. Even as these differences separate us, we have more in
common—even in our experience of HIV—than is generally acknowledged. To recognize our commonalities and explore our futures with
mutual support, we would have to *talk* about our experiences. We
cannot do that if we cannot overcome our fear of self-revelation and
potential rejection, and if we cannot emerge from the isolation that
trauma and shame have imposed on too many. To the extent that they
have been able to find gay communities at all, gay men, young and old
alike, too often find urban clusters of social isolates who live only
in close proximity. As children and adolescents, gay men still often

grow up socially isolated and never completely unlearn the sense of self that experience breeds, a sense of self that interminably sustains the problem.

Thirty years ago, the community activist Eric Rofes—whom I had never before met or seen—asked me to breakfast at a Castro café to discuss HIV-prevention issues. "How will I recognize you?" he asked.

"I'll be the one who looks like he's looking for someone," I said.

"That won't work," Eric responded. "Everyone in the Castro looks like he's looking for someone."

I offered to wear a red carnation, which I did.

# 4

# The Significance of
# Early-Life Experience

Penrose
gives an impression of genuine awareness
signifies
turns to the active role
is actually conscious
is not likely to be wrong
considers natural selection
chooses to evolve

Graves
harbours countless examples
fights in the Civil War
has a more urgent sound
troops, stoops, droops
probably occurred to Browning
puts it at a thousand cavaliers
still hungry and thirsty

Buchan
leaves the rails
seizes ironclads
begins to question me
is backed with German money
proclaims a Holy War
has fallen pretty flat
has been disappointed

—Keith Waldrop, *The Not Forever*[1]

## ERIK ERIKSON AND THE STORY OF QUENTIN

The developmental psychologist Erik Erikson is widely known—he invented the term *identity crisis*—but, in my impression, is often given short shrift by American psychiatry and psychology.[2] I find Erikson's description of human development—succinctly summarized in his Eight Ages of Man—among the most important and seminal contributions in the entire, short history of psychology.[3] Freud—himself a physician—provided remarkable insight into our psychology, but influenced by medical models, his descriptions of psychic processes leave the impression that they are largely autonomous "mechanisms" that exist almost entirely within the organism. Our psychological processes are, in fact, significantly a social product, and in his incorporation of Freud's insights into a *psychosocial* model—a model that accounts for the cultural and social context of an individual's psychology—Erikson provides a description of human development that is compelling, and verifiable by both observation and personal experience. It is an immensely useful model. In working with someone in therapy, I rarely gain as much useful insight from a diagnosis—which largely describes the internal mechanism—as I do from a consideration of how the person expresses the central challenges posed by Erikson's Eight Ages of development. The model is subtle, elegant, and profoundly humane.

Erikson's psychosocial description is important for gay men—particularly young gay men, whose life trajectories are not yet codified—because being gay almost always complicates the developmental experience. A gay child's or adult's experience in each of the Eight Ages—his "resolutions" for each of the developmental challenges—helps clarify his potential vulnerabilities and how he has or has not been able to adapt to the sometimes-traumatic challenges of growing up gay and living as a gay adult. For many gay men, a problematic resolution of an earlier developmental experience may intersect with later-life experiences—isolation within fragmented gay communities and the two epidemics are examples—and this intersection may produce some "composite" trauma. Later-life experiences echo and synergistically layer themselves onto earlier developmental events.

People vary widely in their comfort with introspective psychological exploration, and the discussion of human psychological development that follows thus requires a brief introduction. Young people—who, in their twenties, are usually still working to define independent identities—are sometimes reluctant to acknowledge the relevance of childhood and adolescent experience in their developing adult lives; and older men have often buried the very memory of their histories— much less their contemporary relevance—and can likewise be reluctant to explore them. Because of the stigma so often directed at gay lives, gay men of all ages may also fear psychological exploration as "pathologizing." The reluctance and fear is understandable but, in the discussion that follows, unfounded. What we most fear in self-contemplation is the discovery of vulnerability, much of which is rooted in early developmental influences. But we are not culpable for our early-life histories, and not "weak" for being affected by them: childhood and adolescence are, by their very nature, vulnerable times, and vulnerability carried into adulthood is natural and expected. Any adult who asserts invulnerability is—sometimes unconsciously and sometimes not—armoring himself against feelings of significant vulnerability. In contemplating our selves as they relate to our histories, we discover our *whole* selves, and in that discovery find possibilities for change, for the better. Such possibilities are most easily accessible to young people because they are newly constructing adult lives and identities and thus have a flexibility that older people often lack. But older people, too, often find important benefits in the exploration of selves and histories.

How we got anywhere in life is certainly not entirely a product of developmental experience. Some aspects of who we are as adults are elements of inborn nature. These inborn traits, our nature, and our environment, our nurture, do not act independently. Our nature dictates our individual requirements for "good" nurture and influences how we experience the less-than-perfect nurture that all of us actually receive. The complex interactions of nature and nurture provide a set of provisional—later changeable—developmental outcomes that, together, more or less make us who we are. We are all patchwork quilts of strengths and vulnerabilities. If the elements of nature are the fabric swatches we are handed at birth, our nurture influences how we stitch the swatches together to make the quilt. At any point in life, the assembled, but growing and changeable, quilt is what we and others experience as our character or "personality."[4]

In Erikson's Eight Ages, each age is a period in human development with a central developmental challenge or "task," for which there is a spectrum of possible outcomes or, as Erikson calls them, "attitudes." The tasks, which I will describe individually later in this chapter, present themselves more or less chronologically, beginning in infancy and continuing through childhood, adolescence, and early, middle, and late adulthood. Erikson elaborates on his understanding of developmental challenges and their outcomes: "In describing the growth and the crises of the human person as a series of alternative basic attitudes such as trust vs. mistrust, we take recourse to the term a 'sense of,' although, like a 'sense of health,' or a 'sense of being unwell,' such 'senses' pervade surface and depth, consciousness and the unconscious."[5]

Taken together, the outcomes that emerge from each of the developmental tasks form what we think of as relatively enduring— "characteristic"—personality, which, as Erikson tells us, is an amalgam of conscious subjective experience, behavior in relation to others, and "unconscious inner states." In the aftermath of trauma or loss, however, our self-experience and observed behavior may become uncharacteristic, because earlier developmental outcomes have been rechallenged. We often refer to such experience as *regression*, because we have regressed to—or, much more usefully put, *reengaged*—earlier developmental challenges in an effort to resolve current challenges. Throughout life, reengagement is a normal human process.

The idea of regression—even if we think of it as reengagement— often feels problematic to those who expect consistent, linear "progress" in life and thus experience reengagement as a "setback." Far from being a setback, reengagement is precisely how we *do* progress through life, because it significantly contributes to continuing growth and maturation. Reengagement offers the opportunity to reexamine our earlier responses to developmental challenges and allows us the possibility of improving upon the typically less-than-perfect resolutions we earlier found. The opportunity in reengagement is only realized, however, if we do not simply cling to earlier unsatisfactory resolutions that leave us vulnerable, which would be pure regression. To realize the opportunities in reengagement, we must emerge with new, more ro-bust resolutions. Real progress in human life is made not by moving straight forward in denial of developmental challenges that have left us vulnerable, but by some combination of linear and cyclical move-ment. We walk a more or less straight path, circle back to an earlier waypoint, contemplatively engage it, and emerge from the circle on a slightly different forward trajectory. Each adjustment benefits from an accumulated life experience that has helped clarify the conse-quences of any given resolution. People come to psychotherapy because their current trajectories are leaving them unhappy, and psycho-therapy largely addresses such unhappiness by encouraging contem-plative circling. This is why therapy so often entails talking about the past.

The feeling that we are expected to live "successful" lives on a single, unaltered trajectory—perpetually leaving our pasts behind—makes many people reluctant to reengage earlier, still-pertinent develop-mental experience. Thirty-two-year-old Quentin was one such per-son. He came for his first therapy visit, sat down in the chair in my office that was farthest from mine, and immediately laid out some ground rules:

> "I want to get one thing up front. I know you see a lot of people who didn't, but I had a good childhood, and it's not something I need to go back into."
>
> "That's fine, I haven't even mentioned it," I responded. "How about telling me why you've come to see me."
>
> The ground rules did not last long. "Rick, my partner, and I are having problems, and he thinks it's my fault. He says I act like my father, and I should work it out in therapy."
>
> "And how long has this been going on between you and Rick?"
>
> "It pretty much started when I got HIV. So three years ago, the summer of 2011. I was in Denver for work and had a fling."
>
> "And what does Rick mean when he says you're acting like your father?"
>
> "My father's been angry at my mother for as long as I remember. *She* says he's jealous and controlling—it's a

permanent standoff. I don't know what it's about really. I know she's a bit of a fag hater, and my father's really not, and I think they fight about that. Anyway, she's definitely a loner—withdraws from the family, and my father doesn't like it, even though I think he's sometimes the same way. Is this making any sense? He was once trying to explain to me why they'd had a fight, and he said, 'I'm just trying to get her to come back to the family,' and I thought, 'Well, yeah, and how about you?' I think this all started after the first baby died—my older brother, or he would have been. Or maybe after they realized what I was. Is this making any sense?"

"I think I have the gist of it. What are you? What does that mean?"

"A fag."

"And how old was the baby when he died?"

"I think about two."

"And you were born how long after his death?"

"Oh, just a year or so I think. They don't really talk about it. When I first heard about him, I asked his name and they wouldn't tell me."

"So your mother was still dealing with the death when you were born." Quentin did not respond. "Did you have other siblings?"

"No, just the three of us."

"If Rick thinks you are like your father, is Rick like your mother? Does he 'stand off' from you?"

"Sometimes it feels like he does. His last partner died of AIDS in '02, and I think Rick is still afraid of my being positive. But in the meantime I needed some support about it, and I couldn't trust him to give it. When I asked for it, he'd tell me I was being controlling—'You're being controlling, just like your father.' That's the point I started making. So, yes, to answer your next question and save you the trouble, I'm pissed off at him for this."

After a short time, Quentin became more appreciative of the potential in making some circles back into his history, and it was helpful for us to see which developmental challenges he circled back to. For

Quentin, it was Erikson's first challenge of the Eight Ages of Man: the development of the capacity to trust. Very early in life, Quentin had had difficulty trusting in the care and attention of parents who were emotionally preoccupied—and in conflict with each other—after the death of his older brother. That vulnerability—difficulty in trusting—was reengaged by the loss Quentin felt when he contracted HIV, his fear for his own well-being, his guilt about how Rick would be affected, and his fear that the HIV would damage their relationship. He had lost trust in himself, and he had, again, lost trust in others.

After contracting HIV, Quentin was frightened, but he could not allow himself to trust Rick for support. He reengaged the infantile and childhood feelings of distrust that his parents' inattention and remoteness had provoked. Quentin also remembered that, as a child, he had felt responsible for his parents' inattention—as all neglected children do in their natural, magical egocentricity, a magic that gives them control over the world, but also leaves them culpable for all that goes wrong. Quentin had yet another reason for feeling culpable, one less universal. Even as a young child, he had felt that he was "different," although he did not know why. He once said to me, "After the first one died, then they got the one they didn't want, the gay one."

As a child, Quentin felt responsible not only for his parents' inattention, but also for their conflict with each other, and he recalled feeling that had he been a "better kid," they would have been happier with each other and more available to him. He now felt similarly culpable because of his "fling in Denver," and he anticipated from Rick the rejection he had experienced with his parents. "Rick has already been through this once, and the last thing I should have done was put him through it again." On another occasion, Quentin told me that he and his parents had barely spoken to one another since he told them he had HIV. His mother thought his getting HIV was "stupid" and did not want to talk about it. "Gay people," she said to him on the phone, "should learn how to behave. I don't know what you want from me." Quentin thought it was "stupid," too, and he thought that Rick shared the sentiment, though Rick had never said so. "I let both of them down, and if Rick never talked to me again, I'd get it." The feelings of failure and culpability, rejection and neglect, and loss of trust were once again destructively operative in Quentin's life. The important question for our therapy was whether Quentin could now find a better resolution to this challenge than he had as a child.

In childhood, Quentin had attempted to resolve the untrustworthiness of his parents by developing an unrealistic independence. He became a "good boy," and an important part of being good in the eyes of beleaguered parents is not asking anything of them by being needless. Unfortunately, Quentin's parents may have experienced his independence and apparent lack of emotional needs as Quentin's rejection of *them*, and evidence of his true independence. Such a cycle simply intensifies. Today, Quentin was bringing that same unrealistic independence and apparent lack of emotional needs to his relationship with Rick, even after the Denver fling and all the distress he was feeling. Quentin rarely asked Rick for supportive attention, but when he did and Rick tried to respond, Quentin routinely rejected it: any positive response from Rick threatened Quentin's independence. But Quentin experienced this pattern of asking and rejecting as *Rick's* unreliability, a confirmation that Rick could not be trusted. Even as it was distressing, the confirmation was oddly comforting for Quentin, for it assured him that his independence was realistic and necessary. Rick, in my impression, was simply confused. Quentin was thus re-creating a familiar, intensifying cycle of culpability, neglect, and distrust.

After much exploration of this cycle, I finally forcefully suggested to Quentin that he had never *let* Rick care for him. Quentin hesitated for a moment, looked startled, and then began crying for the first time since I had met him. "No," he said, "I never have." As he said those words, I could see on his tearful face the look of an assertive but abandoned child, one who was in over his head and was frightened. His first-learned resolution of distrust, unrealistic independence, and feigned lack of emotional needs was possibly adaptive during childhood with beleaguered and adversarial parents. But in adulthood, it was no longer adaptive; it was problematic and left Quentin unhappy and vulnerable.

Our tendency in circling back to old challenges is to leave the circle on the same familiar trajectory we learned in earlier life: we simply reenact the challenge and emerge with the same resolution. *This*, as I have said, is "regression." As adults, we sustain earlier resolutions with some combination of three methods. The first is that we choose people like our parents, people who are likely—because of who they are—to play the familiar role and thus assist us in having the familiar experience and arriving at the same resolution. Quentin might have chosen someone unlike Rick, someone distant and rejecting. He did not do that, but he did invoke the other two methods of reenactment: he *misinterpreted* Rick's intentions, and he *provoked* Rick into more distance and rejection by actively refusing Rick's efforts. Such reenactment, regardless of how it is accomplished, is complexly motivated. Sometimes we are simply attempting to learn to tolerate the emotional pain through repeated exposure to it. Sometimes we are hoping to have it come out differently, but without a change in how we resolve it. In either case, the exit trajectory is unmodified, and we have simply unproductively reenacted and relived pain that sits deeply in our emotional memories.

In our discussion of his current challenge—his feelings about his HIV infection and his distrust of Rick—Quentin and I were able to see the roots in his childhood experience. Quentin began to understand that his rejection of Rick's supportive efforts was significantly responsible for what was happening between them, and Quentin was able to consider the possibility of allowing Rick's support and having a different outcome. Allowing that support was frightening because it required a trust in Rick that was unintuitive, and because it threatened the independence that Quentin had learned to rely on. We spent a great deal of time talking about Quentin's considerable fear after contracting HIV, which had been concealed behind his independence, apparent lack of emotional needs, and anger at Rick. Quentin began to envision a revised trajectory, one that might allow him to acknowledge his emotional needs and allow Rick to be responsive. Quentin had learned to allow *me* to be responsive without feeling threatened, and he needed to bring that new capacity to his relationship with Rick.

About a year into our work, Quentin arrived in my office one day and said, "I did something really important, something I never thought I could do." Quentin hesitated. "Rick and I were lying in bed last night, and I said to him, 'Would you hold me? I feel frightened.' I started crying, and he held me. He didn't let go." What had allowed Quentin this important change was his realization that he had still been using an old, no-longer-adaptive resolution to his emotional needs. Because of who Rick was, that resolution was simply destructive.

Quentin's story illustrates the significance of early developmental experience on later life, and how the early and late experiences interact. In working through his relationship with Rick, Quentin had productively reengaged—not simply reenacted—earlier developmental challenges, and found new, more productive resolutions. Such reengagement is almost invariably a component of the process of recovery from trauma and loss. Because too many people feel discouraged about the need to reengage old issues, I must emphasize something that Erikson repeatedly asserts. The objective of each of Erikson's developmental ages is not the complete and final accomplishment of a "best resolution," after which we move on to the next challenge with an assured success under our belts. There are *no* complete successes or failures in human psychological development, and few developmental resolutions go unchallenged in later life. The best outcomes for developmental challenges are *relatively* robust, and provide some useful balance between the two ends of a challenge's spectrum of outcomes. Over time, these accumulated outcomes coalesce into a relatively stable way of experiencing ourselves, behaving in the world, and living in our conscious and unconscious minds. This is the "characteristic self" that I earlier mentioned. When a person's accumulated developmental experience is relatively good—never perfect, but good enough—our characteristic self provides us, in Erikson's words, "a sense of being 'all right,' of being oneself, and of becoming what other people trust one will become."[6] When our characteristic selves shift later in life, it is because new life experience has engaged earlier resolutions that left us with some vulnerability. If our characteristic selves are not changing in response to new experience, it is because we have stopped learning and growing. We have stopped living.

## THE EIGHT AGES OF MAN

The remainder of this chapter presents a developmental overview of issues affecting gay men. In discussing each of Erikson's Eight Ages of Man, I briefly describe four connected topics for each. I present a brief overview of Erikson's description of the particular developmental period, including its central challenge, and the spectrum of possible resolutions for that challenge. I describe how the challenge might have been of particular significance for gay people with their partially different issues and needs, and their possible exposure to an unsupportive—or overtly hostile—social environment. I discuss how life experience in the early and late epidemics might reengage the central challenge of the period under discussion. And I broadly suggest a potentially productive response to the reengaged challenge. While each of the Eight Ages is the first experience with the challenge, all of the challenges resurface and reengage throughout life. No challenge results in a perfect resolution that forever lays the challenge to rest.

### 1. Basic Trust vs. Basic Mistrust

The challenge of Erikson's first stage arises during the infant's first year, but continues to be significant throughout a human life. This challenge or task of developing a capacity to trust clearly describes Quentin's early life and, later, the dynamics of his relationship with Rick. According to Erikson:

> The first demonstration of social trust in the baby is the ease of his feeding, the depth of his sleep, [and] the relaxation of his bowels. . . . The infant's first social achievement, then, is his willingness to let the mother out of sight without undue anxiety or rage, because she has become an inner certainty as well as an outer predictability.[7]

In his concluding remarks on the developmental challenge of trust vs. mistrust, Erikson describes something particularly important for many gay men:

> Even under the most favorable circumstances, this stage seems to introduce into psychic life (and becomes prototypical for) a sense of inner division and *universal nostalgia for a paradise forfeited* [emphasis added]. It is against this powerful combination of a sense of having been deprived, of having been divided,

and of having been abandoned—that basic trust must maintain itself throughout life.[8]

I believe that much of the "paradise forfeited"—the unrealistic paradise of perfect and perfectly consistent parental attention and care—is what we seek in idealized, unconditional, adolescent—and often adult—love. Erikson's idea of "the most favorable circumstances" in infancy includes some sense of deprivation and abandonment, and as adults, we surely experience some of both in even the most supportive relationships. As adolescents and adults, we often feel conscious disappointment in others who are failing to provide the forfeited paradise that we long for. Unconsciously, we often carry disappointment in ourselves because as infants and small children we received less than perfect care—the paradise we would have known had we been worthy of it. Quentin described being "pissed off" with Rick and was disappointed for not getting from Rick what he would not allow Rick to give him. In part, Quentin would not allow Rick to give it because he did not deserve it: he was not "a better kid" for his parents, and he had disappointed Rick with his emotional distance and his Denver fling.

While most people experience a paradise lost, it is often a more conscious experience among gay men than many others, particularly heterosexual men. A sense of loss, longing, and nostalgia characterizes many gay lives, and a sense of disappointment in both oneself and other gay men is common. That gay men often feel themselves disappointing is no surprise, for gay men are taught to feel that simply for being gay. Their disappointment in other gay men occurs through a different developmental influence. Heterosexual adolescents are supported in their hopeful anticipation of a paradise restored through current or future intimate relationships that gay adolescents are explicitly forbidden. For gay adolescents, paradise was not only lost in infancy and childhood, it appears forever unattainable. With relatively few exceptions, we are taught that the futures of gay boys entail deprivation, abandonment, and loneliness. This often leaves gay adolescents with a sense of loss and longing for something they never had and feel they never will. When young gay men do finally learn that relationships are possible—now earlier in life because of the Internet—they still usually engage in those once-forbidden relationships without the interpersonal experience that heterosexual adolescents naturally acquire. Even as the heterosexual adolescent's early anticipation of a paradise restored is unrealistic, the simple teenage hope allows him or her to fall first into infatuation and, from there, begin to discover the realistic possibilities of love. Denied that developmental foundation, some gay men may find themselves in perpetual longing for something that cannot be had, and consistent disappointment when they try to find it. Life in both HIV epidemics has seriously reengaged any early-life tension between trust and mistrust. During the early epidemic, gay men experienced a world gone awry, a dangerous and untrustworthy world that was suddenly populated with lovers and friends who could not be trusted to stay in one's life, or to survive at all. Positive men experienced both the loss of dead and dying positive friends who showed these men their own frightening futures, and the loss of avoidant or stigmatizing negative men. Negative men also felt the loss of those who had disappeared from their lives and often lived with little trust in their ability to remain uninfected. For young men today, the world is still an untrustworthy place because HIV is still a risk, and the social consequences of contracting it can be life-changing within today's self-stigmatizing gay communities. For both older and younger men, the epidemics have too often motivated a tactical avoidance of intimacy, and thus isolation. Those whose early lives echo that of Quentin—whose life was characterized from infancy by an inability to trust—find the challenge of trust all the more difficult.

The challenge for gay men today is to recover some capacity for reasonable trust and intimacy by taking new risks that thoughtfully confront, rather than accommodate, distrust. The restoration of trust in oneself and others is a major task for survivors of trauma and loss, but not an impossible one.

### 2. Autonomy vs. Shame and Doubt

This period of early psychological development—falling between approximately one and three years of age—occurs when the infant first experiences muscular maturation and mobility. In his mobility, he experiences a sense of autonomy, and his first sense of personal choice and will: he is able to crawl or walk off on his own. Some parents are fearful for the child's safety or experience the child's new autonomy as defiance or abandonment, rather than exploration and growth. Such parents sometimes attempt to limit the child with shaming, punishment, or withdrawal when the child—as he inevitably does—returns to them for reassurance. With little parental support, the exploring child soon finds himself feeling overextended and frightened by his self-assertion. Erikson describes the resolution of the challenge as a spectrum extending from a sense of shame, self-doubt, and anger at one end, to a relatively comfortable feeling of autonomy and self-direction on the other. The challenge presents a pull between "holding on and letting go. Erikson explains: "To hold can become a destructive and cruel retaining or restraining, [or] it can become a pattern of care: to have and to hold. To let go, too, can turn into an inimical letting loose of destructive forces, or it can become a relaxed 'to let pass' and 'to let be.'"[9] Erikson describes shame as "rage turned against the self," a self that the child attempts to conceal from others, a self in which the child considers "himself, his body, and his wishes as evil and dirty."[10]

*Doubt*, Erikson writes, is the "brother of shame." In his observation, doubt "has much to do with a consciousness of having a front and a back—especially a 'behind':

> For this reverse area of the body, with its aggressive and libidinal focus in the sphincters and in the buttocks, cannot be seen by the child, and yet it can be dominated by the will of others. The "behind" is the small being's dark continent, an area of the body which can be magically dominated and effectively invaded by those who would attack one's power of autonomy.[11]

Shame and self-doubt are significant issues for many gay men, and early-life stigmatization and the two epidemics have exacerbated both. Because of the sexual transmission of HIV, it is not difficult to imagine that dirtiness, promiscuity, contamination, irresponsibility, retribution, defectiveness, and failure are some of the unrealistic, destructive feelings that people have consciously and unconsciously attached to themselves, as well as to the public event of the two epidemics. For some older men, the decade of Gay Liberation that preceded the early epidemic felt like the self-assertive overstepping of a two-year-old: we got in over our heads, and the frightening epidemic was our punishment and our penance. Young men today often have similar feelings, simply for "overstepping" by living sexually active lives. The fear of "invasion" by HIV—which, among gay men, happens largely through receptive anal sex—reminds one of Erikson's description of our "dark continent . . . magically dominated and effectively invaded." To contract HIV means having our bodies dominated by a retrovirus that we anthropomorphize with intent and purpose, and to which we forfeit our autonomy and control.

Many now-older gay men rose to the demands of the early epidemic with Act Up, TAG (Treatment Action Group), and numerous community-based organizations, all forcefully asserting a gay agenda that demanded understanding, support, and action to quell the emergency. But during those years, many other men retreated from the stigmatizing gaze of society into often-unconscious shame, self-doubt, and quiet anger. Sometimes, today's young men do that, too.

The current challenge for gay men is the discovery or rediscovery of a sense of reasonable, relaxed, purposeful autonomy by confronting conscious and unconscious shame and doubt, and working it through—a topic discussed in following chapters. We need to learn or relearn, as Erikson states it, to "self-govern by the spirit, not by the letter."[12]

### 3. Initiative vs. Guilt

The shift of focus from shame to guilt—which generally begins around the age of five or six—is considered developmental progress: if shame is about hiding from the gaze of others to protect oneself, guilt is remorse about behavior that might harm others. The developmental challenge that Erikson posits for this age is the struggle between initiative—activating ambitions and goals—and guilt. Initiative is built on an earlier-gained sense of autonomy, which is hampered by shame and doubt; and initiative is hampered by guilt: "Initiative adds to autonomy the quality of undertaking, planning and 'attacking' a task for the sake of being active and on the move. . . . The danger at this stage is a sense of guilt over the goals contemplated and the acts initiated in exuberant enjoyment of new locomotor and mental power."[13]

A child or adult might feel guilt about his goals and initiative for many reasons. For the young child that Erikson speaks of in this developmental age, simply having independent interests may feel harmful to an anxious or emotionally needy parent whose distress is aroused by the child's activity, or by the separation the activity brings about. When separation is the issue, the child may feel guilt for harming the parent by "abandoning" her. *She*—the child feels in the moment—needs him more than he needs her, and her apparent distress over the separation seems to confirm the feeling. As the child matures toward adolescence and then adulthood, goals and initiative expand beyond concrete interests and physical activity. For younger gay children who feel "different," and for older children or adolescents who know they are gay, the goal of being oneself and the initiative expressed in pursuit of that goal may be a source of significant guilt. Both the goal and the initiative feel like a new abandonment: the parent had her own hopes and expectations for who her child would be, and in abandoning that trajectory the child abandons her. A psychologically astute thirty-five-year-old gay man— who works in public health on behalf of gay men—briefly related to me a piece of his own developmental history:

> My parents divorced when I was four years old, and while I always denied a fear that I had "caused" the divorce—which I thought was a cliché—I cannot deny that I walked on eggshells for years after, even still today. I was afraid of something more happening that would fracture our already-fractured family. When I came out to my mother and father— at eighteen and twenty years old, respectively—my feelings of shame about my sexuality were compounded by my feelings of guilt about the divorce. I still worried that coming out would cause another fracture. After I told my father, he cried for fifteen minutes before we had to leave the restaurant. It has taken him fifteen years to even acknowledge that my partner is a man and that I am happy with this.

All children, gay and straight alike, share a more universal source of guilt about goals and initiative. The child may experience guilt about excelling when a parent or sibling—a less "successful," less motivated, less talented, or disabled one—cannot. In both childhood and adult-hood, "doing better" than others who are "deficient" or in need is a common source of guilt. This is *survivor guilt,* and many gay men would reengage this early developmental challenge during the later challenge of the early epidemic. A man who was clearly ambivalent about hav-ing a successful life during the early years of the epidemic looked plain-tively at me and said, "All of my brothers are dying. Why not me?" In Erikson's words, "For here the child becomes forever divided in himself."[14]

Survivor guilt is not, as many mistakenly understand it, simply guilt about remaining alive when others have perished. It is guilt about doing better than others, about good fortune in the face of others' mis-fortune, about succeeding when others cannot. It feels harmful and disloyal to those who have not done as well. During the early epidemic, survivor guilt compromised the survival initiative of many thousands of men who, with conscious or unconscious purpose, exposed them-selves to HIV; and the same is sometimes true for young gay men now living through the late epidemic. During the years of the early epi-demic, I knew many men, both positive and negative, who felt guilt about simply hoping or wanting to survive.[15] And I have known many young negative men today who have similar feelings about not con-tracting HIV in the face of friends who have contracted it. These ex-periences of later-life guilt are always exacerbated by an early-life experience of guilt for being gay and thus disappointing others by being oneself.

Because guilt crushes initiative, the inclination of those who sur-vive early developmental or later-life trauma with conscious or uncon-scious guilt is to live constricted, unfulfilled lives that deny life's potential. But it is no man's responsibility to forfeit his initiative—and thus himself—to be something that someone else wanted him to be. The challenge for gay men today is to recognize and acknowledge guilt and attempt to work it through by allowing themselves to have the lives they want. Without unfounded guilt, our lives are more expansive, ful-filled, and happy.

## 4. Industry vs. Inferiority

In discussing the developmental challenges between approximately six and eleven years of age, Erikson touches on a period that is usually significant for gay boys. These are the years during which the gay child is often first aware of feeling "different" from other boys, and he can easily experience that difference as inadequacy or inferiority. Children in this age range are learning to "win recognition by producing things."[16] For boys, "producing things" is encouraged through competitive activities such as sports; but with a sense of inadequacy—and, often, different interests—many gay boys are reluctant to participate.

Even without a strong sense of inadequacy or inferiority, the simple feeling of difference—often experienced as outsiderness—can inhibit a child's productivity. If outsiders do not feel productive within their peer milieu, they must find personally meaningful, independent forms of productivity. Some gay boys do this with academic accomplishment, creative pursuits, or other expressions of talent that more conventional boys avoid. I believe that this early experience of comparative inadequacy and outsiderness is partially responsible for the common high level of resourcefulness, creativity, and originality that I observe among gay men. For those gay boys who cannot find independent forms of productivity, "The child's danger, at this stage, lies in a sense of inadequacy and inferiority. . . . If he despairs of his tools and skills or of his status among [his peers] he may be discouraged from identifying with them."[17]

For many obvious reasons, gay boys often fail to identify with peers, and this experience often endures into adult life. The early sense of outsiderness too easily begets isolation, and for the child, without other options or resources, isolation is often unavoidable. But it is not necessarily unavoidable if the adult is able to find a community of "outsiders" in which he can finally feel insiderness. Unfortunately, the outsiderness of childhood and adolescence too often becomes a way of experiencing *oneself*, rather than one's current circumstances. Too many gay men sustain a feeling of outsiderness even with new lives in potentially supportive communities: new circumstances do not easily recast one's sense of who one is. Erikson succinctly describes the developmental connections between feelings of outsiderness and inadequacy, identity and productivity: "We have pointed in the last section to the danger threatening individual and society where the school-child begins to feel that the color of his skin, the background of his parents, or the fashion of his clothes rather than his wish and his will to learn will decide his worth as an apprentice, and thus his sense of *identity*."[18]

Today, the identities of many older and younger gay men—particularly those with unhappy, long-standing feelings of outsiderness and inferiority—are expressed in contemporary community agendas. If the agendas of the earlier homophile and liberation movements pursued freedom to be oneself, today's agendas are much more focused on finding insider identities through assimilation into conventional social forms such as military service, marriage, and parenthood. These forms, we hope, will allow us to feel "like other boys." Given the powerful synergy between adverse early developmental experience and the stigmatizing, isolating experience of the two epidemics, these current-day agendas make psychological sense. But they are perplexing to other gay men with different personal histories and points of view. The desire for assimilation is understandable for those men who did not find paths to personal—internally rooted—productivity as children or adults, and who continue to experience their outsiderness to mainstream society as inferiority. In contrast, the push for assimilation is perplexing—sometimes repugnant—for men who did find personal forms of productivity in their outsiderness, and who feel they have been able to live more happily and authentically in the expression of their differences. These men have transformed outsider identities into internal assets.

Authentic lives are internally rooted lives. In an authentic life, our life in the external world is relatively coherent with our internally held values and sense of self. The authentic adult life thus seeks validation first internally, and only secondarily from others. The challenge for young adult men today is to discover or rediscover a sense of productivity and adequacy, both of which require and express authentic lives. Some will find authentic lives in socially assimilated forms, others in lives that insist on diversity and differences. The "rightness" of the choice is largely measured by the authenticity of the resulting life. In making this important choice, we are significantly influenced by our developmental experience in adolescence, the fifth developmental age, which Erikson calls Identity vs. Role Confusion.

## 5. Identity vs. Role Confusion

The onset of puberty—usually around the age of twelve or thirteen—marks the end of childhood, the beginning of "youth," and the period during which we first form social and sexual identities among peers. This is adolescence. If the gay boy did not earlier realize that he was different from other boys, he almost certainly will now. And now is the developmental period during which difference—of sexuality, race, interests, talents, and even aesthetics and dress—can be most significant and disturbing. According to Erikson, "The growing and developing youths, faced with this physiological revolution within them [body growth and genital maturity], and with tangible adult tasks ahead of them, are now primarily concerned with what they appear to be in the eyes of others as compared with what they feel they are."[19] Among adolescents, the clannishness that differences spawn is usually a defense against feelings of identity confusion. In remaining within the clan, individual identity feels assured, even as the identity found is little more than a mimicking of currently stylish group identity.

For obvious reasons, these are often emotionally difficult years for young gay people. Their identities are confused not only by the universal turmoil of puberty and adolescence, but because being gay makes them decidedly different from the majority of heterosexual peers. Heterosexual boys of this age often live with nascent, conventional, overly defended male identities, and gay boys, who remind them of now-unacceptable aspects of themselves, are experienced as threatening. For that threat, the gay boy is usually ostracized and often actively abused. The experience of severe rejection, humiliation, and abuse during these years can leave a gay person with a confused, lifelong, highly reactive sense of identity.

In the extremes, the reactive identity can take either of two, seemingly opposing, forms. The first is expressed in an almost-childlike desire to find one's identity in the affirmation and approval of others. Such a man has a persistent craving for insiderness and attempts to find his identity in the apparent fact or the given impression of conformity. This is a man who seems uncomfortable in his own skin and has the feel of someone living someone else's life, while speaking someone else's words. The second form of reactivity inverts the first.

Identity is sought in confrontation of the insider group—the larger, conventional society—with an insistent, sometimes-exaggerated assertion of precisely the differences that mark one as an outsider. This in-your-face approach is assertive, but just as reactive as the approval-seeking approach, and just as likely to be rooted in self-doubt. With a more benign—if never perfect—developmental experience during childhood and adolescence, a gay man's identity might be formed from an organically evolved mix of conformity and difference. This mix provides a relatively balanced, relatively comfortable, internally rooted sense of self—one that is more authentic, resilient, and durable than those of the two reactive solutions.

With often-painful adolescent experience as a developmental foundation, the early and late epidemics have also threatened gay men—not only with outsiderness, but with unwanted identities. For many men, the liberating identities that began building in the years following Stonewall became displaced by an identification with "people who are promiscuous, sick, and contagious." If America had experienced gay men as pariahs before the onset of the early epidemic, the problem only worsened, and many young gay men today feel, resentfully, that they have inherited this legacy from older men. No longer unified by a struggle for liberation or a fight against premature death, gay men today live in increasingly fragmented communities that champion conflicting right and left political agendas.[20] All of these relatively recent changes blur a sense of identity. The challenge for gay men today is to overcome the reactivity born of both adolescent experience and the two epidemics, and to discover or rediscover identities that are internally rooted, self-expressive, and revealed in authentically lived lives. One requisite for this task is the acceptance of diversity among gay men themselves, a diversity that is the inevitable product of the complex social evolution that has taken place over the past half century. The gradually improving trend in America's acceptance of gay people has diluted the meaning of a "gay identity." With that shift, and without unified, single-minded purpose, today's gay communities make one thing clear: taken alone, the fact of being gay is not much to have in common. We must each find ourselves.

## 6. Intimacy vs. Isolation

The first of Erikson's three *adult* developmental ages spans roughly the years between eighteen and thirty-five. During this period, we first grapple with the challenges of adult intimacy, which Erikson tells us is a capacity built on the foundation of a reasonably well-accomplished sense of identity. That hard-won sense of identity—which, in turn, builds on the earlier-accomplished sense of autonomy—must be partially relinquished to allow intimacy. Intimacy thus requires relinquishing some measure of both autonomy and identity. To connect intimately with another, we must surrender part of *ourselves*, just as within the shared physical living space we surrender some of our territory. When the subjective sense of identity—and its underlying foundation of autonomy—feels too unformed or too vulnerable, we are often reluctant to relinquish any of it.

Emotional intimacy can feel as if it threatens to subsume us. Almost all intimate human relationships tread a delicate, ever-shifting, often-contentious line between independence and connection. The fear and avoidance of intimacy, Erikson says, "may lead to a deep sense of isolation and consequent self-absorption."[21] While this is certainly true, some people with a vulnerable sense of identity do enter relationships, but they usually prove problematic if one is hoping to gain an adequate sense of identity *from* the relationship. While relationships often help us discover new elements of identity—which is an important way that relationships help us grow—we rarely *find* an identity. The hope that a relationship will provide one is rarely fulfilled.

Within an accepting and supportive society, one begins in adolescence to form an adult sense of identity. But gay boys are often denied the requisite acceptance and support, and beginning in their teenage years—and often earlier—gay men are often subjected to social forces that actively confuse or prohibit an authentic sense of identity. Gay teenagers often cannot talk to others about their lives and feelings, and they are often actively prevented from engaging in the exploration of relationships that is a natural and supported element of heterosexual adolescence. Gay boys are left with surreptitious sex that must be assiduously segregated from their social lives, and they too often experience that sex with shame and guilt. Because the sex is the only "relationship" they have been permitted to know, the shame and guilt are easily transferred later to potentially fuller, adult relationships. In-tegration of sex and relationships remains difficult, and a deficit of intimacy is one consequence. A gay man once succinctly described the problem to me: "I can't have sex with someone I love." The sex—still attached to the shame and guilt he experienced during adolescent sex—felt as if it devalued or contaminated a relationship with some-one he cared for. This troubling developmental path is not a conse-quence of being gay, it is a result wrought by a society that forcefully imposes destructive developmental limitations and then stigmatizes the result: "Gay men are promiscuous and do not have relationships." Such a society is speaking out of both sides of its toothy mouth.

Speaking about heterosexuals, Erikson makes an important obser-vation about the difference between sex as physical behavior and sex as an expression of emotional intimacy: "Strictly speaking, it is only now [in the Age of Intimacy vs. Isolation] that *true genitality* can fully develop; for much of the sex life preceding these commitments is of the identity-searching kind, or is dominated by phallic or vaginal strivings which make a sex-life a kind of genital combat."[22] As one consequence of the societally imposed limitation on gay adolescent relationships, the sexuality of many adult gay men does, indeed, sug-gest identity-searching sex or genital combat. In having surreptitious sex with other boys—rather than fuller relationships—adolescents are nevertheless seeking to discover themselves, in the only way permit-ted. In adulthood, sex with other men may be the only personal—or social—expression of an identity that some men have known. Such men are still trying to consolidate identities through sex alone.

If, for gay men in truncated adolescences, the experience of emo-tional and sexual intimacy was already disrupted, the two epidemics have obviously compounded the problem. The disturbing emotional en-tanglement of sexual intimacy with HIV, sickness, and death left many men living through the early epidemic avoidant of any sexual or sexually intimate contact. When men did connect sexually, the expe-rience easily mirrored adolescent sex: it was often nonrelational and felt dangerous and, if conducted in defiance of the Condom Code, for-bidden. Older-group men often had such troubling feelings, and for younger- and middle-group men—who have never known a gay life free of HIV—it has been the only experience of sex and intimacy that many have ever had. If, as Erikson asserts, isolation is the alternative to intimacy, the two epidemics have dramatically promoted the avoidance of intimacy and the painful "safety" of isolation.

With all the developmental and historical obstacles that have complicated gay lives and identities, a remarkable number of men *have* found authentic relational intimacy both before and throughout the two epidemics. Those hard-earned lives are the rewards of a remarkable tenacity brought to bear against pernicious developmental influences, and they stand in testimony. Today, the challenge for gay men is to discover, rediscover, or sustain authentic, reasonably robust senses of a broad gay identity that allows sexual and relational intimacy. It is from such identities that the fullest lives flourish.

### 7. Generativity vs. Stagnation

The Age of Generativity vs. Stagnation spans the middle portion of adult life, approximately the ages of thirty-five to sixty-five, and is thus most pertinent for middle- and older-group men. Erikson tells us that generativity is about "establishing and guiding the next generation," although he adds that generativity is "meant to include . . . *productivity* and *creativity.*" The alternative to generativity is "a pervading sense of stagnation and personal impoverishment. Individuals, then, often begin to indulge themselves as if they were their own . . . one and only child; and where conditions favor it, early invalidism, physical or psychological, becomes the vehicle of concern."[23]

For older-group men, formerly productive and creative lives were often disrupted by the demands of the early epidemic. HIV-positive men were often forced by medical issues into early retirement from planned careers or creative work, and both positive and negative men otherwise found their lives redirected by uncertainty, trauma, and loss. Today, I often meet older men who feel that their lives are stagnant and disappointing, but they have given little thought to the influence of the early epidemic, during which they spent ten or fifteen of the normally most generative years of our lives expecting to die. Many people, gay and straight, have feelings of stagnation or disappointment by the age of sixty-five, and the onset of persistent grumpiness is one sure sign. Older gay men, like combat survivors, can often identify the responsible influences.

For older gay men today, the formidable challenge is to acknowledge—rather than deny—the feelings of stagnation or disappointment; to grieve and release the unrecoverable loss of earlier, unrealized generative life; and to use what is left to live as fully, creatively, and productively as possible. Generativity can be realized at almost any age, and I sometimes find myself offering an obvious, often-ignored observation to men who are attempting to grieve disappointing lives: we can only start from where we are, never from where we wish we were. This is sometimes a difficult reality to accept, particularly for those who cannot release their self-blame for what has derailed them. In the hope of redeeming their pasts—and thus themselves—they stagnate in a futile effort to redo what cannot be redone. If they can let go, men often find that creative pursuits, the nurture of old talents and skills, the development of new ones, and the mentoring of the young are valuable, life-sustaining opportunities. The essential feature of a happy human life is a sense of purpose, and from an early age we seek to discover it. In later life, we must often rediscover it.

### 8. Ego Integrity vs. Despair

In speaking of those living in old age—over sixty-five, give or take—Erikson tells us, "Only in him who in some way has taken care of things and people and has adapted himself to the triumphs and disappointments adherent to being, the originator of others or the generator of products and ideas—only in him may gradually ripen the fruit of these [previous] seven stages. I know no better word for it than ego integrity."[24] "Ego integrity" suggests a thoughtful acceptance of one's life and, thus, oneself. In that acceptance, we feel relatively whole and relatively fulfilled by how we have lived; and we accept what *will* transpire, including death. In the alternative to ego integrity—despair—we feel fragmented and at odds with all that we can no longer redo or control, including the inevitability of death. "The lack or loss of this accrued ego integration," Erikson says, "is signified by fear of death: the one and only life cycle is not accepted as the ultimate of life. Despair expresses the feeling that the time is now short, too short for the attempt to start another life and to try out alternate roads to integrity."[25]

Working with hundreds of dying men during the early epidemic, I saw repeatedly that—as young as many were—some died with relative acceptance, and some felt only despair, struggling angrily to the end. Those who died with more acceptance were usually men who felt some sense of personal satisfaction and accomplishment; and they were almost invariably men who, at some point in their lives, had experienced requited love with another man. Those who fought death were too regretful and angry about what could not be redone, and, importantly, too disappointed in themselves to feel any acceptance of death. Thoughtful, authentic self-forgiveness and self-acceptance are the useful resolutions for this age. For those gay men whose productive responses to earlier developmental challenges were significantly obstructed by a stigmatizing and destructive family or society—and by the dislocation, trauma, and losses of the epidemic—simply learning to live with inalterable loss, disappointment, and despair is the final challenge.

## A WORD FOR THE YOUNG

Erikson's Eight Ages of Man provides an inventory of seminal developmental challenges that all humans encounter. The less well resolved, more vulnerable outcomes of these challenges include elements of mistrust, shame, self-doubt, guilt, a sense of inferiority, role confusion, isolation, stagnation, and despair. We all carry *some* mix of such feelings, and gay people are certainly not alone in this developmental legacy. But the life experience that gives rise to vulnerabilities in gay men is often different from—and more truly traumatic than—the experience of heterosexual peers. As described in my discussion of each of the Eight Ages, many gay men today are survivors of a complex trauma rooted in early developmental experience and the two traumatizing epidemics. The two sources of trauma conflate into a "composite" trauma in which developmental challenges that arose in earlier life are reengaged by new trauma and loss later in life. Such composite trauma can feel like a self-sustaining and immobilizing vortex that forever feeds back on itself, obstructing authentic, beneficial change. Every introspective and thoughtful person spends much of his or her life juggling and rejuggling responses to both new and reengaged challenges; but too many gay men have been forced, by family and society, to do too much juggling. Some of us have been truly immobilized by a post-trauma vortex and accomplish change only with difficulty and true empathy and steady help. Others, through their own considered introspection, find ways to substantially break out of the vortex and thus bring beneficial change to their lives more easily. On the whole, gay people in America have found remarkable paths to self-realization—a miracle really, if we consider the noxious nurturing that so many vulnerable young lives are given.

As subjective experiences, early- and late-life trauma have much in common, and importantly, the two act on each other synergistically. In recovery from early-life trauma, the hope is that we will discover lives that are better than they have ever been. In recovery from late-life trauma alone, the hope is more modest: that we will recover the ground lost to the traumatic event, and—with new perspective and insight—perhaps something more. The recovery from either kind of trauma requires the examination of both, for in their synergy, each deeply influences the experience of the other. While this chapter's inventory of early-life challenges and their beneficial resolutions provides objectives for gay men to consider, it does not provide a process for doing so. In chapter 5, I will discuss some of the issues that can obstruct the process, including psychiatric diagnosis, isolation, unacknowledged grief, and problematic substance use. In chapter 6, I will discuss late-life trauma recovery *itself*, drawing on the seminal work of Judith Herman and others. While Herman writes largely about women's rape and combat survivors, her insights are highly pertinent to the trauma that many gay men have experienced, both in early and later life.

Young gay men usually have possibilities for change that many older men do not. Erikson orders the challenges of the Eight Ages as he does for a good reason: our psychological development is to some extent both progressive and cumulative. Progressively, within each challenge the quality of the resolution sets the foundation for challenges that follow. The inability to trust during infancy predicts more difficulty with autonomy, which, in turn, influences the possibility of gaining adequate senses of initiative, industry, identity, and intimacy. Cumulatively, while the eight challenges Erikson describes are never completely resolved, the accumulation of too many unsatisfactory resolutions can make it considerably more difficult to help bring change to unhappy lives. One needs to dig further down through the accumulated layers, and that denser "stack" of developmental events is more difficult to sort, examine, and reconstruct. The longer-standing, more codified histories of older people are often difficult to untangle and reconstruct in useful ways. Older men *do* often make significant changes in their lives, but they do it more slowly, and with more effort. Younger people have accumulated and codified less, and with the resilience of still-developing lives they very often find easier opportunities for useful change. Because of this inevitable—if quite variable—difference between older and younger gay men, much of the remainder of this book is written for young men and their futures. Many of the stories in the following chapters are stories from older men about their younger years, but I tell them, in good part, *for* young men, who may learn much from them.

# 5

# Some Obstructions to Self-Discovery and Self-Realization: Diagnosis, Isolation, and Grief

When the palace was rebuilt, the pictures, burned along with so
    much
else—flammable details of a pile given to the flames—had to be
    painted
again. Painted, necessarily, by artists not from those past times the
pictures came from.
                                        —Keith Waldrop, *The Not Forever*[1]

## DIAGNOSIS: THE STORY OF PAUL

Many readers will notice that I have not yet used the term *post-traumatic stress disorder*. PTSD, as it is now popularly known, is a diagnosis offered in the *Diagnostic and Statistical Manual of Mental Disorders* (DSM), which is conceived of and published by the American Psychiatric Association (APA). Today most often discussed in connection with combat survivors, PTSD is an abbreviation used to indicate a constellation of real-world "signs" and "symptoms" that survivors of trauma sometimes experience. This diagnostic term is thus simply a label for that constellation; and as with much psychiatric diagnosis, the very fact of the label can be harmful and can obstruct the recovery of men living in the aftermath of traumatic combat, early-gay-life experience, or the two HIV epidemics.[2] Gay people were considered "diagnosable" long before the idea of PTSD was conceived in 1980, and the diagnoses have caused untold harm, much of it still unresolved.

Diagnoses of homosexuality or "ego-dystonic homosexuality"[3] remained in the *DSM* through the terrifying first half-decade of the early epidemic, until, in 1986, they were finally expunged. What they left in their wake was a legacy of emotional injury that is still alive today. The stigmatization of gay people has always been a societal problem for which gay people have been blamed; and psychiatry—which has too often been a professional mouthpiece for mindless social norms—has played a significant role in inverting the blame. If the trauma gay people have experienced were more broadly recognized, perhaps PTSD would be the new diagnosis of choice. But the use of the label would likely only do further harm, and it would require an acknowledgment that is unlikely to be made: it would force psychiatry to look at the very trauma it had helped create through the abusive use of diagnosis.

Diagnosis is the foundation of the contemporary conceptualization of "mental health." If we were to take the *DSM* compendium of diagnosable disorders seriously, everyone would fall in one of two spheres: normal and healthy, or abnormal and ill. The 947 pages of the most recent *DSM* offer 265 "disorders" to choose from, many of them specious.[4] But, while psychiatry was pathologizing gay people with diagnoses, society was a step ahead: being homosexual was worse than *having* a disorder, it was *being* a monstrosity. A twenty-seven-year-old man once said to me, "When I left my family and moved to San Francisco to come out, I thought to myself, 'You are abandoning your family so you can be a monster.'" The idea was not this young man's invention, nor was it the invention of Freud. During the 1950s and '60s, many prominent, presumably authoritative APA-member psychiatrists—including the notorious Charles Socarides and Robert Spitzer—supported the idea of monstrosity by describing gay people as diseased, sexual "psychopaths."[5] Such characterizations not only countered the nascent homophile movement for gay civil rights, they furthered the widespread societal stigma and violence directed at gay people and brought untold emotional damage to millions of gay and lesbian Americans. In his wonderfully researched and thoughtful book about the history of early gay-equality movements in the United States, John D'Emilio tells a story about the 1968 American Medical Association annual meeting in San Francisco:

As the AMA prepared for its annual convention in June 1968, the editor of the San Francisco Medical Society *Bulletin* warned the arriving doctors to "be on guard against brigades of harlots and homosexuals." At the convention itself, Socarides spoke of homosexuality as "a dread dysfunction, malignant in character, which has risen to epidemic proportions." When he called upon the federal government to finance national centers for the cure and rehabilitation of the "sexual deviant," homophile [movement] leaders held a well-received press conference where they likened his proposal to a "final solution."[6]

Stigmatization by psychiatry has had the unfortunate consequence of long deterring gay people from seeking help to address the emotional consequences of that stigmatization. The discussion of emotional issues, the feeling goes, risks offering yet another opportunity for stigmatization: troubling feelings suggest the need for help, needing help looks like pathological weakness and personal failure, and weakness and failure validate the stigma. Asking psychiatry for help is particularly problematic because it is psychiatry that defined gay people as pathological in the first place. While this common apprehension about seeking help is understandable, all human beings—even men—sometimes have troubling feelings; and members of societally stigmatized minorities often have more. Members of minorities who are also survivors of trauma often experience troubling feelings, and how could they not? This assertion is not a confirmation of pathology or weakness; it is an acknowledgment of the truth about normal human responses to adversity. Even as our frequent denial of this truth is understandable, acknowledgment of and attention to our feelings are much more helpful. Authentic strength lies in our own thoughtful attention to our vulnerabilities, not our denial of them.

Psychiatric diagnosis does more than stigmatize people and alienate them from potentially useful support. Diagnosis can also reduce the quality of care that people receive when they *do* come for help, because diagnosis is too easily mistaken for insight by both provider and patient. We obviously need to know certain things to be helpful to a person in emotional pain: what he is feeling, how he experiences those feelings, and how he expresses them in his life. It is also usually

helpful to know the history behind the feelings. *After* doing this deductive work, it might then be useful to attach a diagnostic label simply for communicating the observations quickly and succinctly; possibly
for the suggestion of a useful "treatment" approach; and possibly to
help guide further deductive exploration suggested by the diagnostic
label. But in itself, the diagnostic label has told us nothing that we did
not ourselves observe or hear from the patient. The diagnosis has provided a name, not insight.[7] Despite the illusion imparted by a diagnosis, people do not usually "have" an emotional issue in the sense of
having a cold or a bacterial infection.[8] Unlike medical diagnoses, few
psychiatric diagnoses describe an underlying cause with a clearly useful course of treatment or a reliable prognosis. Depression, as one
example, is not something people have, it is an experience, a way of
experiencing oneself and the world. Some people characteristically—
or in the shorter term, in an acute response to life events—have depressed feelings and sometimes live out the feelings in ways that are
problematic and self-perpetuating. The useful deductive investigation
is about when and why the person first became depressed, how he is
experiencing the depression, and how the depression might be creating further problems.

Today, a psychiatric diagnosis often leads immediately to the
use of psychotropic medication, a practice that furthers the avoidance of exploring and understanding feelings. Such medications—
antidepressants being the most widely used today—are appropriate
and useful for some people, some of the time. But antidepressants do
not usually address underlying causes[9] and obviously do not change
the depressing real-world facts of a life. While they are certainly not
"happy pills"—the FDA is unlikely to approve anything that makes
people *too* happy—they do sometimes help shift subjective experience
in ways that allow the person to make useful changes in how he lives
his life. Less usefully, antidepressants can also make unchanged, intolerable lives feel more tolerable by flattening the entire range of emotional experience. If someone is depressed because he is unnecessarily
isolated and lonely, a medication used as the sole form of treatment to
make the isolation more tolerable is a questionable approach.[10] Too
often, the diagnosis of an emotional issue, and the prescription of a
drug to treat it, is the psychiatric equivalent of coffee and aspirin for

fatigue and fever. No deductive investigation is made into what is caus-
ing the fatigue and fever, nor is any attempt made to directly treat that
cause: we simply treat the symptoms and leave it at that. Unfortunately,
the fatigue and fever "diagnosis" legitimizes the prescription, and the
prescription validates the diagnosis: because we have depression, we
use an antidepressant, and the fact that we are using it confirms that
we have the depressive disorder. Chronic "fatigue and fever" is not a
medical diagnosis, and no competent physician would settle for it
or simply prescribe for it without further deductive investigation.
American psychiatry—and the pharmaceutical industry that supports its work—does that all the time.[11]

In addition to the professional *push* for a diagnostic conceptualization of our emotional lives, an important *pull* for diagnosis comes
from those who are being diagnosed. I see two primary responses from
therapy patients who have been given a psychiatric diagnosis—almost
always by someone other than me. One is fear or discouragement about
having a disorder and being labeled ill. The other is relief that a useful
discovery has finally been made, and by virtue of having an identified
disorder, the patient is relieved of fault and blame for his condition.
Sometimes people feel both responses simultaneously, though many
voice only the relief. Therapy patients thus often appreciate diagnoses
and often ask for one. Instead of simply providing it, I usually try to
talk about what it would mean to have one, and our most frequent discovery is that it would relieve the man of uncertainty about his life,
and his feelings of culpability and shame. Many of the abbreviations
for psychiatric diagnoses end in a *D* for good reason: *D* stands for
"disease," "disorder," or "dysfunction," as in ADHD, PTSD, or—a male
favorite and pharmaceutical golden goose—ED, for "erectile dysfunction."[12] The patient "has" a disorder, has an FDA-approved prescription
medication to prove it, and is no longer to blame for his failures—
inattention or hyperactivity, depression or anxiety, or flaccid penis.

Such relief from responsibility is often helpful because it lessens
the ridiculous burden of culpability placed on those who are not "normal" because they are not feeling what they and others feel they ought
to feel. I am completely supportive of the effort to relieve people of
culpability and self-blame for emotional issues, but diagnosis sometimes leads to reinforcing stagnation in the troubled feelings: with a

diagnosis, the patient "has an illness," which is not his doing, and over which he has no control. He identifies more strongly with the feelings, and they become more deeply entrenched in his sense of who he is. If he is told the truth—that the diagnosis is a label for a constellation of feelings and symptoms that we understand relatively little about, but that people do improve even if a definitive diagnosis and course of treatment is unknown—he might have a less-entrenched identification with the problem. He might also build or sustain a realistic hope of *actively* working through the problem, rather than settling quietly in with it, or waiting passively for someone else, or his medication, to "cure" it.

Diagnoses do not in themselves resolve anything, and they do not usually even get people completely off the culpability hook. Few depressed people really feel that they simply have a disease through no fault of their own. They may assert the diagnosis as a defense against anticipated blame from others, but they continue to feel somehow culpable. The sense of culpability—and the shame it breeds—is destructive and keeps our problematic emotional issues entrenched. As a psychotherapist, one of the most useful observations I have made is that everyone plays the best hand he can muster at any particular moment in his life. No one plays his second-best hand because, if he does, the decision to play it is his best hand at that moment. This observation reveals at least two obvious, but sometimes-startling, facts: we are not completely in control of our emotional lives, and we do not conduct our lives in hindsight.

In 2012, I began seeing Paul in therapy. An attractive, noticeably effeminate forty-four-year-old, he had a history of depression starting in adolescence. He had also lived in New York through much of the early epidemic, but had remained HIV-negative. A week after his partner Francis's death in 1998, Paul had attempted suicide with a lethal dose of Francis's medication but had vomited before respiratory arrest. He was psychiatrically hospitalized and, after release, moved to San Francisco. Martin, the San Francisco psychiatrist who had been handling Paul's relatively complex medication regimen for the past few years, suggested to Paul that he see me for "talk therapy." Paul told me that

Martin had diagnosed him as bipolar II[13] after their second meeting. It was the first diagnosis that Paul felt maybe rang true. The medication regimen seemed appropriate for the diagnosis, but the personal history Paul related to me did not obviously support the diagnosis. After I had a decent sense of Paul's life experience and we had had four or five sessions together, Paul and I had a conversation about his diagnosis and what it meant to him:

> "What do you feel about the diagnosis that Martin made?" I asked Paul.
>
> "You mean the bipolar?"
>
> "Yes. Did he make another?"
>
> "No, just the bipolar. I guess I was very relieved."
>
> "Why relieved?"
>
> "That's a good question. I've never thought about it, but I guess to finally just have a sense of what's wrong. It's the first time someone may have put his finger on it, and Martin says he's hopeful that we can get the medication right. He says he thinks I can have a happier life. I've been living with this since I was a teenager, so it gives me hope. We haven't gotten very far with the medication yet, but I'm hoping."
>
> "I imagine the diagnosis also makes it easier for others to understand you."
>
> "Oh, absolutely. People I know have been saying to me for years, 'Why don't you get out and meet people?' Or this and that—everyone has a suggestion—and now they understand that it's more complicated than that. I explain to them what bipolar two is, and they understand. Even my parents understand."
>
> "*Even* your parents?"
>
> Paul laughed. "My father's out in the zone, and my mother isn't a whole lot better. No, she's better, but not what you'd hope for. But I think they're relieved, too, to know what the problem is. I suppose it gets them off the hook, particularly my mother. She's spent years telling my father that it wasn't her fault. And my father's spent years ignoring her by watching TV sports."

"Wasn't her fault for what?"

"Oh, everything. My being gay and girlie, that's the big one, that's always been the big one. Then all the rest of it."

"What's all the rest?"

"*Being sick.* Spending high school hiding under the covers—no friends, no sports, practically every kid in school calling me a fag and punching me—no nothing except straight As, which they didn't much pay attention to. My mother used to say to people, 'Paul is our little genius,' but beyond being able to say that, she couldn't have cared less. I think they were mostly thinking, 'Oh, if only Paul wasn't a fag and such an obvious one.' I think they've rejected my whole life. Definitely my living with Francis for eight years, whom they couldn't stand—he was even more effeminate than I am—and I insisted on bringing him home when I visited. He was the only real friend I've ever had. *The only one, my dearest friend.* But my parents—well, the whole thing, my whole life, not just Francis. I think I was a disappointment to them starting maybe a week after they brought me home from the hospital. I probably threw up on one of them, and that was the end of the romance—if, indeed, there ever was one."

"So the 'bipolar two' helps with all this?"

"I think it gives them a reason, just like it gives me a reason."

"It sounds as if they've been quite hostile to you for most of your life. And your adolescent life at school also sounds filled with hostility. With your parents, does the diagnosis help with any of that? Do your parents express any apology, empathy, support, or anything like that?"

"I'm just remembering that there was a girl, Marilyn, in high school who had something really wrong with her legs, and the kids used to call her 'gimp.' I remember feeling bad for her, but I never talked to her, never made friends with her, even though I think I liked her. I feel bad just thinking about it, because I think I didn't want to be associated with someone else who had a problem—I was afraid, and I let her

down. It would have been, you know, 'the gimp and the fag.'
It makes me feel like calling her up now and apologizing."
Paul stopped speaking and seemed to be thinking about
what he had just said.

"What about getting ahold of her and talking?" I asked.
"It sounds like it might be helpful for both of you."

"What came to my mind was, now she's probably one of
those New Hampshire fag haters, like my father. Maybe she
always was."

Paul had survived a childhood and adolescence with both a very
unsupportive, perhaps hostile, family, and an overtly hostile school environment. Both were exacerbated, I would be sure, by his effeminacy. In 1990, at the age of twenty, he had left New Hampshire and
moved to New York. The early epidemic was on its trajectory to its destructive apex, and gay men were dying, by Paul's description, "almost
as quickly as I met them." About two years after arriving in New York,
Paul met Francis, they lived together for eight years, and Francis died
of HIV-related causes. After the death and Paul's determined suicide
attempt and hospitalization, Paul moved to San Francisco. There, he
had almost immediately found work as an advertising copywriter and,
by his own description, had been "highly successful." When I first met
him, he had worked for the same large agency for many years and felt
that he was well liked within the copywriting group he managed.

Personally, however, Paul remained isolated, had hardly dated, and
lived with a mood he described as "permanently down, except for the
vacations." He had "only the most casual of friends." He had small ral-
lies of mood occasionally—his "vacations"—which were the hypomanic
episodes that Martin had used to qualify the bipolar II diagnosis.
The vacations were brief, however, and only in relation to his baseline
mood might they be considered even *hypo*manic. In my impression,
the up-mood swings seemed reactive to the depression—Paul's attempts to rally himself out from under the weight of his normal deeply
sad and listless mood—but he could not sustain them.

Accounting for the fact that psychiatric diagnosis is not even re-
motely related to science, I could buy the bipolar II diagnosis. But the
origins of Paul's mood problems were readily apparent in his history,

and we did not need a diagnosis to understand them. He had a largely stigmatized first twenty years, and he had learned in early childhood to elevate his mood by entertaining others with stories and skits that garnered approval, deflecting many painful feelings. Paul's mother had a second description for Paul: sometimes, instead of being the family's "little genius," Paul was "our little entertainer." The cheerful little entertainer concealed a deep well of unhappiness that no one talked about. Currently, his "hypomanic episodes" were expressed in entertaining others with lavish and animated dinner parties at his flat, after which he would lie in bed for two days, "which is why I only do them on Friday nights." The guests were "acquaintances, not friends."

While I never questioned the diagnosis in discussions with Paul, with his permission I did have a single phone conversation with Martin. He said to me, "Paul's a very unhappy, very likable guy whom I really wanted to help. I don't know if he's bipolar or not, but that's about as close as I could get. I hope you can do something for him. He's worth the time, and he's smart, he has guts, and he's still motivated after all these years." Even as Paul was hopeful about the possibility of a successful medication regimen, neither he nor Martin seemed to take the diagnosis seriously. Had the diagnosis led to a useful medication regimen—particularly one that did not also significantly limit Paul's life through emotional constriction—that would certainly have been worthwhile. But the medication, in both Paul's and Martin's estimation, had not been of much use, and that was why Martin had wanted Paul to talk with me.

Early in our work together, Paul was doubtful that he had had a traumatizing experience in childhood and adolescence, and that the epidemic and the loss of Francis had reengaged the feelings of the earlier trauma. Part of his doubtful response to my suggestion that he had endured a lot of trauma had obvious origins: he had simply never thought of his life experience in such terms because it was all he had ever known. "It's just life," he said to me, "and everyone has a life. Don't they?" But Paul had another important reason for doubting that, for much of his life, he had lived through trauma. Like many people, Paul experienced the description of adversity as stigmatizing, as an indictment of *him*, much the way people sometimes experience being diagnosed with a "disorder." Paul heard the description of a traumatized life as if it were a diagnosis: a description of something that he "had" or "was," and he was not as comfortable with this "diagnosis" as he had been with the concrete diagnosis of bipolar II. In my developmental description, he clearly recognized his life—it *felt* true—while the diagnosis felt relatively objective and external. History is something we have lived, a diagnosis something we are called, and the history is often more difficult to accept. As Paul began to accept the historical truth of his traumatic developmental experience, other feelings began to come up. He felt that his history was somehow his failure, and that as a result he was "damaged goods." He thought that he should have had the "strength" to be unaffected by his life experience, and that if he was, his "weakness" had allowed it. He told me, "I can accept the reality of my life going way back, but I have never thought of myself as a product of it. It was history, and I guess I thought I was immune. I don't want to be affected by it."

As we worked together weekly for about three years, Paul became progressively more aware that he had survived a string of traumas that culminated in Francis's death, that he was not the perpetrator of that history, and that he had had a normal and comprehensible emotional response to the course his life had taken. He was also gradually able to accept—partly due to my consistent acceptance of him, and my refusal to pathologize his feelings—that he was not culpable because he was gay or effeminate, because he had made a suicide attempt, or because he had experienced some lifelong depression. With this unburdening insight, he let go of a great deal of shame. As our work proceeded, the significance of the bipolar diagnosis waned, and memories of his life experience became more accessible and useful. As a child from Mercury raised by reactionary New Hampshire earthlings, Paul was a resolute and valiant survivor of serious developmental trauma that was painfully revisited in the early epidemic and the terrible loss of Francis. It was in acknowledging and understanding these experiences that he was able to slowly make changes in his current life. He developed more social connections—"More than I've had in *years*"—and, as one result, saw some noticeable improvement in his mood, energy, and engagement in life. With Martin's help, Paul tapered off most of his medication, but he continued on a single drug, the antidepressant Lexapro, which Paul found helpful. His new life was not a fresh start, but it was subjectively and objectively substantially happier.

Some people with adverse developmental histories like Paul's—particularly those who have less characteristic resilience—can be more difficult to help. But Paul *did* have resilience. Martin told me this on the phone, and I first heard it from Paul when he told me that he had persevered in being accompanied by Francis during visits to his parents' home. During our work together, Paul's resilience and tenacity repeatedly made themselves apparent. A more comprehending, generous, and humane developmental experience would have allowed Paul a happier life with more possibilities, and he will probably never completely surmount some of the limitations imposed by what he did have. But, as Martin said on the phone, Paul is worth the time. Paul is one of the honest, tenacious, good-hearted gay men that I have been fortunate to meet and work with. Although not what the earthlings had in mind, Paul is authentically himself. He is an important kind of hero, and one I greatly admire.

## ISOLATION: THE STORY OF SEAN

In gay communities today, isolation is endemic for both older and younger men; and like diagnosis, it is a significant impediment to recovery from trauma and loss. Unfortunately, gay people often grow up in isolation, and this is still true today because of the rejection and abuse that young gay people continue to experience from families, peers, and communities. Gay adolescents are still actively discouraged or prohibited from developing potentially meaningful, intimate relationships and, as adults, often do not know how to relate intimately to others. As children and adolescents—and sometimes as adults—we hide ourselves to avoid detection, reduce our sense of shame, and protect ourselves from potential hostility. For someone who feels unwanted or contemptible, isolation is safety. While it is usually the only implementable option for children and adolescents, it is too often sustained into adult life, and the emotional aftermaths of the early and continuing late epidemics have layered themselves on top of the trauma and isolation first experienced in growing up gay. On the surface, the self-isolation of a trauma survivor makes little sense, for we would expect him to seek much-needed social connection and support. But isolation is an almost-invariable consequence of any trauma, for trauma damages our inborn capacity for attachment to others.

Survivors isolate themselves when others and the world feel dangerous, and when they feel a need to protect and hide an injured sense of self—a sense of self that is often further restricted by the stigma of diagnosis. The idea that one "has PTSD" helps codify a survivor's isolation. Isolation is not a direct response to trauma but a product of the feelings that *are* a direct response. These feelings commonly include fear, anxiety, depression, shame, a sense of a fragmented or damaged self, and a loss of trust in oneself and the world. In remaining isolated—during a gay adolescence or an epidemic and its aftermath—the survivor is attempting to protect himself, and to conceal and cope with feelings. Unfortunately, the isolation also disconnects him from the social, interpersonal, and professional support that might help him emerge from the aftermath of trauma.

Even as isolation is only a marker of underlying reactions to trauma, it often exacerbates those reactions. Isolation creates its own, secondary problems, particularly when it becomes an extended form of life. Despite such secondary problems, we still cannot address isolation without first exploring the direct symptoms of trauma that lie behind it. Because isolation is a visible marker, it is often the only sign of a problem that an outsider—including a psychotherapist—sees, and it may be the only sign that the survivor himself is conscious of or acknowledges to others. Our first useful step is to note the isolation, our second to remember that isolation conceals other feelings that need exploring before the isolation—and any of its secondary problems—are addressed. By nature, few human beings become spontaneously or willfully isolated, and the helpful solution rarely lies in addressing the isolation alone.

The isolation of older gay men in response to the early epidemic has taken many forms. During those years, some older-group men fled the danger and chaos by leaving gay communities for other locales, many of them unsupportive of gay life. Some men who had never entered gay communities remained isolated where they were, often unhappily avoiding the entire issue of coming out. Rather than flee geographically, some men who lived in gay communities remained physically within them but adjusted their social lives to emulate the isolated lives that they had first known as adolescents. Some men fled into seemingly safe relationships that they would not otherwise have pursued, often resulting in two isolated men living together under a single roof. The psychological stress of life in the early epidemic encouraged many forms of exodus, all driven by fear, shame, emotional exhaustion, and a sense of a loss of community—and of self. For those living through the epidemic with their own HIV infection and the stigma attached to it, those with accumulating losses, and those otherwise experiencing trauma, the relational self—the self they had previously brought to social and intimate relationships—often felt injured or lost. In the words of Judith Herman, the long-standing dean of the literature on trauma, "The traumatic event . . . destroys the belief that one can be oneself in relation to others."[14] As one isolated man told me in 1992, "I can't *be around* people anymore. I don't know what happened, but I can't, and I don't see how to be different."

In the years following the early epidemic, it was not just individuals, but entire communities that no longer seemed what they had been. Gay communities were long past the broad, unifying spirit of post-Stonewall Gay Liberation and were no longer united by the common purpose of the epidemic's emergency. Indeed, gay men were seeming to deny that the epidemic had ever happened, because no one wanted to revisit the trauma in conversation with others, for fear of opening up a discussion too painful to revisit, and retraumatizing everyone involved. Living in now socially and politically incoherent communities—a fragmentation that is particularly destructive within stigmatized minority communities—many gay men felt that they had moved "back to Kansas," where they had *no* community and did not belong. As in childhood and adolescent years, these men were again outsiders and alone, scattered emotionally—sometimes literally—to distant corners. Speaking more broadly about the effects of trauma, Herman usefully describes some of the psychological forces behind the disintegration of gay communities following the early epidemic: "Traumatic events have primary effects not only on the psychological structure of the self but also on the systems of attachment and meaning that link individual and community. . . . Traumatic events destroy the victim's fundamental assumptions about the safety of the world, the positive value of the self, and the meaningful order of creation."[15]


The isolation of young men today is rooted in a constellation of influences that are significantly different from those faced by older gay men. Some are familiar and shared with older men, including the early-life experience of outsiderness and isolation that so easily turns an experience of transitory circumstance into a self-identity that is carried into adulthood; and fear and avoidance of HIV—today, realistic or not— and the isolating effect of stigma directed at HIV-positive men. But other influences on young men are less familiar to older men, and oddly, many of these are a legacy of the early epidemic that older men lived through but young men never knew.

The social and psychological aftermath of the early epidemic is very different for older and younger men. While a middle group of men straddles this distinction, older men knew the experience of being gay in relatively coherent gay communities before the epidemic began. Young men have come out into the postepidemic, fragmented minority communities that I discussed in chapter 3, communities in which some men strive for a post-trauma normalization of gay lives that others abhor and reject. Some now-older survivors did emerge from the epidemic still focused on earlier personal and social agendas, but others—particularly middle-aged and older men with money and influence—have sought the ease and security of assimilation into the larger society. This fragmented legacy has been handed to young men who have no firsthand knowledge of the earlier, youth-driven history of gay life in America, a history that describes communities first united by necessary secrecy, then publicly voiced homophile and liberation movements, and finally the truly desperate-to-the-death battle against HIV. The only gay communities young men have known no longer have such cohering purpose, and with the proliferation of gay people in the public eye—also a result of the early epidemic—young men are finding that their being gay is, pure sex aside, little to have in common. For some men, even gay self-identity—which is strengthened by adversity and outsiderness—is no longer as defined in an American society that is slowly moving toward greater acceptance.

Minority groups naturally strive to define themselves, for the individual's self-identity is partly built on that definition. Young men
are—in a way that older men circumvented with ready-made community
purpose—thus required to build from scratch meaningful communities that provide a sense of self rooted in a sense of belonging. Unfortunately, young men today usually share older gay men's socially
enforced deprivation of early developmental experience that might assist that effort. In my experience, too many young men today feel that
they were forced outside in early life and are being forced out again,
with no home to return to. As one intelligent, Indiana-born twenty-
seven-year-old put it to me, "I came to San Francisco to finally find a
gay life, and I've found—almost nothing."

During the early epidemic, gay men began paying significantly
more attention to physical fitness and an appearance of health. The
epidemic offered the never-to-be-forgotten experience of wasting dis-
figurement and death for hundreds of thousands of young and middle-
aged men. The psychologist Brett Kennedy has had a partial focus on
"body image disorders" among gay men,[16] and in a recent e-mail, he described to me his perception of the evolution of such concerns among
gay men, concerns that are today apparent:

> In my psychology practice during the nineties and early 2000s,
> as treatments improved for HIV-positive men, including tes-
> tosterone and steroids for muscle wasting, many positive men
> no longer appeared "sick," and an overly-muscled "healthy"
> look was becoming the aesthetic. So I was seeing a lot of HIV-
> negative men using testosterone and steroids to measure up
> to the HIV-positive men who now had this "advantage." Dur-
> ing this time, especially in the Castro, New York and L.A.,
> the muscled aesthetic became the ideal, as it conveyed not
> only health, but a caricatured masculinity as well. This body
> aesthetic has changed somewhat over the years, and men are
> now opting for a lean and lithe body, but they continue to use
> different concoctions of steroids to achieve the bodies of
> choice. In the mid 2000s, especially in New York, I regularly
> worked in my practice with gay men with body-image issues
> who were attempting to modify their bodies with steroids and

over-exercising. It seems to me that this "crisis" of our bodies really started and is rooted in the impact of HIV and fear of looking sick, competing with those who have HIV, and issues about masculinity. Obviously culture has changed as well into a more health-conscious society that is more focused on physical aesthetics and plastic surgery, so even without direct connections to the epidemic, young gays are seeing older gay men and their bodies, and they are just trying to compete in a competitive world.

The attention to physical appearance has supported a level of objectification—the experience of others as objects rather than people—among gay men that did not exist before the early epidemic. Objectification has an important consequence for isolation: it encourages physical interaction with other "things" to the exclusion of intellectual and emotional intimacy; and a lack of intimacy in one's life—or an internal incapacity for intimacy—is a consequence and a cause of isolation. Particularly among today's young gay men, objectification has found an important ally in Internet sites and phone apps. Both offer illustrated shopping catalogs of available men, not unlike mail-order shoe catalogs or the illustrated menus of Japanese restaurants. If one does not like a particular pair of oxfords or the tuna sushi, he need only turn the page; and the apps are thus particularly appealing to men who are isolated or uncomfortable with socializing, even as they do little to address those limitations.

Because of phone app use, there is now much less personal, face-to-face contact in "live" gay venues such as gay community centers, support groups, clubs, or bars. Scruff promises to help its users "Meet Millions of Scruff Gay Guys in Your Neighborhood and Around the World."[17] Grindr allows a man to "search by Tribe to find your type of guy" and "narrow down guys with a filter feature."[18] *Tribe* refers to classified groups such as Twinks (young and slender), Bears (older, stout, and hairy), Cubs (younger and stout), Gym Bunnies (toned or muscled), Geeks (too busy with other matters to be concerned about appearance and socially awkward?), or Discreet (surreptitious and perhaps not out). This is not an exhaustive list, but it is noteworthy that all but the last group are defined by objectifying physical characteristics.

Each subscriber is optionally allowed to categorize himself for the benefit of others' searches, and within any given tribe, one can refine the search with additional "filters." Filterable information may include preferred sexual acts, amount of body hair, penis size, circumcision or the lack of it, and HIV status, so one could presumably search for an HIV-negative, uncircumcised, Gym Bunny top. But who is that, as a *person*? The appeal of apps is partly rooted in male sexuality—not just *gay* male sexuality—in its most pragmatic, least relational expression. The app experience thus revisits the unhappy, nonrelational, and isolated adolescent experience of many gay men, an adolescence that American society has almost universally insisted on. While, as adults, many with fulfilled lives use the apps largely for recreational hookups, a majority of men use them to address isolation and a lack of intimacy. They are looking for *something*, something substantial and important; but for every connection that truly grows into something meaningful, thousands are merely objectifying, and thus disappointing.

Resources such as phone apps certainly have huge potential, and that potential is sometimes realized. But young men too often tell me that they are isolated by the technology that constructs their social lives. There is a difference between "meeting" someone on an app through agile thumbs and truncated sentences, and the traditional alternative of sitting together, talking, and having a drink. In San Francisco's Castro district, one often sees young men milling past one another on the street or sitting in bars and cafés, with a majority focused on their phones, rather than one another. Many of these men are using the apps in the hope of emerging from their isolation, but when a meeting does result, one could easily imagine that the app's objectifying structure begets objectified, nonrelational sex that largely replicates the unfulfilling, lonely adolescent experience. In his e-mail to me, Brett Kennedy also commented on the history and effects of technology:

> Online dating was the first step, and then as technology advanced, GPS became integrated into the apps, and the ease with which one could get laid increased exponentially—and, I would posit, intimacy was impaired. Many of my young clients will discuss wanting a boyfriend or relationship, but struggle

with their attention span, and with how to engage another person in a more intimate way. I see people creating "rules" to facilitate intimacy—for example, going on an "old school" date (to dinner), and not sleeping with them, trying to hold off on sex to build on the relationship. I remember one guy who was doing this, and he was so excited about someone he'd met, and telling me about their first date. I remarked that he must be excited about the second date, and he said, "Well, on my way home from dinner, I logged into Grindr and hooked up with someone, and then I wasn't so sure if the guy from dinner was really that great, or if it was really worth it when it's so easy to get on Grindr and have so many options, depending on your mood."

Phone apps have certainly not caused the difficulty that contemporary young men are having with intimacy and isolation, but the apps probably exacerbate it: they, too, easily bring to adult lives the early developmental experience of craving—but rarely finding—authentic connection to others. If the adolescent had only a handful of self-made fantasies about connection, the apps offer an implausible million or more for the isolated adult to page through. For those pages that lead to a face-to-face meeting, a large majority end in objectified sex. But men seeking others are usually seeking more than the release of young male libido: they are seeking emotional connection to others and, in those connections, discovery of themselves—and, possibly, enduring relationships. Purely objectified sex is not a probable path to such objectives.

As we have seen, from adolescence forward, gay men have been societally defined by the idea of "the homosexual," which entirely characterizes gay life by its sexual acts. Societal characterizations readily become a self-identity, and it is significantly the identity of the homosexual that we see expressed by young men today: they are more sexually active than any generation since that of 1970s Gay Liberation. As one young man who was unhappy with his social life in San Francisco put it to me, "Most of the guys I meet would fuck a coconut." The active sexual lives of young men *are* supported by the pharmaceutical control of HIV, which often allows sex with relatively little risk of HIV infection; and young men are understandably pushing back against early-life constraints. Young men often feel that older gay men had access to a birthright of sexual freedom that today's young men have been deprived of. And they often feel that the early epidemic—and the role that older men played in it—were responsible for that deprivation. Their feelings are understandable, and young men should explore sexually, but one wonders how their sexual lives leave them feeling. Too many young men today are puzzled by the idea that human intimacy is important, an intimacy that is also a human birthright—whether young men know it or not. Without this understanding, young men may be on trajectories that will only sustain and deepen the perpetual sense of isolation and unrequited longing they knew in adolescence.

Sean's story provides insight into the isolation that often follows trauma, in this instance the trauma of the early epidemic. Sean, fifty-four, had contracted HIV in his early twenties but did not know it until several years later. He was intelligent, ambitious, and independent; in his twenties, he had completed a graduate degree in electrical engineering and had, at age twenty-seven, started his own company, specializing in "redundant high-speed electronic switching." Like many I've seen in therapy following the early epidemic, Sean felt that the problem he wanted to talk about was "isolation and loneliness." The following transcript is an extreme condensation of many months of conversation.

> "When I found out I had HIV, I remember thinking, 'This is what rape must be like.' My body wasn't mine, it had been taken over by somebody who was going to kill me. A year after I got the diagnosis, I was crapping in my pants and vomiting five times a day, and all of that is completely humiliating. I was twenty-nine when I started getting sick, and I've never gotten over that feeling of losing control, even now. I don't trust people. If I'm near someone who has a cold, I feel like 'Don't touch me, don't get near me, I don't want you inside me.'"

"But you trust yourself?" I asked.

"Yes." Sean hesitated a moment. "No. I'd say no, and I don't know how this fits in, but when you ask the question, I'd say I don't trust myself either. Not with people."

"Well, I'm imagining that you came out of that 'humiliating' experience with certain feelings about yourself, feelings that undercut your self-confidence."

"Well, I felt like a pariah then, and I still feel like one. So, now that you're bringing it up, I think it works both ways—don't touch me and I won't touch you. That's how it works, it works both ways. Right now, I don't know if it's trust of other people, or I just feel ashamed of myself. Is being ashamed distrust of myself? This is confused in my mind."

"Ashamed of yourself for what?"

"For everything, I guess. Getting HIV, shitting my pants for two years, everything. When I was a kid—in my twenties—I trusted people—that's part of the story about how I got HIV. I don't know how to put it, but the whole thing—the epidemic and my having HIV—all left me helpless in some way. I'm ashamed of that. I work hard, I'm smart, I have a successful company—did I tell you that we got the contract for some of the control switching on the Boeing 787?"

"Congratulations, but, no, I don't remember you mentioning it."

"You'd look at me and think that HIV had no effect on my life after the [antiviral drug] cocktail, but the truth is that I *do* feel helpless in some way that I haven't been aware of. Being ashamed of myself, is that a lack of self-trust?"

"Well, I don't think shame supports self-confidence, and reasonable self-confidence seems like a prerequisite to self-trust. So, yes, I'd say that shame and self-trust are connected in some way. And to return to why you first came to see me, I can't imagine that shame and helplessness are things you would experience as a good foundation for working on your sense of isolation."

Sean started laughing. "Hardly! I've never made that connection before, which is weird, because it's obvious when you say it. I'll have to think about it, but I'd never made it: 'Hi, I'm Sean, and I'm ashamed and helpless and I'd like to be your friend.' Sounds good, right?"

"Not really."

"No, *not really*. I'm a different person now than I was then, in '83 or whatever. I'm an ashamed and helpless person, and I don't know who I'd *be* with anyone new in my life. I don't know who I *could* be. As I am now, *I* don't like me, so why would anyone else? *'I'm ashamed and helpless and I'd like to be your friend!'* With your simple questions, I realize that I've lost myself."

"And in doing that, you've lost a sense of a personal or larger community."

"Yes, exactly. I don't even know who I am. How would I know who I would be in a relationship, even a social one? It would be a lie from the beginning."

The feelings that had underlain Sean's isolation were not known to him: after contracting HIV, he had isolated himself, with a purely unconscious sense of shame and helplessness. He felt too damaged— or too nonexistent—to allow social or intimate connections, the very connections that might have helped him emerge from the unhappy personal life he had hidden from himself and others, behind an active and successful work life. While Sean's isolation was substantially a product of those feelings of shame and helplessness, the isolation had exacerbated the feelings, for he was now also ashamed of the isolation itself. In continuing our work together, we would make another important discovery. Sean's impulse to isolate himself started long before he contracted HIV, at the age of twelve, when he overheard his parents talking in the kitchen about whether Sean was gay. "There is one thing that sticks in my mind," Sean told me, "which is when my dad said, 'I would rather have a *dead* son than a gay one,' and then my mom said nothing." At that moment, Sean knew for the first time with absolute certainty that he had to hide himself from others. The epidemic and his HIV infection had only perpetuated the plan.

The aftermath of the trauma of the two epidemics and that of the day-in, day-out extended trauma of gay early-life experience have something in common: connection or reconnection to others is an essential step on the path to discovering or rediscovering happier lives that do not remain defined by the emotional aftermath of the trauma. As I will discuss in chapter 6, coming out of isolation is a crucial last step in working through a post-trauma experience. While the exploration of underlying emotional issues that Sean and I engaged in often feels as if it worsens isolation—and it often does in the short term—the exploration is unavoidable. The alternative—jumping directly to the effort to correct isolation itself—is too likely to result in an inauthentic, internally constricted life that is usually not capable of authentic connection or intimacy. Such a life is capable of *apparent* connectedness, if that. On the aftermath of trauma, the reluctance to examine feelings, and isolation, Judith Herman provides a succinct description:

> Because reliving a traumatic experience [by talking about it] provokes such intense emotional distress, traumatized people go to great lengths to avoid it. The effort to ward off intrusive symptoms, though self-protective in intent, further aggravates the post-traumatic syndrome, for the attempt to avoid reliving the trauma too often results in a narrowing of consciousness, a withdrawal from engagement with others, and an impoverished life.[19]

## COMPLICATED GRIEF AND GUILT: THE STORY OF HARRY

Grief is a natural response to the loss of others, and to the loss of oneself as one once was—or hoped to be. Grieving—the working *through* grief—is difficult, but important, in the aftermath of trauma; and the difficulty is often exacerbated by the complication of conscious or unconscious guilt. When—with or without guilt—grieving stalls, so does the life. Judith Herman suggests some important reasons that survivors of trauma "cling to their symptoms":

Symptoms may be a symbolic means of keeping faith with a lost person, a substitute for mourning, or an expression of unresolved guilt. In the absence of a socially meaningful form of testimony, many traumatized people choose to keep their symptoms. In the words of the war poet Wilfred Owen: "I confess I *bring on* what few war dreams I now have, entirely by *willingly* considering war of an evening. I have my duty to perform towards war."[20]

Harry first came to see me for therapy at the age of fifty-eight. Within a few minutes of meeting him, I sensed that he was authentically at ease in the world, without a suggestion of bluff or posturing. But fifteen minutes later, I had another thought: Harry had the ease of a man who had given up, a man with no hopes or plans, a man who was at ease because he had nothing to lose. Then I had still another unspoken thought: Harry could really stand to lose some weight. He was corpulent, his gait and breathing were perceptibly labored, and he was otherwise obviously in poor health, which I would later find out was partly due to erratic medical attention to his HIV, and partly to his overly generous indulgence in "fine food and wines." As I pondered Harry's poor health, it struck me that this man of ease was planning to die and had visibly implemented his plan to that end. Some people experience the prospect of death as a welcome certainty that unburdens emotional pain, and Harry seemed among them. I thought he might have come to talk about his death, but perhaps it was something else.

Harry was a retired attorney who had spent his entire career in a public-interest organization he had founded to legally represent "socioeconomically disadvantaged medical patients." Many of his clients had HIV and were in disputes with medical and disability insurers. Despite his poor financial compensation for the work, he told me that he was happy with it because he had done "a lot of good for people." He had received "a substantial amount of money" through family inheritance and was, by his own description, "well-off." But when he spoke about that, he clearly did it with discomfort. Harry lived alone, and though he had a small handful of friends, he led an almost completely isolated life in the Berkeley hills, overlooking all of

San Francisco Bay, including the city that he and his partner had lived in together for fifteen years. The partner—also named Harry, though his given name was Harold rather than Henry—had died of HIV-related complications at the age of thirty-nine, seventeen years before Harry and I first met. Harry suggested, "for the sake of clarity," that we refer to his former partner as Harry-2. The two had met when Harry was twenty-six and Harry-2 was twenty-four, and Harry-2 had been Harry's only sustained relationship. "Harry-2 was the only one I really cared about; I loved him more than anything in life." When I later asked Harry why he had come to see me, he simply said, "I really ought to have *someone* to talk to."

Although he did not say it, it soon became apparent that Harry was not only lonely, but markedly depressed. It was the kind of quiet, easygoing depression that calls little attention to itself, the kind of depression that could easily be mistaken for a state of peace and enlightenment. Harry appeared to accept this state of being, though he attempted to medicate both it and his loneliness with his food, and particularly his wine. He acknowledged feeling chronic "sadness," but rejected the thought of being "depressed," a word he always spoke in quotation marks. But sadness alone does not entail some features our talks would clearly reveal: profound grief and guilt, chronic insomnia, almost complete isolation, and a nearly complete loss of interest in everything but eating and drinking. What we called it was of no importance, so we called it sadness. Harry did have some fear of *becoming* "depressed," which was, he said, also part of why he had sought me out. He was concerned that any sadness he did acknowledge would place too much expectation on the few friends he had left, and he did not want to burden them. "People," he said softly, "have their own things to deal with, and the last thing they need is me. For heaven's sake, look at me. I'm old, I'm fat, I'm a mess. I'm completely tainted."

In addition to the obvious aftermath of his traumatic experience with the early epidemic, Harry was clearly having feelings about other issues, including aging; but he seemed to have his feelings about aging entangled in feelings about the many he had lost to HIV in their youth. Perhaps he felt that if he had somehow magically held on to *his* youth, he would have been able to hold on to them, for as he aged, they remained forever young and felt increasingly distant. His attempt to hold on to those young men was keeping Harry attached to his grief, which obstructed any grieving that might allow him to move forward. As I pondered this further, I also thought that his feelings about aging were entangled in feelings about having HIV. *Tainted* is not a term we normally associate with aging, but it does suggest a feeling of "being contaminated," which is relatively common, if often unconscious, among HIV-positive men. And, finally, there seemed to be another issue that Harry was entangled in, something from his early-life experience or family history, all of which he would steadfastly refuse to discuss until much later in our work. He did slip one day, saying that he had done to Harry-2 "exactly what I did to my mother."

"What does that mean?" I asked.

Harry responded by shooting me a sharp warning glance and falling into total silence.

"Well, we don't have to talk about it."

Harry shrugged dismissively, as if there were *never* anything to talk about.

Even as he denigrated himself and self-protectively foiled much of our work, I found Harry sympathetic, likable, and intelligent, and I wanted to be helpful. His adult history revealed that he had at one time led a generous, gregarious social life, with many close and intimate friends. "They all died—well, almost all of them," he told me matter-of-factly not long after we first met. Harry and Harry-2 had lived together in San Francisco during the entire early epidemic. But Harry only rarely talked with anyone about that time, and in our conversations, he was reluctant to accept the influence of the epidemic in his current unhappy and isolated life—forget his childhood and family. When I once suggested that the losses he had experienced in the epidemic were contributing significantly to his sadness, he looked surprised: "So many years later? I'm not sure I see the connection."

Over the first few months of our meetings, I realized that Harry lived with a nearly complete catalog of the feelings that obstruct the talking through and working through of grief. Harry had been unable to grieve almost everything that had transpired in his life, including, I speculated to myself, his unmentionable childhood. An accomplished and fundamentally gregarious man had—perfunctory and unsatisfying social events aside—been sitting home alone for the better part of two decades, drinking wine and eating too much. Even with the un-defined specter of his childhood and adolescence lurking around the edges of our conversations, we would—I hoped—be able to untangle this emotional stalemate and set Harry partially free. Some traumas and losses are ultimately ungrievable, but I suspected Harry had enough resilience to allow a happier life. He would, I thought, never have "closure" or anything like it, for his losses had been too great, and survivors of true trauma rarely if ever have authentic, complete closure. But he could have a better resolution than he had: he could reconstruct himself around the inescapable facts of what had happened, which is an important kind of resolution because it allows a sense of personal wholeness. I hoped that would be true for Harry, and I tangentially introduced the topic. It would quickly become clear that Harry's ex-pectation of *complete* closure—which also seemed impossible to him—was one of the important obstructions to any active grieving. Why work toward something when you already know it is impossible?

"Harry, when we talk, when you talk about your life now, I often have the feeling that it is over or nearly so—that you are living as if you were in the last paragraph of a soon-to-be-finished novel."

Harry seemed surprised by my comment and had to think about it before he responded. "Well, it is more or less over. *Isn't* it?"

"Perhaps the way you're living it now. But why are you living it this way?"

"I've lived it—what else do I want? I'm nearly sixty."

"Well, you've lived the part you lived. But what about the next decade or two? Or three? You *could* live to be eighty-seven. No?"

"Probably not if I keep eating and drinking the way I do."

"Maybe not, which suggests one possible motivation to eat and drink as you do."

"If I wanted to kill myself, I could think of better ways to do it and get it over with. I've thought of them, many times. Please don't call the police."

"I'd guess that your chosen way—the eating and drinking—is a compromise that expresses some ambivalence."

"Ambivalence about what?"

"About having a life or not having one."

"Well, I've already said that I think it's over. I'm still alive, I know, but I'm pretty sure it's not going anywhere."

"If you were completely convinced of that—if that were all you hoped for—I don't think you would have come to see me. I think you'd have just stayed at home. I think you're ambivalent."

"Can't we just talk without an agenda? I know that there's a lot that's happened to me, but we are not going to fix *that*."

"*Fix?* Fix *what?*"

"The whole thing, the whole epidemic. Harry, our friends. The whole thing. We are not going to fix that."

"No, I'm sure we're not going to *fix* it. But our talking might allow the beginning of a change in how you *experience* it."

"And what would we change—if I went along with this?"

"Maybe the grief that you live in—finding a way for you to live less *in* it. You call it sadness, but it is more than that, it's grief. You seem to me to be living deeply in grief without being able to mourn any of it."

Harry became angry for the first time in my experience, and his sudden fury startled me. "Do you think, *do you really think* that I'm going to move on from Harry's passing, from all of that, from all the others, from the horror of all of that? *Do you really think that I could or would do that? Do you think I would pretend that none of that happened or mattered? Do you think I would do that?!*"

"You're very angry. About what?"

"I feel furious. *The idea* that I would get over this . . ."

"Harry, I didn't say anything about moving on or getting over it, and I'm not talking about pretending about anything. I was suggesting the possibility—the *possibility*—of some better way to *not* get over it, to not live completely stuck in it.

That's not getting over it, it's more a kind of accommodation. Right now, your life seems mostly about grief. To not feel completely stuck in that grief is one of the reasons I think you drink as much as you do. I can imagine drinking offers a lot of relief. A minute ago, you asked if I thought you 'could or would' get over it. I think you're ambivalent about both the possibility *and your desire* to get over it. These are two different questions, but one influences the other. What you're feeling is confusing, and we'll both have to think more about it."

Harry gave this a moment of thought. "If you asked me what I *really* wanted, I would say I'd like to close the book on the whole thing. 'Find closure' is what old friends used to say to me. People expect me to have closure, and it's one of the reasons I'm so alone now. A formerly close friend once said to me, 'Harry, it's like you're in permanent homage to the epidemic, and it's over.' People can't stand to be around me."

"Well, it's not over, is it? Your feelings are not over. *You* still have HIV—which you're not taking very good care of—and, anyway, it's all ongoing, people just aren't talking about it. In any case, I don't think you'll have 'closure' on something like this, and I can't imagine why anyone would expect that—except that *they* don't want to think about it, and when *you* do, it's emotionally provocative for them. For right now, for *you*, I'll stick with the idea of accommodation. That would be a big improvement, a very big change in your life. I'm talking about *some* grieving of what's happened, not closure."

Harry glanced at the clock on the end table. "It's time to stop. It's past time." He stood up, said goodbye, and walked out of the room.

Harry phoned in sick to cancel our next appointment, and then two days after that, he called again to say that he would be in the following week. He also wondered if there was any way we could meet regularly twice a week. There was, and we started doing that. When Harry appeared for our first appointment for the following week, he sat down in his chair, started crying, and cried for many minutes.

"Can you tell me what's going on?" I asked.

"I was sitting out on the deck the other night—*drinking*, in case you want to know—staring at the scene of the crime, and I started crying. And coming in here brought it all up again."

"And what is 'the scene of the crime'?"

"The city—San Francisco. Our 'city of light.'"

"And the crime?"

"You know the crime. Harry died, I got HIV, everyone else died. And I guess I didn't die. The crime—the crime I know you know about. The crime you've written about. The whole fucking city of crime twinkling away in the dark."

"It's striking me that you moved to your house to get away from San Francisco, but now you sit and stare at it."

"I used to all the time, mostly at night after work. Not much now, but what we talked about last time brought it up again. For several years after I moved into the house, I would stare at the city and imagine that I'd be able to see Harry walking down the street like he always did—from ten miles away no less. I'd imagine it the way it was before the crime, that Harry and I were on our way to the bar and that Harry was skipping, which is how he walked, and I'd skip after him, and we'd run into friends and they'd come with us. We were in some kind of naïve heaven. It's long gone."

"Yes, Harry died a long time ago."

"And I didn't."

"Yes, and that's the second time you've said that today."

"I don't *want* to forget Harry."

"I'm almost sure you never will."

"But isn't that what you were suggesting last time? Get over Harry, find closure, and stop drinking?"

"I don't think I said anything at all about stopping drinking, and I rejected the idea of closure. And, no, not *forgetting*, not 'getting over Harry.' It's something more like integrating Harry's death—all the deaths—into your emotional life in a way that they don't dictate your life. You partly accepted *the fact* of these deaths when you stopped looking at the city from your deck—when you stopped looking for

Harry on the street—but at the same time maybe you also tried to bury the memory of the facts. I'm not sure."

"I feel that if I stop thinking about Harry, I will just lose him again. That it's better to have him like this instead of not having him at all. I feel like I'll lose myself if I lose him. And all the others, too. Around the time I stopped sitting on the deck, staring at the city every night, I think I started drinking more. And that's when my IBS started, too."[21]

"You'd given up hope of seeing him from the deck, of seeing him at all again. I imagine you were experiencing his loss more intensely. That must have motivated the drinking, too."

Harry nodded yes and then seemed to be pondering something. "But there's something else: Sitting on the deck was what I thought of as 'my time with Harry.' And when I stopped that, as you said, I lost him, but I also abandoned him, I abandoned him the way I abandoned my mother. I remember thinking that Harry would be hurt if he didn't see me on the deck, and he would be angry. I was being disrespectful, as if I were saying to him, 'You never meant much to me, or you don't mean much to me now, and I'm going to forget about you.' And the thought of saying anything like that to Harry was unbearable."

"And yet you stopped sitting on the deck," I pointed out, without appearing to notice Harry's first voluntary mention of his mother.

"Well, I stopped sitting there because he wasn't showing up for our date. I'd sit there and stare, and no Harry. San Francisco became for me—that's when it became the scene of the crime. I never go to the city anymore, I can't. I'm afraid of having panic attacks on the bridge."

"Have you had panic attacks on the bridge?"

"No."

"Have you ever had a panic attack?"

"When I realized that Harry was actually dying. Yes, then I had several. They had me taking Xanax every day."

"Going to San Francisco would confirm that Harry is no

longer alive—he wouldn't be there. It would be the feeling of loss all over again. But is there also something else?"

"Like what?"

"I don't know. Some anger at Harry?"

"Well, I'm certainly pissed off at all these people for dying." Harry was silent for a moment. "And for some reason, right now I'm thinking that *I have the right to be alive* and *fuck them* if they don't like it. *Fuck them.* If I feel like showing up in the city, then *fuck them.*"

"Fuck who?"

"All of them."

"All the people who have died?"

"Yes, all of them, including my mother." Harry seemed startled by what he had said and pondered it for a few moments. "But why am I suddenly angry about this?"

"You sound as if you're angry because *they* don't feel that *you* should be alive, that they don't want to see you in the city. Do you feel that you have betrayed them, that you are being disloyal, just for being alive? Do you feel this about your friends, and your mother—whom you've mentioned twice today?" Harry looked startled again, then started sobbing again, and I remained silent through the end of the hour.

As Harry left the office, he said, "Thank you for listening to me today."

"You're welcome," I said. I had borne witness to Harry's grief, guilt, and anger, and he had no one else to do that. More than simply needing "someone to talk to," Harry wanted and needed someone to bear witness to what he had lived through and what he was still feeling about that experience.

As we continued over the following months, Harry became more willing to discuss his parents. He had been raised as the only child in a wealthy, Upper East Side Manhattan family, with an angry, taunting father who seemed perpetually disappointed in Harry: "It wasn't only my life, it was who I *was* that disappointed him, and he always, always let me know that." In Harry's words, his mother was "well intended and relatively loving" with him, but too unsure and frightened to assert herself in either the marriage or in protecting Harry from his father's emotional—and, occasionally, physical—abuse. That abuse was, to no surprise, badly exacerbated by Harry's coming out during dinner at the age of fifteen, which gave his father the opportunity to hurl several pieces of his wife's heirloom china at the dining room walls. Harry's mother was passively accepting of his being gay, but she was too trapped in her contentious and unhappy marriage to offer Harry much support or love. She always called him "sweetheart," but that was about as far as it went. According to Harry, on the night he came out at dinner, the only upset she voiced to either Harry or her husband was about her grandmother's Limoges plates, which were part of a setting, she said, for twenty-four.

"She tried to be a mother, but she was depressed," Harry said, as if suddenly concerned he was being unfair to her.

"*Depressed?* You sound as if you feel the need to protect her."

"She once told me that Beethoven was the most important man who had ever lived, that life without him would have been a lot worse."

"But she was depressed? Despite Beethoven?"

"She spent a lot of her time in bed. *Very* depressed, and I knew that. But she was all I had, and there was nothing I could ever do that made things better. When I decided to go live in San Francisco, I knew that I was leaving her behind in a life she hated, and I felt a lot of guilt. I felt all that guilt again when Harry and I got together because, with Harry, I had something she'd never had. She knew that, and she knew I would never come home again because my father would never allow me to bring Harry. And then on top of it, she left me all that money."

"She left you the money upon her death? You said a while ago that she had died, but that was the first time I'd heard that."

"Yes, her estate—which was separate from my father's—went to me. She died two years after Harry and I got together, almost to the day, and . . ."

We were both silent for several minutes.

"And what?" I finally asked.

"I already know what you're thinking—it's about Harry and my mother."

"What am I thinking about them?"

"I can't say it without crying again. . . ."

"Well, say it and cry, if you can."

"I can't. . . . Oh, it's about abandoning both of them, leaving them to their fates. It was a horrible thing to do. I don't know if I can forgive myself for that because—it's completely ridiculous, but I feel like I killed them."

Then Harry did start crying.

I said earlier that Harry embodied a nearly complete catalog of feelings that obstruct grieving, and guilt was a significant part of that catalog. Guilt about both his mother and Harry-2 had been working in destructive synergy to prevent the grieving he needed. Harry had a lot to grieve: his childhood of abuse and neglect, the loss of his mother, the loss of Harry-2 and the life they had known together, the loss of innumerable others to HIV, and the loss of his youth to his own HIV. When I first met Harry, he lived without any sense of a personal future, and I felt his life had been swallowed whole by the unexamined, undigested trauma of all that experience. Robert Jay Lifton describes people who have lived "immersed" in multiple deaths, and the difficulty they have in absorbing the losses and working through the grief. He might as well have been talking about Harry:

> This aborted mourning can proceed to the extent that the survivor's existence can turn into a "life of grief." Impaired mourning becomes equated with a more general inability to give inner form—again significance—to the death immersion, and therefore to the remainder of one's life. The survivors may then be especially vulnerable to various kinds of psychic and bodily disturbance, as well as to psychological formulations of their experience. . . . Unresolved, incomplete mourning results in stasis and entrapment in the traumatic process.[22]

Harry first came to see me in the hope that our meetings would provide a substitute for a social life, and thus an end to his loneliness, all without having to actively grieve. By numbing his feelings, Harry's drinking had reduced his emotional pain, but it also had its downsides: it assisted his denial of grief and thus obstructed grieving; it posed probable health risks; and it brought up considerable shame. Both the drinking and the shame about it had kept him more firmly locked in his isolation, which was, itself, yet another obstruction to grieving. But the obstructions felt to Harry as if they also had an upside: in his guilt, Harry felt that any effort to work through his grief for a better life was a statement of unacceptable disloyalty to those he had loved. So two feelings—his abhorrence of disloyalty, and his fear of having to relive and reexamine his losses—made a "successful" grieving process a forbidden and ominous task. Drinking was one way to give that task wide berth.

As Harry's denial about his grief and guilt slowly lifted over time, he increasingly accepted the idea that his feelings were worth talking about. One day we had a brief but important conversation that helped:

"I often think, 'What's the point?' Harry said to me out of the blue. I thought I knew what he meant, but I wanted him to tell me.

"The point of what?"

"The point of anything."

"Is there any point in talking about *this*?" I asked.

"I don't know. I'm afraid that talking too much might keep me alive."

"There's your ambivalence again."

"I suppose that ambivalence about being alive has become my biggest strength."

"I think your ambivalence about being alive is very much about the fact that you're here and Harry-2 is not. We'll never change that."

"Talking, of course, is something else I'm ambivalent about. I'm afraid that if we talk too much, I'll come to acceptance of that fact. And I'm afraid that if we don't talk, it will all be moot. And as I am saying this to you, all I'm thinking about is going home and having a drink."

"Is that what you'll do?"

"No, I won't. I want to sit and think about what you just said—actually *think* about it."

Harry felt—not thought—that his survival was a betrayal of those who had died, an expression of "survivor guilt."[23] He felt disloyal simply for being alive, and to make matters worse, he was not only alive, he was fortunate: he had money, he could buy as much wine and cheese as he liked, and he lived without pragmatic worry in a house on a hill with a commanding view. All of *this* good fortune had come from his mother, who had herself been deprived of another of Harry's good fortunes: he had been in love with a man and lived with him for a happy fifteen years. Not even his obviously involuntary, undesired aging was guilt-free, for Harry once told me that in growing older he was "moving on" and leaving Harry-2 behind, "forever frozen in his youth." In addition to these personal sources of guilt, there was another that is routine, if not universal, in the lives of young gay men: in his early years, Harry had lived for two decades with guilt and shame about being gay, and thus a disappointment to his neglectful family of narrow perceptions. With guilt stretching back to early childhood, Harry had intuitively drawn on it to sustain the stalled and unhappy aftermath of his later-life trauma.

## THE AFTERMATH OF HARRY'S AFTERMATH

For Harry, the synergy between his traumatized childhood and the trauma of the early epidemic had been crushing, and he had lived for nearly two decades perched on a hilltop as if he were the only human survivor on earth. He was not feeling good about most of that life, and his only solace lay in his fantasies of seeing Harry-2 from the deck, his carefully tended rhododendrons, and the Beethoven quartets he fell asleep to almost every night. Having relaxed his tenacious denial of the significance his childhood and the epidemic held for him, Harry was able—over more than two years—to put together a reasonably coherent story of his personal history. With that story in mind, he could more fully experience and interpret his feelings and make some sense of how his life had come to be what it was, and how it might be different. He had, in the words of Judith Herman, "reconstructed a coherent system of meaning and belief that encompasses the story of trauma."[24]

For the first time since Harry-2's death, Harry had begun to find a way to live a life that acknowledged the emotional legacy of his childhood and the epidemic, without existing entirely *in* it. Harry slowly reestablished some of his old relationships—which meant driving over the bridge to San Francisco—and they again became meaningful to him. He improved his physical health by adhering to an HIV-treatment regimen, and better, if still less than stellar, eating habits. And he slowly reduced his drinking to levels that did not impair or isolate him. Harry was still not without ambivalence about "whether there's a point," but he had made a clear shift in the balance of doubt: he had been able to incorporate his history into his current life and, once again, took some pleasure in life beyond the tripartite solace that had fortunately, if inadequately, tethered him for so many years. Judith Herman speaks of a survivor of rape and sexual abuse, but she perfectly describes Harry:

> The survivor who has accomplished her recovery faces life with few illusions but often with gratitude. Her view of life may be tragic, but for that very reason she has learned to cherish laughter. She has a clear sense of what is important and what is not. Having encountered evil, she knows how to cling to what is good. Having encountered the fear of death, she knows how to celebrate life.[25]

Harry would never again be a young man skipping with his lover down the streets of San Francisco, and he would never be who he might have been had his early-life trauma and the epidemic never happened. But he had reconstructed his life into something that mattered to him, he had *really* survived. To this day, Harry occasionally calls to make an appointment for a session or two, "to talk about this or that." Now his phone messages always start with "Walt, it's Harry-1." Our convention had always been "Harry" and "Harry-2," so "Harry-1" was something new. What I sensed in the new moniker was a man who was finally able to consciously experience and accept both the love and traumatic loss of Harry-2. People we have deeply known and loved become part of who we are, and unless we forbid the feelings, we never completely lose them. Together, Harry and Harry-2 had become Harry-1, an authentic integration of a past with a present that had been impossible in the emotionally numbed, internally fragmented life that Harry had been living when I first met him. Harry is, once again, relatively whole. When I return Harry's calls now, I usually say, "Harry-1, it's Walt," and when I do, he laughs.

## WHAT *ABOUT* HARRY'S DRINKING?

When I first met him, Harry had a significant attachment to his wine, and it made our work more difficult. Substance use is elevated among gay men, as it is in most disadvantaged, stigmatized, or traumatized communities. Substance use—which is now often indiscriminately referred to as substance *abuse*—is usually treated as a problem of "addiction." Addiction has become a common primary diagnosis for not only imbibed or injected substances, but for sex, the Internet, shopping, and smartphones. Addiction seems to have become an apt description for any activity that someone engages in more often than he or others feel he ought to. Steeped in the idea of addiction as a diagnosis that identifies the primary issue, many psychotherapists today would not have accepted Harry for therapy until he "cleaned up." That would have been a mistake and a damaging disservice to Harry. With me, he was straightforward about his drinking, he was not intoxicated during sessions—which *would* have seriously interfered with the work—and we were able to usefully address other issues, the true primary issues that lay behind the drinking.

Applied to purely behavioral issues such as sex, the Internet, and shopping, the use of the term *addiction* is a misleading metaphor. Sex and other behaviors may become compulsive, but they are never addictive, and the distinction between an addiction and a compulsion is important. In its original medical use, an addiction described a distinctive biological process: a cellular response and adaptation to a substance; the development of physiological tolerance; a need for escalating dosage to maintain the effects; and cellular renormalization, craving, and other withdrawal symptoms on abrupt cessation of use. While many substances initiate this biological process, many others do not. Behavior never does. Even when the substance is biologically addictive, addiction often remains an inadequate primary diagnosis, particularly if psychological insight is the objective. As discussed earlier in this chapter, such diagnostic labeling too easily leads to the idea that giving a name to signs, symptoms, or behavior provides explanation or insight. The specious diagnosis of addiction supports the popular idea that the substance use or behavior is the fundamental issue, and that the diagnostic label is the name of something that the person has, often a "disease" or "disorder." In that construction of human experience, the "cure" is to stop the use or behavior.[26]

Harry's drinking was psychologically motivated and it provided a lot of benefit. He had not been able to find another way to contain his grief and guilt, and the alcohol assisted the psychic numbing that protected him from seemingly unbearable pain. The alcohol may also have forestalled his consideration of a more succinct approach to suicide, even as alcohol sometimes helps implement that act. At home, and more or less drunk a great deal of the time, Harry had only three things keeping him tethered to life. But alcohol was also contributing to his destructive isolation and, most likely, to his poor health and to an earlier-than-necessary death. The drinking might also have been elevating, rather than lessening, the suicide risk, a thought I discussed with Harry on several occasions. Alcohol is a mood depressant, but it often elevates impulsivity, and many suicides are initiated on impulse. All of these troubling secondary problems made drinking an impossible longer-term solution.

Even with the considerable risks, Harry's drinking was keeping him afloat, and he knew it. To stop drinking, he would have to convincingly feel at least the glimmer of an alternative, and in our early work together, I routinely acknowledged the benefits. My useful role was not to try to convince Harry that he ought to be interested in the longer term. I could only encourage him to stay connected for right now, so that we could investigate the issues, and he could answer the question for himself. "There are things," I said early on in our work, "that I think could be clarified that might allow you to feel different about your life." Harry knew the shortcomings of the "drinking solution" and hardly needed a reminder, and my acknowledgment of the benefits allowed him to feel heard and understood. Shortly after our first meeting, Harry had said to me, "I knew I had to tell you about the drinking, and I thought that, when I did, you'd throw me out the door like most of my friends have. I'm glad you didn't."

My only early requests of Harry were that, for the sake of productivity, he show up at our meetings sober, and that he talk to me if he had defined suicidal thoughts. He never drank on the nights before our meetings, and the supportive regularity of our relationship had pushed suicide further from his mind. Early in the work, I did once remind Harry that alcohol was a central nervous system depressant and that CNS depressants support what Harry and I had agreed to call "sadness." Only over time did I also introduce two other ideas about drinking, both related to psychic numbing. The first was that alcohol induces a physiological—rather than trauma-induced—numbing, and that regardless of its origins, numbing interferes with the work of talking through issues because it makes one less conscious of one's feelings. The second was that numbing supports disconnection from others and isolation, which deepens feelings of loss and grief. "Altogether, it's quite a litany you've got there," Harry commented, and for a long while, he kept drinking. He could not imagine tolerating his internal life without it, and he might have been right—it might have been intolerable. Before Harry could stop drinking, we needed to find insight about why he drank as he did, insight that might reveal a glimmer of credible hope for a different kind of future.

# 6

# Emerging from Trauma, Loss, and Isolation

> I have a terrible habit of remembering the death of people who are
>     still
> alive, killing them off by an act of memory.
> *False* memory, I suppose I should call it, but sometimes a person
> whose death I remember *is in fact dead* and my memorial in that case
> seems no different in character.
>             —Keith Waldrop, *The Not Forever*[1]

Many in today's gay communities hold the hopeful idea that the Supreme Court decision on gay marriage—and a concurrent shift of social perceptions in a handful of small American enclaves—will end developmental trauma for young gay people. This is simply not true, and to know that, one need only look at the torturous history of African-Americans following Lincoln's signing of the Emancipation Proclamation, 150 years ago. For gay lives, the granting of legal rights and authentic acceptance are two different issues in a society steeped in phobic aversion to real diversity. Current legal protections are only the opening scene of act two in a three-act play that will almost certainly stretch into the wee hours of yet another morning.

For young gay people, it is the acceptance and support of the *family* that is most developmentally significant. In my current psychotherapy practice, I see many men in their twenties, and—regardless of the local community and larger society in which they live—those who have support from immediate families clearly evidence the least developmental harm. Even when a young man has grown up with persistent rejection and abuse from adolescent peers, the authentic support of parents is a powerful, if not entirely adequate, antidote. "We love you, we support you, and we want to help" is a magical offering for the child and young gay adult. Unfortunately, this magic is still too infrequently delivered by insecure, frightened, and conformist families, and the developmental trauma of a large percentage of young gay people thus continues unabated. No legislation, judicial decision, or broad societal acceptance matches the influence of authentically supportive parents—or, by itself, repairs damage already wrought by a family. It is from the family that we learn to experience ourselves as lovable, or not.

## WHAT IS TRAUMA?

Trauma entails two components: the objective event itself, and the individual's subjective experience of that event. A traumatic event is usually defined as anything an individual experiences as threatening to his own life, safety, or well-being, or the lives, safety, or well-being of others whose endangerment he has personally witnessed. The endangerment may be physical or purely psychological, and in their nearly universal stigmatization, gay children and adolescents often experience both. The early epidemic also qualifies as a traumatic event for many men. Before the introduction of the ELISA HIV test in 1985, a majority of gay men in urban communities witnessed four years of multiple deaths, and many felt that both they and those around them might already have "it" or would have it, at a time when, whatever it was, it was almost certainly fatal. For middle-group men, the childhood and adolescent exposure to the connection between gay men and untreatable AIDS traumatically threatened their futures. For younger-group men who have lived only in the late epidemic, the stigmatizing social consequences of HIV infection often make seroconversion—or just the fear of it—traumatic. HIV still carries a long-standing legacy and is still too often experienced as the consequence of forbidden and "dirty" sex, and the fate of fags.

The subjective response to any traumatic event is highly variable, and those left with vulnerabilities from difficult earlier developmental experience are often more deeply affected than those with more benign or supportive histories. Stigmatized minorities—whose sense of well-being is already threatened by prejudicial treatment and marginalization—may be more badly affected by trauma than socially empowered groups. Because of their commonly stigmatized histories, gay men may, as a group, be more vulnerable than some others. A history of marginalization is important because the quality of social support before, during, and after the trauma is critical to the psychological outcome. "A supportive response from other people," Judith Herman tells us, "may mitigate the impact of the event, while a hostile or negative response may compound the damage and aggravate the traumatic syndrome."[2] While within their own communities gay men were often highly supportive of one another during the early—if not the later—epidemic, astonishingly little support came from outside. The larger society, presidential administrations, and many families of origin seemed set on letting gay men die, which they did, in the hundreds of thousands.

The characteristic resilience of any individual—the capacity to adapt and cope, which is probably partly inborn and partly developed—significantly affects the subjective experience of trauma. Herman discusses a study of combat veterans in which the "symptom patterns" of traumatized survivors—for example, a tendency to express trauma in active anger rather than passive depression—were found to be related to "individual childhood history, [preexisting] emotional conflicts, and adaptive style."[3] Herman connects resilience to measures of sociability, active coping, and self-confidence. Resilience assists survival, and as a group, gay men have shown extraordinary resilience in the face of the two epidemics. Out in the world—without an epidemic—just being gay has forever demanded resilience. From an early age, gay people must learn to think introspectively about their own and others' feelings, and to circumvent or adapt to adversity. Compared to heterosexual men—group for group—I am sure that gay men are less rigid and more authentically resilient. *White* heterosexual men often unconsciously coast on assumed social privilege that is sustained with rigid, conventionally male posturing. Rigidity is not resilience, it is brittle, and it belies the vulnerability it attempts to conceal. It is difficult to imagine a group of "rigid and brittle males" successfully mustering the competence and tenacity that gay men have brought to the two epidemics for more than a third of a century. In this sense, gay men had a developmental advantage: for many, adversity bred authentic strength.

## HOW TRAUMA AND LOSS INTERACT: THE STORY OF AARON

Authentic strength is rooted in the capacity to acknowledge feelings that those with less strength would repress or deny. Gay men have a lot of feelings to acknowledge and consider, and the two epidemics have upped the ante. Aaron, who agreed to talk with me for this book, had lost himself during the early epidemic. When we met for three hours in January 2015, he was living by himself in Oakland, California (in San Francisco's East Bay), and had been on a psychiatric disability for eleven years. He told me that he had been diagnosed with depression, although his current therapist often suggested that this was "not the whole story." In my first impression of him at the door, Aaron was tall and attractive, although thin and with a slightly constricted manner. As we started talking, he seemed emotionally flat—subdued, and with a limited range of affect. His language itself was expressive, but strikingly in contrast to his consistently flat delivery; the discrepancy suggested several nonexclusive possibilities. The first, that a significant emotional shift had occurred later in life, after his language was well developed; the second, that Aaron had been a precocious child with formidable language skills, but a nearly lifelong flatness of affect; the third, that any antidepressant medications he might be using were flattening his affect and delivery. And finally, I had a feeling that Aaron very much wanted to connect with me, and "being interesting"—which he was—was part of that effort. I began the conversation by asking Aaron about his history.

"Therapists always start there, don't they?"

"Where would you like to start instead? We could start there."

"No, that's fine, I was simply commenting. I grew up in San Diego with my parents, and my older brother, David, who was my best friend, and my younger sister, Sarah. I came out to all of them when I was twelve—David first— and that went well. David was very supportive. I know it's a cliché, but it was a loving family, and I'm still very close to my father—we talk on the phone a few times a week or so. In '94 I moved to San Francisco and pretty quickly got a teaching job at UC Santa Cruz. Then in 2004, I went on disability for my depression. What else would you like to know?"

"What were you teaching at Santa Cruz? And I'm also thinking that you mention talking only to your father."

"Oh, American literature, which is what I majored in at Brown, and then in graduate school at Berkeley. I'd intended to go on teaching, and I wanted to write—you know, a half dozen Great American Novels."

"Did you? *Do* you write?"

"No, I haven't been able to. First the teaching and then, you know, the depression. I somehow never got to it."

"Do you think you might? Is that something you still want to do?"

"No, not really, if I'm honest."

"You said that you were still close to your father and talked with him on the phone regularly. But what about the others, your mother, and your two siblings? You said that David *was* your best friend."

"Sarah is living in D.C.—she's a lawyer and works for the Labor Department—a very bright bulb. Very busy." Aaron stopped.

"And . . . the others?"

"My brother and mother?"

"Yes, I was thinking of David and your mother."

"When I was fourteen, my mother was driving David up to L.A. to have his knee looked at, at UCLA. He was very into sports, and he'd injured it playing basketball. I'd go with him all the time and watch him play, but it wasn't at all my thing. As I told you earlier, we were best friends, particularly after I came out. He protected me from other kids' harassment. I was walking around school with gay slogans pinned to my chest, and I got a lot of taunting and physical harassment. I had a SMITHS button on my T-shirt,[4] and kids would call me a fag—all the usual stuff, *all* of it. But they were afraid of David, who fended them off."

After several moments of silence, I said, "And so David and your mom were on their way to UCLA . . ."

Aaron proceeded flatly. "My mom was driving, and they were killed on the 405 [freeway] when a pickup truck jumped the center rail. The driver was a gardener, and they said he'd had a stroke and lost control. He had a lawn mower in the back of the truck, and it flew out and went through another man's window and killed him, too, and there were other cars involved. According to the paper, the 405 was stopped for two and a half hours."

Aaron stopped for a minute, then suddenly continued, "It was a Tuesday, and when I got home from school, my father was sitting in the kitchen crying and told me. He said, 'Aaron, your mother and David were killed in a car accident this morning,' and he came over and hugged me—very tightly—and I remember being just blank."

Aaron stopped, but appeared unemotional. After several minutes, I asked if he wanted to talk more about what had happened, or if he wanted to talk about something else.

"I don't think I could say much more. I was blank when it happened. My father—he cried for years, the smallest thing would provoke it. That night—the day my father told me—I slept in David's room and never moved out. I cried that one night, sleeping in David's bed, but not much after that, really only that one time. His bed smelled like him. I never moved his things out of the room either, even the sports paraphernalia and the sailboat 'art' that was all over the walls. My room was still intact next door, but I hardly used it. I moved my clothes into his room and added them to his clothes, and as I got taller, I started wearing his clothes, too. I still do, like *this* shirt. When I go home now to visit my father, I still sleep in David's room. He—my father—calls it *my* room, and when he does, I correct him and say, 'David's room.' My therapist says I'm trying to be David for my dad, and that my dad is trying to reassure me that he wants me to be me. I don't know, but it sounds like there's something to it, it's just not all of it. Whatever, what to call the room is about the only thing we disagree about."

"I imagine this is all very painful, and I'm sorry for opening it up. Do you feel like continuing?"

"No, it's fine, we can go on. At this point, I'm curious about where you're going."

"Well, I don't really have an agenda, and I'm concerned about this being painful for you. But I wanted to know about your experience in San Francisco, and now I'm thinking that, emotionally, it had to have connected to your mother's and David's deaths. . . ."

"Oh, I've spent the last fourteen years in therapy talking about it. It's all mixed up together. I wasn't a particularly social kid, and I wasn't when I lived in San Francisco, and I'm still not. I'm about as gregarious as Rip Van Winkle, but without the village kids following me around. When I got to San Francisco—which my father was very worried about because of AIDS—it was '94, and it was a fucking mess, much worse than I'd imagined. I just had *no idea* until I saw it—it felt like Bosnia. I tried some to make friends, but almost everyone I met would be dead before the sun came up. It was the teaching that kept me afloat, and the driving from the city down to Santa Cruz. When I got the job, my father bought me a new Subaru and I loved it. Alone in the car, back and forth twice a week, was my refuge. I'd play tapes of Bartók string quartets or something, and the whole thing would go away. And the teaching gave me something interesting to do, and I can't imagine I would have survived without that. In the city, I lived with two roommates, and one of them, Harris, had a fox terrier who was very affectionate— *needy* I'd say—but crazy. His name was Atman—after Schopenhauer's dog, do you know about that?[5]—and he'd go wild if you left him alone for five minutes, he'd be bouncing off the ceiling. It turned out that Harris was Atman's sixth owner—the others had all died. There were a lot of dogs like that in San Francisco. So Atman and I became friends, and he would sometimes sleep in my room, on the pillow pushing up against my head. Atman, you could say, was the one friend I had who didn't die."

"Your two roommates?"

"No, they both died. Harris last, after Frank, and then I became Atman's permanent number seven."

"This is the accumulation of an awful lot of death and loss."

"By the time Harris died, I had the income from teaching, and my father helped me out, and Atman and I continued living in this huge railroad flat on Fell Street that had practically no heat, and the plaster was literally falling off the walls. It was cold and empty, and falling apart, like the world. I liked it. I liked being alone there. It was near Golden Gate Park, and Atman and I would go for long walks while I went over lesson plans in my head—Atman on his purple leash that Harris had gotten him as a birthday present on his made-up birthday date, because no one even knew how old he was. We would walk over to the lake and sit on a bench and look at people milling around the lake as if they had normal lives. It was very calming. And then we'd go home, I'd give Atman his canned chicken, and I'd have a burrito and a beer and go to bed."

"It sounds as if Atman was your sole relationship."

"We were always together. He'd go in the car with me to Santa Cruz lying on my lap, and then into class. I had a sheepskin pad for him—another birthday present, from me—and he'd sleep on it during class, or in my little office when I was working or meeting with students. You know— *Santa Cruz*—you can do anything. Dogs in class were the least of it. I once had two guys sitting in the back quietly jerking each other off during class, while I was giving a lecture on Twain. The other students who noticed just looked amused. I liked the spirit of the place. Atman was small for a fox terrier, weighed twelve pounds, and you could carry him around under one arm and he loved it, as if he'd been born to be carried around, and sleep on your head. The only thing you couldn't do was leave him alone."

"And other friends? Did you have any, or were you trying to make new friends?"

"No, you know, at a certain point you give up. While I was living in the city, I had *acquaintances* at school, and a few in the city, but no real friends. I'd given up on that." Aaron paused. "After Harris died—well, I liked him. We sometimes slept together—mostly no sex—just sleeping together for the companionship. He was very sweet. He was kind. I liked him a lot. You know, sometimes we hardly slept because we'd talk all night in the dark." Aaron stopped for a minute or two, staring blankly as if trying to remember something; then, apparently giving up on the recollection, he continued, "After Harris died, I decided, 'Enough is enough.' I made a conscious decision not to do it, that there was no point. People seem to have forgotten, but even after the new drugs *a lot* of people died. So, at a certain point you say to yourself, 'I am not going to do this anymore, it's hopeless.' Lee—my therapist, I don't think I told you his name—thinks I made that decision when David died, but I don't know. I was only fourteen, but David was the best friend I've ever had, so I've talked a lot about that in therapy. Lee once said, 'You give me the feeling that you were in love with David,' and I told him I probably was. No sex, though, but I'd thought of it."

"And do you think you were also avoiding HIV in avoiding people during the years in San Francisco? It was certainly something that a lot of people felt endangered by."

"I knew a lot of people who were in more or less a panic about it. But no, I never worried about HIV for myself, it wasn't in the cards—I wouldn't let it be. I never got fucked, and regardless of what some people said, it was obvious that's how you got it. When I was a teenager, yes, but later on I stopped, I realized it was too dangerous. I've never explained this to my father, who's still worried I'm going to get AIDS, and I probably should tell him so he can stop worrying. But it's hard to talk with your father about getting fucked, though I know he knows about those things. So, I think 'abstinence' has been a loss in my life, but I've lived with it well enough, I guess."

"And do you have sex of some kind with others now?"

"No, not really. Every now and then, but rarely. And if I do, it's careful sex."

"*Careful* sex sounds like a bit of a contradiction, no?"

"Lee has said that—several times."

"And how did you respond when he said that?"

"I don't think I've ever responded to that observation." Aaron seemed resolute about honoring the tradition.

"Are you comfortable telling me about other parts of your current life? I'm wondering what you think about the disability. How do you understand it?"

"I think I just sort of progressively sank. Starting around 2000, I had more and more difficulty motivating myself. I was tired of driving back and forth over the mountains to school and exhausted with the teaching. I couldn't write, and I think I just threw in the towel at a certain point. I'd started therapy with Lee, which was good support, but I couldn't turn it around. I don't know, but I think all the earlier stuff had just accumulated on me . . . and I'm not sure I know what else to say. A dog isn't enough, but Atman died around that time anyway—the vet thought he was about fifteen or sixteen, and he'd gotten pretty sick—and that obviously didn't help either. The best I can say is, I sank. It was like watching a barge on the Mississippi with a hole in it—it sinks. I was worn-out."

"The 'earlier stuff'?"

"All of it, all those years. You said it, an awful lot of loss."

"And that loss stretches back to your childhood. Did you then—or do you—think of suicide, if that isn't too intrusive a question?"

"It's occurred to me, I've talked about it with Lee. But

no, I wouldn't do that to Sarah, and particularly my father.
The way Mom and David died, I couldn't do that to him
again. And for some reason that I don't really understand,
I wouldn't do that to David. It's a feeling I don't really
understand."

"Have you talked with Lee about that?"

"No."

"It might be helpful."

"I should bring it up. Maybe I will. Maybe there's still
time to understand something."

"Why do you wonder if there's still time? Time before
what?"

"I don't know why I said that. It feels like it's all
happened already—that my life is pretty much over. I don't
know what I could learn now that would make it different."

"I would probably be more optimistic about that."

"And I probably wouldn't."

Aaron's concluding remark is an unhappy one for a man of forty-
seven with a good possibility of another three or four decades of biological life; but his feelings are understandable. He had obviously had
a serious developmental trauma in adolescence, and this history almost
certainly left him more vulnerable to what he experienced during the
early epidemic. Even as Aaron was trying to connect with me and willingly talked about himself and his history, he still felt largely inaccessible, sealed away and out of reach, as he had been during the depths
of the epidemic in San Francisco. From the brief time we spent together, I sensed that Aaron's adolescent trauma had left him with a
learned capacity for *constrictive defenses*, a possibly once-useful capacity that was now inhibiting any recovery from the later trauma. Constrictive defenses—unconsciously invoked to defend against pain—usually
include denial, repression, and, sometimes, psychic numbing. To
paraphrase another dean of trauma recovery, the psychiatrist Robert
Jay Lifton, if repression is a kind of forgetting, psychic numbing is the
loss of ability to experience the emotional power and meaning of
things that *are* remembered.[6] Aaron told me that he was "blank" after
his father told him about the freeway accident, and in my brief con-

tact with him, he still showed considerable numbing about the horrible event. He had told me the story of the accident "on the 405" as if it were a collection of facts gleaned from a newspaper report. That night, he had moved into David's room, where he had been able to cry, but he never left the room to return to his own, and he never cried again.

Psychic numbing is a common reaction to trauma, particularly to *extended* trauma such as the two epidemics. Numbing helps one endure the traumatic experience by allowing dissociation from frightening, painful feelings and, thus, from the significance of the enveloping event. *During* the event, numbing is thus often helpful, particularly if it is not so profound that it interferes with one's ability to pragmatically respond in useful ways. When sustained long after the event, numbing is problematic: disconnection from feelings fragments one's internal life and obstructs interpersonal connections. Internally fragmented, we are left with no whole, authentic self to bring to others. Because psychotherapy is substantially about talking through feelings—with the purpose of reconstructing the internal fragments into a relative whole—someone exercising significant numbing can be difficult to work with productively. Numbing is more subtle and elusive than more "active" symptoms such as manifest depression and overt anxiety, and psychotherapists often miss it. Numbing depletes vitality, and like the overuse of repression, it can leave behind an internal life almost completely incapable of feeling. Herman comments on why constrictive, "negative" symptoms can be difficult to detect: "They lack drama: their significance lies in what is missing." To the person's detriment, such symptoms are often interpreted as long-standing character, and are never explored.[7]

Lifton tells us that numbing can "readily outlive its usefulness and give rise to later patterns of withdrawal, apathy, depression and despair."[8] This sounds a lot like Aaron's current situation, in which precisely those feelings had almost completely removed him from a social life. With a history of childhood trauma—including the peer abuse during middle school and high school, against which he ultimately lost David's protection—the epidemic presented more losses, and an invitation to again use the constrictive defenses he had learned after his mother and David were killed. Aaron's numbing in response to those deaths—losses that might well have been better resolved with conscious grieving—left Aaron with a developmental vulnerability that would later resurface, in the duress of the early epidemic. During our talk, Aaron said to me, "Atman and I were not unalike. We both had a lot of loss, and when things got bad, we both took a nap." Scary dreams aside, nothing else is as numbing as being asleep, which is one of the important reasons we value it. But full-time sleep is another matter.

Pondering our talk further, I began to think about the balance of trauma and loss in Aaron's life. He seemed to present a mix of middle- and older-group experiences. Beginning in his early twenties, he had exhibited the cautious constriction of life most commonly seen in middle-group men; but he also now lived with the depression and isolation of older men who had been through the wringer. I only partly believed Aaron's feeling that he had experienced little "primary" trauma in the epidemic; while he insisted that he never felt personally endangered, he *did* witness the endangerment and deaths of many others. These included the friends he had made after first arriving in "Bosnia," and his two and only roommates, Frank and Harris. When Aaron first told me of Harris's death, I had seen feelings rising in his throat, but he quickly swallowed them. If Lee thought Aaron had been in love with David, I thought Aaron had also been in love with Harris: Aaron had been too hesitant in talking about him, and too insistent on the idea of (just) "liking" him.

Aaron's childhood trauma had left him more unconsciously vulnerable to later trauma, but his long-standing constrictive defenses had protected him from exploring both experiences. Had he been able to more consciously work through the early trauma and loss, the emotional toll of the epidemic might have been more usefully approachable. Even with the conscious pain that process would have raised, it might have helped Aaron find a more connected and happier life. By the time I met him, he had clearly lost trust in both himself and the world. His trauma and loss, and his once-useful—but now-obstructive, if calming—constrictive defenses had stranded him on a remote Pacific island that was on no one's map. On Aaron's island, the possibility of rescue by sea or by air seemed not even a fleeting thought. Rescue from *what*? *For* what?

## OUR GREAT UNMENTIONABLE

With help, Aaron might have been able to consider those two questions, and he might have found a way to a different life than the isolated and unhappy post-traumatic life he had landed in. In *Trauma and Recovery*,[9] Judith Herman offers help, all of which is pertinent to gay men who have survived early-life developmental trauma or the later-life trauma of both epidemics. Herman suggests four stages of "recovery" for the survivor, only broadly rendered here: coming out of isolation by first connecting in formal or informal therapeutic and healing relationships; finding a position of safety from the threat; actively remembering and talking about the trauma and feelings connected to it, and grieving the losses; and rebuilding a life in the larger world. But lest we understand the "recovery paradigm" too concretely, Herman cautions us that her stages of recovery are not to be taken too literally, and that each stage does not conveniently resolve itself fully so that we may move on to the next: "Oscillating and dialectical in nature, the traumatic syndromes defy any attempt to impose such simple-minded order."[10]

To even initiate navigation of this "oscillating" process, survivors must acknowledge that an affecting trauma has occurred, and that they live with the emotional aftermath. Early-life stigmatization and abuse continue to be a very significant problem for gay people in America; and both the horrible realities of the early epidemic and the more subtle terrors of the late one speak for themselves. But to the serious detriment of survivors, adequate acknowledgment of and response to these events has inexcusably eluded both gay communities and the larger American society.[11] As Herman points out in the opening line of *Trauma and Recovery*, "The ordinary response to atrocities is to banish them from consciousness."[12]

It is more often the society—rather than the individual—that banishes atrocities from consciousness. For gay men it has been both. For many such as Aaron, the "self-banishment" reflects an understandable desire to avoid revisiting pain, and doubt about the ultimate utility of that effort. But for many gay survivors living with the psychological aftermath of a destructive adolescence or an epidemic, shame and guilt—about histories for which these survivors blame themselves, even as they have no plausible culpability—keep them jailed in an un-examined self-banishment that hides them from both themselves and the world. Shame and guilt shrink us internally and provide a sturdy foundation for the constrictive defenses of repression and numbing. With those defenses at the gates, we feel protected from ourselves and from the world, and the self-banishment quickly becomes impenetrable and seemingly unchangeable. While we may feel relatively safe, the costs are high.[13]

## THE FOUR STAGES OF RECOVERY: THE STORY OF RALPH

The needs to clarify psychological distress; overcome isolation; surmount shame, self-doubt, and guilt; and find meaning in a post-trauma life are all issues still confronting many gay survivors of early- and later-life trauma. All are well illustrated in the story of Ralph. A sixty-one-year-old, HIV-negative survivor of the early epidemic and former long-term resident of San Francisco, Ralph tells a familiar story—but with a better outcome than many. It offers useful insight for other older men who lived through the early epidemic, as well as for much younger men who have lived through other traumas, but have the youthful advantage of resilience and still-evolving futures.

With his lover, Tom, Ralph had been cofounder of a successful San Francisco clothing manufacturer with a chain of stores in several major cities. A few years after Tom's death from complications of HIV, Ralph sold the company. He was financially well-off, and several years later he moved to Laguna Beach, a Southern California coastal town with a significant gay community. After the move, Ralph's new partner of two years, Kevin, continued to run a small architectural-design-and-construction firm. I had first met Ralph many years ago in the middle of the early epidemic, and I asked him if he would have a conversation with me for this book. Unlike the many who wanted to avoid revisiting painful memories, he seemed eager to talk about his experience in and after the early epidemic, and we spoke on the phone for several hours. The following is a highly condensed transcript from that conversation.

"I'm glad you asked me to do this because normally no one asks to talk about it. I'm sitting here staring at a picture of Tom on my desk, and the first thing I find myself wanting to say to you is that *I'm damaged*. We're supposed to be strong and move on, but this is part of my being, it's who I am, I feel it inside me. Kevin is forty-eight and was not really around the epidemic, and he's different, and I can't talk to him much about it. It's hard to describe the damage, but it's given me a certain seriousness, a feeling that bad things happen, like around the corner, and then the optimism comes crashing down. I feel changed. Tom was one of the first to get sick, and we kept it a secret because we feared that people would stop patronizing the stores. A lot of guys have moved here [to Laguna Beach] from San Francisco, and I see such blankness in older gay men here, and when I visit San Francisco, they're shut down, and younger men are just detached from the whole thing. Very occasionally an older man will bring it up, usually as a political thing, and I'm surprised even by that. Then if you get them going, suddenly they're talking about how many people they knew who got sick and died, how scared they were, how relieved they are not to have HIV, or how hard it's been having HIV. But this is rare, and I've mostly had to work through it on my own.

"The day Tom was diagnosed was the worst day of my life. It wasn't just that he was dying, it was everything. Several times a week, we'd go for a long drive after work—sometimes four or five hours—just to be alone, no one else around, no phone, barely talking, just gliding along in the dark. It was our own world and it was peace. Tom once said, 'When we're alone in the car driving, it's the only time I feel safe.' I felt the same way. One day when Tom was really sick and looked terrible, we had arrived back in the city on our way home at about one in the morning. We were waiting at a red light, and a car pulled up alongside, and the guy looked at Tom and started shouting, *'AIDS, fags, AIDS!'* I don't know what the guy said—this was San Francisco I'm talking about! I felt terrible for Tom, but *I* was traumatized by this, too, I was shamed by it, even though I wasn't positive. I felt like Tom and I were successful gay people, but this made me feel like trash, that I'd never be valuable enough. It was like being back in junior high and high school, which was a terrible time for me, all those feelings, and here it was happening again.

"Ours was a gay business, a very successful one that didn't cater particularly to gay people, but to all of San Francisco, including a lot of tourists, and other people across the country. We wanted to show them we could do this, but there was a lot of stigma about the owners being gay. There was very obviously a feeling that gay men couldn't do it, couldn't really excel at something like this, and to really excel, you had to sort of duck down a little, stay under the radar, and not make yourself too conspicuous. So I was dealing will all this, and then there's the epidemic going on, and Tom is dying. The best thing we could think of was hiding out in the car. And then that asshole starts yelling at us, and after that I would never look at people in other cars. I could hardly look at anyone."

I asked Ralph if he thought of himself as a "survivor."

"That's hard to say because I was never sick—I guess you're not supposed to say you're a survivor if you're negative, but I've pushed through a lot of fear and heartache, and I've had to work hard—deliberately—to build a satisfying life. You know, I never had anal sex because I always had hemorrhoids. I guess you could say that hemorrhoids saved my life. My doctor once asked me if I wanted to see a therapist—he thought I might have emotional things to work out because I wasn't having anal sex. So I don't know if I'm a survivor, I guess I really am. I see a lot of negative men around me that I think of as survivors, though I haven't heard anyone use the term.

"A lot of them are incredibly isolated—they're very isolated, and I try to extend myself not to let that happen. I have them over for dinner. I've become sort of the gay Perle

Mesta[14] of Laguna Beach, the hostess of the town. One man said to me, 'You're my only social life,' which shocked me. So I make a big effort to keep a community going, mostly with the dinners and barbecues and then other kinds of things like camping trips where six or eight of us will go up to the mountains for four days. I try to plan things so I can get people together who are compatible and can talk to each other. I've taken this on as my responsibility, and not just for them, but for me. It's so easy to just drift off and suddenly realize that you haven't seen anyone in a month. I lived like that for years after Tom died and before I met Kevin, and I don't want to do it again.

"There are also five of us, the English Muffins we call ourselves, who get together for breakfast a couple of times a week, and these are guys I can really talk to—about anything. I started it on Meet Up a few years ago,[15] but then we went private. The Muffins are my therapy now. We talk about a lot of serious things, feelings about everything, and two of them also lost partners, but all five of us lived through AIDS. Two are [HIV-]positive. Without the Muffins, I would probably have a therapist again.

"I guess I didn't mention Marty. After Tom died, I felt completely lost and I was in therapy for about two years and that helped a lot. Mostly Marty just sat there and listened to me, and it's amazing how helpful that was. Every now and then he'd say something incredible, a flash of light. I remember one day I said to him that I felt I must be boring him, that I was just talking about the same things week after week, and I felt like I was just digging myself in deeper just going over the painful past again and again. Marty said, 'You're feeling broken, in pieces. By talking, you're finding ways to put the pieces back together,' or something like that. It was very, very helpful. Slowly, during and after the therapy—I'm talking four, five, six years after—I had gained confidence.

"Then, when Kevin and I moved down here, I started to work with kindergarten kids as a volunteer, and it's made me happier. I've been doing it for years now. Children need help,

they are not sick, they're not dying, they're enthusiastic
about life. Terrible things have not happened to them.
Helping them gives me purpose, a reason for my life. Tom
lived most of his life helping other people. If things go down
the tubes and we have another Republican president, I'll just
volunteer more. I'm stronger than a lot of people, but it's
there—the damage. I'm not one of those people who want to
live forever, but I never say this to people because they get
mad at me. The AIDS thing shaped that in me. So, am I a
survivor? I could say that I've learned again to have a satisfying
life, but when it's over, it won't be a huge tragedy. Tom used to
say to me that at the end he would have died twice—the first
time was the diagnosis, the second time when he died. I'll
have died twice, too. The first time was when Tom got
diagnosed.

### Stage One: Emerging from Isolation

Judith Herman discusses attention to isolation as a prerequisite to her
three stages of recovery, but does not include it as a distinct first stage.
I give isolation the emphasis of its own stage because many gay men
carry a lifelong history of stigma and consequent isolation, and any
later-life trauma only builds upon and exacerbates that experience.
Even as human connections and community are fundamental to
recovery from trauma, isolation is now endemic in gay communities.
Ralph intuitively understood this and was able, as the "Perle Mesta"
of Laguna Beach, to reintroduce himself into a communal life that
helped provide meaning. Echoing much of Erikson's work, Herman tells
us that in post-trauma isolation, we have lost "basic capacities for trust,
autonomy, initiative, competence, identity and intimacy. Just as these
capabilities are originally formed in relationships with other people,
they must be reformed in such relationships."[16]

In Stage One, the connections that help restore our "basic capacities" are found in many different forms. Other people and whole communities bear witness, which, in itself, is validating and strengthening
for a survivor. The witness is able to listen caringly and without vi-
carious traumatization; he does not participate in denial of the trauma;
and he does not dismiss the emotional aftermath as unintelligible or

unwarranted. The witness *recognizes* the survivor, and that recognition provides the foundation for the survivor's recovery of himself. Marty listened to Ralph while Ralph "put the pieces back together." Relatively few heterosexual Americans have the experience that would allow them to bear witness to a gay survivor of the epidemics, and gay men must largely provide such witness for one another. Our bonds as gay men carried us through the epidemic, and they can help us through the aftermath. But we need to both speak and listen to one another, form groups of men to talk about their histories and feelings, and sometimes seek individual psychotherapists when that is possible.

The Medius Institute for Gay Men's Health was founded by Spencer Cox and John Voelcker to define and publicize the current issues in gay men's psychological health. Both men were engaged survivors of the early epidemic. Medius was essentially an effort to initiate Stage One, to gain attention and support for those dwindling away in unaddressed isolation, emotional pain, and destructive substance use, and its white papers were penned in an intelligent, well-researched, eloquent voice. Cox and Voelcker were met with a veritable wall of disinterest and denial. But the busy agendas of gay communities must make room for a "Medius agenda" that stands shoulder to shoulder with the other agenda items that have garnered so much public attention. Commenting on Vietnam combat veterans, Herman tells us that they "refused to be forgotten. Moreover, they refused to be stigmatized. They insisted upon the rightness, the dignity of their distress."[17] Gay survivors of *gay* wars must also refuse and insist.

## Stage Two: Safety

My Stage Two is Judith Herman's first formal stage of recovery. Moving survivors to a place of both physical and emotional safety is widely considered the first stage of recovery from any trauma. With others' help and on his own initiative, Ralph slowly built a sense of emotional safety. During his teenage years, he had felt endangered; and during the early epidemic, he and Tom had again found themselves in a dangerous world, in which they felt safe with each other only during their midnight drives—*safe* before the traffic-light verbal assault that had revived memories of painful personal histories. In grief, and without companionship following Tom's death, Ralph sought out a therapist, then began a relationship with Kevin, and ultimately moved from the concentrated trauma in San Francisco to the relative peace of Laguna Beach. It was through his connections to his therapist, Kevin, the Laguna Beach community, and children who had "not had terrible things happen to them," that Ralph found a sense of emotional safety. When we spoke, I sensed a man who had surely been injured by early-life and later trauma, but who had also now constructed a purposeful life, largely free of a sense of present danger.[18]

Today, many gay men carry a variable mix of trauma from the ongoing late epidemic, the fifteen-year early epidemic, and early-life stigmatization and abuse that originated in the family and often continues into adulthood. For such men, a sense of physical and emotional safety is often more elusive than for survivors of acute, later-life, shorter-term trauma. Because it is ongoing, the late epidemic does not permit absolute physical—and thus emotional—safety for sexually active young men. Even as prevention approaches such as PrEP provide excellent, if imperfect, results, the possibility of contracting HIV remains, and today about 2.4 percent of all gay men contract HIV annually.[19] Although HIV is no longer the threat many feel it to be, it is still a threat of considerable medical and social significance.[20]

Particularly on behalf of young men, we *could* significantly reduce the level of physical threat and its emotional consequences if gay-community leaders and spokespeople focused on the issues of the late epidemic. We have had HAART for more than twenty years, and it has provided HIV-positive men significant assurance against HIV-related illness and death; and it has made the transmission of HIV from those on regular HAART regimens virtually impossible. For HIV-negative men, we also have approved pharmaceuticals for both post- and pre-exposure treatment and prophylaxis, known respectively as PEP and PrEP. Both provide high efficacy against established new infection. These powerful interventions come with an obvious catch: they are available only to informed people with access to money or medical insurance, HIV-knowledgeable care, and supportive physicians who do not stigmatize gay lives and sexuality. One would have expected gay community agendas to focus on these important needs, but on the whole, they have not. It is young gay men—the future of gay male communities—who most suffer the consequences of this inattention.

The majority of gay men have lived in a hostile world for much of their lives, and in the aftermath of adult trauma, they need not a restoration, but a first experience of safety. American society is still largely hostile to gay people, and the emotional aftermath of trauma in such a world leaves many gay men with a sense of self that is characterized by internal division, self-doubt, and isolation that is meant to conceal shame and the "shameful self" from others. The authentic acceptance of gay people would provide an authentic sense of emotional safety; and if that acceptance were felt only by gay men themselves, it would transform gay lives beyond anyone's wildest hopes for legal victories. The absolute conviction of gay people about the right and rightness of *gay* lives might even, over time, transform a society whose stigmatization is now only nurtured by the shame of gay people themselves. It is in authentic, unstigmatized lives that people find emotional safety. That objective cannot be accomplished by individuals alone: "emotional safety" is not simply an internal state, it is a sense of safety in the world and the company of others.

### Stage Three: Grieving and Talking Through

Recovery from both trauma and loss requires grieving. For clarity of discussion, I divide grieving into two consecutive stages, *talking through* and *working through*, although the actual process is never that defined and linear. Many imagine that grieving is painful—which is true—and, less true, that the pain invariably begets nothing more than pointless, self-indulgent "wallowing in the past," from which one should simply "move on." Such advice is often heard from and for gay men living in the aftermath of traumatic early-life experience and the two epidemics, and those caught "wallowing" do often feel shame for their weakness and self-indulgence. As a psychotherapist who has worked with many survivors of trauma and loss, I know that simply moving on is rarely productive, and that usefully conducted talking and working through are powerfully reparative. Only with active grieving in the aftermath of trauma do we find partially restored— or new—authentically expansive, rich, and humanly engaged lives.

The first step in grieving—in which we allow ourselves to bring painful memories to consciousness—is the step we most often hope to avoid. Unfortunately, this step is an essential part of the foundation for a useful grieving process. Herman describes it as "the recovery and cathartic reliving of traumatic memories."[21] Most gay people already know this first step: it begins with the private, conscious acknowledgment of who one is, which gay people often call "coming out to myself." That coming out entails remembering and reliving traumatic memories of life in the closet. The next step is to seek support by coming out to others, and with the support of those witnesses to begin searching for a gay life by grieving the loss of the life that came before. In the grieving, we work through the loss of an old self that we and others had hoped for or expected; and unfortunately, we must often grieve the loss of family, previous intimate relationships, and both casual and important friendships. Only in grieving and relinquishing these losses can we make room for a new sense of self and the life it might offer: a life born of a sense of relative wholeness and self-acceptance. An authentic life.[22]

Grieving almost invariably requires support by others who bear witness. As they first bear witness for us, we learn to bear witness for ourselves, and to then bear witness for others, who, in turn, bear further witness for us. This is the nature of a supportive community: we mutually listen to, comprehend, and care for one another. From Marty's first bearing witness for him, Ralph learned to bear witness to his own life, and then later found a community of men who mutually bore witness for one another. In his grieving—for both Tom and for who he had been before his trauma and loss—Ralph found healing. All useful psychotherapy is fundamentally about bearing witness: the therapist helps a person discover and be himself in the presence of another, and that experience of caring and acceptance helps heal a previously fragmented and divided self. At the end of his long, thoughtful process, Ralph was not "one of those people who want to live forever," but he *had* found a way back to a satisfying, connected life with a sense of purpose, pleasure, and reasonable happiness.[23]

In my impression, Ralph was probably as healed as any survivor of serious, long-term trauma can be, and for good reason: he did not relegate his feelings to unconsciousness, he actively explored them. As with consciously forgotten but disturbing dreams, in the aftermath of real-life trauma the feelings live on in us. They live on most enduringly, disruptively, and destructively when we deny and imprison them—preserved like spores—in our unconscious, where they continue to have undesired and unrecognized influences on our conscious lives. Ralph allowed his feelings into consciousness, and he talked them through, but that was not enough. Even when feelings are thoroughly talked through, we discover that insight alone—unimplemented and unconnected insight—does not change a life. One simply remains fixed in the traumatic memories, which can beget more pain than resolution, the very outcome that many fear. Ralph needed to go beyond the exploration of his feelings, and he did. He implemented his insight in new connections and purpose.

### Stage Four: Working Through and the Story of Bill

Herman calls this final stage of recovery *reconnection*, but in talking about gay men, I am calling it *working through* for two reasons. First, because of long-standing developmental histories of trauma and isolation in a world of stigmatizing families and communities, many young gay men have nothing to *re*connect to. They must find authentic connection for the first time in their lives. Second, the idea of "reconnecting" too easily implies the often-heard, simplistic notion that the solution to trauma and isolation is to "get out of the house, make some friends, and be social." That is not at all Herman's intent, and as she well knows and articulately states—and the story of Bill illustrates—this stage of recovery is a complex internal effort, undertaken in a social context. "Reconnecting" is not about simply *acting* socially in the world.

The need for social connection in this critical final stage of recovery is one of the important reasons that therapy groups are so helpful for working through, an approach that Herman discusses:

> Such groups afford a degree of support and understanding that is simply not available in the survivor's ordinary social environment. . . . Groups provide the possibility not only of mutually rewarding relationships but also of collective empowerment. . . . The group as a whole has a capacity to bear and integrate traumatic experience that is greater than that of any individual member.[24]

Gay communities have something important in common with small, structured "survivor groups." Whether from early- or later-life trauma, gay communities—particularly those of younger men just coming out in the world, or older survivors of the early epidemic—are often groups of men living with feelings of alienation from family, society, and other gay men. *Groups* of such men might thus hold the power "to bear and integrate traumatic experience that is greater than that of any individual member." This is why so many young men migrate to gay communities in search of working through early developmental trauma. Whether our communities and community politics are actually up to the task is another matter.

When he first came to see me, Bill, forty-seven and gay, was living alone in San Francisco. His father had died when Bill was seven; a single child, he had continued to live with his working mother in Idaho Falls until the age of fourteen, when his mother died following a surgery. Having grown up with his parents in borderline poverty, Bill then moved to live with his well-to-do aunt and uncle in Salt Lake City, where he stayed until the age of eighteen. Then moving to a rented room, Bill supported himself for a year with odd jobs, before moving to San Francisco. He had known since the age of twelve that he was gay, but because of the strong stigma attached to it in Idaho and Utah, he had done little exploration. Bill arrived in San Francisco on his quest for self-discovery in 1987 at the age of nineteen and bore firsthand witness to the spiraling epidemic.

Bill had a lot of strengths. He had grown up with a great deal of necessary independence and responsibility and had developed an authentic, resolute self-sufficiency. After moving to San Francisco, he dated a bit, but he had never had a sustained relationship. Shortly after arriving, he began working as an "escort," which he continued for two years, and he told me that it had been a "fun way to make a decent living and learn more about sex." He described his clients as "usually nice, generous, older married men, and I was almost always the top, which I prefer." The clients often took Bill to "fancy" restaurants, and he began thinking about "the importance of mushrooms." When I first met him for therapy in 2015, Bill was the founder and owner of a twenty-year-old company that grew and distributed "specialty mushrooms for high-end Northern California restaurants and gourmet groceries." He was financially successful and said he enjoyed his work. He continued to date, now only sporadically, and felt he was "somewhat depressed and lonely." He presented himself as cheerful, animated, and gregarious, but I sensed a limited range of feeling behind the presentation. Unmodulated cheerfulness often suggests underlying emotional constriction, and Bill seemed *too* cheerful, particularly for a man who was living with so little companionship and intimacy.

During our initial work, much of what we discussed was Bill's history of loss and trauma. For the first time, he was slowly able to recall, reexperience, and discuss the trauma of his childhood, and the trauma during his first decade in San Francisco. He recalled tremendous emotional pain at the time of his father's death, which had occurred in a violent work-related accident in which his father's face and upper torso had been badly burned. Bill had "forgotten" most of this, but in our conversations he was slowly able to recall an astonishing amount of detail. He told me that it had been a closed-casket funeral despite his angry, seven-year-old's protest. He had wanted to see his father, and no one would tell Bill why he was not allowed to, except that "something had happened to his face."

After the funeral, Bill was out of school for about a month, and he recalled his mother having to plead with him to eat. As an enticement several weeks after the funeral, she bought him his favorite, rocky road ice cream, which he also refused. "If you let me see Daddy," he yelled at her, "I'll eat it." She was off work "for quite a while" and stayed in her bedroom with the door shut for the entire day. While Bill and I were focusing on this period in his life, he told me that the night before our meeting he had been thinking about his father, and imagining how proud he would have been about Bill's success in business. But while having these thoughts, Bill had suddenly had what he described as "a strange physical reaction":

> "I was sitting in a dining room chair eating, and suddenly my body started shaking, and my eyes started watering."
>
> I waited for Bill to continue, but he did not. "Were you crying—sobbing?"
>
> Bill sat silently for several minutes without responding,

then suddenly said, "Maybe that's what it was. I know I was very upset about my father. I've never done that before."

"Cried? As a child?"

"I don't know, I don't remember."

What Bill had experienced as "a strange physical reaction," he learned to recognize as an expression of emotion or grief. During his years in San Francisco, even while working as an escort—a "fun way to make a decent living"—Bill now recalled being terrified of becoming infected, sick, and dependent on others. He had almost completely repressed that fear of HIV, focusing instead on the task of remaining self-sufficient. That self-sufficiency had started early in childhood: by the time he was nine, two years after his father's death, he had learned to have the house clean and dinner prepared before his mother arrived home from work. "My mother worked very hard, but was a slob, and a very mediocre cook. I wasn't a *good* cook, but I was better than she was, and I'd stand on a step stool at the stove and make some pretty good dinners that I found in magazines." His mother was thankful for the dinners, but she also warned him, "If you tell people about this, they're going to think you're a fag." At the age of nine, Bill didn't quite know what she meant, but he uncomfortably sensed that she was right about *something*, and he never told anyone.

Against the possibility of losing his self-sufficiency in San Francisco, Bill had been "meticulously careful" in his sexual activity and amassed a "good stash of money." I once said to him, "In a relationship, you'd be like the man who has everything—you wouldn't know what to give him for Christmas. You appear to need nothing from others, and people feel that." Bill accepted my comment as a compliment for what he considered his primary virtue and only later understood its connection to his loneliness. His admirable and authentic independence and self-sufficiency hid a lifetime of grief that he had never allowed himself to experience or think consciously about. Now that he had clearly survived and then some, he had begun feeling that he had nothing purposeful or important in his life, particularly a relationship. He now often sobbed in grief about all that he did not have and had never had.

Bill and I spent a considerable amount of time talking through his grief and then working it through. As he acknowledged and experienced the grief, he came to feel both stronger and weaker—stronger because, in recognizing the emotional needs he had always had, he now understood himself more authentically; and weaker precisely because he had these needs and could no longer live with the self-sufficiency that he had always thought essential. "I feel as if I've met myself for the first time in my life, and it's scary, and I'm pretty sure I don't like it." As Bill further explored and settled into some acceptance of his feelings, the next step would be working through his insights by implementing them in an attempt at a relationship that he very much wanted. For several months, Bill had been dating Kenny, and—though Bill was more reserved in his description—my observation was that he had become very attached. He spoke about Kenny a lot, sometimes almost with a certain rapture, and on a Tuesday, Bill came in and told me about their spending Sunday night together at Bill's house:

"We were lying in bed cuddling—spooning—and talking about the movie we'd been to. I was looking at the skin on the back of his neck, and the next thing I knew I was weeping and just clutching him. I couldn't let go of him. I was very embarrassed."

"Why embarrassed?" I wondered.

"I don't know—for him to see me like that. And he wriggled around so he was facing me—I think I had practically suffocated him, holding on to him like that—and he said what *you* always say to me: 'Tell me what you're feeling,' and then I just started sobbing again and I couldn't stop."

"It sounds as if Kenny offered a supportive response."

"Yes, I thought about that, and I think that's part of what's bothering me now."

"How did you answer him? What *were* you feeling?"

"I couldn't answer him, I didn't know. I said, 'I don't know.'"

"And why would his supportiveness bother you?"

"I don't know. Do you know?"

"Maybe, I'm not sure, but it would be better to know what you think."

"I think I'm afraid of needing him, that that's what I've been afraid of all my life. When I was looking at the back of his neck, at his beautiful skin, I was thinking, 'This is a person with a body—he could get something, it could just go in through his skin, and he could die. And I couldn't bear that.'" Bill felt silent.

I waited before responding, "In an important way, other people are all we have in life. But we sometimes lose them. You've already lost a lot of people. Falling in love is a risk."

Bill was silent for a moment, then began sobbing.

Bill's own analysis of what had happened that night with Kenny was a reminder of how much insight Bill had gained in our talking through his lifetime of loss and trauma. In the next step, working through—which would not be his reconnection, but his first adult connection—he would have to consciously incorporate his insight into how he lived. I described the process to Bill: we "flag" certain issues and situations that provoke familiar, problematic responses, and we learn to consciously recognize the flagged items as they come up in our lives. Feeling attachment to others—and thus dependence—was an important flag for Bill. When a flag comes up, we think about the situation and possible responses to it, and about what each of the possible responses would mean and accomplish. We then make conscious choices to not respond in habitual, destructive ways; we decide to behave differently and evaluate the outcome. Over time, I told Bill, this process of working through changes how we experience ourselves, how others experience us, and how we experience our lives.

"But this seems impossible," Bill objected. "When I told you about that night with Kenny, I didn't understand it until two days later."

"What's important is that you did finally understand it, which was a real accomplishment. And you *did* express feelings to Kenny, even if you couldn't articulate what they were about. Anyway, two days is pretty good for something that complicated. With practice we get more familiar, faster. It's a slow process."

"How slow?"

"I don't know—*slow*. The idea isn't to be perfect, to expect yourself to always be on the spot. You know, you can apologize later to someone and change the outcome then. Some things you can redo and some you can't. A week later you can explain to Kenny what you were feeling if you want to. Over time, these efforts bring incremental, little changes, and the accumulation begins to change our lives. It's slow, and you need to have patience with yourself. What I'm describing here is how we change—the only way we change. We don't change just because we understand something, we change when we put our understanding to use."

Bill and I still continue to meet occasionally when he has something to talk about, and he is now barely recognizable as the person I first met. The resolute cheerfulness is gone, and in its place one senses an authentic, more complex person, one who is *appropriately* cheerful. Bill and Kenny now live together, and Bill continues to grow by working through his still-increasing insight. On a recent visit, Bill said to me:

"When you said *slow*, you meant *slow*."

"I don't know, you seem like a different person from the man I met a few years ago. In any case, it's a lifelong process—that's how we grow. When we stop growing, that's the end."

"Oh, I know I'm completely different. When I think about it, I'm really shocked at how little I understood before. But I'm hardly perfect. I'm still learning"

"If you were perfect, you'd be the first one. Give yourself some slack for the wonderful work you've done. *Really*, give yourself some slack."

Bill has, I think, significantly recovered from his lifelong, composite trauma. He now lives with a kind of genuine lightness, spontaneity, and—most important—sense of himself in connection to others that was unimaginable when I first met him. But Bill is not *over* his grief; he is more consciously aware of it than he had ever been. He has truthfully revealed himself to himself and has come to some acceptance of the grief he has lived with. Herman describes the complexity of self-exploration and resolution:

> The goal of recounting the trauma story is integration, not exorcism. In the process of reconstruction, the trauma story does undergo a transformation, but only in the sense of becoming more present and more real. The fundamental premise of the psychotherapeutic work is a belief in the restorative power of truth-telling. In the telling, the trauma story becomes a testimony.[25]

On another recent visit, Bill said to me, "I don't really know what therapy is exactly or how it works. But I know that over the last few years—well, I don't know exactly how to put it—I'm living in my own life for the first time. It's very different, a very different feeling. And I have Kenny, which would have been impossible before. I don't really understand how it all happened."

The answer was relatively simple: Bill had become himself by having someone support him in finding and being himself. He had had a witness, and for that now had a richer, if more complicated, life.

# 7

# Gay Men's Relationships

When the road was put through, two kings, by their embellishments
(for example: a veneer of blue enameled bricks), invested it with a
splendor which made it the wonder of their world.
—Keith Waldrop, *The Not Forever*[1]

A human society is not a *thing*; it is a group of people living in more or
less tight proximity with a tradition, and thus a collection of explicit
rules and unspoken expectations. Sanctioned formal institutions, social stigmatization, and the long arm of the law attempt to enforce
these norms. Those who are willing to comply are enticed by a host of
benefits, including a common language, riches, a fire department, and
weekly garbage pickup; those who are not willing are deprived, marginalized, and punished. With the Constitution and the Bill of Rights
presumably underpinning American society, we might expect an acceptance of diversity and true equality, but we would be dreaming. For
a land almost entirely populated by immigrants, America is conspicuously intolerant of real diversity, racial and otherwise, and that intolerance has burrowed deeply into the emotionally intimate lives of its
citizens. Human beings—with the probably unique capacity to self-
consciously fear their own dreams, desires, and impulses—live in perpetual anxiety about human emotional life, and thus society, unraveling
into chaos. This is one important reason that America has an appointed committee of nine black-robed justices who ultimately decide
who can be in love with whom, and how that love may be expressed.

Such social and judicial attempts at regulation too often crush the potential richness of human life and have left too many gay people living not as themselves, but as social mimics, or as recluses who have made the fears of others their own. A full century after the Emancipation Proclamation and the end of the American Civil War, interracial marriage—"miscegenation"—was still illegal in many American states. In 1967, the Supreme Court struck down antimiscegenation laws, which changed the official rules, but not the feelings of a probable majority of fearful—and thus hateful—Americans. It took another half century for the black-robed committee to strike down laws prohibiting gay marriage, which has also changed the rules, but not, on the whole, societal feelings. What is most astonishing about these two long-standing social conflicts is that American society ever meddled *at all* in such personal matters of feeling. And it has been not only the law, but also societal stigmatization and shaming that have driven the meddling—meddling that has left deep, disfiguring emotional wounds, passed on from one generation to the next. African-Americans and gay people are still attempting to heal these wounds.

## THE HOPE

Society continues to offer the socially constructed idea of marriage, which is the same, often humanly unrealistic, relationship it has always been, now slightly modified by a larger potential population of participants. This traditional, socially constructed idea of a relationship is granted social status with family celebration, legal rights and protections, and financial incentives. But actively or by default, society prohibits such benefits for relationships not socially constructed and treats many as if they did not exist. For prohibited or ignored *emotionally* constructed relationships, the important substance of the relationship—the bonding, companionship, love, trust, and intimacy— is dismissed by a society that fears diversity and the social disorganization it seems to threaten. Emotionally constructed relationships are instinctual and central in human life: *everyone* has a relationship, has lost a relationship, or has simply longed for one. Whatever the experience—have, had, or longed for—our internal lives are inextricably woven around how we relate to others emotionally. As adolescents approaching adulthood, the prospect of a relationship fills us with aspiration and longing: "If only there were *someone* I could love," a gay seventeen-year-old once said to me, "I would feel okay." Having found another young man with whom he experienced six months of elation, he later said, "I could be wrong, but I think the whole relationship thing is overrated. It's much more complicated than I thought." Relationships are, indeed, complicated. The seventeen-year-old had not lost his hope, but he had realized that for gay men the complications are usually even greater.

As a group, gay men quite naturally crave both socially constructed and emotionally constructed relationships. Everyone craves social acceptance to some degree, and all people—even men—instinctually crave companionship, love, and emotional intimacy. These two cravings—for acceptance and love—are inborn and are reinforced by the dependency and vulnerability experienced in infancy and childhood. In the adolescent aspirations and adult lives of gay men, both cravings are strong, but often difficult to distinguish. Many intuitively feel that what they crave emotionally can only be had within a socially constructed relationship. "Serious and meaningful" relationships have long been defined by conventional heterosexual marriage, which is the only model for relationships that many know. In reality, most relationships between two men are emotionally constructed, personally conceived inventions. As a group, gay men have been remarkably successful at relationships that work, which is, in the face of pervasive social expectation, wonderful evidence for the occasional triumph of the human spirit over fearful social meddling. For the heterosexual who wonders which man in the gay couple is "the wife," the useful answer is probably "You are ignorant of the emotional complexity and potential richness of human life. We are trying to dig out from under *your* mess and find and be ourselves."

Because of the assumed authority of conventional relationship models, gay men, young and old, often feel that "relationships" are, for them, out of reach. Although they are not alone in these feelings, gay men seem to approach the prospect with an unusual amount of both aspiration and doubt. Gay men are not alone in using longevity as the marker of success, with little attention to the actual human experience of the couple. For many, the existence of "long-term gay relationships" is evidence for the viability of relationships between men. In themselves, gay relationships are no more unavailable or problematic than any other relationships, but gay relationships must persevere in a society that is, still today, largely obstructive. The major obstruction is the imposition of heterosexual relationship models, which are too often cited to assert the idea that gay men without them die alone and lonely. I have heard this cliché repeatedly—once as a personal warning to me, at the age of twenty-two, from an eminent, usually insightful psychoanalyst and family friend. The implicit message was that without a conventional heterosexual relationship—meaning, without *being* heterosexual—I would have *no* relationship.

The truth is that *within* relationships, many people, gay and straight, both live and die alone and lonely. In this unhappy human dilemma, gay men sometimes fare better than others because of the broader possibilities that relatively convention-free gay relationships allow. These possibilities include the nurture of a "second family of choice," which does not rely on the often-contentious, fickle nature of biological families. In 2018, American society still teems with ill will for gay people, marriage or no marriage, and even without ill will, there is a great deal of well-meant but misplaced doubt about gay relationships. Recently back from a 2015 family Thanksgiving in Texas, a sensitive and perceptive twenty-six-year-old gay therapy patient, Tom, related a brief conversation he had had with his mother. "I know that your Republican friends don't want me to be gay," he said to her, "but what do *you and Dad* have against me?" His mother's probably well-intentioned response was "Men don't have relationships, and your father and I just want you to be happy." Such warnings—which are significantly evolved from the idea of the homosexual, and from utterly unfounded confidence in conventional relationships—have predictable consequences. They tend to fulfill their own prediction. Dismissing, stigmatizing, or prohibiting gay relationships, society would then use the *result* of those influences to demonstrate that gay relationships do not work or do not even exist in any substantive, human, emotional sense. Tom returned from the family visit with his determination to live as a gay man intact. He also still carried hope for a relationship, but the hope lived in a shadow of fear that his mother might be right:

"I'm sometimes afraid," Tom said, "that I will never find someone to be with. I don't think I know how to do that, I don't know if it's possible. I know we can't, and I'm not asking you to, but I suddenly had the feeling that I wanted you to hug me. I feel very lonely and I'm scared."

"You'll find someone," I glibly promised.

"How can you *know* that?" Tom asked with irritation.

"You're right, I apologize, I can't *know* that. I think I was trying to avoid the pain and fear you're obviously feeling, I think I was simply avoiding it because it's painful for me to see you feeling this way. But I know you, and I think it's possible, and it's something we have to try to work on."

## THE HOPELESSNESS: THE STORY OF MICHAEL

*Some* sense of hopelessness about relationships is experienced by all but the rosiest of people. But among gay men, hopelessness is more frequently articulated than it is among heterosexual men; it is more likely to be about the very possibility of a relationship rather than its quality; and it is a feeling much more likely to have been first experienced during developmentally formative adolescent years. The imbalance of hopelessness between gay and straight men is perhaps clarified by the suggestions of a disturbing piece of research from 2011. In the United States, only about 60 percent of men who have had sex with men self-identify as gay.[2] The 40 percent who are not gay-identified are almost certainly not even entertaining the idea of a relationship with another man. They are having sex, and as the homosexual model dictates, sex has no meaning beyond the physical act. For men who *are* gay-identified and have had thoughts of relationships, my social experience and thirty years as a psychotherapist suggest considerable hopelessness, even in the age of Internet dating and legally approved gay marriage.

I began working with Michael in 2012, after his thirty-eighth birthday had instigated his decision "to see someone to talk to." Michael lived alone in a spacious flat in San Francisco's Cole Valley, was a published novelist, and had both a public following and a robust private social life.

"I am embarrassed—*ashamed* really—to even tell you why I'm here," Michael said as he sat down in his chair on our first meeting.

"We don't have to talk about it right now. Perhaps you can tell me something else about yourself and your life, and at some point when you're more comfortable, we'll come back to it."

"It's that I've never had a relationship, and I just turned thirty-eight. I believe that you'll have nothing but contempt for that. I have nothing but contempt for myself. It seems like a terrible failure, an inadequacy within me that I will never be able to correct. When I was eighteen and at Brown, I met someone named Paul, who told me he was gay, and we started having sex, which continued for most of the school year. I didn't even think of myself as gay—don't ask me how I reconciled that, because I have no idea, I suppose it was all unconscious. I was much more into him than I acknowledged. I spent that first summer between terms in England, and I received a letter from Paul ending it. He said, 'This isn't going to work for me.' Those were his words. I was bereft and suicidal for the next seven weeks, and waiting for my return flight home, I was planning to jump off the Dover cliffs. Nineteen years old, *not* gay, and suicidal over another boy. I was living with a family in Dover, and I'd walk to the cliffs—a stretch with no fence— and sit, day after day, looking at the Channel. One day about three weeks after I'd gotten the letter, a sweet, rather decrepit elderly couple walked by, and the old woman looked at me and said, 'Luv, don't sit so near the edge.' I can't tell you why, but at that moment I started to cry, and I gave up on the idea of jumping. I've dabbled with other guys since Paul—here and there, for a short time—and nothing has worked out, it's all come to naught. It's a failure I'm very ashamed of."

"There's a lot to talk about here, but what do you think about how the old woman affected you?"

Michael thought about it for a minute. "I think she

made me feel that she cared—that someone loved me."
Michael tried to restrain himself, but he started sobbing.

Beneath his apparent career and social "successes" lingered a hopelessness that described both his past and future: Michael's history of self-professed "failure" felt, to him, like proof of his future. He once told me that the only future he could "seriously fantasize" was one of "complete, uninterrupted solitude." His time writing gave him that solitude, and he hoped, he said, to extend it to his entire life. "I have the idea of getting a house along the North Coast, and telling no one where I've gone. Even as I fantasize about this, I know it's a desperate move, but it's the only one I can think of as possible."

Psychologically, if not socioeconomically, Michael had a family and developmental background shared by many gay men. His parents were wealthy, and his mother, who came from an even wealthier New England family, "placed great value on social position." For her, a gay son was not part of the plan, and Michael had waited until he was thirty-two to come out to her. Michael described his mother as "intensely asexual," and when he did come out to her, she said only, "I don't want to hear *any* of the details." Michael had never seen affection expressed between his parents, his father had never been affectionate with him, and his mother was only affectionate in the most perfunctory ways she imagined a mother "was supposed to be with a child."

Michael thus led a familiar gay adolescence in which sex and emotionally constructed relationships were rigidly segregated from each other, leaving him feeling that a relationship with another man was a hopeless aspiration: "Like planning your future around winning the lottery," he once told me. He was, of course, not forbidden socially constructed peer relationships with other boys, but the construction clearly excluded any romantic or sexual feelings. Michael had sporadically explored his sexuality, but the explorations were mostly onetime sexual encounters, and the sex was "mostly not good *at all*." It was only with Paul that Michael had a *relationship*, a connection of friendship, companionship, romantic feelings, and sex. This was Michael's first and only emotionally constructed relationship. For both boys, it was distorted by the developmental influences of earlier adolescent experience, and neither knew where to go with it. At the time, Michael did not even think of himself as gay, and that, Paul wrote Michael, "isn't going to work for me." Michael once summed up his year with Paul: "We were like two orphans stranded in the wild. We had no idea where we were, who we were, or how to care for ourselves, much less each other."

Even as Michael had had sporadic sex with other boys through his teenage years, he had no conscious gay self-identity, and the conscious identity would probably have left him even more hopeless about the prospect of relationships. At the age of sixteen, Michael began to focus on writing and thus initiated not only his creative life but also his plan for a life in isolation: "I remember being aware that I needed a way to have a life alone, even though I had no idea why it would have to be that way." As we continued our work together, Michael realized that he had lived as a teenager "with a truly crushing sense" of longing—and loss—for something he had never had, even as he did not know what that something was. "I lived with a kind of gnawing or craving. It was just some kind of diffuse, very deep painful desire that I've never really understood or resolved." These feelings were so familiar and per-vasive that Michael had assumed that everyone privately held them.

Michael said something else important: "When I am alone, I rel-ish the solitude itself; it's something I have always lived with and now welcome. What bothers me is when it starts to feel like annihilation, as if I am ceasing to exist. I feel that a lot." Human life exists substan-tially in companionship and intimacy with others: in some important sense, life without these connections does not subjectively feel like a complete existence. With all the hopeful gay social and political suc-cesses of recent years, there are still too many gay men who, like Michael, feel that life and love with another man is impossible. Lurk-ing among the feelings that sustain such hopelessness is one that is often overlooked: *self-doubt*, which is largely an internalization of so-cial influences, but takes root and develops a life of its own. The ongo-ing external prejudices of a stigmatizing society easily mesh with the internal feelings, and together they readily sustain a persistent self-doubt that propagates its own prediction. Michael doubted his via-bility in relationships, Paul's letter had confirmed that doubt, and two decades later Michael still lived with it. In our work together,

Michael and I would increasingly focus on his self-doubt, which, for all his external successes in life, remained profound.

Much of the push for marriage equality has been motivated by the desire to overcome hopelessness about gay relationships, as well as the self-doubt that drives much of the hopelessness. But self-doubt is an internal problem and will never be fully resolved by political victories, or the external approval that such victories hope to realize. Over time—probably decades—the legalization of gay marriage will likely shift the larger society's and gay men's acceptance of *the fact* of gay relationships. The question is whether this change will also shift acceptance of the actual nature of gay relationships, or if in marriage gay people will be expected—and expect themselves—to mimic the socially constructed idea of traditional heterosexual marriage. If legal marriage raises acceptance of gay relationships without compromising their emotional construction, this will be a truly important victory. If, instead, the acceptance is predicated on "normalizing" gay relationships by molding them—at least in appearance—into conventional heterosexual forms, the change will become a significant additional source of hopelessness for gay men. Mimicking and misrepresentation are inauthentic, and inauthentic lives *feel* hopeless. To be authentic, relationships between men must continue to express gay sensibilities, including the social, emotional, and sexual diversity that naturally characterizes relationships between men. The possibility of legal marriage raises the challenge of remaining oneself in an authentic and meaningful way—however "being oneself" is understood by each man himself.

## THE FEAR: THE STORY OF AMADO

Conventional social values obstruct relationships between adult men in many obvious ways: by forbidding them, stigmatizing them, minimizing or denying them, and by prohibiting their public expression. There is not a single gay man alive in America who has not sometimes felt self-conscious or fearful about touching a lover in public. This alone is a human tragedy, and for gay men, many such socially engineered tragedies are experienced at a very early age. In childhood and adolescence, many gay boys internalize socially promoted ideas that make relationships feel less plausible and natural. In addition, gay boys and young men often develop other feelings that bear on relationships. These feelings are the roots of much self-doubt and include guilt, fear of risk and loss, fear of disappointing others, and fear of emotionally needing too much and having too little to give back. The overarching feeling is fear of rejection. Michael felt many of these things, and depending on the particular developmental experience, all people, gay and straight, have the potential for such feelings. Gay men, however, are often particularly vulnerable: feeling guilt about being oneself, feeling disappointing, and having unfilled emotional needs are a common legacy of growing up gay in a hostile family or society that demands conformity as the price of acceptance. In such a family or society, just being gay can feel like an irrevocable failure that will taint all relationships, including, paradoxically, relationships with other gay men.

When I first met him, Amado, an intelligent, handsome thirty-six-year-old Latino, carried many feelings from childhood that, as an adult, made relationships a foreboding prospect. We began working together in 2012, and it was "relationships or, I should say, the lack of them" that he wanted to talk about. Amado had grown up in San Jose, California, the oldest of four children. He had a stay-at-home mother who raised the children and took care of the household, and a seaman father who worked on oil tankers and was away for extended periods. As the oldest child by seven years, Amado had significant responsibility for the younger children. He also served as "my mother's companion when Pop was away." In 2012, Amado was living by himself in San Francisco's East Bay, and working at an automobile plant near his own home, and about a half hour from his mother and his childhood home. Despite the considerable demands of his early-life domestic responsibilities, Amado had graduated from San Jose State University, continued his education, and earned a graduate degree in manufacturing design engineering. At the auto plant, he worked as a quality-assurance supervisor and was responsible for a large group of quality-control inspectors on the plant's assembly line. "Helping my mother keep things in one piece at home," Amado told me, "was the perfect training for my career."

Amado—a name given by his mother, meaning "beloved" in

Spanish—decided at the age of nine or ten that he was gay. He had always been necessarily closer to his mother than his seafaring father, and his mother, Amado thought, had intuited his gayness, though, to this day, they had never explicitly discussed it. He had also never discussed it with his father, who, now retired and at home, had never raised a question about his thirty-six-year-old "unattached" son.

"Would he be disapproving if you told him?" I wondered.

"You've got to be kidding!" Amado responded. "Tell me you're kidding."

"I don't know your father, so help me."

"This Latino man, a sailor, this man who wanted me to go to the California Maritime Academy and follow in his footsteps, this man who told me, his eldest son, when I was twelve, that if I took a shower every morning, people were going to think I was a *pansy*? This man who thinks the man's only job in the family is to barbecue meat? He would *hate* me for being gay." Amado was first laughing and then visibly upset, and we sat silently for several minutes.

Then Amado suddenly continued, "My father, he made me hate who I am. I've never told you this, but the first time I had sex with a man was at the Oakland docks. When I was a teenager, I used to drive up there to meet men. They were working on the ships, and a lot of those guys were gay."

"Seamen like your father? Men you were seeking attention from?"

"I guess so."

Further conversation made it clear that, in many ways, Amado had been fortunate in his relationship with his mother. She was emotionally sensitive and insightful, affectionate and supportive, all largely without placing inappropriate emotional demands on him. From this valuable experience, Amado knew how to have a relationship, and he understood the meaning and value of companionship and intimacy. Throughout his childhood, Amado's mother had been heavily encumbered by her responsibilities, and she needed his help. Even as a child he had been acutely aware of that. Sitting in my office, Amado revealed a pathos that was quiet but unmistakable, and he remembered having had similar feelings during his teenage years. And in Amado's account, his mother had "always seemed kind of depressed."

"It sounds as if you were very important to your mother," I suggested.

"What does that mean?"

"That you were indispensable to her."

"I *couldn't* give her any more than I did. I needed my own life, too," Amado quickly responded.

"Did you feel I was suggesting you should have given her more?"

"Yes."

"Maybe I misstated things. I didn't intend that, and I don't believe it. My impression is that you gave her a great deal, as much as a child and teenager could possibly have given without entirely forfeiting his own life."

It was Amado, not me, who held a sense of failure about what he had given his mother. He had never, he felt, relieved her of her burden, "and I certainly never made her happy." As a child, he had experienced the two objectives as reasonable expectations of himself and had, in falling short, never been comfortable having his own needs or voicing them. Anything he did for himself felt injurious to his mother and only exacerbated his sense of failure. As a child, Amado had been a voracious reader—"San Jose Library's biggest customer"—but he had never spent a moment in his books without nagging guilt about shunning his responsibilities around the home. Now, even as an accomplished and emotionally sensitive adult, Amado held feelings of failure and guilt and imagined that he would disappoint any man with whom he might have a relationship. "I also feel," Amado once told me, "that I would smother anyone with my neediness, and they'd go running for the hills. That's what I feel about you. I don't know how you can sit there and listen to me whine. I think I am one of your problem clients, and that you'd like me to just disappear."

Whenever Amado and I turned to the subject of possible *current* relationships, all of these feelings surfaced as impediments. Failure, disappointment, and neediness were, in his perception, all that he had to offer another man. Amado and his father rarely spoke about anything, and when they did, Amado said he could "see the disappointment written all over his face, top to bottom and ear to ear." That disappointment was simply about Amado's being gay, which as a pubescent child Amado had decided was the reason his father was so little at home. Still not having explicitly discussed being gay with either of his parents, Amado was convinced that his father knew and held only contempt for him. "My mother, I guess, is probably just disappointed and sad."

Failure and disappointment were not only Amado's idea of how his parents felt about him, they had also become his sense of who he was. It would be a long time before he stopped assuming that this was the only person he had to offer to a relationship. For now, Amado needed to remain alert to the feelings and, particularly, to how he played them out. I told him that in putting the feelings into action in potential relationships, he would receive ongoing confirmation that the feelings were valid; and in not pursuing relationships at all, his conviction that relationships were impossible would only deepen. And we both agreed on something else. When a man Amado had met at a party said that he liked Amado and wanted to get to know him, Amado had responded, "The more you get to know about me, the less you'll probably want to know."

"Okay, let's stop right there," I interrupted.

"Well, that was what I was feeling. I liked him, too, and I guess I was trying to be honest. I was warning him."

"I know that you *feel* that, and we both understand why, but I know you well enough to know that those feelings are not true. All you will get back from playing out such feelings is confirmation that the feelings are true. Very few people you said that to would want to see you again."

"A pretty bad opening line, I guess," Amado conjectured.

"Terrible."

"Well, we're definitely in agreement on that," Amado responded, and we both started laughing.

One point about this exchange should be made clear. I was not suggesting that Amado attempt to deny his feelings about himself, or that he behave inauthentically with others. I later explained to him that by *acting* differently—by not acting out long-standing, substantially unrealistic feelings—he would get different results. Those results would begin to slowly change his self-experience and his sense of what he had to offer another man. We often consider our feelings, and then decide not to act on them: this is thoughtfulness, not inauthenticity. In my much more objective observation, Amado is a man of kindness, loyalty, intelligence, humor, and emotional insight. He has a lot to offer, and he is "probably not bad to look at, or at least that's what people tell me." Amado and I have also spoken about other fears that influence his potential relationships,[3] and as I write, he is dating a bit and trying to thoughtfully consider his feelings and actions and note the effects of his opening lines.

## THE FANTASY: THE STORY OF BRICE

As groups of men go, there are none as emotionally introspective as gay men, but, at the same time, none as unrealistically idealizing of relationships. In gay communities, Cinderella's prince is known as Mr. Right, and every man who is not irrevocably hopeless imagines that someday he might find him. Sometimes an obvious fantasy seems the only alternative to intractable hopelessness: while scrubbing the kitchen floor on hands and knees, one does not think about a better life, one dreams of life in the palace with the prince, who is perfect in every emotional, intellectual, and physical detail. Gay men have a solid developmental foundation for intractable hopelessness about relationships and, thus, a lot of motivation to dream. Both the history and the dreams are frequently evident in how gay men pursue relationships, and how they experience the ones they *do* find.

"I have felt completely alone for my entire life," thirty-one-year-old Brice said plaintively to me. "I have wanted to be unequivocally and passionately loved forever, for as long as I can remember, and in my [ten-year, current] relationship with Peter I have never felt it." Even as I knew that Brice's wish for unequivocal, unconditional love was impossible, I understood what motivated his feelings. I was sympathetic to the emptiness and pain he felt, and I wanted to support his hope for something better than what he currently had.

Brice had grown up as an only child to two young parents—both twenty when Brice was born, and both preoccupied with financial struggles and their own significant and enduring marital conflict. They had little to offer him, but both attempted to use him as a companion. His father dragged him to sport events because Brice's mother had no interest—and neither did Brice—and when his father left him at home, his mother used him as an emotional companion to assuage her loneliness and depression. "Whenever my father took me to a game, I felt like a dog on a leash, and when my mom hugged me, I felt like she was smothering me and sucking my life away. It was like being hugged by a vampire. Neither of them did *anything* for me." Neither parent seemed to get enough from him, and Brice grew up feeling that he received little from others, and had nothing to offer. This feeling of inadequacy was extrapolated into most of his life, and despite undergraduate and graduate degrees, and a successful business career—all firsts in his family's history—Brice experienced himself as an almost complete failure in love and life.

Significantly as a compensatory response to how his relationships with his parents had left him feeling about himself, as a young adult Brice was living out a two-part fantasy. The first part was about himself: he would fantasize that he had everything to offer because he was Brice, the attractive and successful businessman. The second part was about relationships and was predicated on the first: that he deserved and could find a man who would give him everything he wanted. When part one of the fantasy collapsed, which it often did, Brice was once again "a nobody" and lived in depressive discouragement about himself, and hopelessness and anger about relationships and how they left him feeling. He would then slowly rally part one of the fantasy by working out at the gym. As the gym time improved his self-experience and mood, he would tell me that he was "feeling very attractive." But the two parts of the fantasy worked bidirectionally. Brice not only believed that being attractive would garner a relationship, he believed that the unconditional love of the relationship would make him feel valuable. The problem was that the two-part fantasy was a bootstrap operation. Brice needed a relationship to make him feel good about himself, and he needed to feel good about himself to have the confidence to pursue and endure any real-life, necessarily conditional relationship. Cinderella may have found a prince who offered unconditional love, but Brice had found only real people. Many, including Peter, *did* have much more to offer than Brice's parents had, but none had everything.

At the age of twenty-one, Brice had begun a relationship with twenty-nine-year-old Peter, and it had, in fact, provided Brice with some important things. He and Peter were good companions, and in my perception they had an honest, human connection with the kind of variability and compromise that characterize almost all couples. When he was in a part-one downswing, Brice felt lucky to have *anything* and lived in fear of losing Peter. But when Brice shifted into a part-one upswing, he felt he had better options, and the relationship seemed like a nearly complete disappointment. During the upswing, Brice would say that Peter's love—love that Brice acknowledged—was equivocal and conditional, and that Peter had never expressed his love in ways that Brice wanted him to.

"And what would that be, how do you want him to express his love?" I asked.

"I want him to make me feel loved and *desired.*"

"But another person can only love and desire you, he cannot make you feel that way. You've told me many times that when Peter tries to embrace you, you pull away. Are you allowing him to express his love and desire for you? Are you *accepting* that?"

"*That* kind of embrace," Brice responded angrily, "is not what I want. And I don't need you to tell me this is all my fault."

In this "parallel process," Brice had rejected my attempt at a clarifying interpretation, just as he rejected Peter's efforts to express love. As with his mother, the hugs left Brice feeling only further depleted and worthless, and my interpretation had affected him similarly. He experienced my question as an accusation, an assault like his mother's and Peter's embraces. Brice and I were eventually able to discuss what he wanted from Peter, and it sounded like an adult relationship that met an infant's instinctual expectation of unconditional, perfect love and care. The problem is that no infants receive perfect love and care, and no adults—or very, very few—experience truly unconditional love from another adult. Brice's fantasy of a relationship that would finally and forever make him feel valuable was making any possible, real-world relationship feel intolerably deficient. No relationship could make him feel the way he wanted to feel about himself. Only he could do that.[4]

Brice's isolation and the impossibility of any relationship during his painful, adolescent years left him with only fantasy to retreat to. The fantasy of a relationship not only provided a safe haven, it gave him something that a real relationship could never give. The fantasy relationship could never be disappointing because it was entirely his own creation, and it could never be taken from him because it was entirely his. Fantasies are not subject to the real-life laws of physics, and they thus excel in supporting bootstrap operations. In inventing his fantasy relationship, Brice could also feel that he was a person who deserved it. It was thus not only the fantasy of a relationship, but also a fantasy about himself as the person he felt he was not, but wanted to be. The fantasy helped him feel perfectly lovable and desirable to an extent that no one really is, and that no real relationship could possibly confirm. Fantasies are almost always fantasies of perfection, which is an important reason we have them. Unfortunately, fantasies of perfection often leave us inattentive to the possible and actual. From Peter, Brice received much more than he was often able to recognize.[5]

Early-life fantasy about relationships has another curious twist, one that often carries problematically into adult life. The adolescent's hopelessness about relationships first motivates conscious fantasies of idealized relationships that then become fantasies of idealized relationships that have been had *and then lost*. The prefantasy hopelessness is incorporated into the idealized fantasy itself. Because the idealized relationship has become a relationship lost, the man is more in pursuit of the loss than of the relationship itself. Men who consistently court other men and then back away are sometimes expressing this transformation.[6] In 2001, I first understood this process in writing a note to myself following a weekly session with Lou. Then thirty-three years old, Lou had never experienced an ongoing relationship with another man and was afraid he never would. Most of what Lou and I talked about was relationships, which Lou felt he had been fervently working to accomplish since his teenage years. At the time of my session note—here reproduced almost verbatim—Lou was simultaneously dating two men, Andrew and Richard.

> Lou feeling that he is "ratcheting up to a new crisis" in the unbearability of having Andrew gone for 3 weeks; his dissatisfaction with Richard, feeling depressed when Richard is around because he doesn't need Lou the way Andrew does; Lou's conviction that his current emptiness will be interminable, just as it felt interminable before he came out and had sex; filling that emptiness with fantasy; fantasy as idealization and then actually pursuing the idealization rather than Andrew himself; Lou *idealizing even the loss of Andrew, as if the relationship is more about the loss than its actuality*; the longing experienced by gay men, the discouragement about it; the expansion of every current loss into everything his life is about, just as it was in adolescence; is he trying to lose me too with his erratic behavior (missed appointments, etc.)? Lou ends the hour by asking me to tell him what his "options" are.

In thinking about Lou and his feelings, I realized that we feel loss not only about relationships we have had and lost, but also about relationships we have never had. For Lou, loss had become his sense of what a relationship was, and like many other men, he pursued not relationships, but the feelings of loss that relationships aroused. Because his initial adolescent fantasy about relationships was now almost purely a fantasy about losing them, Lou pursued the romance of loss. If the loss was painful, it was also a predictable, loyal companion that he had long lived with and now trusted. The loss of relationships had become Lou's emotional sustenance, even as he still consciously held the idea that he was actually pursuing relationships.

## WAYS THAT GAY RELATIONSHIPS WORK

Not that you would know it from the idea of "the homosexual" or conventional, socially constructed models, but relationships between two men are, in many ways, like those between any two human beings. Some are wonderful, some are good, some are good enough, and some languish in unspoken tragedy. All relationships are too emotionally complex to completely decipher, and gay relationships carry the obvious, additional burden of widespread disapproval. But gay relationships potentially offer at least three benefits that distinguish them from heterosexual alliances. They may draw on a "male camaraderie" that is rooted in both the inborn and acculturated male sensibility; they are relationships between two men, one or both of whom may possess a more inclusive blend of male and female sensibilities; and they offer sexual possibilities—and, thus, a breadth of emotional expression—that are often unavailable to conventional heterosexual couples. Gay relationships are usually an inside-out process that helps surmount the limitations of the outside-in, socially constructed relationship that would dictate expected and "appropriate" feelings and behavior. In today's American society, one man simply loving another is still an inside-out form of life.

Male camaraderie is often beneficial for gay male relationships, even if it has roots in the limiting and problematic "pure-male" sensibility. One need only think of a football team to conjure up pure-male camaraderie, or, more on topic, the element of male camaraderie in the relationship of Morris and Billy, whose blended sensibilities were introduced in chapter 1. Their solution to "who gets to be on the bottom" was to arm wrestle, an obviously male solution to a distinctly unconventional male dilemma. But male camaraderie and a "gay camaraderie" are not mutually exclusive, at least in gay relationships: the sensibility that allowed Morris to experience Billy as "a beautiful, sweet, gentle woman" had been accomplished through an expression of male sensibility, a contest of physical strength. Both kinds of camaraderie are bonding, and Morris and Billy were bonded in both their conventional male strengths and the important strength of "feminine" sensibility, without which intimate relationships are invariably problematic.

Most men have a mutual understanding of one another that I am not sure is possible between men and women. The two genders—significantly as a consequence of the developmental gender split described in chapter 1—so often find each other indecipherable. After thirty years of conducting psychoanalysis, Freud himself is reputed to have once asked, "What does a woman want?" A 2016 Google search seemed to confirm the ongoing bewilderment of both genders: the entry *What do women want?* provided 1.07 billion results in 0.35 seconds, the first of which was headlined "Listen Up, Fellas, Here's What Women Really Want." A search on *What do men want?* provided 1.03 billion results; and a search on *What do gay men want?*, a meager 178 million. Notably, the searches on men and women both returned results that largely informed men about what women wanted *from* them, and vice versa. Exploration of who men and women *are* was largely absent in the responses. The results for gay men were much more about the discovery of what it means to be gay, rather than what a gay man might want from another. On the whole, gay men have thought a great deal about who they are and already know who other men are and what they want.

Because gay men in relationships usually share not only biological sex, but some variable measure of both inborn and acculturated male sensibility, gay relationships can suffer some of the limitations that a pure-male sensibility introduces into any intimate relationship. The emotional opacity of pure-male sensibility interferes with the expression of intimacy and mutual support, the conscious clarification of problems, and the mediation of solutions. Women—and men with some internalization of women's sensibilities—are thus usually necessary for any enduring, intimate relationship. In the polarizing acculturation of the traditional gender split, men are taught to do things only indirectly for others—for example, by providing economic support. They are expected to go *out* into the world and are taught to respond to emotional conflict with withdrawal, denial, anger, or aggression. An intimate relationship between two men does not even exist when both are relating through withdrawal, denial, anger, or aggression. When such relationships endure, they are largely built on the bond of conflict, which is, unfortunately, the only way some people—especially men—know how to experience connection. Think again of football.

As adults, we continue to grapple with the feelings of helplessness and dependency that are first necessarily experienced in infancy and childhood. Struggles over the balance of power are thus significant in most adult relationships. In gay male relationships, the struggle also exists, but its resolutions are often somewhat different from those of heterosexuals. How two men structure power in the relationship cannot—and need not—rely on traditional gender roles, which have done little good for anyone; just as gay men must invent themselves, they must invent their relationships. One of the important inventions is—to borrow, and slightly reconstruct, a concept from the family therapist Jay Haley—to find some balanced integration of *complementarity* and *symmetry*.[7] It is this balance that provides stability and bonding within any relatively happy, intimate relationship. In complementarity, partners balance power by complementing each other's differences; in symmetry, they find balance in equity. This "two-type" balance can be particularly difficult for young men, who, in their twenties, are often still struggling for an adequate sense of autonomy and identity. In my therapy work with gay couples, I am inclined to think of "successful" relationships as a balance between two conflicting requirements: mutual support for each man's individual needs and personal growth; and the fundamental relationship requirement of being emotionally bonded and together. The former relies significantly on complementarity, the latter on symmetry, and a relatively happy relationship allows some measure of both. For young men, the need for personal growth often overpowers the capacity for togetherness, which becomes more available with greater maturity and a more assured sense of self. For men of all ages, the balance between two men requires invention, and invention is most needed and available in unconventional, emotionally constructed relationships.

A useful balance within gay relationships is often expressed partly through sexual practices. To meet the emotional needs of both men, Morris and Billy explicitly pursued symmetry in their versatile sexual life. In some other gay relationships, sex more clearly expresses complementarity, in which each man is largely the top or the bottom: a partner who holds the balance of power outside sex may be more sexually passive and receptive. Nonsexual matters also offer a range of solutions to the balance of complementarity and symmetry. If an older partner holds the authority of age, experience, or money, the younger partner may balance that with special skills, greater experience with gay life, physical appeal, or the simple fact of greater height or physical strength.

## SEX

Money and sex are both often experienced as measures of power and control and are the two common relationship hot spots for both gay and straight couples. Gay men's forced adolescent segregation of sex from relationships, the stigma attached to "homosexual sex," the conventional acculturation of males, and the inborn nature of male sexuality are four influences that conspire to create sexual issues for gay couples. The most common issue is probably the waning or loss of sexuality within the relationship, which, contrary to popular perception, is most often initiated in longer-term heterosexual relationships by the male. Males, straight and gay, withdraw from sex for many reasons, but one of the most common is fear of humiliation for not being able to "perform." For gay couples, the male sensibility that motivates withdrawal is likely to be more or less doubled. As a result, the incidence of diminished sexuality is probably higher among gay couples than straight ones.

Diminishing sex within gay relationships can follow from other issues also seen in heterosexual relationships, including broadly based power struggles, anger, and emotional withholding. But in gay relationships, diminishing or absent sex also often has distinct developmental roots: gay adolescents and young men are often limited to sexual lives that allow only highly eroticized, libidinal "sport sex" that is focused on novelty, orgasm, and demonstrations of prowess and performance. Such sex largely excludes—often even forbids—the expression of emotional intimacy, which is precisely what is needed to sustain sex in longer-term relationships. Ongoing relationships require at least some transition from pure sport sex to "relationship sex" that remains erotically engaging, but also communicates intimacy, affection, and attachment. Sex *can* be one of many ways that two men share their lives.

The transition from pure sport sex to something more emotionally inclusive is often difficult for those with a more purely male sensibility. A beautiful, potent body engaged in hot sex with the beautiful body of an idealized stranger is what all men, but particularly gay men, have been acculturated to believe is the definition of "good sex." Long-term partners usually know way too much about each other—and each other's imperfect bodies—for either to buy the "I'm hot, you're hot, let's fuck" approach that characterizes most gay adolescent, and much adult singles, sex. When the male sensibility cannot make *any* transition from pure sport sex to relationship sex, both gay and straight couples experience a "loss of sexual interest." Against this loss, straight couples often have an advantage: they have some measure of feminine sensibility in the game, a sensibility much more attuned to emotional expression.

Among gay men I have worked with in therapy, those with no previous sexual experience with women almost invariably have more difficulty understanding the idea of relationship sex. In contrast to the feminine sensibility, the male sensibility appears to have an inclination, probably partly inborn, for sex split off from emotional connection. In split-off sex, an enduring erection and an orgasm with profuse ejaculate appear to be the measures of "success." These measures—based on the ridiculous presumption that involuntary erection and ejaculation are a personal accomplishment—make sex a test of physical performance. Even as connection and self-discovery are often the unconscious motivations, the performance model drives most adolescent sex, and it is the conspicuous theme of most pornography. For both gay and straight boys, Internet pornography now offers an easily available correspondence degree with a major in sex, from a third-rate faculty with a poorly conceived curriculum. When gay men meet after graduation, they quite naturally share what they learned in school. Despite similar education, straight adolescents do have a developmental advantage over gay boys. Straight boys are clearly in training for relationships with girls, not simply sex. With girls who are "relationship material," straight boys are expected to *act* as if sex, feelings, and relationships were somehow related. Thus the transition from sport sex to relationship sex is something many straight boys have at least anticipated during adolescence, perhaps only as an obligation to the unintelligible nature of women.

In contrast, the gay adolescent is usually taught that gay sex is "bad and dirty," and he is rarely in training for any relationships he wants. The inclusion of sex in relationships or relationships in sex feels like forbidden cross-contamination. This training—in keeping sex and feelings separated from each other—supports a conventional male sensibility that can be difficult to unlearn. The training easily extends into adult life, and even men with a highly developed gay sensibility—which includes some feminine sensibility—still often carry unconscious feelings that they must protect primary relationships from the contamination of sex. They protect their partners from the degradation that sex would inflict, and they protect themselves from being seen as sexually emotional beings by the men with whom they live their daily lives. With purely erotic sport sex unsustainable—and unacceptable—within a familiar, long-term relationship, men sometimes find themselves sexually aroused only by objectified, idealized strangers who would not hold sex against them and would not, themselves, be degraded by sex. Sport sex detached from feelings is what the idealized sexual object is for.

Human beings are among the two or three most sexually active of the mammalian species and are certainly the biggest blabbermouths. Nevertheless, we have extraordinary difficulty *talking* about sex. In the United States, we live in perhaps the most erotophobic, sexually shamed society in the Western world, and the consequences are immensely destructive. Because gay men have been forcibly defined by sex—again, the idea of *the homosexual*—they have less reluctance than most to talk about sex *with me*, but they still have difficulty with intimate partners, with whom they most need to talk. I have seen innumerable gay couples in therapy who were having little or no sex and were both troubled by that; but they had never had anything but the most fleeting, superficial conversation about what is often the elephant in the relationship room. In working with couples, I thus often initiate a discussion of their sexual lives by asserting what ought to be obvious and would be in a less fearful, more perceptive society: human lives are naturally erotic, and sex is one of the important and pleasurable ways we share and communicate. "If you share a hike in the hills, a movie, a meal, or a bed," I sometimes ask, "why not your bodies?" Many gay men have never heard such an obvious affirmation of human sexuality. Many have never allowed themselves to even think such a thing.

Sometimes a couple's sexual life mutually diminishes, but more often than not, one of the two would like to have sex and repeatedly tries, but is too often rebuffed. The desirous partner finally abandons the effort, in feelings of rejection, undesirability, hurt, and anger. His rejecting partner retreats still further in resentment of the expectations and often-unconscious feelings of failure and guilt. The hurt, anger, and guilt are displaced into other conflicts—often about money and decision-making authority—but the sexual issue itself remains undiscussed. Other expressions of affection—simple ones, such as touching, hugging, and kissing—are avoided in all but their most perfunctory forms because they threaten to provoke the entire cycle of sexual approach, rebuff, hurt, anger, failure, and guilt. As a result, the two men often drift apart emotionally, not only because they do not have the shared bond of sex, but because they must maintain distance to keep the unspoken sexual issue unspoken. If the anger and guilt are not too destructive, gay couples can often sustain a male camaraderie that assists the relationship—but not always. A majority of gay couples who come to therapy because they are "fighting too much and thinking of splitting up" have not had sex in a long time. But they rarely connect the issues.

As with all couples, gay male relationships do not *require* an ongoing sexual relationship. Many relatively asexual gay relationships are happy enough without it: two men live together, love each other, and find support and companionship in their arrangement. Sometimes, one or both seek sex outside the relationship, *one* more often than not. Unfortunately, some gay men also feel shame about asexual primary relationships. They feel they "should" be having sex and experience their asexuality as a confirmation that there is, indeed, something "unnatural" or wrong with gay relationships—or at least theirs. They also often feel shame about outside sex, which in America is rarely an acknowledged part of conventional, socially constructed relationships. With no a priori purpose of helping gay couples initiate or reinstate sex, the question I usually ask is *why* they do not have sex together. More often than not, their history reveals that early in the relationship the two men were sexual, but the sex waned, sometimes rather quickly. But why, as they got to know each other more deeply and intimately, was this natural human expression of sharing, affection, intimacy, and bonding progressively excluded?

Two answers are typically offered by one or both members of the couple. They are "bored" with the sex they have, and one or both are "no longer attracted" to the other. (The latter explanation is almost always revealed without the other partner present.) Both of these issues—but particularly the latter—are experienced as indecipherable, autonomous, and unchangeable internal facts. In truth, both boredom and a lack of attraction *can* be addressed, but not simply with the revival of sport sex. Sport sex relies on two elements that no longer-term relationship can reliably provide: novelty, which would fend off boredom, and an idealized partner who would thus be more readily experienced as "attractive." Complete novelty and idealization are usually possible only with strangers.[8]

## SEXUAL INTEREST AND THE STORY OF LESTER AND BILL

One of the most striking things about couples stuck in the conundrum of desired-but-diminished or absent sex is that they have lost the capacity for play—a capacity that all children have, but many adults have lost. The idea of "boredom" is obfuscating because if it alone were the reason that partners were not having sex, they would simply do something interesting, something novel and engaging—something playful. Novelty and play are intuitive, and when we cannot play, something is actively, if unconsciously, obstructing it. Some gay couples with waning sexual lives have told me that their sex consists largely in watching pornography together, while separately masturbating. This is a kind of sport sex stimulated by others' sport sex, an often pleasurable, shared activity that expresses male camaraderie. But within adult relationships, it is not quite mutual play; it is the enactment of a substitute for mutual play that is as likely to distance the two men as to support their connection and intimacy. It has its unconscious purpose: the avoidance of true mutual play allows men—and teenage boys, who commonly engage in such activity—to conceal feelings from each other that might otherwise be revealed.

By its very nature, play is spontaneous and thus requires an acceptance of uncertain outcomes. *Sexual* play involves both an uncertain internal—emotional—experience, and the possible revelation of that experience to another. With a stranger who knows nothing about us, and about whom we know nothing but our fantasy, such emotional self-revelation often feels safer. The interaction thus provides an opportunity to both experience and reveal feelings we normally repress or conceal. If the encounter does not feel safe enough, we can always feign responses that a stranger accepts but a longtime partner would easily perceive as false. The partner already knows us well and, we sometimes fear, will use our self-revelations or emotional vulnerabilities against us. To avoid that risk, we avoid play.

If children have the advantage of intuitive, natural play, adults *could* have another advantage: a mature self-confidence resilient enough to allow the uncertainty of play. Sexually, young men sometimes strike a balance between the two, for they remain closer to early-life play, even as they have developed some measure of maturity and resilience. As men age further, self-consciousness can begin to constrict resilience, as it did for thirty-four-year-old Lester, whom I first saw for therapy in 2014. Earlier in his relationship with Bill, they had sex often, but after seven years together Lester told me they rarely did, "maybe three or four times a year if we're lucky, and it's usually no good."

"It would be helpful if you and Bill could be more *playful* with each other," I said.

"What does that mean?" Lester countered, with discomfort in his voice and bewilderment on his face.

"I'm thinking of *fun*—emotionally expressive and spontaneous *play*."

"I have no idea how we'd do that."

"How about, while he's standing at the stove scrambling eggs, you walk up behind him and lick him on the back of the neck."

Lester looked stunned. "You're kidding!"

"No, I'm serious. Why would you not do that to a man you love?"

"*Lick* him on the neck? While he's making breakfast?"

"Why not? Sex, in part, is just adult play, or it *can* be. When you two were still having good sex, I imagine that licking went on. Why is this suggestion so surprising?"

"There's a big difference between sex and licking Bill on the neck while he's cooking."

"Which is what?"

"I don't know. In sex it's expected, but the thing you're describing—he wouldn't expect it and I'd look foolish. Childish. I would feel stupid."

"Children know how to play, and you haven't really forgotten. Would you try playing in some way—an idea of your own—and pay attention to what feelings come up? It would be helpful."

"I'll think about it."

"What does *I'll think about it* mean? 'Probably not'?"

"Probably."

As Lester and I continued our weekly meetings, I realized that he was, indeed, very uncomfortable with the simple playful gesture I had suggested. He had revealed his emotional life to me, and he had a developed gay sensibility. But beginning early in childhood, he had also learned to conceal feelings—particularly "gay-looking feelings"—by avoiding spontaneous, playful behavior. Lester had always felt uncomfortable emotionally revealing himself to Bill, and early in the relationship Bill did not know Lester well enough to detect the restraint. It was primarily Lester who had begun retreating from sex, and when I pointed out his emotional restraint when he did have sex, he said, "I have to admit that I once thought sex was about feelings." But he had little actual experience with emotional-expressive sex, and he had always been uncomfortable with what it might reveal, both of himself and of Bill. Sex with Bill had always been largely an exercise in trying to present the person Lester imagined Bill wanted him to be: mature, strong, and "masculine," though Lester did not often feel like any of those things. In fact, Bill had never expressed such expectations, and I told Lester that I thought they were more a projection of his feelings about himself than an accurate sense of what Bill expected. Lester's capacity to play with Bill seemed hog-tied by a confusing and tangled interplay of misperceived expectations, containment, and posturing.

With almost-exclusive experience in purely erotic sport sex before the relationship, Lester and Bill had constructed a sexual life that was emotionally unexpressive and disconnected, and—now that the purely erotic component had waned with familiarity—simply boring. The sport sex they had both known *had* been a kind of play, but a relatively rote, constricted male play that was more about performance than emotional connection and affection—think, yet again, of football. When I first suggested it, Lester had thought of spontaneously licking Bill on the back of the neck as a violation of that male protocol: it would express a perfectly normal need to give and receive affection that he was reluctant to acknowledge in himself, to reveal to Bill, and, probably, to discover in Bill. As Lester put it, "Bill's and my idea of *play* is Monopoly." Like their sexual life, Monopoly had rules, and the rules allowed them to reveal much less of themselves. My persistent suggestion was that they do something more interesting, and to do that, they would have to allow play and its uncertainty. They would have to be willing to let go of the idea of a conscious performance, express themselves spontaneously, and then work through what they had discovered in themselves and revealed to each other. Without this change, their sexual relationship would remain "boring" and possibly allow their entire relationship to slowly drift apart.

## ATTRACTION AND THE LOSS OF ATTRACTION

During our work together, Lester had mentioned only in passing the other often-mentioned impediment to sex within ongoing relationships: loss of attraction. Both attraction and its loss are usually experienced as somehow-autonomous, immutable feelings, often elusively explained with words such as *type*, *chemistry*, or *spark*. All three are certainly parts of the human experience, but as often used, the terms provide an incomplete understanding of attraction, and particularly the *loss* of attraction in otherwise bonded and loving relationships. A *type* is often about physical appearance, but it sometimes includes a certain "type of person"—an intellectual nerd, a kind man, or a sports hero—that the physical presentation suggests. (Attractions to types are often tied to associations learned from early-life experience, sexual or otherwise, and the connection is often unconscious.) The ideas of chemistry and spark seem rooted in something broader—a sense of the total person—rather than just the physical appearance. It is this broader idea of attraction that suggests something important about the loss of attraction: it is rarely a simple loss of physical attraction, a single brain synapse somehow suddenly and irrevocably disconnected. Loss of attraction is connected to a shift in other feelings. In this construction, the loss of physical attraction is only one result of some mix of conscious and unconscious feelings that *can* be understood, and sometimes changed.

The feelings that can influence a loss of physical attraction are legion: boredom in sex with a familiar partner; a learned need to objectify sexual partners; long-standing, unconscious feelings about particular physical characteristics; negative nonsexual feelings about the partner; negative feelings about sex itself; and negative feelings about oneself.[9] But the loss of attraction with someone we know and love is almost always emotionally complex. A therapy patient, Tom, told me that he continued to love, but had lost sexual attraction to, his partner, Farley. When Tom told me that Farley had "gained at least fifty pounds," I simply accepted Tom's stated aversion to "fat men," but I also asked why Farley had gained so much weight. Tom told me that Farley had lost his job two years earlier and had become depressed. "Farley spends his time lying morosely on the sofa, eating ice cream. He even sometimes spends the night there."

"He's withdrawn from you," I said.
"Exactly. But what's that got to do with his being fat?"
"How do you feel about his withdrawal?"
"I'm furious. And I'm disgusted by his passivity."
"Feelings like those could make Farley *feel* sexually unattractive. You may not find weight attractive, but you tell me you still love him, and if you *make love* to Farley, you make love to a person, not a body. You're telling me that it's the body that's the whole problem."

As we worked on the feelings behind the loss of attraction, Tom realized that his feelings for physical types—he liked lithe men, which Farley had once been—were the smaller part of what obstructed Tom's sexual desire in the relationship. Helpfully, Tom had "a very strange dream" in which he walked into the bathroom, saw Farley standing in the shower, and was shocked to see that Farley had not male genitals, but a vagina. In discussing the dream, Tom realized that Farley's passivity and weight both feminized him. Farley had lost his male body definition, and the weight created a literal barrier that held Tom off physically, just as Farley's depression held Tom off emotionally. Farley's "lazy life on the sofa" expressed more of a desire for ice cream than for Tom, and Tom felt hurt and abandoned, and that made him angry. Consciously, Tom had experienced all of these feelings as a "loss of attraction."

When we deeply know and love someone, he *feels* beautiful, and it is a normal—if inhibitable—human response to feel physical attraction. If we do not recognize that feeling as sexual attraction, we must sometimes reconstruct our idea of what sex is. When, with time and familiarity, a partner is experienced as a whole person, sex with him can no longer be *purely* erotic sex. A pure history of sport sex leaves many men with three legacies that can be problematic in long-term relationships: they become accustomed to objectifying other men as sexual objects; they are familiar with only the purely erotic component of sex; and they learn to "split off" sex from relationships and from their day-to-day lives. Lester no longer experienced Bill as sexually attractive because the erotic component of their sex had waned, and they had segregated sex from the rest of their lives. Like their Monopoly evenings, sex was a discrete *diversion* from the relationship, rather than a natural, fluid extension of the communication and companionship they routinely shared. This was one reason that "sex" in the kitchen—even if it was only an affectionate lick—was so unimaginable to Lester. The very idea conflated day-to-day life with something that was "supposed" to be both discrete and discreet. If the discrete component arose from Lester's experience with sport sex, which has nothing to do with feelings or relationships, the need for discretion was spawned by our culture: an erotophobic and shaming society, in which sex is treated like defecation, which is never spoken of and occurs in its own special room—the so-called bathroom, which is most often used for its toilet—behind closed doors. Presumably, no one knows what goes on in the special room or has to think about it—but everyone does, because everyone uses it. In Lester's family, "sex was never once mentioned—by anyone." After much conversation, Lester was no longer shocked by the idea of "sex in the kitchen," but he remained reluctant to implement it. He told me that he had had many sexual experiences with other men in what he called "ABC sex"—sex in alleys, baths, and cars—but that with Bill, the rare sex they did have was reserved for the bedroom. None of his ABC experiences involved relationships, or even friendships, and with Bill, Lester continued to segregate sex. Like ABC sex, their sex was not on the continuum of their lives together, it had its time and place. "Sex has nothing to do with the rest of our lives," Lester told me.

"And *that*," I responded, "is precisely my point."

From adolescence, Lester had experienced sex, not as communication with another person, but as a physical behavior with another body. This is a male inclination anyway, but now that Lester had not a body but a whole person on his hands, he did not know how to think about sex, and he needed to reconstruct his idea of what it was. The reconstruction of ABC sex into relationship sex would not provide the kind of transcendent, blindingly white-hot sexual experience he experienced in his young, ABC days. But it would also not abandon erotic pleasure; it would be sex that integrated that pleasure into a physical expression of sharing, companionship, intimacy, and love, all of which Lester and Bill both felt and valued.

"It would be more like," I suggested to Lester, "having dinner, seeing a film, having coffee and cake afterward to discuss the film, and then going back to the car for a blow job in the parking lot—all just for the fun of it. You and Bill would do all this together, and the evening would be meaningful. When we spend such an evening with someone, it is an evening with another person we value and love, not an evening with someone's body. Sex is a natural part of such an evening."

As I spoke those words to Lester, I had another, unvoiced thought: when a lover dies, it is less the loss of the physical presence that feels so impossible, than the loss of the *mind*—the entire, unimaginably rich internal life that had become a seamless part of our own internal life. We had nurtured our shared mind with companionship and talk, and also with the metaphorical act of sharing our bodies. We had *entered* each other, in both senses of the idea. In such a relationship, we do not have sex, we make love in a private, two-person world that feels as large and timeless as the entire universe. *That* is relationship sex in its purest, most powerful expression, and we are fortunate, I thought, to find that other person once in a lifetime. "Lester," I said, "you and Bill would really benefit from reconstructing your sense of what sex *is*. You might find magic."

## A SONGBOOK FOR YOUNG MEN

How gay people experience their relationships is significantly influenced by how American society treats those relationships: today, gay men still live on the fringes of a heterosexist society that is only narrowly comprehending and supportive of emotionally intimate relations between men. Current public gay agendas suggest that marriage is the solution for this marginalization, even as the Pew Research Center reports that America has seen "decades of declining marriage rates," and that today the "share of American adults who have never been married [is] at an historic high."[10] One obvious explanation for a gay inversion of the larger social trend is the common gay adolescent experience of hopelessness about ever finding someone to love and be loved by. A legally binding marriage with socially defined expectations can feel as if it will finally allow the seemingly impossible to be real and permanent. Like many heterosexuals, gay men sometimes pursue marriage as a form of ownership that ensures "fidelity" and locks in a partner for life. But gay men *have* found good and enduring relationships without marriage, and we know that for millennia socially constructed marriages have been fraught with conflict, furtive and deceitful nonmonogamy, and acrimonious separations and divorce. So what else motivates gay people to marry?

Gay relationships *are* now most readily accepted and supported when dressed with the crown jewel of the heterosexual social plan, legal marriage. Society has famously bestowed rights, privileges, and protections on those wearing the jewel, and the *pragmatic* appeal of legal marriage is thus obvious. But why have gay agendas pushed for marriage, rather than the decoupling of marriage from rights and privileges for all citizens? And even with the lonely adolescent experience in mind, why *emotionally* would LGBT people want to participate in a heterosexual convention with such a problematic history, a convention that has also served as the standard against which gay lives have been stigmatized? These questions are important because, among all the rights and privileges gay communities have pursued over the last half century, legal marriage is the one aimed squarely at deconstructing and reconstructing gay relationships—and thus at the core of what it means to be gay and live a gay life.

Among gay men, the most often stated, nonpragmatic reason for marriage is simple and compelling: many couples wish to make a personal statement of commitment to each other—through participation in a social institution that has long stood as *the* icon of commitment. In taking mutual vows, men hope their relationships will feel more valuable to themselves, and—though not as often explicitly stated—less marginalized by others. Even as adults, a large majority—particularly those within stigmatized, marginalized groups—seek approval for their lives and hope that approval will find expression in acceptance and love. In June 2015 (shortly before the Supreme Court decision on gay marriage), the Human Rights Campaign (HRC) appealed for donations with the idea that marriage "in all 50 states" would allow gay people to "be welcomed in their communities as married couples."[11] The language suggests that the issue at hand is *others'* welcoming acceptance of gay relationships, but it only implies that marriage might allow gay people to feel differently about their own relationships. The implication relies on an unstated idea: if others held more esteem for gay relationships, then gay people could feel more esteem for them, too. More broadly and succinctly, gay people need others' esteem to feel esteem for themselves. Given human life as it is often lived and experienced, there is some truth in this idea; and with the beginning of a shift in American social values, the idea even offers some hope. But this is not the whole truth for gay people living in America today.

An outside-in approach to the development of self-esteem is necessarily how children grow: the esteem of adults is internalized by the child, providing a foundation upon which he slowly constructs a positive, internal sense of self. But for adults, the esteem of others is rarely adequate when the internal sense of self has been significantly injured by early-life stigmatization and shaming: there is no adequate, internal foundation of self-esteem on which external contributions can stand. Without that foundation, one is attempting to fill a bottomless hole that swallows the external esteem almost as quickly as it is delivered. Such a life requires an impossibly consistent flow of outside esteem and is a wobbling and too-vulnerable life: whenever the flow stops, the internal life collapses again. Such a deficit of self-esteem must be explored and changed internally, and legally mandated rights and privileges—even with their obvious justice and longer-term possibilities—will rarely, by themselves, accomplish that end. As adults, those with difficult early-life experience must usually work for a reasonable measure of inside-out self-acceptance.

Even if legal marriage were to "legitimize" gay lives and relationships in the eyes of society and gay men themselves, another issue stands between gay men and truthful conventional marriage: as traditionally defined, marriage is inconsistent with much of gay male life as it is actually lived. Marriage is a binding legal agreement that specifies commitment to hell-or-high-water, lifelong, monogamous relationships that are traditionally focused on the breeding and rearing of children. It is no coincidence that within six months of the Supreme Court decision favoring gay marriage, the Human Rights Campaign made "the right to adopt a child in their home state" its number one agenda item.[12] Elementary school bullying—which is a primary source of the inadequate self-esteem that outside-in esteem will not repair—was number two on the list. Job security against firing for being gay—probably on the Monday following Saturday's celebrated and publicized wedding—was number three. Such an agenda is heavily biased in favor of older men. Some older men *do* want children, and they should clearly have the right to adopt; but early-life bullying and job security are much more immediate and critical issues, particularly for gay children and young men, who are the future of gay life in America. For many younger men—and many older ones, too—the HRC's old-man agenda feels like pandering for acceptance by attempting to weave gay lives into an often-meaningless heterosexual social fabric. If older gay men wish to adopt and mentor, the young gay men ignored by today's community agendas would be a valuable place to start. Young men must know that, even as they live in increasingly conventionalized communities, they will not be marginalized by their own communities for leading "unconventional" gay lives. In the pursuit of acceptance through conformity, stigmatized communities too easily marginalize their own nonconformers, and the persistent celebration of marriage as the crowning achievement of gay people in America is a step in that direction.

Were it not for developmentally imposed adolescent hopelessness about relationships, the pragmatic benefits, and the fight against social marginalization, it seems unlikely that many gay people would even consider marriage as a model for their lives. Everyone already knows that half of all marriages fail, and it is likely that half of the other half should be mercifully terminated. But what are the alternatives for gay people? As a gay man and a psychologist, I know that the idea of anyone independently deciding on the form and content of his life and relationships is an idea more easily suggested than implemented. Among social animals, the outsider's default aspiration is to be on the inside; and for the *highly* social human animal, assimilation through marriage—with the actual construction or mere appearance of a "normal life"—has obvious appeal. Gay men have usually grown up as outsiders, and outsiders often hope to present themselves as "just like" insiders and receive the benefits and approval that insiders grant other insiders. But psychologically, the question remains: Are men who fall in love with other men and get married just like heterosexual men in conventional marriages? Both gay lives and gay relationships have a long, necessarily independent history of improvisation and invention, largely born of a gay sensibility. Without traditional social models to draw on, gay men have had to discover ways to be themselves in a manner that straight men with a ready-made life plan never have. For gay men, married or not, the task of discovery persists.

The benefits of improvisation and invention are considerable: they allow us to *be* and *live* as ourselves. Gay lives and relationships are often more expressive of the natural, inborn range of human feelings and experience than conventional marriage models prescribe or allow—for men and for women. Relationships between gay men—human, good, and valuable relationships—are not only expressions of traditional romantic love, they are also often fraternal, paternal, non-monogamous or polyamorous, and communal, and they are often thoughtfully and honestly so. Society—and some gay men—critically judge such unconventional inventions and use them as evidence that gay relationships do not work—even as the same inventions are non-explicitly or deceitfully implemented in many heterosexual unions. The improvisations and inventions of gay male couples are obviously not, in themselves, problematic or pathological; they are simply inconsistent with the *stated* terms of conventional marriage. The useful measure of success for gay relationships must not be how society experiences, but how gay men experience, their lives together—how relationships do or do not support the happiness, satisfaction, and growth of those involved.

Gay men crafting their lives and relationships must try to reconstruct one important principle that society and its conventional relationships have persistently distorted. This is the principle of *fidelity* as honesty and truth. Fidelity is not about the appearance or reality of monogamy, or guarantees of lifelong love that no one can honestly make. Fidelity—the real fidelity that makes relationships important and humanly decent—is simply about being truthful. When a relationship does not provide something one partner needs, is otherwise in difficulty, or clearly no longer works, fidelity is respectfully saying this and empathetically talking it through. If gay people are to live *their* lives, it will not be by mimicking a society that only accepts relationships that follow its rules—rules that it does not actually honor. *That* society has insisted that its love is somehow better or more real than that of gay people, which is an obvious untruth. *That* society—fearful that in others' freedom it will see its own limitations, deceptions, or envy—has demonstrated prohibitions and hatred for unconventional forms of bonding and love that have persisted for millennia against all odds.

Some gay men do truly desire conventionally defined marriages; others need them for acceptance and approval or assurance
of ownership; others dismiss marriage as irrelevant to their lives. One
consequence of this newly possible diversity is that gay communities
today feel less coherent. They *are* less coherent, but this suggests
growth, not fragmentation—but only if gay men do not marginalize
one another. The early years of the Mattachine Society and "homosexual rights," the post-Stonewall Gay Liberation movement, and the
early epidemic all fostered a coherence within gay communities that
was significantly formed around fights against active oppression or
emotional and physical death. This is the kind of "forced coherence"
that beleaguered minorities often experience, but it is misleading. For
gay men, those three historical periods created many strange bedfel-
lows, men who, in any regard other than their fight against a common
enemy, would have found little of interest in one another. If communities of gay people today have evolved into something more diverse—
and the diversity is allowed and supported—all the better. The
married Smiths, living with their two adopted children in a Chelsea
rooftop condo, have never had much in common with the Radical
Faeries in rural Tennessee—other than societal oppression and the
slaughter of an epidemic. Today, they have less of both enemies, and
less to unite them.

So-called gay communities in America have always been more defined by their outsiderness than by the diverse characteristics of their
insiders. Even as gay men share many feelings—including, of course,
the famous "homosexual feeling"—there has never been "a gay community" in any emotional or relational sense. I have spoken with
innumerable young men who grew up as outsiders and moved to San
Francisco's Castro in the hope of finding a sense of belonging in a large
outsider community. Many have been deeply disappointed, and many
live in loneliness and a new form of outsiderness, still hoping that "the
gay community" will take them in. Even as they wait, they also blame
themselves for somehow not making it happen, just as they blamed
themselves for their outsiderness when they were children and
adolescents.

Fortunately, the disappointed hopes of these young men is significantly a problem of scale, a problem rooted in the misperception that

an "American society" exists. America is not a coherent society or community, but an *idea* that leaves many Americans feeling like outsiders; and the communities in which young gay outsiders then seek belonging and insiderness—"the Castro," "West Hollywood," and "Chelsea"—are also just ideas. From within such gay male geographic communities, young men must find their own *real* communities of four, six, or eight devoted and enduring companions. *That* accomplishment is important and affirming, and everything a human life could hope for and need. The futures of young gay lives will not be transformed through assimilation into gay communities seeking seamless internal unity, or through assimilation into an often-ugly, contentious, and divisive American society. The transformation will happen when, one by one, each man discovers who *he* is and makes a life for himself that expresses that self-discovery. Gay lives will be diverse, but all will share one important aspect: they will be honest lives that stand on authentic self-acceptance.

When they were young, today's older gay men had no socially constructed models for their lives, unless they were willing to live largely false lives: "bachelor" lives or heterosexual married lives, often paralleled by secret lives that sustained adolescent histories of ultimately unfulfilling, surreptitious, and relationless sex. The alternative to a false life was an authentic, emotionally constructed life with another man that demanded discretion and secrecy, or indiscretion and the risk of painful marginalization. Today's young men have more choices, which is both an opportunity and a danger. In navigating this broader range of possibilities, young men have an advantage over older men: their emotional trajectories and lives are not yet codified, and their futures are almost entirely in front of them. Young people are curious and resilient, and even when emerging from adverse early-life experience, they hold a capacity for discovery and change. But in working with gay men in therapy for a third of a century, I am most struck by one great tragedy: in childhood, most have been handed a rule book of limitations to live by, rather than a songbook of possibilities. Young gay men *can* and must find ways to allow themselves to sing. All the diverse forms that true gay life has improvised constitute a special universe that should not be relinquished to meet the expectations of a pathological society. In

that universe lies something wonderful: men in love who have discovered themselves and, by their own invention, are among the
splendors of human life on earth. The life of Matthias Johnston—a
life I was fortunate to share—is such a story of discovery and self-
discovery, and I tell it to the best of my recollection in the following,
closing chapter.

# 8

# The Life and Times of Matthias Johnston

A day, considered as a span of time, period gone through. "God is
my witness," cries the knight, "never shall it be said to my reproach
    that,
for fear, I failed to leave by the door I entered."
                                    —Keith Waldrop, *The Not Forever*[1]

Almost from start to finish, Matthias Johnston's life was his own invention, and he would leave by the door he entered: by his own account, he was gay at the age of six, and it is certain that he died gay at
the age of sixty-seven. As a child and teenager, he survived abuse and
rejection, but with support from a handful of others, he forged a life
that was humanly intimate, artistically productive, and, above all else,
largely self-accepting and authentic. Matthias was always Matthias, a
fact I can attest to, for I knew him for fifty of his sixty-seven years. He
was one of the most courageous people I have known, and it sounds
too simple to say, but it is true: Matthias was gay, and he was a hero
for simply being and living as himself.

Born in Texas to fundamentalist parents descended from, in Matthias's telling, "dour Norwegian stock," he moved with his family to
Fairbanks, Alaska, when he was three months old. There he was raised
in an eight-foot-wide, forty-foot-long trailer with his older brother, Haakon, his mother and father, and his mother's beloved cat, to which
Matthias was profoundly allergic. His mother, Betty, was the intellect in
the family, but she was deeply disappointed in her own narrow and impoverished life—"narrower than the trailer we all squeezed past each

other in, and just as shabby," Matthias once told me. Betty survived on a diet of movie-star and true crime magazines, and although she never admitted it, Matthias was sure that she dreamed of being Lana Turner. This fantasy conveniently included both Hollywood stardom and murder: Johnny Stompanato, Turner's gangster boyfriend, was stabbed to death by Turner's teenage daughter, Cheryl, in the master bedroom of their Beverly Hills home. For Betty, the Lana Turner fantasy was thus encompassing and complete.

Matthias respectfully described his father as "a dolt" whose saving grace was that he rarely opened his mouth. He would occasionally bark a reprimand or demand, but he usually forgot his purpose a moment later. Matthias's brother, Haakon, was not bright like Matthias and their mother, he was more like the dolt. Haakon was terrified of life, particularly the emotional life that lived inside him, and he took it out on Matthias. Matthias had always felt that Haakon was "definitely gay," and when Haakon moved back to Texas at the age of twenty-nine, Matthias conjectured that Haakon had done it "to find cowboys to fuck." Instead—or perhaps in addition to sexual pursuits—Haakon opened a fundamentalist church of his own, and the enterprise quickly became a hugely successful television ministry, broadcast throughout the Western world. As Matthias would himself become a playwright, this was clearly a family with show business in its blood, if you discount the dolt and the cat.

Matthias's family was a very hostile place for a smart and precocious boy who dreamed only of other boys and realized he was gay at the age of six. While better than poor Cheryl's childhood, Matthias's was certainly in the running. There was the cat, with which he was trapped in a trailer hardly large enough for the cat alone, much less the five of them. He spent his childhood blowing his perpetually runny nose on dirty clothes from the laundry hamper because his father told Matthias he was wasting Kleenex if he used more than two a day. Matthias's father and Haakon mercilessly teased the obviously feminine Matthias—I have seen photographs, and he was an exceptionally delicate and beautiful child—and taunting peers in grammar and high school only made it worse. Matthias once told me that he had been beaten so many times by gangs of boys that the only thing that had saved him from multiple bone fractures was the heavy outdoor clothing he wore for the Alaskan winters. When I first met him as a seventeen-year-old, Matthias had a slightly crooked nose on his still-beautiful face, but for me, it only added to his presence and charm. *He* experienced it differently.

Behind her dreams of stardom and murder, Matthias's mother had a whole other hidden story. Betty was filled with shame. She had married a man from the wrong side of the tracks in Ropesville, Texas, and her parents were deeply disappointed in the direction her life was taking, and they let her know it in no uncertain terms. But it was worse than that: Betty was pregnant with Haakon before the wedding. With a hostile father, brother, and cat in the trailer, and bands of ruffians outside, as a young child Matthias had sought companionship and solace from his mother, but got it only sporadically. She was socially very self-conscious and would clean the trailer with disinfectant, rags, and Q-tips before any visitors—all women from her fundamentalist church—were allowed in. And she had a peculiar way of presenting the family to these God-fearing cronies. Betty introduced her husband and Haakon by name, and would then point to Matthias and say, "And this is our little artist." Judging by her extreme reaction when she finally realized that Matthias was gay, she had had little conscious awareness of this very obvious fact. She had always known that *something* was wrong, and she was as ashamed of Matthias as she was of herself, and Matthias knew it. Betty had more than shame; she had rage. In Matthias's telling, you could practically smell it in the confines of the trailer, even with the disinfectant. Without warning, she would every now and then unleash that rage on Matthias, but no one else. The little artist seemed clearly bound for something she had never allowed herself, and she was envious.

Matthias tried to find refuge from his living nightmare in books, writing, drawing, and painting, all of which only heightened the ignorant ire of his father and brother. Betty was secretly impressed, but never said so, because his obvious talent continually reconfirmed her feeling that Matthias was headed for something she would never have. By the time Matthias was fifteen, he had read all of Victor Hugo's novels, beginning with *Les Misérables*, which, precociously at age ten, he had retrieved from the Fairbanks library thinking it must be a story about a family living in a trailer. By the time he was sixteen, he had the almost-certain distinction of being the only person in Alaska who had read all ten volumes of the *Memoirs of Casanova*. And he had also worked his way through the entirety of *Remembrance of Things Past*, most of which he had not completely understood, though he *had* detected that he and Proust had something important in common. In his reading, writing, painting, and drawing, Matthias had created a completely private world, a world that took him out of the trailer and into a life that survived on the dreams he would eventually follow. His English teacher at school, Hortense Twain, had a soft spot for Matthias, and she encouraged and supported him with book suggestions, and small gifts of writing paper, watercolor pads, and paint sets. She was actively admiring and once told Matthias that she thought he was one of the best authors she had read since Mark Twain, who, she assured Matthias, was no personal relation to herself. Matthias, of course, already knew Mark Twain, front to back and top to bottom.

One night, Matthias told his family at dinner about a compliment Miss Twain had given him for a short story he had recently finished. Matthias's father pointed at him, looked at his wife, and fairly shouted, "What's the matter with this boy? He's *your* son." Matthias knew exactly what his father really meant and was terrified by the apparent discovery. He flushed with embarrassment and then started to cry. "And that's just the kind of girlie shit I'm talking about," his father continued, still shouting at Betty. Matthias ran to his bed at the front of the trailer, and as he rushed past, Haakon said under his breath, "It's about time you learned about pussy." Matthias lived almost entirely in his self-made, private world because he had to. It was within that world that he was working feverishly on his future, whether he knew it or not. "It's what kept me alive," he much later told me. "That and Hortense Twain." He kept all the fruit of his labors stacked in a cardboard book box under his bed, which was the only personal space he was allowed in the trailer. By the time he was sixteen, the box was ready to burst, and so was Matthias.

Three times, Matthias had thought about killing himself, the first time at the age of twelve. The night of his humiliation at dinner became the fourth time, four days after his sixteenth birthday on February 11, 1963. This was no empty threat or a "cry for help," because

Matthias knew exactly how he would do it. In the summer, the Chena River flowed right behind the family's trailer, and everyone in the neighborhood used it as a garbage dump for everything from kitchen scraps to broken lawn chairs and worn-out car tires. When the river froze during winter, it was still the dump, and the garbage would pile up, sometimes three or four feet high, before the thaw sank it or floated it downriver. On the coldest possible winter night, Matthias planned to crawl out onto the ice and hide under the piles of debris and freeze to death. Jack London had told him it would be euphoric and quick, and Matthias needed nothing more to recommend it. No one would find his body under the garbage, and in the thaw, he would sink or float away and be forever free of Alaska, and the horror of his family and schoolmates.

Though it was plenty cold enough, Matthias did not initiate his plan the night of the humiliating dinner. He had also been considering an alternative, one based on the advice and assistance of Miss Twain. She had told Matthias that he had "real talent," and that there were many possibilities in life. He *did* have dreams, and her ideas engaged him. Miss Twain thought Matthias would do better down in the Lower 48, maybe New York, or even San Francisco, and she quietly told him that one day after class. And Miss Twain told him how he could do that—*after* he graduated high school—and gave him a copy of the Fairbanks bus schedule, in belief that it would bolster his hope and get him through that last year at Fairbanks High. She also handed Matthias a plain, sealed envelope, with his name handwritten in fountain-pen ink on the front. Inside there were seven twenty-dollar bills. "You need to pay for the bus ticket," she said, "and have a little left over to get started. It's all I can afford. I hope it's enough." Matthias thanked Miss Twain and promised he would finish school and keep the schedule and envelope in the box under his bed. But the night of the horrible dinner, one more year felt completely impossible, and Matthias realized that he had to break his promise to the only person in the world who liked him and had shown him kindness.

Matthias had always been an outsider to his own life, an exotic tropical bird swept into a cold, hostile landscape by a quirk of the jet stream. He was freezing to death in a hateful world of abuse, fear, humiliation, and shame. The trailer felt as if it were shrinking daily, and the wretched nineteen-year-old cat had still not died. After school let out for the summer preceding his senior year, and five months before the Kennedy assassination in Dallas, Matthias implemented Miss Twain's plan instead of his own. At 3:30 a.m. on June 6, 1963, Matthias left a brief unaddressed note on the kitchen table telling his family that he was leaving and would not be coming back, and warning them not to look for him. *If you locate me, I will never let you bring me back here, no matter what,* the note concluded, and he signed it *M.* Under the note he placed a sealed envelope addressed to *Miss Hortense Twain, for The Recipient Only.* It was a thank-you note. Then, with his duffel bag on his back and his heavy cardboard book box in his arms, Matthias trudged over an hour to the bus station, where he bought a one-way ticket to Grand Island, Nebraska. During the trudge, he had thought about Miss Twain's suggestion of New York or San Francisco and decided that New York was farther away, and thus the better option. But Grand Island was as far as he could get on half of his $140, and that's what he settled for. He was headed in the right direction for New York, and maybe Grand Island *would* be grand. In the trailer the next morning, the dolt was infuriated and wanted to call the police. Matthias's mother slapped him twice in the face and said, "For once in your life, leave that goddamned boy alone." The dolt and Haakon were shocked. Betty had used the Lord's name in vain, and she was *angry.* When Matthias left, her dreams for herself left with him, and she would never forgive him for abandoning her. *He,* she realized, would have a better future. She would not.

Three days later, Matthias rolled into Grand Island, and from the bus window it didn't look grand, and as it turned out, it wasn't an island at all. But Matthias was nevertheless thrilled to be so far from Fairbanks, and even after paying for food during the trip, he still had fifty-nine dollars and change in his pocket, which felt like a fortune. More fortuitously than anyone could have imagined, the bus station was a short walk from the airport, and Matthias hiked over with his knapsack and box to watch the airplanes land and take off, and to find something to eat. As he sat on a bench, a handsome boy a year older than Matthias walked by, and Matthias asked him if he knew where to find food. Matthias and Mike would become friends, and Mike's family would become Matthias's own for the following year. Mike's father,

Mr. Markey, owned the fixed-base operation on the airport that sold fuel, serviced planes, gave flight instruction, and provided transportation and assistance to transient pilots. He offered Matthias a job as a line boy, and Matthias learned to drive a "follow-me" truck to lead aircraft to parking spots and refuel them. He and Mike worked on the line together, and one night shift when there was little traffic to attend to, Mike introduced Matthias to his first sexual experience, in a darkened hangar, under the wing of a twin-engine Beechcraft Baron that belonged to a Nebraska Republican U.S. senator. The blow job was a revelation. Matthias and Mike became best friends, the first real friend Matthias had ever had, except for Miss Twain.

Mr. Markey thought Matthias a good learner, a hard worker, and "an upstanding young man" and, in addition to expanding his paid duties, offered him free flight instruction. Mr. Markey was a retired navy flight instructor in F-104 Starfighters, and he would personally conduct Matthias's training. He also often took Matthias home for dinner, where Mrs. Markey found that she liked him, too. She was a student counselor at Nebraska University at Kearney and was uncomfortable with Matthias's living in a rented room on the east edge of town. She decided the family would take him into their home. He roomed with Mike, Mrs. Markey mended his clothing and bought him some new things, and after he showed the family what was in his box, she insisted that he immediately apply to a good college and finish his last year of high school in Grand Island. She would help him with both. All the while, in the luscious privacy of their bedroom, Mike was teaching Matthias more about the human body than he had ever dreamed of. Matthias finished his year at the Markeys' with a junior degree in sex education, a private-pilot license with instrument rating, a high school diploma, and acceptance at Wesleyan University with a full scholarship, including room and board.

Matthias had managed to save $600 from his part-time job at Mr. Markey's, $140 of which he mailed to Miss Twain at the high school address. He placed the money in an envelope, wrapping the seven twenties in a sheet of paper on which he wrote, *Please do not tell anyone where I am. I am fine, and I finished high school here. I am going to college in Connecticut, which is near New York. Mrs. Markey, the mother in the family I am staying with, helped me with getting into school, and her son Mike is my best friend. Thank you for everything. From your appreciative student, Matthias.* Even as the trauma of his earlier life was still alive and churning within him, Matthias now had a glimpse of the futures that Miss Twain, Hugo, Casanova, Proust, and the Markey family had suggested were actually possible. In just one year, Matthias had three new people who liked him—which made a total of four including Miss Twain, and anyway, Mike counted for at least one and a half—and this helped Matthias feel that dreams might not always be just dreams. His thoughts of the Chena River and Jack London's solution had slowly receded from consciousness; but inside he was still injured, haunted, and fearful, even as he was determined not to live in those feelings. He would try to accept what the world was now offering and see if he could really be part of it. Even with all he had endured, Matthias was strong, and it was not just the kind of strength some people use to hide their injury. It was real strength. Matthias made no effort to hide any part of his internal life, he showed his vulnerability, too. It was just not the whole story.

The first week of August 1965, the entire Markey family drove seventeen-year-old Matthias to the bus station in the Markey Aviation company van. Matthias said goodbye to everyone, thanked them for everything they had done for him, shook Mr. Markey's hand, then kissed Mrs. Markey on the cheek, then Mike. Mike blushed. Mr. Markey pretended not to see the kiss for Mike, but Mrs. Markey saw it, and she understood. She put one arm around Mike and the other around Matthias and gave Matthias a second kiss and said, "I know you and Mike are going to miss each other. But, sweetie, you need to make your own life. I hope it's a wonderful life. And please stay in touch so we know how you're doing." Then she kissed Matthias on the cheek again and quietly whispered in his ear, "This is from Mike." Now Matthias blushed. He boarded the bus, and once seated, he waved goodbye, and all the Markeys waved back. The magic carpet to his future—and to mine—released its air brakes with a whoosh and lumbered out of the station, pointed at Connecticut. From his view through the smeared window next to his seat, Matthias thought Mike was tearing up, but wasn't sure. On their last night in bed together, with Mike faced away from him in the dark, Matthias had said something he had learned from Casanova: "You know I'll always love you." Mike had not responded, and Matthias thought Mike was also crying then because Matthias could feel a slight tremble in Mike's body and the mattress. "I *need* to go to college. *I want to be a writer,*" Matthias pleaded. Without turning his head, Mike answered with a choked "I know." Matthias stroked Mike's back for several minutes, and the two soon fell asleep together, resting up for the morning departure. When you're seventeen, you can sleep through anything.

In my freshman year at Wesleyan University in Middletown, Connecticut, I went almost every morning to Downey House, the school's post office, general store, and café. There I would have an egg-salad-and-bacon sandwich on dark whole-wheat toast, three or four cups of coffee, and six or eight Gauloises Bleues, which I had found out were the cigarette of choice for teenage sophisticates. In 1965, that was my idea of a healthy way to start the day, and no one said otherwise. As it turned out, Downey House was not only the venue for my morning constitutional, it was how I first met Matthias: kudos to Gauloises because, very early in our first term, Matthias walked up to me and asked if he could try one. With no sense of being gay myself, I was immediately and completely transfixed by this other seventeen-year-old. He was tall but delicate, and incredibly beautiful, and he had a quiet, firm voice, and a small gold loop in each ear. In 1965, the earrings were definitely something one noticed. When friends asked why the guy they saw me hanging out with had earrings, I explained it was because he was from Alaska. For the occasional few whose qualms seemed unallayed by the explanation, I sometimes added, "And it's very cold there."

Matthias and I quickly developed a routine of doing egg salad and bacon, coffee, and Gauloises almost every morning, and we talked a lot about all kinds of things. He was much more erudite than I was— among other things, I had never even heard of Casanova, much less read all of his accounts of adventure. We never explicitly discussed it, but Matthias knew he was gay. I had no idea I was—I did not even have the idea that *he* was, though, in retrospect, the whole situation was completely obvious. In my conscious understanding, I just liked him, and I wanted to be near him. For me, having sex with another boy did not define an internal or social identity, or a way of life. For as long as I could remember, I had thought that physical attraction between boys was something everyone felt, and that some acted on it, others not. I had come from a family very different from Matthias's. When I was twelve years old, my father had walked into my bedroom to find me playing naked on the bed with a friend, Robbie, who was "spending the night." My father seemed only a bit surprised and said with a chuckle, "Oh, I'm sorry, I didn't know you kids were busy, I was just going to say good night," and he turned and walked out of the room. Robbie was mortified, which puzzled me at the time, because I had no sense that we were doing anything that someone might object to. When I told my father the next day about Robbie's concerns, he said, "This is nothing to worry about. Robbie's parents have probably told him some stupid things. It's something you'll make your mind up about when you're older." Unlike me, Matthias had grown up with adversity that concisely defined him. As an outsider, every aspect of his outsiderness defined who he was. By the age of seventeen, Matthias had developed an acute sense of identity as a gay person, and because of his family and others, it was an identity that caused him a great deal of pain. I would decide or discover that I "was gay" only later in life. For the time being, I just liked being with Matthias, which, after all, is most of what being gay is about.

Matthias had something else that immediately and completely engaged me, even though I did not yet completely understand it. His entire internal life was willingly in view, like a landscape that allowed you to see from the rain-soaked Connecticut hills to the horizons of the western deserts. He revealed everything. He was vulnerable and strong, frightened and courageous, hurt and kind, and he was both a stalwart lone survivor and a generous friend. He was completely in view, and completely intimate. We remained "best friends" throughout our four years at school together. Matthias had a dual major in English and theater, with a soft spot for Ibsen, Strindberg, and Chekhov, all of whom, in Matthias's telling, wrote stories about families living in trailers. I went into philosophy, with a focus on Nagarjuna, Schopenhauer, and particularly Wittgenstein, all of whom, I later realized, I pursued in hopes they would help me find myself. My family had not lived in a trailer or anything close, and it had not been cruel, but it was a mess in its own disturbing way: Matthias and I had both been orphaned at the age of sixteen. For me, it was because both of my parents had died of illness; for Matthias, because it was either him or them. With Miss Twain's help, he had decided it would be *them*, and he had irrevocably orphaned himself the day he got on the bus and headed south. This connection, and others I did not fully understand, quickly made us the kind of friends who no longer have to say anything to have a conversation. Sitting in silence over our egg salad or Gauloises, we would both suddenly burst out laughing in unison, look each other in the eye, and have a communication that felt profound. Matthias and I shared an acute sense of both the hopeless, floundering comedy and the wonderful potential of human life, and we did not need to speak of it out loud. Life was horrible and terrific, and we both knew it. We could make each other laugh with a sideways glance.

Matthias and I soon developed another important, lifelong bond. Because of his familiarity with aviation in Alaska—which is crawling with airplanes—and the flight training Mr. Markey had given him, Matthias concluded that I should also learn to fly. I got lucky, and my well-to-do stockbroker maternal grandfather thought it was "a worthwhile enterprise for a young man" and offered to pay for it. I began lessons at a small flight school at Chester Airport, just south of Middletown. I was immediately enthralled by the feeling of a takeoff or landing, the view of Earth from the cockpit, the challenge of it, and even the smell of the planes. They smelled like freedom. And it was *flying*. I usually managed two lessons a week between Wesleyan classes, papers, and exams, and over the next two years I gained a commercial license and instrument rating. I had logged more than six hundred hours of flight time, and like Matthias, I felt it was something I had always been meant to do. Flying gave me a sense of competence in the world that I had never before had, a competence that seemed to extend to everything. To be able to break the bounds of Earth is a transcendent experience, even if it is also a cliché. When you can fly a plane really well, you can do anything, and both Matthias and I felt that.

We found something else in flying, something I don't think my grandfather had in mind when he mentioned the "worthwhile enterprise." In the small planes we flew out of Chester, Matthias and I necessarily sat very close to each other, shoulder to shoulder and thigh to thigh. I allowed myself to be only marginally conscious of the meaning of this physical intimacy, for it felt like a natural extension of my desire to be with him. In the plane, I was able to be with him far above and free of the narrowness of human life on the surface, which might have been a clue, but was not at the time. I touched him whenever I had the chance, and he liked it. My grandfather was still willingly footing the flying bill, and before we graduated from Wesleyan, we had accumulated a total flying time of almost a thousand hours each. That was a lot of time in the cockpit together. My logbook was filled with entries such as *Chester—Portland, Cessna 150, 2.1 hours, w/ M*. When Matthias flew left seat—meaning pilot in command—his entries were similar, but ended in *w/ WB*. WB was code for "Wally Burger," because almost no matter where we flew, I had a hamburger when we got there. When we flew to Portland, Maine, it was a lobster roll, but we weren't usually that lucky.

During these years, I was also dating girls, while Matthias had found a boyfriend of sorts, perhaps better described, I thought at the time, as a "sex buddy." My dating was okay and I met several girls I liked, and we had sex, but these good connections never had the emotional intensity I felt in sharing a sandwich, a flight, or a touch with Matthias. He described his boyfriend, Hank, as "swell," which, from Matthias, seemed damning. I met Hank many times, and he was a likable guy, and was devoted to Matthias, which made me both happy and jealous. Hank wanted to become a lawyer, an idea Matthias bemoaned. Hank was from a very hoity-toity Philadelphia society family that had bred a long line of fancy lawyers. I would occasionally remind Matthias that Hank cared about him and was kind. Hank was also steady and solid, I would continue, which could not fairly describe either Matthias or me. With those words, Matthias would relent a bit and give Hank his due.

Just before the beginning of the winter term of our sophomore year, Middletown was unbearably cold and gray, and Matthias and I did something that would begin to change my life. We decided to drive up to Cape Cod and stay a long weekend at the Provincetown Inn, which is as far out on the Cape as you can go without falling in the ocean and floating to France. We filled a single brown-paper grocery bag with clothes and a toothbrush—which we usually shared when away from school—and tossed the bag into the backseat of my yellow, three-cylinder Saab and headed northeast. Like Middletown, the Cape was also desolate in winter, but unlike Middletown, it was not a *morose* desolation. The pounding ocean gave the Cape life, like a Dostoyevsky story about human suffering told as a landscape. It was a living, breathing desolation, rather than the silent corpse of a Middletown winter. The Cape felt like *our* kind of desolation. The inn itself *was* a bit morose. We were two of probably only six or eight guests in the entire sprawling, creaky establishment, which, in the off-season, seemed almost exclusively manned by a jocular, elderly fellow we came to know as Mr. Henry.

Matthias and I had not even talked about what we would do for three days, and it was too cold and windy to spend time wandering on the beach. After we checked in, and without discussion, we went to our room, took off our clothes, and got in bed together, where we spent the next three days embracing, interrupted only twice a day by room service from Mr. Henry. Our interminable erections were impossible to overlook, but we never had "sex." Matthias was sensitive to my ambivalence and was waiting for me to make my decision. And I think he also felt, as I did, that sex might somehow destabilize our relationship, something we both valued too much to risk. We stroked each other's face, back, and chest, and we kissed. Then we napped, woke up, and started all over again. Both eighteen, Matthias and I were profoundly in love, but I had not even named the feeling, and certainly did not know what to do with it. Neither did he.

On our last morning in Provincetown, Mr. Henry arrived at our room with breakfast. With a towel wrapped around his waist—and an obvious, unmanageable erection—Matthias opened the door, and on the cart with the two covered dishes of bacon and eggs was a large white two-layer cake. It was decorated in awkward pink script that read, *Happy Lifes for Mathis and Walter.* Mr. Henry told us that his wife had made it especially for us, and we did not breathe a word about the spelling of our names or the plural form of *life*, for the intent was obvious, and we wanted to be appreciative. We thanked Mr. Henry and asked him to thank his wife, and after he left the room, we started giggling and could not stop. When we finally did, we ate the entire cake, pink letters and all, for as Matthias had pointed out, we couldn't leave any of it behind and hurt the Henrys' feelings. *Then* we ate our breakfasts. The entire weekend—from the moment we first undressed to Mrs. Henry's cake—had felt as if it were happening in a different time and space than anything I'd known before. I felt fortuitously disoriented by an experience that transformed my life internally and should have changed the way I lived it in the world. But it would not until a decade later. During that decade, whenever I thought about whether or not I "was gay," I always thought of Provincetown and the little blue room in the inn. And I remembered the cake, which had offered me a message I was still ignoring. Mrs. Henry was no scholar, but she was certainly a seer.

After our weekend, we returned to school for the winter term, remained best friends, and spent most of our time together. But we never talked about what Provincetown meant. Matthias continued his writing and theater work, and I continued my philosophy and started seriously in photography, suddenly inspired by Henri Cartier-Bresson and Lee Friedlander. Matthias also continued his relationship with Hank, which had by now advanced well beyond sex-buddy status. "Hank," Matthias told me, "wants to do public interest law, which is a big relief. He wants to do gay rights stuff. *Go, Hank.*" I could tell that Matthias was finally in love with Hank, and I said so. Then Matthias stared at me and said, "But you *can* be in love with two people at once." I asked him whom else he was in love with, and he continued to stare at me without saying a word. I had asked a stupid question, and I stared back, not knowing how to say what I should have said.

I had a favorite aunt, Janet, who lived on the banks of the Connecticut River, about a half hour south of Middletown and a few miles from the airport where I did my flight training. Janet, my mother's sister, was worldly and a bon vivant, and also a bit of a drinker, mostly bourbon and Campari, but one at a time. About a week after Matthias had essentially told me he was in love with me, he and I drove to Janet's for Sunday dinner, as we often did. On the way there in the Saab, Matthias touched my thigh and brought it up again: "You know, you *can*. I *know* you can love two people at once." I quietly responded, "Yes, I know. I believe you," and I glanced briefly at his eyes and then looked back at the road. This brief exchange must still have been written on our faces when we arrived at Janet's. Well into the meal, Matthias left the table to go to the toilet, and Janet took the opportunity:

"I like Matthias a lot," she said. "He's delightful and he's funny and smart, and he's very attractive. You two have something going on, and you should think about it. You won't find many like him. Just give it some thought." Waiting for a response, she reached over and affectionately rubbed the back of my hand, which was lying flat on the table. I had listened carefully and was thinking it over. I said, "I *do* think about him." She smiled and started to say something else, but Matthias walked catlike back into the room. He realized we had been talking about him, and later, as we pulled onto the road to drive back to school, he wanted to know what we had said.

"Was she warning you about me?" he asked cautiously.

"*No*, birdbrain," I said as I hit him on the arm with the back of my hand. "Where do you get that idea? She really likes you, and she said you were beautiful and smart, and she wanted me to think about it."

"Think about what?" Matthias was making me think about it all over again.

"Matthias, *she can tell we're in love*. She wants me to think about that—in a good way. She wants us to get *married*—I don't know what she wants. She wants us to be *together*. She's worried about me being an orphan. She thinks you're the perfect person for me, and—"

"And what did you say to her?" Matthias interrupted.

"She's probably right."

"About what?"

"That you're the perfect person for me. She's probably right."

"Did you say that to her?

"I said I *do* think about you." I turned my head to him. "Matthias, I think about you *all the time*." With one hand on the wheel, with the other I suddenly gripped his arm, as if he were the only thing on earth holding me upright. We did not speak out loud again until we arrived back at school.

With all of these feelings, and all the time Matthias and I would spend together over the remainder of our years at school, I still had my girlfriends, several of them. But I did think mostly about *him*, often about him in the blue room, which was precisely the weekend Aunt Janet would have envisioned for us. She never knew about Provincetown, and I regret never having told her.

For his senior thesis, Matthias did a production of Ibsen's *A Doll's House*, which he directed. Mine was a short film called *The Dinner*, which, in my mind, was a capsulation of Wittgenstein's ideas about language. Matthias loved it, as I loved his *Doll's House*. After four years together, we finally graduated in early June 1969, "the year of the double blow job," according to Matthias. "It will be another hundred years before this happens again, and we should make the best of it," he said. While other students, including Hank, paraded in their caps and gowns to the delight of their families, the two orphans went to O'Rourke's Diner at the north end of Main Street and had steamed cheeseburgers and coffee. A few days later, Matthias and Hank would move to New York City to pursue work in theater and law school, I to San Francisco to work with a small group of other photographers, in what we grandly called Alfa Photojournalists Cooperative. I think we meant *Alpha*, but so it goes when you're enthusiastic and twenty-two.

The night before our departures, Matthias asked that we spend the night together at my off-campus apartment, but I was concerned about how Hank would feel about it. Matthias told me he had already told Hank about the plan, and "Hank," he said, "has always known about Provincetown and fully understands our relationship and its importance in my life. Hank said to give you his love." For the first time since our visit to the inn, Matthias and I spent the night together, and we embraced and kissed almost to sunrise. For me, it was a stunning revelation all over again, an experience I had never quite felt with a girl. After our morning sandwiches, coffee, and Gauloises, Matthias and I returned to my apartment. The plan was for him to go home to Hank's apartment and drive down to the city in Hank's Austin-Healey 3000, their belongings stuffed behind the seats and tied to the rack on the top of the trunk. I would pack and prepare the Saab for the drive to the West Coast. As we were about to part, Matthias gripped both my arms, looked me straight in the face, and said, "You know that we can never have lives without each other." I did not know exactly what he meant, but I knew he was right and started tearing up, and then crying. Still holding my arms, he stood and watched me for a minute, then, like a cat, began licking the tears off my cheeks. Then he kissed me gently on the mouth, and as deftly and quietly as a cat, he released my arms, turned, and left the apartment. I wondered if I would ever see him again.

I sat on the edge of my bed for probably an hour. I felt empty, but panicked. Then, in a flash of anger, I suddenly had the thought that, for a guy who was as allergic to cats as Matthias was, he did a very good cat impersonation. My anger was about his leaving, but I also knew immediately it had been the right thing to do. Hank was *good* for Matthias. Hank knew he was gay, and I had no idea who I was. Matthias was smart, sensitive, and loving like a cat. He was irresistible like a cat. I loved the smell of his breath and his body. But he was also complicated, quirky, and vulnerable, for he lived with a lingering hurt and self-doubt deeply rooted in his sixteen years in the trailer with his envious, untrustworthy mother, his dolt of a father, and a brother who offered only abuse. Matthias needed someone steady and smart like Hank. I had never had a cat, I wouldn't even know what to feed one, and I could not conjure up an image of living with Matthias in New York or taking him to San Francisco. Then I thought, *You do not even know if you are a cat person or not. You do not deserve Matthias.* I started to tear up again and realized that I loved Matthias so deeply and irrevocably that I would give up anything for him. Even him. That thought lingered for a moment, and then I remembered that I wanted to make Ohio that night. I looked around the room to make sure everything had been packed, then went downstairs to clean the Saab's windshield and check the tires for the long drive ahead. A *car* I knew how to care for. As I rolled out of Middletown, I thought to myself, *This Saab is your only relationship.*

Matthias and I ended up at opposite ends of the country, and I was frightened by my loneliness, which was making me as morose and empty as a Middletown winter. I felt I had not only lost Matthias, but in some way I did not completely understand, I had lost myself. Those were the days of expensive long-distance phone calls, but that did not stop us, and we would also write long letters to each other at least weekly. After my $150 rent for the apartment on San Francisco's Divisadero Street, calls to Matthias and Hank were my biggest expense, one I could barely afford. Perhaps not coincidentally, it turned out that 1969 was not only the year of the double blow job, but the year of the

Stonewall Riots, the birth of Gay Liberation. The riots occurred two weeks after Matthias and Hank moved into their grubby apartment on East Eighth, between Broadway and Lafayette. Hank, who had been accepted at NYU Law, was elated and inspired by the riots, and the coincidence of events would inform his career for the next fifty years. Later, Hank and I would become much closer, and we would talk often. I admired his kindness, intelligence, devotion, and tireless work for the lives of gay people. Even before I decided I really was gay, I knew that Hank was also working for me. I had fallen in love with him, too.

Matthias began working as a stage manager for off- and off-off-Broadway productions and was writing plays on the side. All the plays were family stories, and of course the families always ended up badly. I read every one, and I loved them. Seven years after his arrival in New York, one of Matthias's plays was finally produced off-off-Broadway, and word of mouth got it seen and extended, and suddenly it had real press. One of the New York papers sent a well-known critic who described it as "the most promising new work this reviewer has seen since *The Glass Menagerie*." With some casting changes, the production was finally moved to Broadway, and seemingly overnight Matthias was the golden boy of New York theater. He received a Tony for the first play, while his following play was also running to nearly sellout audiences at a second theater, the Belasco on West Forty-Fourth. Matthias was grateful for the recognition, but never trusted others' interest in his work or, much more important, in *him*. His tenacious self-doubt hounded him through every success, and his episodes of depression and withdrawal continued, now worse. He had become a celebrity, "someone," he told me on the phone, "whom I have never met and don't want to know, because I wouldn't like him." Hank thought Matthias's new celebrity was bad, but not *that* bad, and though Matthias was suddenly exploring a celebrity's access to any sexual companion he desired, he and Hank kept working through their relationship. Hank wrote me:

> Sometimes I'm so angry at him, but then I think to myself that Matthias struggles with all these other men because he is still looking for himself, and for *you*. Even as I sometimes want to just run away, I adore him, as I know you do. It's a complicated life we three have been living together for all these years. But it's been mostly wonderful, and I would never want you

not to be part of it—some of the others he drags in now and then I could definitely do without. I love you as Matthias does. For Matthias, and for you.

One benefit of all the financial success was that Matthias's invested income could easily support the two of them, allowing Hank to continue the wonderful work he did, work that mortified his hoity-toity family because it barely paid enough to keep cat food in the house. And the money would do something else. Hank had always handled the finances because the task was entirely beyond Matthias. After two movie deals for his plays, and another in negotiation, Hank told Matthias that they had plenty of money to fulfill a dream Matthias had had since the age of twelve: he could have his own plane. Matthias bought a new Beechcraft Baron, the same model of plane under which he and Mike had first explored each other's body in the darkened hangar at Markey Aviation. "The movies," Matthias warned me on the phone, "are too miserable to even contemplate seeing, but the Baron is wonderful." Matthias kept the plane at Teterboro Airport in New Jersey, just west of Manhattan, across the Hudson and Hackensack Rivers. When he was twelve, a plane had been part of his fantasy about fleeing his family, and now flying was his real-life refuge and solace. After a bit more than a year of additional flight training, for which he earned a commercial license and twin-engine rating, he flew the Baron to Grand Island to visit the Markeys. "I feel such gratitude to this family," Matthias wrote me, "that after I landed and was taxiing behind the follow-me to the Markey hangar, I thought my heart would burst. I have no way to really thank them for the year they gave me." The letter described the gifts he had brought for Mr. and Mrs. Markey and Mike, and they seemed thoughtful, personal, and extravagant, but I imagined the family was simply glad to see him, now more or less grown-up. *Mike,* Matthias's letter continued, *is now the assistant manager at the FBO, and he lives with a boyfriend, to his father's tolerant consternation, and his mother's delight.* The letter closed as Matthias's letters to me almost always did: *I miss you terribly. Love, Matthias.*

By phone, I had spoken to Aunt Janet the day before—she wanted my advice on a new Polaroid camera—but early the following morning,

New Year's Day 1981, she suddenly died of a heart attack. On first hearing the news in a 4:00 a.m. call from her lawyer, I had my life's only panic attack: my teeth started chattering uncontrollably, and I thought I was suffocating. Matthias, Hank, and I went together to the memorial service in Connecticut. Even if, in her perception of things, Matthias and I had never resolved our relationship, she had come to treat us as a couple, and she included Hank in "the couple." She had become a good and generous friend and surrogate mother to all three of us, and we were all left bereft by her death. Two months after the memorial, Matthias phoned me. He had decided to visit his parents, which he had not done since leaving the trailer in the middle of the night, eighteen years earlier. He wanted to see if there was "anything to salvage," and I imagined that Janet's death had inspired the impulse: Janet had taken us in, and now we were orphans again. Hank still had his family—it was not *altogether* hoity-toity—but Matthias and I did not. Haakon had arranged Matthias's "family reunion" at his Texas ranch on the outskirts of San Antonio. Matthias proposed that he would fly the Baron to Oakland, just east of San Francisco, and after spending the night, we would proceed to San Antonio the next morning. After the visit, he would fly me home. At the time, I was in graduate school, but it was an offer I would not refuse. I badly wanted to see Matthias, I wanted to fly the Baron, and I was curious about the miserable family I had never laid eyes on. Matthias said he could not bear to go alone, and Hank, who was terrified of flying, would not accompany him. When I met Matthias on his arrival at Oakland Airport, I saw that the tail number on the Baron was N123HW. "'Hotel whiskey'? 'Hank and Walt'?" I asked. "Or did they just assign that number by coincidence?"

"No, I picked it, it's 'Hank and Walt.' I might have done 'whiskey hotel,' but I didn't want to hurt Hank's feelings." *Hotel whiskey* is the international pronunciation for *HW*, used for clarity in radio communication. *N* stands for United States registry, and one can guess the meaning of 123.

I had something of my own to surprise Matthias with. I had been dating a woman, Diane, whom I knew from graduate school, where we were both pursuing a degree in clinical psychology. I was very fond of Diane—she was funny, kind, and smart, and she was beautiful. But about a month before Matthias came to Oakland to pick me up for the family reunion, Diane and I were making love on a Sunday afternoon. I suddenly realized—clearly and unequivocally for the first time—that I wanted this person in my bed to be Matthias. I gently pulled away, sat up, and said to Diane, "I want to be gay." She reached over and touched my arm, kissed me on the hand, smiled, and said, "Then you should be." She understood and probably always had. We would remain good friends until she and her then husband retired many years later and moved to Costa Rica.

Following that Sunday epiphany with Diane, I thought a lot about living as a gay man, and what would change, if anything. I realized that my reluctance had not been about the stigma attached to being gay, because I had been lucky enough to have had almost no exposure to that misfortune. My reluctance had been much more rooted in the loss I'd experienced in childhood, and in my fear of wanting someone—wanting *anyone*—as much as I had wanted Matthias from the day we met. Relationships with women had been relatively manageable: they did not bring up the uncontainable emotional and physical desire, and the almost complete forfeit of an independent self that I felt when I was with Matthias. Together, he and I were essentially one. In that fusion, I was no longer the autonomous orphan survivor who could take care of himself, I was now a man who needed someone else whom he did not have. I *did* need someone else, and that realization made me cry with both relief and terror. The question was not whether or not I was gay, but whether I could survive a real, full relationship, whether I could allow myself to be completely in love. Terror or no terror, I now accepted my need; I wanted a full, self-acknowledged relationship, and I was already in love and had been for many years. The night before we left for San Antonio, Matthias and I made completely unconstrained love for the first time since we had met, sixteen years before. If someone had seen us, they would have thought, *These two men are trying to devour each other. And they're taking all night.*

The next morning we had a late start for San Antonio. We drove to the airport, fueled, and preflighted Three Hotel Whiskey, got a weather briefing from the Flight Service office, filed a flight plan, received a clearance, and were soon climbing through the stratus "marine layer" hanging over the airport. We had an initial cruise altitude of eleven thousand feet, with forecast good tailwinds. Emerging into the brilliant sunlight above the gloomy stratus layer that topped out at seventeen hundred feet brought up all the elation I had felt with Matthias the night before. He was wonderful, the Baron was climbing like a rocket to the moon, and the enroute weather was impeccable. Because our departure had been so late, we decided to stop and spend the night in Santa Fe. I slept in Matthias's arms, he in mine, and I dreamed of something wonderful that, in the morning, I could not quite remember, except for the feelings of elation and gratitude.

Early the next day, after refueling, a check of the oxygen system, and a preflight, we proceeded contentedly enroute, expecting a relatively easy arrival into San Antonio in time for lunch. Weather forecasts for the enroute portion and for San Antonio had been fairly good, but they were not to pan out. With weather, what you see is what you get, and what we got conspired with a mess of morning rush-hour departure traffic from San Antonio. Marginal visibility at the airport, unforecast scattered thunderstorms in the vicinity, ice, and heavy traffic would result in reroutes, long holds, and irritable pilots and approach controllers. It was nerve-racking. Only twenty-two miles west of San Antonio, air traffic control was keeping us at nineteen thousand feet, an altitude we had long before requested to clear the tops of some building cumulus that threatened ice and a bumpy ride. Once east of the buildups, we had been promised something lower, but it was not forthcoming. We were still too high to get down easily for the approach, we were still on oxygen, and we were now completely in cloud. The air mass was moist, and the outside air temperature was minus two centigrade, just below freezing. The onboard Bendix radar showed serious precipitation only east and southeast of the airport, and that would not be the problem. Rime ice—rough, clumpy ice—had begun slowly building in the corners of the windshield and then, much more rapidly, on the propellers and airframe. All the deicing equipment was on. The windshield and prop tubes were slinging alcohol antifreeze everywhere, and the wing and tail ice-removal boots were pumping. When I again requested lower from air traffic control—this time for the arrival *and the ice*—the controller said, "Unable, stand by for lower, I have outbound traffic climbing out below you."

Over the next two or three minutes, Matthias was hand flying the nearly crippled plane magnificently, but he had gradually been adding small increments of power to maintain altitude against the weight and aerodynamic drag of the accumulating rime. We still had no descent clearance, and with both engines now at full power, Matthias looked at me and said, "It turns out that airplanes are just like the rest of life— it's easier to go down than up." We laughed. I glanced at the vertical speed indicator in front of me and realized that we were descending at almost three hundred feet per minute. Matthias saw the startled look on my face. "Go for it," he said as he looked back at the instrument panel, and I made the call pilots hate to make: "Antonio approach, Three Hotel Whiskey is declaring an emergency. We're unable to maintain altitude with an ice load, descending at three hundred feet per minute, leaving eighteen thousand two hundred. We need an immediate descent to eleven thousand." A declaration of emergency grants the pilot complete authority, and the controller's immediate response was "Three Hotel Whiskey, cleared to eleven thousand, maintain current heading." Matthias immediately started down rapidly, but as we got lower and into warmer air, chunks of melting ice broke loose, making an unnerving racket as they hit the fuselage and tail. A circuit breaker on the panel popped, and I saw that we had lost the flashing beacon on the top of the vertical tail, probably to an ice strike. Also unnerving was the irritation in the approach controller's voice as he directed other aircraft out from under us. It all sounded like mayhem. Down at eleven thousand and free of our ice load, we were no longer San Antonio approach's favorite aircraft. For forty minutes we were vectored here and there and finally put in a holding pattern sixteen miles northwest of the airport.

After fifteen minutes of flying ovals, I roughly calculated that we had significantly less than an hour of fuel remaining. We had burned a lot of it while trying to fight ice and gravity with maxed-out engines at nineteen thousand. I tapped Matthias on the arm and pointed at the fuel gauges, then at the communications microphone. He knew what was coming and nodded affirmatively. As second-in-command of approach control's least favorite aircraft, I made the call: "Approach, Three Hotel Whiskey is declaring critical fuel." Only then were we released from the hold and blessedly given an approach and landing, with an instruction to keep our speed up. They were probably thrilled to get rid of us, and we hustled down the approach corridor on the Instrument Landing System, and used nearly a mile of runway before turning off onto the congested taxiways for a twenty-minute crawl to the ramp. We spent the first half hour talking to the shop foreman at the FBO about replacing the tail beacon, which had been completely shattered and torn from the wiring harness. The rest of the plane looked undamaged, but the shop would inspect it carefully, and the foreman said he thought he could do it all that afternoon. We spent the next forty-five minutes at the FAA office, doing paperwork on the declaration of emergency. Then we walked to the terminal and had doughnuts and coffee to steady our nerves. Matthias looked exhausted and was very quiet.

As nerve-racking as it had been, our troubled arrival into San Antonio would prove to be a picnic in the park against the horrible drama that awaited us at Haakon's "ranch mansion" south of town. Johnston Ranch was the home of the world's second most financially successful television ministry, and the entire cast of *Les Misérables* that Matthias had fled seventeen years earlier awaited us there. Sitting in the passenger seat of our rental car enroute to the ranch, Matthias suddenly gripped my arm and said, "This is a terrible mistake." I looked over at him and he looked stricken and pale, his normally relaxed, beautiful face contorted in a way I had never quite seen it. I pulled to the side of the highway and shut down the engine. Matthias looked over to be sure I had the emergency flashers on, then released his seat belt, reached over and embraced me, and started weeping. We sat gripping each other for a long while, and I told him that we could drive back into town and find a hotel, that I would do whatever he wanted. He wanted only to weep out thirty-four years of grief that still lived inside him and knotted his guts. With my white cotton handkerchief, I wiped his face and nose and realized that I was doing exactly what my father had done for me when I was a child. I brushed Matthias's hair back from his face. I rubbed his neck and stroked his back. There seemed no way to quell the grief. After another five or ten minutes, he suddenly sat up, took the handkerchief from me, blew his nose, and said, "Let's go ahead. It will be the last time I see them, and I need to tell them why." He put my handkerchief in his pocket, and then kissed me on the cheek. I restarted the engine, turned off the flashers, and pulled back onto the barren highway that led to the ranch.

We were admitted through the security gate at the bottom of the drive by a rotund man with rosy cheeks, dressed in a gray security guard's uniform. He looked like a pink-and-gray cow wearing a cowboy hat and a six-shooter. The magic word was *Matthias*, and the gate swung slowly open under careful bovine supervision. After several minutes climbing the long drive to its crest, the mansion came into view. The gussied-up twelve-bedroom, redbrick, white-trimmed behemoth was laid out like a vast single-story motel without all the doors, just a row of white-framed windows evenly spaced across the facade. And an ornate, completely anomalous large dome was perched on the roof right above the hugely oversize front door.

When Matthias noticed the parking lines painted on the drive near the house, he said, "Haakon always was a controlling asshole, like his father. Park across a line."

"Meaning *your* father?"

"That, too."

Matthias had transformed himself since our roadside stop. Now he looked as if he had appraised the situation and was ready to go into combat and emerge in one piece. Before he got out of the car, I pulled him toward me and wiped the corner of one eye, which still held a remnant of tears. He then gently slid his finger across my upper lip. "Nothing there," he said, "I just wanted to touch you."

A dignified-looking Hispanic woman in an un-Texas-like black-and-white maid's uniform greeted us at the door. She led us into the domed rotunda and told us that she would tell "the reverend" we had arrived. In the center of the rotunda stood an elevated, life-size crucifix, and around the base of the sculpture lay a lifeless, odorless ring of white plastic flowers. Matthias looked at Christ and said, "Five foot ten, I'd say." Christ's face and body looked as if they had been crafted at Madame Tussauds—shiny, smooth, and too perfect—or perhaps even by the hand of a skilled mortician. This was just the foyer, and it was frighteningly downhill from here. A voice suddenly boomed from the far side of the rotunda, and when a large man in a white suit and bolo tie emerged—he looked as if he'd been eating too many cows—I knew from his air of self-importance that it must be Haakon. He walked toward Matthias with his arms outstretched as if to embrace him, and Matthias backed sharply away, more, I thought, out of instinctual fear than hostility. Haakon stopped, extended his hand to shake, and Matthias ignored it, instead turning to me and saying, "This is my lover, Walt." Haakon responded that Mom and Dad were going to be happy to see Matthias. If the family itself were not enough, the house was crawling with Siamese cats—at least six by my count—attended to by the maids, and Haakon knew well of Matthias's allergy. I realized that the trauma that still churned inside Matthias was going to allow no reconciliation with *this*. He really *had* come to tell them why he would never see them again, and he did and would not.

Matthias's mother, Betty, had grown morbidly obese since Matthias had last seen her, but in his perception she had shrunk internally to better fit into the unhappy life she had always led. She spoke in a pinched, staccato voice that made her sound like the dummy of a not-good ventriloquist, and almost everything she uttered was platitudinous and empty. She seemed terrified of saying anything meaningful, and although I could see she was intelligent, only a thimbleful was actually showing. Matthias's father, like Haakon, was not intelligent, and they both mostly bellowed like cows. But in the faces of both cows, one also saw the potential for meanness. After a half hour of painfully forced and empty chatter, we sat for "late luncheon" at the behest of a maid, and Matthias apparently decided it was time. He began to unleash a measured, quietly expressed rage that I had never quite seen or imagined in him. Moments after he started, he turned to me and asked if I was okay. Haakon quickly took the opportunity to offer me a tour of the ranch in the middle of lunch, and I said, "I love Matthias, and I will stay here if he wants me to." Matthias walked around the table, put his hands on my shoulders, kissed me on top of my head, and then returned to his seat at the table.

As if presiding over court, Matthias initiated a recitation of transgressions for which he would never forgive the family that sat before him: a detailed, chronologically ordered catalog of the specific events that comprised sixteen years of emotional and physical abuse, humiliation, and neglect. The attending maid scurried from the room. The

dolt and Haakon sat stone-faced. And then halfway through the catalog, Matthias suddenly stood and pointed at his father and then Haakon
and said, "Don't you, don't either of you, think *even for an instant* that
you will ever again talk to me as you did in the trailer—don't think I
will tolerate that for an instant. With your religion, your plastic cruci-
fixes and self-importance, you are both liars and hypocrites, and neither of you will ever again *talk* to me at all. You—and your *lives*—are
unforgivable."

Matthias turned quickly to his mother without pointing and spoke
more softly, with a just-perceptible sadness. "And you, the only intelligent adult in that trailer, who sat around as if you had no role in this
family, no responsibility as a parent, no responsibility to a child, and
allowed all this to happen. I *tried* to find a way to love you because
you were the only possible friend I had. You gave me nothing back,
and for that I will never forgive you. I *know* you live in pain—I knew
it when I was eight—but that's *your* pain, and you've never done anything about it. You've made your life with two idiots, and you'll live
with it, but I will not. You should never have had a child."

Beginning to tear up, Matthias sat down again and was silent for
several minutes. Betty started to speak, and he interrupted her and
asked her to be quiet, and then he proceeded chronologically to finish
the catalog of transgressions. No detail would go unmentioned, many
too awful to repeat. One by one, the horror of the stories made *me* tear
up, and I found myself silently vowing that I would never allow anyone to hurt Matthias again. By the time he was done more than a half
hour later, he had laid out at the dining room table not only a catalog of
horrifying, painful transgressions, but also a completely crafted text
of a gay artist's manifesto that would not tolerate or excuse abusive
treatment. Matthias knew, I knew, and even Betty in her shrunken
heart knew that everything he had said was true. His father and Haakon seemed to know nothing. Matthias's hurt, his strength, and his
rage, all of which I already knew, had never before seemed so monu-
mental, or so moving. This time *I* walked around the table and kissed
Matthias on the back of his neck and massaged his shoulders. His
mother looked down at her lap, his father winced, and Haakon mooed.
One by one—Betty first—the three left the room, and Matthias and
I sat, now side by side, and finished our lunch.

We should have gotten out of there while the going was good, and we considered making the long drive back into town and finding a hotel. But we were both exhausted, and we decided to stay until the following morning. We did our own brief tour of the ranch, and the only beautiful thing about it was the handsome young ranch hands. They looked as if they had been culled from a model agency's portfolio, and it was difficult to imagine that Haakon had selected them for their nonsexual skills or ranch experience. Matthias again speculated on Haakon's sexual proclivities: "Christ hanging in the foyer, he's peddling his crap on TV to millions, and fucking boys behind the corral. That's my big-shot brother." Everything else on the ranch was just as preposterous: it had that ridiculous, cheap, overwrought look that the rotunda suggested, as if the entire ranch had been delivered as a piece, decorator-selected from the local Walmart high-end shop. Like the family itself, the ranch was completely false and soulless, with a single exception.

We spent much of the rest of the afternoon in the kitchen with the elderly Mexican cook, Lela, who had made the wonderful lunch that, as Haakon described it, Matthias had ruined. Matthias and I had not had a *good* time at lunch, but we *had* liked the food. We chatted with Lela for almost two hours, and she told us about her family and growing up in Mexico, her two children, her divorce, and her second husband, whom she seemed to adore. When Matthias asked her if a Catholic could divorce and remarry, she seemed to entirely dismiss the question with a wave of her arm and something in Spanish that neither of us understood. Lela was real, a wonderful discovery in this humanly empty, tortured house. Against her polite protestations, we helped her with the dinner preparation—a couple of sous-chefs—then went upstairs to shower together and dress in fresh clothes that didn't reek of San Antonio approach controllers and the perspiration they'd inspired. On the way up the stairs, Haakon had stopped us and said that, in *his* house, we would have to stay in separate rooms. Matthias had responded, "Fuck you, we'll be out of here in the morning and you can have the place disinfected. *You*, you'll get over it—as you've managed to get over *every* truth—before we've reached the main road." Haakon mooed again, but said nothing.

By arrangement with Lela, Matthias and I had dinner in our room, including a beautiful small chocolate cake she had made just for us. In the middle of the night I awoke, and I could feel Matthias through the mattress, shaking and sobbing next to me. I put my arm over his waist and pulled myself next to him. Pressed against his back, I whispered, "I love you," and pulled myself still closer, but he continued crying, and without releasing him I returned irresistibly to sleep. Very early the next morning, the family was still in bed, and we went to the kitchen to say goodbye to Lela, who was already busily at work. We thanked her for last night's dinner and the beautiful cake and apologized for not being able to stay for breakfast.

We left for the airport and ate breakfast there. We paid the shop bill for the beacon repair and inspection, did the usual flight preparations, and soared gratefully away from Texas, returning uneventfully to Oakland with a no-mess, no-fuss straight-in approach to Runway 27-Right. Matthias spent the night, and in the morning I drove him back to the plane. As I watched Three Hotel Whiskey climb and disappear into the marine layer still blanketing Oakland, I thought what an extraordinary man he was. To have survived such a family and then found an authentic life and substantial self-acceptance seemed heroic. He was winging his way first back to Grand Island to visit the Markeys, then back to Teterboro and Hank. I imagined him breaking out on top of the marine layer into the brilliant sunlight, and the image echoed my vision of what had happened in Texas. In both, I wanted to believe, he had freed himself from gloom. But for Matthias, it would never be all sunlight. He would never again see or communicate with his family, and he would live his own life, but he would always carry the injury and pain.

Back at school the Monday after our return from San Antonio, I was swamped with papers and exams, including a final in my perpetual nemesis, inferential statistics. Ten days later, I realized that Matthias, Hank, and I had not talked or written, which was very unusual. I felt an instant of panic. I tried to dismiss the feeling with the thought of Matthias buried in script changes during rehearsals for a production of his new play, *Full Turns*. Then the panic returned and I thought of an aircraft accident—but, no, Hank would have called me. Then I finally thought of Matthias in emotional pain, and my panic turned to grief. I recalled his sobbing in the middle of the night at the ranch mansion, and we had never talked about it. I called their New York number, and Hank answered. Matthias, Hank told me, had been depressed and withdrawn since his return and was having difficulty writing. Hank wondered what had happened in San Antonio because Matthias had refused to talk about it, and I told Hank he should wait for Matthias to tell him. I asked if Matthias would come to the phone. He was sleeping, and Hank said that he would ask him to phone me. Matthias did, hours later.

"What's going on, are you okay?" I asked.

"I've been very down. I was ashamed to call you."

"Ashamed of what? Were things okay with the Markeys? What are you ashamed of?"

"Oh, the Markeys were fine. They're sweethearts. I'm ashamed of what you saw with my family—of them and of me. The whole thing. I know I hurt you, just letting you meet them, and I'm ashamed of myself, because when I see them, I realize how damaged I am. I know you can see that."

"Matthias, for shit's sake, you were a hero in San Antonio. I have never loved or admired you more. You did what you said you were going to do—what anyone would have to do with a family like that and survive—you told them the truth. That you came from that family and have made the life you've made—it astonishes me. I can't think how to tell you what I feel for you. I love you all the more since San Antonio."

Matthias did not respond, and the next voice I heard was Hank's.

"Matthias handed me the phone and he's on the sofa crying again. What did you say to him? Are *you* okay?"

"I told him I love him more than ever since San Antonio. I told him he was a hero for what he did there. *He was.*" Then I started crying, Hank started crying, and we agreed that we would have to talk later. Just before we hung up, Hank said that Matthias wanted to say something else to me and handed him the phone.

Still crying, Matthias said, "I realized as we were climbing out of San Antonio that now I'm really an orphan. Janet is dead. And my family's dead."

"Matthias, you were an orphan the day you were born. You already know this, but you and I, we are both orphans. We have each other, and we have Hank. We are orphans, but we are both living with two people we love. We have *us*."

The next day, we all spoke again, and Matthias was doing better and had returned to his script revisions. During this conversation, I said something to Matthias that, on his deathbed, he would tell me he had never forgotten:

> You can't just *get over* a family like that. It would be impossible for anyone. You get rid of as much of them as you can, and for the rest that stays with you, you just have to try to not live it out. You've already done that. You've made a hugely different life, a life they could never understand. You're a hugely different person. Hank and I love you for *you*. It has nothing to do with them. I hope that giant crucifix falls on their heads.

Matthias laughed when I mentioned the crucifix, and at the time I thought he'd more than half believed all of what I'd said. The disbelieving part of him remained submerged in that murky, muddy, leftover self-doubt that would cling to him for his entire life. But half a Matthias would have been enough, more than enough. Only half of him was still a monument to the goodness in human life.

Nineteen eighty-one turned out to be a very bad year. It was not only the year of Janet's death and the San Antonio confrontation, but the year that the AIDS epidemic opened on Broadway for early previews, with a July 3 piece in *The New York Times* about a "rare cancer in homosexuals." The entire audience of gay men was terrified, and there would be little in Matthias's, Hank's, or my life that was not changed by an epidemic that ran completely unabated for an unimaginable fifteen years. *Everything* changed, as if the very color of sunlight had changed, shifting our perceptions of everything. Well into the initial chaos, Matthias said to me, "It's like flying a plane that's shedding parts, one after the other—like the tail beacon going into San Antonio. I'm waiting for the whole tail to come off." Everyone was waiting for the whole tail to come off, and I lived much less in trepidation for myself than for Matthias and Hank: we had no idea who already had whatever it was that people had. I couldn't imagine being left behind and alive without them, it seemed *impossible*.

One day early in 1982, Matthias phoned and said, "I got bad news on Tuesday."

My heart seemed to stop, and I felt a complete woodenness that left me unable to speak.

"Are you there? I started saying that I heard Hortense Twain had died."

I began breathing again, coughing and gasping for air, grateful and furious, furious that Matthias had let me think, even for an instant, what I had thought. "*You bastard*. The next time, *start* the sentence with *Hortense Twain*."

Matthias apologized. This tiny event had instantaneously filled me with horror. As it would eventually turn out, none of the three of us contracted HIV, and Matthias would once tell me that he was not sure if this was a blessing or a curse. It *was* a blessing, but a complicated one, because, as Matthias and I discussed many times over our later years together, neither of us any longer felt he wanted to live forever. We had seen enough death that we knew it could sometimes be the blessing. *Hank*, he wanted to live forever.

In that same startling conversation about Miss Twain's death, Matthias first told me about something else—meeting Mason.

"*Maison*, like French for 'house'?"

"No, like *mason* jar. Or Perry *Mason*. He's an oboe player and a genius besides, but you should see the way he looks. I first ran into him last Tuesday, on the south side of Columbus Circle. He was standing on the street in the cold, playing his oboe for nickels and dimes, and almost everyone was ignoring him. I put a dollar bill into his oboe case, and after listening a few minutes longer, I added a twenty. The playing was incredibly beautiful and plaintive—it turned out he's studying at Juilliard on a scholarship—but *the way he looks*. He's small and scrawny, his head and face are the shape of a large cantaloupe, his eyeglasses are broken, he has long, filthy hair, he's covered with acne, and his teeth are sticking out in every direction. He looks like Sneezy and Bashful rolled into one. As I stood there and listened, I thought, 'I need to make him a sandwich.' And then I realized that, after that, I had to immediately get him to a dermatologist and an orthodontist. And an optometrist. I don't know what it was, but—well, Hank and I have decided to take care of him.'"

Their desire to take on Mason wasn't difficult to understand, par- ticularly if you took his personal history into account: his childhood had been too much like Matthias's. He was a gay kid who grew up in western Ohio, so close to the border that the family might as well have been living in Indiana. Mason's parents were what today we'd call Mike Pence Republicans: fairly well-off, sinister, and creepy fundamental- ists who were determined to crush the human spirit, including their son's. But Mason had had too much inborn intelligence and will to go along with *that* plan, and his parents retaliated with severe neglect, punctuated by intermittent, harsh reprimand. His physical appearance was indisputable evidence of the neglect, and his confused, but still- seeking, virginity at the age of nineteen told the rest. As Mason said of his parents, "They hate me." And Mason shared something else with Matthias: at the age of eighteen, Mason's high school music teacher had told him that he was inordinately talented and suggested that he look into Juilliard. In defiance of his parents' prohibition, he took the bus to New York and never went home again. They had told him that New York was a "sinful, filthy place, unfit for human life," but Mason liked it immediately. After two auditions—the attending faculty had thought the first was too good to be anything but a fluke—Juilliard accepted him and provided not only a complete scholarship, but a room and a small stipend for food and other necessities. Mason supple- mented the stipend with his Columbus Circle performances, which brought in another two or three dollars a day, if he was lucky. When Matthias brought him home to meet Hank—this was before the physical remake—Hank knew immediately that they would have to help this socially awkward but kind young genius. Mason seemed to be living alone in an internal world entirely of his own making, for his unusual intelligence had made him very eccentric. Oddly, that intelligence also made him vulnerable and uncertain: he understood too much, and every thought or decision raised a hundred paths or possibilities, a labyrinth that most people could not even track. Matthias and Hank couldn't do much about all *that*—at least not directly—but they could give Mason a sense of family and acceptance for the first time in his life. They could do what the Markeys had done for Matthias, and they could even help socialize him by enlisting the assistance of his psychologist uncle, which was me. Always in charge of the finances, Hank started "the reconstruction of Mason" by quadrupling his Juilliard stipend and taking him clothes shopping to supplement the single pair of jeans, two pairs of underwear, and two shirts he had arrived with in New York. Matthias handled the doctor's appointments, and the dermatologist and ophthalmologist were fine; but Mason would have nothing to do with an orthodontist: he was convinced, perhaps quite correctly, that any tooth work would change his embouchure and thus his future. They left the crazy teeth alone.

By the time I first met Mason in person, his skin had substantially cleared, he'd had a shampoo, and he was wearing a new pair of granny glasses. His teeth were still frightening, but so what? Something about him was so direct and authentic that one couldn't help but like him, even if his eccentricity was often puzzling. *I* wanted to make him a sandwich. What I learned about him—he knew I was a psychologist and thought of me as his "Uncle Walt," so he talked freely—was that he knew he was gay, but he had little idea about what that meant. "My parents tried to make me hate who I am, but I don't want to hate myself. Should I find someone to have sex with? I've never done that." When I was in town and Hank and Matthias were both busy, Mason and I would often have lunch together, and we'd talk about all sorts of things. He'd gained some social connections to other young gay men—Juilliard was a treasure trove—and had even had sex, about which he had a lot of questions. So we'd talk about that and whatever else was coming up in his life.

About two years after I first met him, Mason found a boyfriend, a sophomore swim-team captain from NYU. On the surface, their relationship seemed completely implausible, for Brett was as beautiful as Mason was homely. I was delighted for Mason, and on first meeting Brett, I knew almost immediately that he was honest and kind and cared a great deal for Mason. Mason's mind could run circles around the swimmer's breaststroke, but unlike many others, Brett seemed unintimidated by that mind—he seemed to appreciate it. They would more or less stay together for many years, and they would have their ups and downs, but their bond was always solid, if inexplicable. They made me think of a quiet, twenty-five-year-old mare serving as paddock companion for a high-strung champion Thoroughbred: her presence steadied and calmed him and improved his race. Heaven knows, Mason's mind needed calming, and he needed the kindness that seemed to fill Brett's heart. For many years, their paddock would be a small apartment over a noodle bar in the East Village, which Hank happily paid for when "the kids" were short on cash.

During those years, I was often in New York for work, and I almost always spent time with Mason, for he had become part of our family. If Matthias and Hank were my brothers, companions, and lovers, they had also given me a son to share—and, in Brett, a son-in-law. They would fret about Mason, his life, and his future, for they loved him as one loves one's child.

"I would stand in front of a moving bus to protect him," Matthias once told me.

"I would too," I said, "but we also have to let him live his life."

Matthias nodded affirmatively, and so did Hank.

"But what about *HIV*?" Matthias asked, suddenly anxious again.

I assured him that Mason and I had discussed it a lot and continued to do so. "You know, Mason's life has to come from him, not from us, and it will—he's *strong.*"

Matthias knew that, but he also feared that, in the aftermath of a wretched childhood like Matthias's own, Mason would suffer as Matthias had. He was almost certainly right, but like Matthias, Mason would also make a life for himself, and it would be his own life, it would be authentic. Mason's inner strength was written all over his Sneezy and Bashful face, and he *was* a survivor.

While Mason's life seemed to be getting better and better, the epidemic got worse and worse. Emotionally, it derailed us in many ways, but it also rallied us. As Mason continued his studies at Juilliard, Matthias, Hank, and I became activists in different ways. Matthias pulled back from the theater and writing, worked with Act Up and the Treatment Action Group, and assisted Hank when he needed it. I started writing and speaking about the lives of gay men in the epidemic, and the psychological issues in HIV prevention. Hank worked tirelessly—sometimes to the unhappy exclusion of Matthias and me from his life—on various issues, serving as pro bono counsel for both the National Gay and Lesbian Task Force and Lambda Legal, which he considered the only two LGBTQ organizations worth supporting. His values were defined, and he gave short shrift to anything that fell short, significantly influencing both Matthias's and my perceptions of what was important in the current "gay agenda." Hank was interested in gaining legal equality and protections, not acceptance, and was the first person I knew to recognize the issues of queer, gender-queer, and transgendered people, at a time when "gay men" still largely shunned them. "I'd, of course, never say this in court," Hank once told me, "but if this society doesn't like us, *fuck 'em*. I'm sick of people trying to pander to overcome prejudicial, often illegal treatment. We need to fight, not pander." His priorities included HIV discrimination, inequity in health care, job discrimination and security, legal impediments to HIV prevention, sexual liberty, gay-related racial discrimination, gender discrimination and abuse, and other prejudicial treatment that threatened the health and welfare of LGBTQ people and still does. Matthias always called it "Hank's BLT work," but deeply admired it, even as he felt shut out and missed Hank. So did I.

Matthias, Hank, and I tried to squeeze in our relationship around our time with Mason and Brett, the immediate demands of the epidemic, and Hank's work. But even with all the havoc on the ground, Matthias and I managed to sustain our flying life. When in New York, I would stay with them at their new apartment on West Eighty-First, between Columbus and Amsterdam. It was a block from Central Park, where the three of us would usually walk in the evening after dinner, summer and winter. This became a family tradition that calmed and centered us. At the end of my visits, Matthias would fly me back to Berkeley in Three Hotel Whiskey, particularly when ominous weather fronts were not bisecting the country. Our time in the plane together was still our refuge, and during the epidemic we were more than ever in need of refuge. I treasured being up in the air with Matthias, and it gave us some time alone. Anyway, Hank was busy.

Enroute to Berkeley one sunny Monday, sightseeing over Nebraska at eighty-five hundred feet, Matthias and I came to understand something about our bond more clearly that we ever had. One of the most engaging things about flying is that everything has to be done *really* well, because even small details can be matters of life and death. The epidemic had made daily existence on the surface a matter of life and death, and we were both peculiarly comfortable with that. In both flying and the epidemic, we were strangely in our element. Young orphans are made suddenly aware of the dangers in life and live daily— probably forever—with a shadowing sense of potential emergency or death. Matthias and I lived together in that shadow. From the air, human life on the surface always looks deceptively peaceful, and as we thought and talked about the lives of orphans, Three Hotel Whiskey purred contentedly, and the checkered landscape of Nebraska slid placidly beneath us. But with all the sightseeing, thought, and conversation, Matthias and I were both continually scanning the aircraft panel instruments for irregularities or problems, and we were scanning vigilantly for possible conflicting traffic. All pilots and all orphans scan like that. Matthias and I were both pilots and orphans, and we scanned like that in the plane and in life. We existed together in that unspoken vigilance.

After a period of silence and a tiny adjustment to the right engine's fuel mixture, Matthias suddenly said, "The sweethearts live right over there." He was pointing in the direction of Grand Island, which was 150 miles south of our course, and nowhere in sight. I knew he wanted to stop to see them, but before I could say anything, he pointed through the windshield at something I hadn't yet seen. It was the minuscule black speck of an approaching aircraft, and the next instant we had a call from Minneapolis Center: "Baron One Two Three Hotel Whiskey, Center, traffic eleven o'clock, two miles, eastbound, showing ninety-five hundred feet, closing fast." I responded, "Center, Three

Hotel Whiskey, traffic in sight," and then went back to my thoughts. I knew that Matthias thought about the sweethearts often, but today we couldn't stop for a visit because I needed to get back to Berkeley for work the following morning. Before I'd even finished the thought, the oncoming traffic, a Cessna 421, passed a thousand feet overhead at a closing speed of maybe four hundred miles per hour.

In 1985, at the age of thirty-eight, I had a startling experience—I met the second man in my life whom I loved unequivocally. This was Robb. On a visit to New York three months after I'd met him, I already knew what he meant to me, and I had to talk about my feelings with Matthias and Hank. I intuitively felt that we had a problem to discuss, but Matthias had solved it long ago. While we were still in school, he had said to me, "You *can* be in love with two people at once." In thinking about his statement seventeen years later, I realized that being in love with only one person was a social idea. It was not an in-born human trait or need, and certainly not a useful assumption about how life ought to be lived. Before Robb, I had already been in love with two men at once: Matthias, Hank, and I had been lovers for almost two decades, and with more happiness and much less conflict than most couples I knew. Now there was also Robb, and he was not an alternative, he was part of our lives. Matthias and Hank accepted him and came to love him almost as I did, initially because I did, and then because they did. The four of us became an *amour à quatre* of our own making, and we would remain grateful for one another, and for our family, for the next seven years.

For six of our seven years together, we had all known that Robb had HIV. I think Matthias and Hank were more realistic about the probabilities, but I was a fantasist, even as I had watched the epidemic hack its way through gay communities for almost a decade. In the summer of 1992, the four of us—and Mason and Brett on and off—spent a relaxed, do-nothing August at the Truro house just south of Provincetown that Matthias and Hank rented for the summers. Salmon or lobster on the outdoor grill was the really big event of the do-nothing week. We did this most Augusts, but this year for Robb was *too* do-nothing: he had always loved lying in the sun and swimming in the surf, but now he couldn't even walk the two hundred yards to the shore. Matthias and Hank were worried, but I insisted Robb was simply tired and needed rest. Back in Berkeley three months later, on Thanksgiving night—four days before Robb died—I called Matthias and told him that he and Hank had to come immediately, that Robb was now certainly dying. They left Teterboro the next morning in the Baron, which always terrified Hank, who survived in the plane on Valium, earplugs, and an oatmeal-colored sleep mask. Robb died on the Monday evening after their Saturday arrival. I was completely bereft, for, although it had been a seven-year family relationship, Robb had been *my* Hank. Matthias and Hank were deeply grieved, and I had no doubt that they loved Robb. But I often thought they were as grieved about my grief as they were about him. All three of us had had innumerable losses eleven years into the epidemic, but for me this was the worst. "Wally Burger, you will always have me," Mathias said repeatedly in an effort to comfort me. Once when he made that promise, I stared at him and said, "We should be so lucky." He stared back. We sat stare to stare for a while. Then we burst out laughing or crying, or both. It was one of those times when you couldn't tell what you were feeling. But one thing was certain: it was impossible that Matthias and I would *always* have each other, and we both knew it and always had.

For a long time after Robb's death, I expected the entire planet to come to a standstill. Inexplicably, life continued as it does, even after something as horrible as this. I was back in therapy to talk about Robb, and I was working on my first book, which was about living in, and only possibly surviving, an epidemic that had gone on for a decade and seemed interminable. Matthias continued his activism, and Hank, of course, was up to his ears in his heroic battle with American society. Matthias, Hank, and I remained as close as we had ever been and spent a lot of time together. To Matthias's and my delight—and Hank's horror—the Baron would get a lot of exercise over the next twenty-two years. In addition to the usual airborne jaunts—which included Berkeley and the Markeys—Mason and Brett would move to Los Angeles, where Mason had been offered a position in the L.A. Philharmonic, and Brett would become a swimming instructor at UCLA. Matthias would visit them at least twice a year and usually fly them up to Berkeley to see me. Three Hotel Whiskey was an essential part of our family, and we had come to know her so intimately that we started just calling her Whiskey—unless we were talking to air traffic control, when we used the full tail number stamped on her registration.

Just as Matthias, Hank, and I slowly aged over the decades, so did Whiskey. Matthias took meticulous care of her, but she was necessarily not quite what she had been when he bought her in 1979. In thirty-five years of flying, Matthias and I had put more than six thousand hours on the airframe and had run through four pairs of factory-new engines, three sets of deicing boots, two paint jobs, and two interior refurbishments. The paint jobs were always in the original factory colors, white with thin red and gold stripes, which neither Matthias or I much liked. But, as Matthias pointed out, "It's the only decent way to treat her, and besides it's authentic. She is what she is." In April 2014, thirty-five-year-old Whiskey was just back from her annual teardown and inspection, and Matthias phoned me, as he always did, with a detailed report. You'd have thought we were talking about our child. The annual had gone fine with nothing special of note, but he had replaced the instrument vacuum pumps and alternators on both engines, just for assurance on this critical equipment. He had also changed out the two vertical-speed indicators, one of which had become erratic in old age. "When I look at my body," Matthias said, "Whiskey's doing a lot better than I am." "But she's only thirty-five," I said. "You're sixty-seven. Maybe you need a paint job, maybe white, with red and gold stripes." We laughed. I didn't care how old he was. I still thought he was beautiful.

Six weeks later, Matthias called me for maybe the tenth time since the Whiskey annual report. "I got some bad news yesterday," he said quietly.

"The last time you said that, an eon ago, Hortense Twain had died. Surely she's not died again?"

Matthias laughed, but it was a peculiar, unsteady laugh that made me uncomfortable. "Wally Burger, this is serious."

Because of the way he said it, I felt suddenly immobilized, frozen and breathless.

"The headaches I told you about, it's a glioblastoma, a brain tumor. It's the size of an apricot, and Sloan Kettering says there's nothing really to do about it, but they can try this and that. And Hank and I talked about it last night after I got the news, and he wants me to, but

I'm not going to do the radiation or chemo or the other crap that will accomplish nothing. I can't fly, I can't pick you up. Take United."

I couldn't respond, and we sat silently on the phone for several minutes. I could hear his breathing, and I realized that I would know that sound anywhere, that it was as distinctive as his voice. And it was not just his breath I heard, it was the entirety of our fifty-year relationship, which had truly begun with Matthias enveloping me in his breath and arms and spirit as we lay in bed together at the Provincetown Inn. Only half believing that I was about to lose all of him, I tried again to speak, but my throat felt in spasm, twisted shut. Finally squeezing it out, like Mike in the dark the night *he* lost Matthias, I said, "I'll take a flight tonight and get a car into the city. I'll be there by morning. I love you." I hung up the phone and left for the airport without a suggestion of baggage, not even a book. Matthias, Hank, and I shared clothes anyway, and Matthias and I still shared a toothbrush. "Hank wants his own," Matthias had told me with a laugh many decades earlier. "He believes in germs instead of love."

I arrived in New York, and the headaches got worse, and then unbearable. Give or take a blurry, lost day or two, three weeks later Matthias died in the Eighty-First Street apartment, in a springtime morphine stupor. The mouth and golden tongue I had known for fifty years had slowly stopped talking, and the breath I had cherished inhaling since Provincetown had ceased. Matthias lay completely still for the first time in his life, and mine. Unlike Robb, who had died much too young and was angry, at sixty-seven Matthias seemed completely at peace. In Hebrew, the name Matthias means "gift of God," and in the New Testament, Matthias is chosen as the apostle to replace the traitor Judas. *My* Matthias was both of those things. He was a gay man who was my greatest gift in life, and a man who was always completely honest and completely himself. Just before he lapsed into muteness, he had barely whispered something to me, so quietly that I had to put my ear inches from his mouth. In a slow staccato series of weak exhalations that barely formed words, he said, "Don't let them near me." I knew whom he meant, he meant his family, and I nodded an affirmation and kissed him. With Central Park lit in springtime blossoms visible through the east windows, I sat on the edge of Matthias's bed and held his hand. He would never speak again, and the family would never get near him. Hank and I made sure of that. At the age of sixty-seven, Matthias departed life through the door he had entered, the door he himself had made when he left the family's trailer fifty-one years earlier, at the age of sixteen.

From a background of adversity and terrible abuse, Matthias had forged his way to the only honest life his frightened, troubled family had ever spawned. He had escaped the future they had written for him, and had reimagined a life for himself that was hugely better: he had lived as Matthias, and no one else. He had also remained, as he once told me, "someone who lives on a slow river of sadness," like the Chena that flowed behind the trailer and served as a garbage dump for the sad family that lived there. But even with that sadness and all the hurt that lurked beneath it, Matthias had always found a way to give more than he took, and to truly love. From my fifty years with him, and my brief seven with Robb, I had learned more about myself and about human life than I ever imagined there was to know. Together, these two men and Hank had helped me live a life of self-acceptance, authenticity, and love. For all that, I am inexpressibly grateful. They were men of integrity and courage, and in their struggles to be themselves, they took no prisoners.

# An Afterword for
# Young Men's Futures

Treacherous
marshes, threatening
scenery

ill-seen when most
observed

I go to the
masquerade as Is

—Keith Waldrop, *The Not Forever*[1]

With Robb and Matthias gone, there were Hank and me, and Mason
and Brett, now living out their complicated but loving adult lives in
Los Angeles. Following Matthias's death, I remained in New York for
a long while, and we tried to begin digesting the indigestible loss. We
left Matthias's studio at the east end of the apartment completely
untouched, with its staggering heaps of papers, books, photographs,
handwritten notes, paintings, memorabilia, and unfinished scripts. It
was a room Hank and I wanted to leave as is for the rest of our lives,
because it was a monument to all that Matthias had been and accomplished: it was proof that he had arrived at the masquerade as *is*. Just
staring around the room, I could almost hear his voice, and sometimes
imagined I could even feel his touch.

From his deathbed, Matthias had asked me to keep Whiskey, but
last requests aside, she had to go. Aside from the significant costs of
maintaining and operating her, Hank would never voluntarily set foot

in the plane, and at the age of sixty-seven, I was no longer as sharp or motivated as I'd been in younger years. Serious single-pilot operations in a complex, demanding twin-engine plane were no longer my idea of challenge or fun, and I had never so much as scratched a plane. It seemed worth getting out while the going was good. Anyway, Whiskey had been Matthias's and my world together for thirty-five years, and I wanted to leave that memory intact. Without Matthias, Whiskey was no longer an exhilarating world of intimacy and freedom, she was simply an airplane. An enthusiastic young man from Oregon bought her for a song and a dance. After the sale was completed, he and I shook hands, and I stood on the ramp in the fresh early-morning air to watch him climb out of Teterboro. As he raised the landing gear after takeoff, I imagined I could hear the familiar sound of the wheels clunking into the fuselage wells, this time on a life I would never again have. Soon, the white, red, and gold plane became a black speck on the western horizon, and the end of that life was sealed. The energetic young Oregonian would make Ohio in a bit over an hour and be home by early evening if weather didn't foul the plan. I wondered who would meet him at the airport, and then imagined it would be someone he loved. In my thoughts, I wished him half as good and loving a life as the one that Matthias, Hank, Robb, and Whiskey had given me. He should be so lucky.

Hank and I very slowly returned to our ordinary lives, and it was both Matthias's death and Hank's ongoing work that, after twenty years of note making, finally catalyzed my beginning to write this book. The writing was inspired by the sixty-seven years of Matthias's life and the twenty-nine of Robb's, and by the searching, heroic lives of the hundreds of gay men I have worked with in therapy over the past three decades. Everyone who comes to therapy is there to find and be himself, regardless of his stated reasons. I have felt enduring admiration for these men, and their capacity for trust, perseverance, and ultimate self-acceptance, often against serious odds. Over time, many have been able to find themselves and live that self out.

Today's gay communities would like to think that they bask in the light of a new golden age of acceptance and self-acceptance, but that is significantly untrue. Some of today's young gay men *have* had the good fortune to grow up in supportive families and communities. But the vast majority have not grown up in Manhattan or San Francisco, or in families that read *The New York Times* and Jacques Lacan. They have grown up in upstate New York or California's Central Valley—or Wyoming, Oklahoma, or South Carolina. In itself, being gay is as natural as breathing, and in a society truly accepting of natural diversity, we would accept ourselves as we are, no questions needed or asked. Shame, self-rejection, and self-contempt are feelings imposed from outside, toxic feelings we hear expressed by others and take in. Once internalized, the feelings are a Trojan horse, a gift from the Greeks, a gift that unleashes internal havoc by creating lives that are twisted by a divided self. The "gift" becomes a self-assault. Many men can unlearn the gift, and today's slowly shifting social values provide an opportunity, particularly for young men who are still working to find themselves and the lives they will lead. For older men with more entrenched trajectories, the unlearning is possible, but more difficult. Men of all ages *do* change, and the millions of gay men who suffered difficult starts but now live with authentic self-acceptance stand testimony to the possibility. The men whose stories I have related in this book stand testimony. Robb, in his too-short life, stands testimony. Matthias stands testimony: "Don't let them near me" were his last and final words.

Despite all the genuine successes, too many expressions of apparent self-acceptance are inauthentic. Many adult gay men still seek society's approval as a substitute for self-approval, an effort to swap apples for oranges. That effort rarely, if ever, leads to an authentically full and happy life. While Hank and I were trying to work through our feelings about Matthias and his death, Hank said to me:

> Think of how Matthias started out, and what he did with his life—he *liberated* himself. Half the time, the gay liberation movement is really the "Please like us, we were born this way" movement. Liberation is about insisting on our own lives, not seeking *their* permissions for a diversity that harms no one. If society is going to hang the acceptance of gay people on our conforming, I'm out of the conversation, but not without insisting on my rights. I'm like Matthias and Robb and you. I like being gay. I want to be gay, and I'm going to be gay. Our lives and how they got this way are no one else's business.

And then, of course, I listened to the attorney's lecture on the U.S. Constitution and the Bill of Rights, and the protections guaranteed all citizens, "black, brown, yellow, white, gay, gender queer, and straight." Like Matthias and Robb, Hank is a man of self-acceptance and authenticity. With those strengths in the offering, these three men became my lovers, brothers, and best friends. They were my family, and like all families, it was not without its rough times and problems. But it was the family we wanted it to be, a family of self-acceptance and mutual acceptance, a family of honesty and authentic connection, a family of love. It was *our* family. It was a gay family.

With everything that *has* improved in today's American society, and all the gay declarations of political victory and pride, the Trojan horse still lives inside the gates of too many lives, particularly those trespassed by hostile families during childhood and adolescence. As a psychotherapist and a socially observant gay man, I see those lives often. In shame, many of us still bargain with the horse, and our biggest bargaining chip lies in trying to live lives that inauthentically mimic the lives society would have us live. This cycle of shaming and shame is a malignant ecology that will endure forever unless *we* reject it: let us find our own ways to invent honest and loving lives.

# Notes

## INTRODUCTION

1. Walt Odets, *In the Shadow of the Epidemic* (Durham, NC: Duke University Press, 1995).
2. "The National HIV/AIDS Strategy and the Mpowerment Project," Center for AIDS Prevention Studies UCSF, accessed January 23, 2015, http://www.mpowerment.org.downloads.national_hiv_aids_strategy_MP_email.pdf.
3. Ibid.
4. "HIV in the United States: At a Glance," U.S. government, accessed December 7, 2014, https://www.aids.gov/hiv-aids-basics/hiv-aids-101/statistics/.
5. "Expanding the Impact," Centers for Disease Control and Prevention, accessed December 7, 2014, http://www.cdc.gov/nchhstp/newsroom/HIV FactSheets/Epidemic/Transmission.htm.
6. "CDC Warns Gay Men of 'Epidemic' HIV Rates," LifeSiteNews, accessed December 21, 2013, http://www.lifesitenews.com/news/epidemic-1-2-of-gay-men-will-have-hiv-by-age-50-if-current-rates-continue-w.

## 1. ARE GAY MEN HOMOSEXUALS?

1. Keith Waldrop, *The Not Forever* (Richmond, CA: Omnidawn Publishing, 2013), 37.
2. Harry Oosterhuis, "Sexual Modernity in the Works of Richard von Krafft-Ebing and Albert Moll," U.S. National Library of Medicine, accessed September 21, 2015, http://www.ncbi.nlm.nih.gov/pmc/articles/PMC3381524/. Krafft-Ebing was the author of *Psychopathia Sexualis*, although the term *homosexual* had earlier been used by an Austro-Hungarian journalist, Karl-Maria Kertbeny. See Robert Beachy, *Gay Berlin: Birthplace of a Modern Identity* (New York: Alfred A. Knopf, 2014).

3. John D'Emilio, *Sexual Politics, Sexual Communities: The Making of a Homosexual Minority in the United States, 1940–1970*, 2nd ed. (Chicago and London: University of Chicago Press, 1998), 21.

4. Ibid., 18.

5. Stigmatization is almost purely projection onto others we consciously or unconsciously identify with—people we fear being like—and stigma is obviously not reserved solely for gay people. A society relies on projection to protect its sense of "integrity" against all kinds of minorities: in America, Caucasians—*all* of whom are immigrants, many of mixed origins—experience racially different populations as a threatening violation of "white integrity." Only in the face of diversity do Caucasians have any Caucasian identity. Similarly, the larger American society so assumes the normality of heterosexuality that heterosexuals do not consciously experience a heterosexual identity. Like non-Caucasian Americans, gay people—who have lived since the invention of the word *homosexual* with a defined outsider identity—find this kind of assumptive, unconscious identity completely unfamiliar.

In the late nineteenth century, defining one group as homosexual necessitated defining the rest of society as something else, *something nondeviant*. Therefore, not surprisingly, the popularization of *homosexual* was quickly followed by the invention of a term for another new identity, the *heterosexual*. Having invented the term *homosexual*, the Austro-Hungarian journalist Karl-Maria Kertbeny used *heterosexual* to identify those who were not homosexual. (See "How Male Same-Sex Desire Became 'Homosexuality,'" LGBT History Project, accessed September 23, 2015, http://lgbthistoryproject .blogspot.com/2012/05/how-male-same-sex-desire-got-its-name.html.)

Although Kertbeny discussed the issues perceptively and sympathetically and intended the language to be neutral and nonprejudicial, the two terms would eventually prove troubling. Today, *homosexual*—as opposed to *gay*—has become a stigmatizing term, while *heterosexual* has not, and this difference suggests something important. Because homosexuality has always been the deviance, *heterosexual* means *not* homosexual, or free of deviance. *Homosexual* means *non*heterosexual, or abnormal, and the implication of abnormality makes the term stigmatizing.

6. Long Doan, Annalise Loehr, and Lisa R. Miller, "Formal Rights and Informal Privileges for Same-Sex Couples: Evidence from a National Survey Experiment," *American Sociological Review* 79, no. 6 (2014): 1172–95, https://doi .org/10.1177/0003122414555886. The study is based on data collected in December 2010, prior to the 2015 Supreme Court decision on gay marriage.

7. Subjects were a selected random sample from the U.S. population.

8. Doan, Loehr, and Miller, "Formal Rights," 1184.

9. Ibid., 1185.

10. Ibid.

11. Ibid., 1186–87.

12. This study was first published as "The Power of Love: The Role of Emotional Attributions and Standards in Heterosexuals' Attitudes Toward Lesbian and Gay Couples," in August 2015 by Oxford Journals and may be found at http://sf.oxfordjournals.org/content/94/1/401. The study's lead author,

Long Doan, provided me with a prepublication draft of the study, and I worked from that unpublished version, which was all that was available at the time of my research.

13. John M. Becker, "Straight People Embrace Marriage Equality, Reject Gay PDA," Bilerico Project, accessed December 15, 2014, www.bilerico.com /2014/11/straight_people_embrace_marriage_equality_reject_g.php.

14. Long Doan, Lisa R. Miller, and Annalise Loehr, "The Power of Love: The Role of Emotional Attributions and Standards in Heterosexuals' Attitudes Toward Lesbian and Gay Couples," prepublication draft obtained from Long Doan, December 17, 2014, with permission for limited citation.

15. Throughout the twentieth century, gay sex was largely treated as a pathological behavior, but even when it was not, it was still not seen as humanly important. This prejudicial misperception found expression throughout the early epidemic in public opinion and public health messages that thoughtlessly suggested that gay sex was unnecessary and dispensable. Despite the nearly universal, centuries-long experience that condoms interfere with intimacy, gay men were expected to readily adopt them as an *every-time*, *lifelong* measure for anal, and even oral, sex. The incredulity about gay men's noncompliance with the Condom Code—much of it from gay men themselves—is a measure of how little the gay sensibility behind gay sex is understood or acknowledged, even by gay men. If men would not use condoms, they were often then told that anal sex was dispensable, despite its having, for many gay men, the same emotional significance that vaginal sex has for heterosexuals. Frottage—the rubbing together of bodies—was often suggested as an alternative for gay men, but not for heterosexuals.

16. For many heterosexual men, two men displaying affection for each other suggests that being biologically male provides no assurance of heterosexuality, and the display threatens the heterosexual's identity, usually unconsciously. The fragility of heterosexual male identity is revealed in a pernicious American tradition: those heterosexuals who would try to deny the simplest, most human expressions of affection between two men are the same people who routinely watch fictional drama—or documentary reports of real-life events—in which males affirm their heterosexual identities by beating or shooting one another to death. Violence is the male interaction of choice because it is the only way many men are able to engage intensely with other men. It is a kind of—*truly* perverse—intimacy.

17. *Cathexis* is from the Greek, but in James Strachey's English translations of Freud, Strachey used the term to translate from the German *Besetzung*. A German friend described one meaning of *Besetzung* as a "spark or electric charge," another as "military occupation or filling."

18. In Freud's description, libidinous energy—the libido—is primary and fuels cathexis. In my understanding, a particular cathexis still determines *how* libidinous energy is directed, and in this sense, cathexis is primary in understanding what it means to be gay. Everyone has libido, and there is no difference between heterosexual and homosexual libido; the only differentiation is in how an individual expresses libido. If the engine—the libido— powers the car, it does not steer it, and the steering is what defines the route

of travel. My point is that same-gender sexuality is secondary to and follows from same-gender cathexis.

19. Doan, Miller, and Loehr, "Power of Love," 22.

20. *GLAAD Media Reference Guide—AP and New York Times*, GLAAD, accessed October 5, 2015, http://www.glaad.org/reference/style.

21. Ibid.

22. "gay (adj.)," Online Etymology Dictionary, accessed August 13, 2014, http://www.etymonline.com/index.php?term=gay.

23. "gay," Oxford Dictionaries, accessed August 13, 2014, www.oxforddictionaries.com/definition/english/gay.

24. Another aspect of gaydar is probably the unconscious perception of pupillary dilation, which occurs naturally with sexual attraction. Most people are not aware of this phenomenon, but I believe that gay men are unconsciously sensitive to it, just as most people are. Pupillary dilation is not only a sign of sexual interest, it is unconsciously interpreted as a sign of availability by the other party, who may return the communication with his own involuntary dilation. Gay men often detect each other through eye contact alone; and they know that straight men are often uncomfortable with sustained eye contact and avoid it, except in intimidation or overt aggression.

25. Some women are threatened by a gay man's lack of sexual interest because they rely on "attractiveness" as a source of social power, self-worth, and identity. Women who encounter disinterest can experience it as a threat to their feminine identity, and to the conventional social construction of gender that supports that identity. Such threatened women are sometimes hostile to gay men. Some women with more independently defined identities can become emotionally intimate companions of gay men. For these women, intimacy may feel less attainable with competitive women, and nearly impossible with heterosexual men, many of whom lack the developed capacity for emotional transparency and expressive intimacy.

26. Homophobia in heterosexual men is much more about their own emotional insecurity than about gay men. In seeing certain things in others, these men fear seeing something undesirable in themselves. The solution is often an "inhibited projection," which, like projection, is self-protective. Unfortunately, both projection and inhibited projection diminish and distort our perception of others. Many straight men who are not actively homophobic are unable to recognize the sensibilities of gay men because of a need to remain blind to those in whom they might uncomfortably recognize something of themselves. An astonishing number of heterosexual men assert that they "have never known a gay person," which can rarely be true.

27. Properly speaking, *sex* is used to describe biological differences, *gender* to describe socially influenced differences.

28. Donald Trump, the U.S. president as of 2017, is one notorious and extreme example of a fragile male identity hidden behind a doggedly "masculine" presentation that is, in turn, bolstered by pathologically narcissistic defenses. Told by his authoritarian and emotionally distant father that there were only two kinds of people—winners and losers—Trump was sent as a teenager to military school to become a winner. He revealed to classmates that the three

men he modeled himself on were Clint Eastwood, James Bond, and Hugh Hefner. Trump's extreme sensitivity to criticism is an obvious indication of the fragility behind his exaggerated male presentation. When he appeared to be losing the race in the last weeks of the campaign, Trump told a group of supporters, "I don't know what kind of shape I'm in, but I'll be happy, and at least I will have known, win, lose, or draw . . . I will be happy with myself." His concern with what shape *he* is in, and his conviction that he will be happy with *himself*, instead of concern for the election and the country, are obvious expressions of his narcissism. But apparently the assertive male presentation that is driven by a nearly delusional narcissism was compelling for millions of American men, and more than a handful of women. In Trump, men saw the man they wanted to be, women the man they wanted. (Trip Gabriel and Ashley Parker, "Hillary Clinton Makes Pitch for Mandate and a Swing-State Sweep," *New York Times*, accessed October 21, 2016, http://www.nytimes.com/2016/10/22/us/politics/donald-trump-hillary-clinton.html.)

29. "What Does the Bible Say About Man and Woman?" accessed October 31, 2015, http://www.openbible.info.
30. Waldrop, *Not Forever*, 37 (also cited at the chapter head).

## 2. STIGMA AND SHAME

1. Waldrop, *Not Forever*, 19.
2. In the most recent available figures (2014) from the Federal Bureau of Investigation, LGBT people were at the top of the list of minorities subjected to hate crimes, followed in descending order by Jews, Muslims, blacks, Asians, Hispanics, and whites. LGBT people today are approximately twice as likely to be targeted as blacks. Haeyoun Park and Iaryna Mykhyalyshyn, "L.G.B.T. People Are More Likely to Be Targets of Hate Crimes Than Any Other Minority Group," *New York Times*, June 16, 2016, http://www.nytimes.com/interactive/2016/06/16/us/hate-crimes-against-lgbt.html?_r=0.
3. Soumya Karlamangla, Abby Sewell, and Laura J. Nelson, "Boy's Alleged Abuse Described in Graphic Grand Jury Testimony," *Los Angeles Times*, August 18, 2014, http://www.latimes.com/local/countygovernment/la-me-gabriel-fernandez-20140819-story.html#page=1.
4. Ibid.
5. "Anti-Defamation League State Hate Crime Statutory Provisions," Anti-Defamation League, accessed February 14, 2015, http://www.adl.org/assets/pdf/combating-hate/ADL-hate-crime-state-laws-clickable-chart.pdf.
6. Benjamin B. Wagner, U.S. Attorney for the Eastern District of California, "Civil Rights Prosecutions: Hate Crimes," U.S. Department of Justice, accessed February 14, 2015, http://www.justice.gov/usao/priority-areas/civil-rights/hate-crimes.
7. Ibid.
8. "3 Whites Indicted in Dragging Death of Black Man in Texas," CNN.com, July 6, 1998, http://www.cnn.com/US/9807/06/dragging.death.02/.
9. Liz Hamel, Jamie Firth, Tina Hoffman, Jennifer Kates, Sarah Levine, and

Lindsey Dawson, "HIV/AIDS in the Lives of Gay and Bisexual Men in the United States," Henry J. Kaiser Family Foundation, 4, accessed October 29, 2015, http://files.kff.org/attachment/survey-hivaids-in-the-lives-of-gay-and-bisexual-men-in-the-united-states.

10. Twenty-six percent of respondents cited "equal rights"; 24 percent, "marriage equality"; 20 percent, "HIV/AIDS"; 8 percent, "employment discrimination"; 7 percent, "general health"; and 7 percent, "violence, hate crimes or bullying."

11. Ibid., 16.

12. "Stigma and Discrimination," Centers for Disease Control and Prevention, accessed November 11, 2015, http://www.cdc.gov/msmhealth/stigma-and-discrimination.htm.

13. Personal communication, October 11, 2014.

14. Medical care providers often stigmatize or refuse LGBTQ people. This is a significant problem in the United States, and GLMA: Health Professionals Advancing LGBT Equality has worked on addressing the issue for decades. Discrimination is seen not only in private primary-care medicine, but in specialty medicine, dentistry, emergency rooms, and hospital settings. See http://glma.org/.

15. "Gay and Bisexual Men's Health: Mental Health," Centers for Disease Control and Prevention, accessed February 14, 2015, http://www.cdc.gov/msmhealth/mental-health.htm. According to the Centers for Disease Control:

> Homosexuality is not a mental disorder, but homophobia, stigma, and discrimination have negative effects on the health of MSM [men who have sex with men], lesbians, and other sexual minorities. The negative effects of social marginalization can be found in adolescent and adult MSM. For example, research has shown that MSM and other members of the LGBT community are at increased risk for a number of mental health problems. Research also has found that, compared to other men, MSM are at increased risk of:
>
> - Diagnoses of Major Depression during adolescence and adulthood;
> - Diagnoses of Bipolar Disorder; and
> - Diagnoses of Generalized Anxiety Disorder during adolescence and adulthood.
>
> MSM are also at greater risk for other health threats that often occur in conjunction with mental health problems (i.e., comorbidities). These include greater use of illegal drugs and a greater risk for suicide. For example, MSM are more likely than other men to have attempted suicide and to have successfully completed a suicide attempt. The HIV epidemic also has had a profound impact on the mental health of MSM. The disease affects those men who are living with HIV, and loved ones of those living with or having died from HIV.

16. "Thirty Years of HIV/AIDS: Snapshots of an Epidemic," amfAR, accessed February 20, 2015, http://www.amfar.org/thirty-years-of-HIV/AIDS-snap shots-of-an-epidemic/.

17. Chris Geidner, "13 Times the Reagan White House Press Briefing Erupted with Laughter over AIDS," BuzzFeed, accessed March 23, 2015, http://www .buzzfeed.com/chrisgeidner/times-the-reagan-white-house-press-briefing -erupted-with#.ky3QgG20R.

18. "Thirty Years," amfAR.

19. Philip M. Boffey, "Panel Disagrees over AIDS Risk for Public," *New York Times*, October 4, 1985, http://partners.nytimes.com/library/national/science /aids/100485sci-aids.html.

20. Ibid.

21. Philip M. Boffey, "Federal Efforts on AIDS Criticized as Gravely Weak," *New York Times*, October 30, 1986, http://partners.nytimes.com/library /national/science/aids/103086sci-aids-2.html.

22. "Thirty Years," amfAR.

23. I will discuss the idea of "addiction" more fully in later chapters, but a brief note here seems useful because of its importance for Peter. In its original medical use, *addiction* describes a physiological process of cellular response and change in the presence of a drug and development of tolerance and withdrawal symptoms—because of cellular adaption—when the drug is discontinued. Applied to behavioral issues involving sex, eating, shopping, and Internet browsing—or medically nonaddictive substances—the idea of "addiction" is a misleading metaphor that has ridden the coattails of 12-step programs that were originally about alcohol or other drugs. Addiction is a discrete, biological process that has, in itself, no human meaning. Peter's sex had important meaning for him and, obviously, none of the biological processes of addiction. Sexual desire may become problematic, however, when it is acted out *compulsively*. Compulsive behavior is the result of attempting to address emotional issues with ineffective solutions. Engaging in sex to fill an emotional need that sex—in the particular way one is having it—does not fulfill is an obvious example. When the ineffective solution is invoked repeatedly—always to no, little, or only temporary satisfaction— the pattern becomes a compulsive, repetitive behavior. This is still not an addiction. One important distinction between addiction and compulsive behavior is that compulsive behavior often has emotional meaning, while addictions, per se, do not. Although addictions may have been initiated by something meaningful, once under way they become a biological process that is independent of the original meaning. Much of the representation of compulsive behavior as addiction seems an attempt to skirt meaning. Compulsive behavior needs to be understood, addiction simply stopped, perhaps with medical help. How one first became addicted to a substance *is* something that would usually be worth understanding. Unless a drug is simply forced on an unwilling victim who becomes quickly addicted, most addiction is initially motivated by something meaningful: something motivates a person to attempt to alter his consciousness.

## 3. OUR TRIPARTITE COMMUNITIES TODAY

1. Waldrop, *Not Forever*, 103.
2. "Basic Statistics," Centers for Disease Control and Prevention, accessed October 7, 2017, https://www.cdc.gov/hiv/basics/statistics.html.
3. The developmental assumptions used to determine the age range of each of the three groups is as follows. People would first have been able to be cognizant—if not entirely comprehending—of the connection between gay men and the epidemic beginning at about age eight. They would become cognizant of being gay at age twelve. The first gay sexual experience beyond childhood play would have occurred at age sixteen. Men would have first come out and associated with other gay men at the age of eighteen. I have made these rough assumptions based on three decades of doing psychotherapy with hundreds of gay men, and based on the approximately forty interviews I conducted in preparing this book. Obviously, for many individuals, these ages would be different. They are means and give us only an impression of who might fall into which group.
4. Other psychological issues span all three groups. Denial has been a significant part of how gay communities have psychologically managed the epidemic, and this is still true. Partly as a result of shame, gay men in all groups—in different ways—have exercised denial about HIV in both the early and the late epidemics. We use denial against experiences that are frightening or painful, but we also use it to banish external and internal facts that feel shameful—because the shame is painful. There is no apparently easier way to try to reduce stigma and manage shame than by having the stigmatized, shameful fact go away. One expression of denial of the epidemic is our "normalization" of HIV in gay communities. We have "medically institutionalized" AIDS, and HIV infection is now widely considered a "chronic manageable disease," comparable to diabetes or hypertension. HIV *is* now endemic—rather than epidemic—in our cities, and it *is* largely medically manageable. The normalization of HIV *has* helped positive men with troubled feelings about their infections, and it *has* helped reduce shame. But HIV is still an infection of medical consequence, and perhaps most important, HIV has significant social and psychological meaning seen in few—perhaps *no*—other chronic manageable diseases. It would often be useful for the positive man to consciously acknowledge this meaning rather than deny it, because it would help him confront and address the feelings around it. HIV has changed the interpersonal and sexual experience of all positive and negative men, and this is true for all three groups. HIV is not *nothing*, normalized or not.
5. The concurrence of these three important influences has created a significant problem for many older-group men. Although isolation is common among both positive and negative older-group survivors, it is more common and even more problematic for those who are HIV-positive. But not only older-group men experience isolation. All three groups experience it, but for different reasons. The problem, however, is usually more etiologically and psychologically complex in the older group.

6. "HIV/AIDS and Older Adults in the United States," *Today's Research on Aging* 18 (December 2009), http://www.prb.org/pdf09/TodaysResearchAging18 .pdf.
7. "HIV Among Older Americans," Centers for Disease Control and Prevention, accessed March 19, 2015, http://www.cdc.gov/hiv/risk/age/olderamericans/.
8. Ibid.
9. Ibid.
10. Jane Gross, "As More Cases Arise in People over 50, a Silent Group Slowly Gets Help," *New York Times*, March 16, 1997, http://partners.nytimes.com /library/national/science/aids/031697sci-aids.html.
11. Lipodystrophy is a redistribution of subcutaneous fat, as a result of long-term use of antiviral medications and, possibly, of HIV itself. Lipodystrophy is usually visible in the face (as sunken cheeks and temples), in thinness of the arms and legs, and in elevated abdominal fat levels.
12. Let's Kick ASS is a valuable San Francisco–based organization, founded by a long-term HIV survivor, Ted Anderson, in 2013. It offers an opportunity for new, supportive community, but on a larger scale than what Luis and Mark had put together with their new friends. ASS is an acronym for "AIDS Survivor Syndrome." In 2016, the organization's mission statement read:

> Let's Kick ASS—AIDS Survivor Syndrome is a national grass-roots movement of long-term survivors, positive & negative, honoring the unique and profound experiences of living through the AIDS epidemic.
>
> We envision a world where long-term survivors infected with and affected by decades of HIV live long, healthy, dignified, engaged, meaningful and productive lives, free from stigma and discrimination.
>
> We know that restoring a sense of meaning and purpose is vital to reclaiming our lives, ending isolation, and envisioning a future we never imagined.

13. The Condom Code was the primary HIV-prevention message throughout the early and, now, late epidemic. The code is that every gay man—without regard to his own or his partner's HIV status—use a condom for every sexual interaction, regardless of the particular form of sex. That meant that both insertive and receptive anal and oral sex were included. For a time in the late eighties, it was even briefly suggested that a rubber dental dam be used for kissing because HIV had been discovered in saliva. More men were frightened by the seemingly impossible, monolithic Condom Code than were adherent to it.
14. The interview with Franklin, a pseudonym, was conducted face-to-face in Berkeley on October 3, 2014.
15. "HIV Testing and Risk Behaviors Among Gay, Bisexual, and Other Men Who Have Sex with Men," Centers for Disease Control and Prevention, 6–7, accessed December 22, 2014, http://www.cdc.gov/mmwr/preview/mmwrhtml /mm6247a4.htm. CDC figures for self-report of unprotected anal intercourse

(AI) are higher in this group than in younger-group or older-group men. Approximately 57 percent of HIV-negative middle-group men reported unprotected AI in the twelve months preceding a November 2013 survey. For HIV-positive men in the same age group, the figure was 63 percent. Many men of all ages have railed relentlessly against this second-course behavior and stigmatized both middle-group and younger men for it. Older men forget how they felt and behaved during the self-discovery and elevated libido of youth, and they expect young men to adhere to their more mature feelings and behavior. Human beings—particularly young ones—learn little from others' experience, particularly in matters that are rarely talked about or are talked about only with discomfort, reserve, and misdirection. Younger men do not have the waning libidos of older men and will learn little about "appropriate sex" from them. The expectation of older men—and many younger men who are denying their own feelings and experience—is that sex be conducted in a rational and sensible manner, that perpetual assumption of so much unhelpful HIV-prevention work. The expectation is in vain, particularly for young male human life. Older men must recognize that younger men are developmentally different, and that many middle-group men are survivors of childhood trauma about the entanglement of gay identity, sex, and death. As Franklin's story makes clear, much developmentally useful experience is hindered by the early trauma of HIV. Because of trauma-induced developmental delay, many middle-group survivors are still discovering themselves as sexual gay adults.

16. Grindr is a mobile phone application on which the user has a profile and a photograph, and the app shows profiles and pictures of other users, also providing their distance from the user's present position.

17. A coherent counterphobic process may underlie and employ breakthrough episodes. People sometimes make entire careers rooted in counterphobia; pilots who are afraid of flying are one example I am familiar with. AIDS-prevention educators are another, and I have known several educators who became HIV-infected through breakthrough episodes that expressed an underlying counterphobic process. Counterphobic processes are seen in many, but most often in middle-group men, because of childhood trauma triggered by early knowledge of HIV and its consequences. These men's lives are often shadowed by a persistent, haunting fear from a young age.

18. Hamel et al., "HIV/AIDS in the Lives," 3.

19. Ibid., 19–20.

20. "HIV Testing and Risk Behaviors," CDC, 7.

21. "HIV Among Older Americans," CDC, 3.

22. The interview with Jason, a pseudonym, was conducted face-to-face in Berkeley on November 11, 2014.

23. *ddf ub2* means "drug and disease free, you be, too." *Clean* means "no infections and HIV-negative."

24. Gary Feldman, M.D., personal communication, October 11, 2014.

25. Henry David Thoreau said, "The youth gets together his materials to build a bridge to the moon, or perchance a palace or temple on the earth, and at length the middle-aged man concludes to build a wood-shed with them."

26. The simple epidemiological observation that, in the United States, HIV is seen most frequently in gay men has often been experienced by gay men as a stigmatizing and shaming indictment of being gay. The epidemiological observation feels like "You have AIDS because you are gay, and you have caused the problem of AIDS by being something that you shouldn't be anyway." The feeling is that AIDS further soils the gay identity. Thus many gay men have insisted that AIDS is not a "gay problem," which is true—it is a problem within gay communities—but overlooks the epidemiological point. Epidemiological facts do not assert causes. The effort to dissociate group identity from AIDS has often had the unfortunate effect of redirecting public funds from the groups most in need of it. This has been true in both gay communities and African-American communities, which have also often tried to dissociate themselves from AIDS. All stigmatized minority communities have an aversion to being associated with problems, particularly when the implication is that the problems are self-induced.

27. Peter Staley, "Gay-on-Gay Shaming: The New HIV War," *Huffington Post*, February 28, 2014, http://www.huffingtonpost.com/peter-staley/gay-on-gay-shaming-the-new-hiv-war_b_4856233.html. The reference to "Truvada whore" is about the disturbing controversy surrounding pre-exposure prophylaxis, or PrEP, which may be the most effective prevention measure we have ever had. Gay men still make up the largest group in new infections in the United States, but many gay men deny that and find the statement of that fact stigmatizing.

28. For those interested in the history of HIV prevention for gay men in the United States, please see Odets, *In the Shadow of the Epidemic*; and two articles, Walt Odets, "AIDS Education and Harm Reduction for Gay Men: Psychological Approaches for the 21st Century," *AIDS & Public Policy Journal* 9, no. 1 (1994), http://waltodets.com/Articles/AIDS_Education_and_Harm_Reduct/aids_education_and_harm_reduct.html; and Walt Odets, "Why We Stopped Doing Primary Prevention for Gay Men in 1985," *AIDS & Public Policy Journal* 10, no. 1 (1995), http://waltodets.com/Articles/Why_We_Stopped_Doing_Preventio/why_we_stopped_doing_preventio.html. The full text for the two articles is available at the URLs listed.

29. Over several months in 2014 and 2015, I asked several dozen gay men how often an infection occurs from an exposure through receptive anal intercourse (RAI) and through insertive anal intercourse (IAI). Not a single man knew the answer to either question or had even a rough estimate. RAI results in an infection for every two hundred to three hundred exposures; IAI, an infection for every thousand to twelve hundred exposures for circumcised men, with higher rates for uncircumcised men (because of the cell structure of the foreskin). *Remember that these figures are group statistics that do not predict for any single individual in any single sexual act or series of sexual acts.* If the winning odds on a roulette wheel are one in thirty-six, the result of any single play of the wheel is never predictable from that ratio.

30. Today, the code usually, but not always, excludes oral sex. Virtually no gay men use condoms for oral sex, and there is no evidence that oral sex transmits HIV, except in rare circumstances. The possibility of infection exists

with ejaculation in the mouth when wounds are open to the bloodstream in the receptive partner's mouth—for example, immediately after oral surgery. The past thirty years have seen a small handful of possibly documented cases of such transmission. According to the CDC (http://www.cdc.gov/hiv/basics /transmission.html):

> The highest oral sex risk is performing oral sex (fellatio) with ejaculation in your mouth. However, the risk is still low, and much lower than anal or vaginal sex. Factors that may increase the risk of transmitting HIV through oral sex are oral ulcers, bleeding gums, genital sores, and the presence of other sexually transmitted diseases (STDs) (which may or may not be visible).

31. Although I have been speaking about the Condom Code, instruction about HIV testing is similarly problematic. From the beginning of the early epidemic, public health attempted to establish six-month testing as the community standard, although I have never heard a credible rationale for the six-month interval. An astute thirty-five-year-old—born in 1980, a member of middle-group men—who was an early reader during the writing of this book wrote me a note about his experience with testing:

> In addition to the Condom Code, another "good gay" behavior that became ingrained in my generation is the ritual HIV test. I'll never forget my first HIV test, and while I had already made the connection between gay and HIV, this experience really solidified the syntonic relationship, as you call it. When we met I mentioned to you that most of my work experience has been within Public Health organizations, and Public Health has made routine HIV testing into as important a "good behavior" for gay men as the Condom Code. . . . Public Health's mission is to "stop HIV," and with HAART, they are now counting on identifying/diagnosing and treating all cases, in order to slow the spread of HIV. This is indeed the premise of British Columbia's multi-million dollar "seek and treat to optimize" HIV prevention (S.T.O.P.) program. The thing is, routine HIV testing does very little to alleviate any of the root issues you describe in your book. It's a false assurance. You've done the "right thing" making sure you know your status. It's your "duty" as a gay man. But this is in the service of some tangential goal. Just like the Condom Code, it reinforces shame and denial.

32. Social marketing is sometimes associated with another concept, *diffusion of innovation*, and the two are often used together, though backed by slightly different concepts. In this discussion, I will use the term *social marketing* to refer to elements of both concepts. The two share the idea that people pass through "psychological stages" in their willingness to adopt new attitudes or behavior. This psychological model is simplistic. The "stages of change" are

awareness, knowledge, persuasion, implementation, and confirmation. This is exactly the set of stages two people might use in deciding where to have lunch. The model leaves out a great deal of what transpires psychologically in "persuading" people to "implement" condom use during sex. The first and second stages are superfluous for most gay men in the United States—they already know about HIV and condoms—and the last stage is possible only through unreliable self-report by people who have been subjected to social pressures. This unreliability is known as social-desirability bias.

33. James W. Dearing, "Social Marketing and Diffusion-Based Strategies for Communicating with Unique Populations: HIV Prevention in San Francisco," *Journal of Health Communication* 1, no. 4 (1996), https://doi.org/10.1080/108107396127997.

34. Social-desirability bias is the underreporting of socially undesirable behavior or attitudes and the overreporting of socially desirable ones. This limitation must be considered in any research based on self-report. In my experience, gay men consistently underreport the practice of anal sex, particularly receptive anal sex. People underreport the fact of *being* gay, which makes U.S. Census data on LGBT people suspect. The percentages are almost certainly higher than reported.

35. Susan Kippax, an Australian researcher, coined the term *negotiated safety* in a 1993 paper called "Sustaining Safe Sex." Her belief was that informed negotiated safety was a better long-term solution than many shorter-term measures such as condoms, and her longitudinal study of gay men supported that idea. The idea was largely ill received and very controversial in the United States.

36. Negotiated safety—like every other prevention approach for sexually active people—is not a way to eliminate *all* possibility of infection. It is a *risk-reduction* strategy that, in Lyndon's life, allowed the physical intimacy that he and Tim valued. In all areas of life, we accept some risk for things we value, and driving an automobile is an obvious, everyday example. But if gay sex is treated as a dispensable activity, then risk reduction feels inadequate, and we expect *risk elimination*. Unlike heterosexuals, gay men in the United States are usually expected—and publicly expect themselves—to adhere to a risk-elimination standard. As one result, Lyndon had never heard the term *negotiated safety*, had never heard the generic practice discussed by prevention workers or friends, and had never received support for clarifying and refining "the arrangement" with Tim to improve—not ensure—its reliability. Lyndon and Tim were both ashamed of and uncomfortable with what they were doing and avoided any discussion that brought it to consciousness or the attention of others. I had asked Lyndon a simple question—whether he thought he could avoid HIV for his lifetime—and his confused response was that no one had ever asked him that. Thoughtful prevention education would have raised *that* question for sure.

37. Hamel et al., "HIV/AIDS in the Lives," 4.

38. Ibid., 34.

39. Ibid., 3.

40. See note 34.

41. James Krellenstein, personal communication by phone, December 6, 2014. Krellenstein has been particularly active in support of Truvada PrEP, the controversial FDA-approved pre-exposure prophylaxis.
42. The World Health Organization has stated that the use of PrEP is "strongly recommended" and that there is "high quality evidence" of its efficacy. For more information, see the following link, first accessed October 2016: http://www.who.int/hiv/topics/prep/en/.
43. It is now widely accepted that the proper treatment of HIV infection with multidrug regimens lowers viral blood levels to a point that does not allow HIV transmission. In lab test reports, this is labeled *undetectable*.
44. The CDC currently reports oral contraception as 91 percent effective against pregnancy, which is virtually identical to the efficacy cited for Truvada PrEP against HIV. For condoms, the reported efficacy against pregnancy is 82 percent, while for HIV, it is in the 70 to 75 percent range. All of these efficacy figures partly reflect inconsistent use, but in both contraception and HIV prevention, the use rate appears significantly higher for the oral pill than for the condom. Unlike a daily pill, condom use must be implemented in the altered consciousness of sexual arousal. Pills are more readily implemented as a long-term strategy, but condoms ultimately remain a tactical approach that relies on rational behavior in an irrational state of consciousness. Sex *is* irrational, which is a significant part of what makes it humanly valuable. Pills are also much less disruptive of the sexual and emotional experience than condoms, which have been disliked and avoided by men for centuries. Gay men are no different, nor should anyone expect them to be. For efficacy data, see the two following links, both accessed April 2016: http://www.cdc.gov/reproductivehealth/unintendedpregnancy/contraception.htm and http://www.aidsmap.com/Consistent-condom-use-in-anal-sex-stops-70-of-HIV-infections-study-finds/page/2586976/.

## 4. THE SIGNIFICANCE OF EARLY-LIFE EXPERIENCE

1. Waldrop, *Not Forever*, 22–23.
2. American psychiatry often finds Erikson's developmental, observationally derived description of human experience unsophisticated for its lack of a "scientific" or medical model, and clinically less useful because of Erikson's relative disinterest in diagnosis. Psychologists are sometimes more engaged by Erikson's work, but some emulate psychiatry and lean more on diagnosis.
3. Erik Erikson, *Childhood and Society*, 2nd ed. (New York: W. W. Norton, 1963), 247–74.
4. I believe that perceived "personality" is more usefully thought of as a combination of character, style, and sensibility, which I discussed more fully in chapter 1, in the context of a "gay sensibility."
5. Erikson, *Childhood and Society*, 251.
6. Ibid., 249.
7. Ibid., 247.

8. Ibid., 250.
9. Ibid., 251.
10. Ibid., 251–54.
11. Ibid., 253.
12. Ibid., 252.
13. Ibid., 255.
14. Ibid., 256.
15. In the late eighties, I conducted a therapy group for HIV-positive men, all doing badly with their medical issues. Those doing less well often unintentionally dominated the group's conversation. Once, a group member, Karl, talked for the first twenty minutes about the side effects of his medications, including constant vomiting and debilitating diarrhea. When I pointed out to other group members that they were unusually quiet that evening, one previously silent man responded, "We should let Karl talk. He threw up five times today. I only threw up twice." Everyone laughed and all immediately turned their focus back to Karl. No one who was feeling better than Karl would speak and call attention to himself. When the group had dwindled to three survivors, I began seeing the three men individually and discontinued further group work with seriously ill HIV-positive men. In those days, *positive* meant "dying"—in short order for those who were symptomatic. Those men with the most advanced clinical illness unintentionally set a standard that other men were reluctant to exceed. Feelings for those doing less well were clearly producing premature suffering and death among those who were otherwise healthier. This is the group that I mentioned in the introduction: four men died in a single week, following a meeting in which one of the four was so ill that he was barely able to speak. The relatively healthier men in the group could not aspire to do better than the one man who obviously could not survive.
16. Erikson, *Childhood and Society*, 259.
17. Ibid., 260.
18. Ibid., 260–61.
19. Ibid., 261–62.
20. The gay political right—the assimilationist wing—rallied around Andrew Sullivan's book *Virtually Normal: An Argument About Homosexuality* (1995), which, broadly speaking, posited that homosexuals were "virtually normal." Michael Warner, from the other side of the argument, countered with *The Trouble with Normal: Sex, Politics, and the Ethics of Queer Life* (1999), an argument for difference and diversity. In 1993, Bruce Bawer had released a book, *A Place at the Table: The Gay Individual in American Society*, which is usually credited with initiating the political-right gay agenda. It argued for gays' finding a place at the larger society's table.
21. Erikson, *Childhood and Society*, 264.
22. Ibid.
23. Ibid., 267.
24. Ibid., 268.
25. Ibid., 269.

## 5. SOME OBSTRUCTIONS TO SELF-DISCOVERY AND
## SELF-REALIZATION: DIAGNOSIS, ISOLATION, AND GRIEF

1. Waldrop, *Not Forever*, 102.
2. While the American Psychiatric Association (APA) was preparing a new edition of the *DSM*—the *DSM-5*, released in 2013—the U.S. military asked the organization to change the PTSD diagnosis to PTSI—post-traumatic stress *injury*. The military thought—I believe correctly—that the idea of having a "disorder" was discouraging too many combat soldiers from seeking help, but the APA refused the request. The APA appears to take some pride in its euphemism for "illness."
3. *Ego-dystonic homosexuality* referred to homosexual feelings in men who found the feelings alien and wanted to be "cured." That the feelings were significantly an internalization of social stigma was overlooked, and "reparative" therapy was widely considered the solution.
4. The *DSM-5* is a carefully constructed *political* document that attempts to appease the conflicting theoretical orientations of APA members—the psychoanalysts and the behaviorists, and almost everything in between. As a politically compromised document, the *DSM* often neglects useful clinical realities, and it casts people with diverse emotional lives as diagnosable "cases of disorder." Undoubtedly, someone at the APA thought it important to maintain PTSD as a disorder, despite the possible benefits of allowing combat survivors to experience themselves instead as injured. *Disorder* implies that the person is psychologically ill—as opposed to emotionally *affected*—and it is not a term that is usually accurate or necessary, particularly if it obstructs useful attention to the person's feelings. For good reason, we do not describe a soldier with a leg wound as *crippled*, we describe him as *injured*: the former is subjective, stigmatizing, and entrenching, the latter objective. People have feelings of all kinds, and those who have survived trauma often have significant feelings that are comprehensible and appropriate responses. Such feelings are not an illness, disease, or pathology, they are human life as we have always known it. If we were not trying to hide from ourselves the reality of all the horrible things people do to one another, perhaps we would not find it so compelling to hide the consequences of those horrible things behind the label *illness*. We are much more tolerant and accepting of prejudice, stigma, abuse, and combat than of the consequences of those brutalities. *We* did not do it to the survivor of trauma—*he* has an illness. This is a reassignment of blame that we see often, perhaps even typically, in the aftermath of trauma, which is a *social* problem.

   The social problem lurking behind diagnosis is revealed in some implications of the *DSM* term *disorder*. In addition to being a euphemism for *illness, disorder* implies *out of order* in the courtroom sense of the phrase: messy, disruptive, and not according to the rules. Disordered things—and people—are "out of place." A person diagnosed as disordered has departed from the "normal" order of human life that we expect him to have, and in doing so, he disrupts our lives. The idea of being out of order—having a disorder—is the reason that the discussion of diagnosis is important for gay men.

5. Participating in the antihomosexual movement alongside Socarides was another powerhouse in the APA, the psychiatrist Robert Spitzer, of Columbia University, which had, in 1967, been the first university in the United States at which a gay student organization had formed, the Student Homophile League. Dr. Spitzer figured significantly in the stigmatization of gay people in the United States. *The New York Times* once described him as "a major architect of the modern classification of mental disorders," considered by some "the father of modern psychiatry." Spitzer was the chair of the committee that prepared the *DSM-III*, released in 1980. Homosexuals had long been sacrificed in the political compromises operating behind the publicly authoritative face of the *DSM*. But in the *DSM-III* that Spitzer chaired—only thirty-eight years ago—homosexuality was, for the first time, *not* diagnosed as a disorder. So far, so good for Spitzer and the *DSM*. The political compromise, however, was that the *DSM* committee replaced the old diagnosis with a new one, *ego-dystonic homosexuality*—which was defined as homosexuality in a man or woman uncomfortable with his or her sexuality and wanting to change it.

It is inexcusable that a group of intelligent clinicians was unable to recognize and acknowledge that the alienation from their sexuality—the dystonia—that some gay people feel is the creation of a pathological, stigmatizing society. Ego-dystonic homosexuality is not a clinical problem or disorder, it is a societal problem. The political significance of this new diagnosis was that it left open the door for careers devoted to "reparative" or "conversion" therapy, a widely practiced, highly destructive, and thoroughly discredited "treatment and cure" for homosexuality. One could well imagine that many of these careerists were hoping that they could constrain their own homosexual feelings by successfully treating such feelings in others.

Despite Spitzer and others—who continued to believe that homosexuality was a "treatable disorder" that could be "cured" in people who were "motivated"—ego-dystonic homosexuality was, by popular demand both within and outside the APA, finally removed from the official diagnostic lexicon in 1986, in a revised edition of the *DSM-III*, the *DSM-III-R*. It took six years—including the first five years of the early epidemic—to wrangle the politics this time around. Six years of wrangling was not only enough time to kill thousands of adult gay men with HIV, it was enough time to accommodate approximately twenty-seven thousand youth suicides in the United States. A high percentage of the losses were among gay youth, whose suicide rate is about three times that of heterosexual youth.

Following the release of the *DSM-III-R*, the ever-determined Spitzer met with a group of "ex-gays"—gay people who professed to be successfully cured—and continued his work on reparative therapy. In 2003, with the two epidemics tucked well away from public consciousness, Spitzer published a methodologically shoddy study in the *Archives of Sexual Behavior* that appeared to validate the efficacy of the practice. The APA officially disavowed support for both the study and the idea of reparative therapy, but that did not stop the use of Spitzer's fallacious work to further injure gay people. It was of little help that in 2012—nine years and another fifty-seven thousand youth suicides later—Spitzer himself, at the age of eighty, finally denounced his own study. In the same year that Spitzer came around, talk of gay marriage was ubiquitous; California was considering legislation to make reparative therapy illegal (which passed); and the World Health Organization described reparative therapy as "a serious threat to the health and well-being—even the lives—of affected people." Writing to the *Archives of Sexual Behavior* in 2012, Spitzer said, "I believe I owe the gay community an apology."

6. D'Emilio, *Sexual Politics, Sexual Communities*, 216.

7. In medicine—which, in the pursuit of credibility and respectability, psychiatry has, from its beginnings, tried to emulate—diagnosis *does* often provide insight. Medical diagnosis is deductive: if a patient is suffering from fatigue and fever, blood tests discover a particular bacterial infection, and *then* we name it. In this diagnosis, we have something useful. The benefits of medical diagnosis include an understanding of the symptoms and the potential for currently unseen symptoms and complications; a course of treatment; and a plausible prognosis. The identification of the bacteria provides the diagnosis, not the fatigue and fever. Although it misrepresents itself, psychiatric diagnosis functions almost exclusively at the level of fatigue and fever—it labels symptoms as if they were underlying disease processes. Psychiatric diagnosis is thus largely an inductive procedure. The diagnosis is a "meta-name" for a constellation of symptoms—but it presents that meta-name as the causal issue. Depressed feelings and other symptoms are named *depression*, and depression is the cause of the depressed feelings and other symptoms. The diagnostic name gives rise to the implication—or explicit statement—that a person "has" something, a kind of psychiatric equivalent of a bacterial infection. Finally, having "discovered" the psychiatric diagnosis—presented as the cause—the further implication is that we know what to do about it and can fix it.

8. Certainly some organic—physical—conditions can, as one example, cause depression. Prescribed or over-the-counter medications, structural brain anomalies, $B_{12}$ deficiency, thyroid dysfunction, and several disease processes are among the medical problems that can produce a subjective sense of depression. Recreational substance and alcohol use are other relatively common physiological causes of depression, even as they are often attempts to self-medicate depression that preceded their use. Note that these are all medical diagnoses.

9. How psychotropic pharmaceuticals function is widely misrepresented and misunderstood, which supports much of the popular and misleading conceptualization of diagnosis and "mental health." Many drug manufacturers and care providers imply—or explicitly promote the idea—that depressed serotonin levels in the brain cause depression. This misleading description implies that the "disease" of depression has a physiological cause. What we actually know is that selective serotonin reuptake inhibitors (SSRIs)—such as Prozac, Zoloft, Celexa, and Lexapro—raise serotonin levels. We do not know that this change corrects the underlying cause of depression because no one has demonstrated that low serotonin levels *are* the cause. Low sero-

tonin levels are only associated with depression, but that association could be explained in a number of ways. For example, low serotonin levels may be the result of depression, and a third, unaccounted-for or unknown factor might well affect both mood and serotonin levels. It is, however, true that raising serotonin levels—and whatever else the drug is affecting, which is a lot—sometimes reduces the subjective experience and behavioral expressions of depression. Acetylsalicylic acid—aspirin—also sometimes reduces the experience of headache. This well-established effect does not prove that low acetylsalicylic acid levels cause headaches. FDA psychotropic-drug approvals require that we start with a diagnosis, because any drug in the approval process must demonstrate efficacy in treating something specific— a diagnosed illness or disorder. The FDA will not approve a psychotropic drug because it helps people with an undiagnosed malaise "feel better." *Those* drugs are scheduled and illegal, although some are probably as effective and harmless as their prescribed counterparts. Part of the importance of distinguishing cause from association is this: the efficacy of pharmaceuticals is now too often being used to validate the legitimacy of a diagnosis and, by implication, the presence of a "disorder." The medication is cited as substantiation of the existence of the disorder that the medication is treating. Disorders and medications are used to simultaneously validate each other, which is peculiar science.

10. The use of psychotropic medication as the sole approach to treatment has increased dramatically over the past thirty years because of newer pharmaceuticals. This is not usually because the newer drugs are more effective, but because they are safer and lower in some undesirable side effects such as sedation and weight gain. This is particularly true of antidepressants, which are now routinely prescribed by primary-care physicians rather than psychiatrists. Older antidepressants were more dangerous in overdose, had more undesirable side effects, and sometimes required careful monitoring and ongoing adjustment of dose or type. Because of these complications, people were referred to psychiatrists for prescribing and monitoring, and psychiatrists were more likely to see the need for additional forms of treatment. The changes in drugs and prescribing channels have led to the much more common use of psychotropics as sole forms of treatment. This is exactly what pharmaceutical companies and third-party payers would like to see.

11. People quite naturally want to understand why they feel as they do, and they often look to diagnosis for the answer. But a psychiatric diagnosis is usually a poor explanation, little more than "You are depressed because you have depression." The desire to understand the cause of our feelings stretches back to at least the fourth century B.C. and Hippocrates' four bodily humors. Hippocrates was a physician, and in his medical explanation, an imbalance among the four humors—phlegm, blood, yellow bile, and black bile—was responsible for people's moods. In the late nineteenth and early twentieth centuries, psychiatric diagnosis began to be more useful—or so I think—but it was still not medicine or science, even as it attempted to mimic both. Always driven by narrow cultural and social values and expectations, inductive

psychiatric diagnosis is today also driven by some other important influences. In the United States, our entire system of third-party-payer health care— insurance payments—requires a diagnosis for reimbursement, and the amount of reimbursement is usually based on the diagnosis. A physician or psychiatrist requires a diagnosis to responsibly and legally prescribe medication; and a medication—antidepressant, anxiolytic (antianxiety), and antipsychotic are examples—requires a diagnostic category to receive Food and Drug Administration approval. The immensely profitable world of psychotropic medication is founded entirely on diagnostic labels that the APA provides in the *DSM*. Additionally, pharmaceutical companies themselves now sometimes spur the "discovery" of new diagnoses to legitimize new drugs—or new uses for old drugs, which is often even more profitable—and the FDA often accepts these constructions. Good business is sometimes found in providing a solution to a problem that no one knew he had.

12. Now that pharmaceuticals are available to address the physical symptoms, erectile dysfunction is routinely treated as a medical issue. It is more often than not an emotional one, even as diabetes, prostate problems, aging, and other truly medical issues sometimes play a role. Emotional withholding, generalized anxiety, sexual-performance anxiety, resentment and anger, poor self-esteem, and troubling conscious and unconscious feelings about sex and sexuality are the more common causes of erectile difficulties. The indiscriminate medicalization of the problem is an end run around emotional issues that might otherwise be productively explored.

13. The diagnosis bipolar II describes depression punctuated with periods of *hypo*manic activity. In contrast, bipolar I describes full manic episodes. The latter can be quite distinctive to an observer, the former less easy to discern.

14. Judith Herman, *Trauma and Recovery* (New York: Basic Books, 1992), 53.

15. Ibid., 51.

16. Body dysmorphia—known to the APA as body dysmorphic disorder or BDD—describes someone habitually and distressingly focused on specific, sometimes-imagined details of his or her physical appearance. It is classified by the APA among obsessive-compulsive problems and is associated with problematic psychological and social functioning, and a high rate of suicidality.

17. Scruff.com, accessed June 20, 2015.

18. Grindr.com, accessed June 20, 2015.

19. Herman, *Trauma and Recovery*, 46.

20. Ibid., 183–84.

21. IBS, "irritable bowel syndrome"—which usually entails diarrhea—often keeps people isolated. It may be exacerbated by alcohol and may also have a psychogenic component.

22. Robert Jay Lifton, "The Concept of the Survivor," in *Survivors, Victims, and Perpetrators*, ed. Joel E. Dimsdale, M.D. (Washington, DC: Hemisphere Publishing Corporation, 1980), 124.

23. Many of the feelings that Harry revealed are components of "survivor guilt," a well-known but widely misunderstood idea. Among the obvious signs were Harry's repeated assertions that he had been too helpless during the years

of the epidemic and had never done enough for Harry-2, "who was a much better person than I ever was." Harry had offered me numerous conjectures about how he might have saved Harry-2's life, all of them unrealistic. Many gay survivors of the early epidemic are vulnerable to survivor guilt for at least two reasons. The first affects all marginalized minority communities: the individual identity is—or is expected to be—strongly affiliated with the group identity, which enhances the sense of disloyalty when any individual in the group "does better" than other group members. The second is that gay men often already carry guilt from early in life. That guilt is often carried seamlessly into feelings of new guilt connected to the epidemic. Having felt in early life that they had failed their families by being gay, in the epidemic they felt they failed their "new families" of gay comrades by not keeping others alive, or by not dying with them. Guilt comes easily—and inauspiciously—to too many gay men. Being the best—"the best little boy"— or living perfectly motivates many gay men. Such aspirations do not always represent the pursuit of excellence alone; they sometimes represent the pursuit of redemption. During the early epidemic, the extended, uncontrolled slaughter—and the meanings that were attached to it—made the accomplishment of both excellence and redemption difficult to realize.

During the years of the early epidemic, prior to 1996, survivor guilt was largely experienced by HIV-negative men. They appeared to be the only people in gay communities who *could* survive. Survivor guilt among these men became a significant part of a psychological epidemic hidden behind the HIV epidemic itself, and the guilt contributed to the unconsciously motivated HIV infection of many. In those years, innumerable HIV-negative men told me stories of impulsively exposing themselves to HIV shortly after the deaths of friends and lovers. Today, with countless HIV-positive survivors of those years, survivor guilt is experienced by both negative and positive men, because they are now all survivors of an epidemic that killed more than six hundred thousand.

It is important to distinguish the *direct* psychological effects of living through the epidemic from effects mediated by guilt. Guilt introduces complications into grieving, and unless the guilt is identified, the relatively simpler process of grieving is inhibited. Guilt can misdirect or entirely stall grieving, and Harry's was significantly stalled by guilt. Like many survivors of the epidemic, Harry repeatedly rejected the idea of survivor guilt by telling me that he was "not guilty about being alive." But he was doing his best— through medical neglect, eating, drinking, and isolation—to see that he would not be alive much longer. His behavior was, by different means, very similar to the behavior of negative men who, in feelings of guilt, unnecessarily exposed themselves to HIV. The life Harry was leading was not only a direct response to his unprocessed grief, but an expression of guilt—not guilt about being alive, but guilt for continuing to live when his friends and Harry-2 could not. The guilt was about doing better than others, about leaving them behind, and about being disloyal. During our talks, Harry often said something like "I don't know why it was Harry, it could as well have been me." When I would say, "But it wasn't you," Harry was invariably silent, sometimes irritated, and often tearful. Surviving Harry-2 made him very uncomfortable. He was experiencing guilt about having something that Harry-2 did not have. Harry had life, Harry-2 did not.

The following description of survivors, by the psychiatrist Michael Friedman, is characteristic of many men surviving the early epidemic; but Friedman's discussion is about survivors of the Nazi Holocaust. Friedman is citing the work of another researcher, William Guglielmo Niederland, a German-born American psychoanalyst:

> Typically, after struggling to begin a new life and often succeeding, these people succumbed to a variety of symptoms like depression, anxiety, and psychosomatic conditions. . . . Niederland believed these symptoms to be identifications with loved ones who had not survived. His patients often appeared and felt as if they were living dead. Niederland believed that these identifications were motivated by guilt, which he called survivor guilt. The survivors experienced an "ever present feeling of guilt . . . for having survived the very calamity to which their loved ones succumbed." (Michael Friedman, "Toward a Reconceptualization of Guilt," *Contemporary Psychoanalysis* 21, no. 4 [1985]: 520)

Friedman usefully expands in his article on Niederland's original, narrower conception of survivor guilt as a response to literally surviving disaster. Friedman includes the idea that survivor guilt is not only about having survived, but also about feelings that one

> could have helped but failed. . . . It is a guilt of omission. It is the guilt of people who believe they have better lives than those of their parents or siblings. The greater the discrepancy between one's own fate and the fate of the loved person one failed to help, the greater the empathic distress and the more poignant one's guilt. (Ibid.)

24. Herman, *Trauma and Recovery*, 213.
25. Ibid.
26. True biological addiction to a substance is a discrete, autonomous physiological process that, like a bacterial infection, has, in itself, no human meaning. But biological addiction does not make the addiction a disease, and certainly not a disease for which a psychiatric diagnosis is the name. Even with biologically addictive substances, people rarely sustain use simply because they are addicted. People are psychologically motivated to *start* using, and they experience benefit from the use; but the idea of a humanly meaningless disease process dismisses both of these important subjectively experienced facts. Although the addictive properties of some substances can help to sustain use, people usually also continue because the underlying emotional issues have never been addressed and the person continues to experience benefit. Psychiatric diagnosis and the idea of disease aside, the

very term *substance abuse* is prejudicially dismissive of the motivations and benefit that many people experience.

## 6. EMERGING FROM TRAUMA, LOSS, AND ISOLATION

1. Waldrop, *Not Forever*, 102.
2. Herman, *Trauma and Recovery*, 61.
3. Ibid., 58.
4. The Smiths were a gay British rock band led by Morrissey.
5. The philosopher Arthur Schopenhauer, who lived alone for several decades in later life, had a series of standard poodles, most named Atman, which is Sanskrit for "self," "true self," "soul," or "essence."
6. Lifton, "Concept of the Survivor," 122. Although Aaron's emotional flatness was obvious and pervasive in our conversation, not everyone employing psychic numbing appears flat. A person using numbing is sometimes animated and social; but the animation feels forced, and feelings about remembered events are absent or seem inauthentic.
7. Herman, *Trauma and Recovery*, 49.
8. Lifton, "Concept of the Survivor," 121.
9. While Herman's work is aimed at those working professionally with survivors, it offers much useful understanding for other readers.
10. Herman, *Trauma and Recovery*, 155.
11. A reparative effort must come from both gay communities and, spurred by that effort, from the larger society. Herman succinctly describes the consequences of community silence following trauma:

> The response of the community has a powerful influence on the ultimate resolution of the trauma. Restoration of the breach between the traumatized person and the community depends, first, upon public acknowledgment of the traumatic event and, second, upon some form of community action. . . . Returning soldiers have always been exquisitely sensitive to the degree of support they encounter at home. . . . After the First World War, veterans bitterly referred to their war as the "Great Unmentionable." (Herman, *Trauma and Recovery*, 1)

The epidemics—both of them—have become our Great Unmentionable, not only in America at large but a within gay communities. Because gay people have made them an unmentionable, it is no surprise that the larger American society—the very one that ignored the decade and a half of the early epidemic while it slaughtered hundreds of thousands—is now also not mentioning it. Twenty years after HAART, in recognition of those who have died we have the Names Quilt, an astonishing, privately made and funded fifty-four-ton tapestry that is relegated to memory and a warehouse, but cries for a permanent, Washington, D.C., museum. In San Francisco, we have the National AIDS Memorial Grove, which occupies seven-tenths of 1 percent of Golden Gate Park. This tiny, neglected parcel of land next to the publicly maintained tennis courts was rehabilitated with private money and by a handful of volunteers. The Grove is hardly "national" in origin or importance, though it was declared so by President Clinton in 1996 at the behest of Nancy Pelosi, eight years after its rehabilitation began. On the subject of public recognition and memorials, Herman talks about the importance of the Vietnam War Memorial in Washington, D.C., for combat veterans. Unlike the Grove, the Vietnam memorial was a federally funded project. In Herman's words, the memorial wall was "probably the most significant public contribution to the healing of these veterans. . . . The 'impacted grief' of soldiers is easier to resolve when the community acknowledges the sorrow of its loss" (Herman, *Trauma and Recovery*, 71–72).

While the experiences of surviving Vietnam combatants and gay survivors of the early epidemic are significantly different, they have many similarities. The loss of young comrades, the violence—in the case of AIDS, the gruesome, disfiguring medical conditions that people suffered and others witnessed—and the widespread stigma that returning veterans and gay men experienced are all similar. There is also at least one significant difference, one of proportions. Over the twenty-year duration of the Vietnam War, 58,209 Americans died. In the first twenty-nine years of the two HIV epidemics in the United States, the toll has been 636,000. Part of the objection to my comparison will be that Vietnam veterans were "fighting for their country," and gay men were fucking. My response is that gay men—in asserting their freedom after centuries of crushing stigmatization—were fighting for their humanity, and for their lives and the lives of those they loved. Everyone in a fight claims to fight for humanity, which is sometimes true and sometimes not. In the decade before the epidemic began, it was true for gay men in America.

It must be made true again. The Quilt and the Grove—although wonderful and appreciated—are very small gestures in a national context, and it is important to note that they are almost entirely the work of gay people. The two virtually hidden gay monuments imply, but do not elaborate upon, the importance of attending to our psychological aftermath. If we are still waiting passively for society's recognition, support, or action in response to our Great Unmentionable, it will never come to be. America is now much more responsive to the idea of assimilating us—into forms of life that effectively deny the epidemics—than in understanding, respecting, and helping us as we are. To usefully respond to the trauma and losses of the epidemic and the social and psychological aftermath, it is we who must muster the same proactive, heroic effort that we brought to the epidemic itself. We must insist on creating, if not a national standard, a gay community standard that recognizes the social and psychological aftermath, and actively supports the public and personal work needed to address it.

12. Herman, *Trauma and Recovery*, 1.
13. Remembering, reexperiencing, and verbalizing painful feelings is probably the essential step in grieving and recovery. Trauma survivors understand-

ably avoid the process because it is painful, and because they often fear that the pain will lead to nothing useful. But other important feelings also motivate us to avoid grieving in the aftermath of trauma. Among the most significant and most obstructive are shame and guilt. While these two feelings are common in the aftermath of purely perpetrated traumas such as rape and the Holocaust, they may be among the most prominent obstructions to grieving among gay survivors of our two epidemics. Unfortunately, shame and guilt add significantly both to the inventory of what must be painfully revisited, and to the total task of post-trauma recovery.

For many gay men surviving the epidemics, shame and guilt are felt about a confusing mix of many things: being gay, having sexual lives, and feeling culpable for the epidemic itself because it was a "gay epidemic." Many men feel further shame about revealing emotional vulnerability in the aftermath, which is thought a confession of weakness that might be used to further stigmatize gay lives. Much of our shame is unconsciously rooted in a single fact: the two epidemics among U.S. gay men are largely a biological consequence of receptive anal sex. In the minds of many critics, including many gay men themselves, anal sex is an unacceptable, unmentionable, and dispensable behavior that—unlike vaginal sex for heterosexuals—is of little or no emotional significance or human importance. The unconscious summation of this argument is clear: anal sex is *bad*, and we have an epidemic to prove it. The epidemic was our failure, simply for being who we are. But a bit of corrective perspective is required. Had HIV thrived among U.S. heterosexuals as it has in most of the world, it would not have been experienced as a "heterosexual epidemic." It would have been an epidemic of hapless, sympathetic victims who, in the aftermath, required active support. For the survivors of the six hundred thousand who had died, we would have had a federally funded AIDS Post-Traumatic Stress and Family Rehabilitation Act.

As a result of shame and guilt—and, in fairness, exhaustion from the epidemics—our communities have done an astonishingly poor job with their aftermath. We have failed to internally direct attention and resources to it, and we have virtually abandoned the effort to gain assistance from the larger society. Our community standard is silence, as is that of the larger society. During the early epidemic, had Act Up not insisted that "silence is death," many fewer of us would have survived at all. Today, our own silence colludes with the silence of the larger society, and silence still equals death. This is now emotional death that leads to isolated lives that feel not worth living, self-neglect, and, often, premature physical death. As communities that were once focused on restoring a sense of emotional and physical well-being to gay people who had been traumatically stigmatized and abused for being gay, our silence about the aftermath of the epidemics is inexcusable.

14. Perle Mesta was a well-known Democratic Washington socialite and hostess during the 1940s and '50s and was appointed by Harry Truman as ambassador to Luxembourg after the Second World War.

15. MeetUp.com is a website for people who would like to start or join "common interest" groups. Within or near metropolitan areas are hundreds of groups, including many specified as gay.

16. Herman, *Trauma and Recovery*, 133.
17. Ibid., 27.
18. While Herman often speaks of safety in the context of formal therapeutic relationships, she provides an idea of the importance of the issue, regardless of the context:

> Trauma robs the victim of a sense of power and control; the guiding principle of recovery is to restore power and control to the survivor. The first task of recovery is to establish the survivor's safety. This task takes precedence over all the others, for no therapeutic work can possibly succeed if safety has not been adequately secured. (Herman, *Trauma and Recovery*, 159–60)

19. "Expanding the Impact," Centers for Disease Control and Prevention, accessed December 7, 2014, http://www.cdc.gov/nchhstp/newsroom /HIVFactSheets/Epidemic/Transmission.htm.
20. With widespread use, today's medications offer the possibility of actually ending the epidemic. To do that, we need not end all new infections; we need only put the rate of new infections into a descending trend. When, for each potential exposure, the statistical probability of actually contracting HIV progressively declines, the epidemic eventually "self-extinguishes." If we progressively remove a single number from a roulette wheel between each spin, the gambler is given lower odds of losing on each following spin. His losses would progressively decline, and when no numbers were left on the wheel, his losses would end.
21. Herman, *Trauma and Recovery*, 25.
22. The entire grieving process—both talking through and working through—is, in description, relatively simple. We allow the process to begin by acknowledging—rather than denying—our trauma or loss and its emotional import. Then, within supportive relationships, we talk through the trauma or loss by remembering, reexperiencing, expressing, and gaining insight into our feelings about that history. We also gain insight about how our feelings have distorted our sense of self, and we work to reconstruct that post-traumatic self into a new form that reclaims some of our old self, but also acknowledges the changes that are now part of us. We then begin working through by taking our insight and partially reconstructed self out into the world, where we find new ways of being in it, and of relating to others. This is a good description of the path that Ralph found for himself. Following Tom's death, Ralph spent two years talking to and being listened to by his therapist, Marty. Ralph told his story and experienced and thought about his feelings; he gradually "put the pieces" of himself back together; he regained some sense of confidence in himself and the world; he connected with Kevin; and he went back into the world and constructed a new life that was authentic and supportive. As in all grieving, Ralph's process was not a simple, linear moment progressing irreversibly through consecutive stages. While the linear concept of talking through and then working through as two distinct, consecutive steps may be didactically clarifying, people actually experience much more to and fro, but with a forward trend. We talk

through, gain insight, and reconstruct a sense of self, then go into the world and implement these changes. Our experience in the world allows further insight and an adjusted sense of self, and we then go back again into the world with *these* changes. The forward trend is driven by a contemplated, continuing dialogue between ourselves and others; and in this dialogue we are able to move through grief. The to-and-fro movement with a forward trend characterizes not only the grieving process but all learning and growth in human life.

23. The actual processes of talking through and working through require a bit more explicative detail. Talking through begins with revisiting the trauma and our feelings about it. Herman calls it "reconstructing the story" (Herman, *Trauma and Recovery*, 175–95). In the context of his pretrauma life—and beginning with a story that is often fragmented, incoherent, and incomplete—the person establishes a linear, factual narrative of the traumatic event to which the listener bears witness. The person then begins to remember, re-experience, and verbalize his feelings, and to tie them to the facts of the narrative. The verbalization and contextualization of the feelings helps to put into language something that before was pure feeling—disturbing, but unformed, elusive, and unutterable. The recounting makes the event of trauma or loss concrete, and the reconstruction of feelings into language gives us the opportunity to think and talk about them. This process is very much like the traditional analysis of dreams, from which we often wake with only *feeling*. In reconstructing the chronological narrative, we can begin to consider the meaning of the story and thus understand the feelings that accompanied it. As with the interpretation of dreams, in talking through we translate feelings into words; cognitively consider the feelings; and gain insight into them. With cognitive insight—rather than unformed, pre-verbal emotion—we begin the process of working through in the world. During the working through, we are able to observe how we bring our feelings and sense of self into the world and make conscious and considered decisions about how to play—or not play—them out. We *incorporate* our insight into our ongoing lives. This incorporation allows us to actually move forward and out of a life characterized by the trauma and loss.

24. Herman, *Trauma and Recovery*, 214–16.

25. Ibid., 181.


## 7. GAY MEN'S RELATIONSHIPS

1. Waldrop, *Not Forever*, 63.

2. "How Many People Are Lesbian, Gay, Bisexual and Transgender?," University of California at Los Angeles School of Law, the Williams Institute, accessed July 23, 2014, http://williamsinstitute.law.ucla.edu/wp-content /uploads/Gates-How-Many-People-LGBT-Apr-2011.pdf. The study reports that 19 million Americans (8.2 percent of the total adult population) self-report that they have engaged in same-sex sexual behavior. The most recent U.S. Census reports that approximately 5 percent of the population identifies as gay. Thus it seems possible that as many as 39 percent of men who

have had sex with men do not identify as gay. Anecdotal evidence would suggest that this figure is at least plausible, if imprecise. Additionally, self-report surveys about such topics introduce a social-desirability bias that is likely to skew the report of "socially undesirable behaviors" to the low side.

3. Amado (a pseudonym) and I spent considerable time trying to understand the emotional dynamics of his relationships with his parents, because those dynamics informed the possibilities of current relationships. He had a sense of failure and guilt about both parents, but for different reasons. Amado felt he had never done enough to assist his mother or make her happy, and he had simply done nothing for his father, as evidenced by his father's absence. But Amado had an emotional alliance with his mother, and one of the feelings they shared was abandonment by Amado's father. Amado's pathos, which mirrored his mother's, was partially rooted in that shared experience: his father was the first man that Amado would never deserve or have. Amado was left feeling that there was something deeply lacking and deeply unacceptable not about his family, but about himself. He had nothing to offer others, and like his mother, in the end he would find only abandonment. When Amado pushed back from the man at the party with his "terrible" opening line, he was, in anticipation, encouraging that man's abandonment. And Amado was also, we later discovered, reacting to another fear that the possibility of relationships always brought up: a feeling that any relationship he had would only further his mother's feelings of abandonment. Just as he needed another man, she needed him.

4. Brice's fantasy of a relationship was partly rooted in a particular, not-uncommon developmental experience: conspicuously inadequate and neglectful parenting that left him feeling worthless. In the child's intuitive, if simplistic, understanding, if he was worth something, he would be receiving better care. Much of Brice's relationship fantasy also suggests a more pervasive experience among gay men. His poor sense of self-worth—the core motivator in his fluctuating, bootstrap dilemma—was further diminished simply by the fact of being gay. Even as Brice insisted on an "out and proud" posture in his adult life, he had a great deal of unconscious discomfort about being gay, often expressed in concern about his body and his distinctive manner of speech, which he thought "looked and sounded" gay. His out-and-proud assertions often felt overwrought and compensatory, and the downswings in his cycle did bring out considerable conscious shame. That shame had been firmly established in his adolescent and later-teenage years by relentless teasing and harassment from peers.

5. In discussing Brice's fantasy, I am also describing narcissism, which is significantly about using others to feel better about oneself. In such narcissism, there is little concern about the relationship as a whole and a significant lack of interest in or empathy for the partner. Narcissism is one compensatory response to self-doubt and poor self-esteem.

6. A multitude of motivations lie behind the pursuit of others followed by retreat. The fear of abandonment is a common one. The pursuer abandons before he is abandoned and thus retains a feeling of control, rather than helplessness. The fear of revealing oneself as undesirable is another motivation

for retreat, as is the desire to be, oneself, pursued. In the latter, the partner retreating from the relationship tests the desire of his potential partner. Often, multiple issues lie behind chronic patterns of pursuit and retreat.

7. Haley, who died in 2007, was a well-known, influential advocate of family and brief therapy, and the author of many books on these subjects. He largely conceived of relationships as symmetrical *or* complementary, but I believe that the two often exist simultaneously in different facets of the same relationship.

8. The absence of sex in ongoing relationships is not always a fundamental issue; it sometimes follows from other conflicts. These can include struggles over autonomy, control, or power, or feelings of emotional neglect or abuse. In such struggles, "sexual withholding" can be unilaterally or bilaterally employed as a weapon. The refusal of sex is sometimes the only retaliatory measure that a partner feels he has the power to implement. Sexual withholding is a formidable, destructive weapon, and it often only exacerbates underlying conflicts. These conflicts in combination with the sexual withholding itself easily merge into a unified, growing rift that can make the relationship feel impossible. When underlying conflicts encourage sexual withholding, they need to be separately addressed, and their expression through sexual withholding must be clarified. With that clarification, "boredom" and "loss of attraction" can then usually be addressed through, respectively, the reimplementation of play and a reconstruction of how we think about sex within relationships.

9. A lack of play may lead to boredom with sex, and boredom may contribute to the loss of arousal and attraction. The objectification of a sexual partner is usually learned in adolescence, but is impossible within a long-term intimate relationship that provides too much mutual knowledge. Early-life sexual experiences often create enduring learned associations between physical types and sexual gratification or hurt and abuse. When we feel negatively about a partner for other reasons, we can experience him as less physically attractive. When, as the children of an erotophobic society, we feel bad about sex itself, we are reluctant to experience our emotionally intimate partner as sexual, for fear of harming him and the relationship. When we feel negatively about ourselves, *we* feel unattractive, but often project that feeling onto the partner, withdraw from sex, and experience loss of attraction. These kinds of feelings are hugely more approachable and changeable than the seemingly autonomous internal phenomenon of "falling out of sexual attraction." Again, the question to be explored is *why*.

10. Wendy Wang and Kim Parker, "Record Share of Americans Have Never Married," Pew Research Center, September 24, 2014, http://www.pewsocialtrends .org/2014/09/24/record-share-of-americans-have-never-married/.

11. A June 2015 solicitation letter from the Human Rights Campaign (HRC) opens with four bulleted agenda points, the first of which is "Making it possible for same-sex couples to get married in all 50 states—and be welcomed in their communities as married couples." Number four on the list is "Creating safer and more welcoming schools and colleges, hospitals and businesses, churches and synagogues." Priorities two and three are about a federal

ban on discrimination, and the election of people "who will take a stand for LGBT rights."

12. A December 2015 solicitation from the HRC lists current priorities as (1) adoption rights, (2) elementary school bullying, and (3) antidiscrimination laws to protect gay people from losing their jobs for being gay. The HRC bills itself as "the largest, strongest and most experienced civil rights organization in the country," and its voice is undoubtedly prominent, if only unevenly supported in gay communities.

## 8. THE LIFE AND TIMES OF MATTHIAS JOHNSTON

1. Waldrop, *Not Forever*, 34.

## AN AFTERWORD FOR YOUNG MEN'S FUTURES

1. Waldrop, *Not Forever*, 70–71.

# Index

abandonment, 129, 330*n6*
academics, 135
Act Up, 132, 292, 327*n13*
addiction, 183–85, 309*n23*, 324*n26*;
    compulsion distinguished from,
    183–84, 309*n23*; diagnosis, 183,
    184; sex, 69, 70, 183; *see also*
    *specific addictions*
ADHD, 150
adolescence, 6, 16–17, 24–25, 32, 72,
    73, 77, 80, 94, 120, 129–30, 133,
    135–38, 153–54, 155, 164, 187,
    205, 302; abuse, 137, 257–65;
    developmental gender split, 35–47;
    homosexual identity and, 32–33,
    35–47; identity vs. role confusion,
    137–38; industry vs. inferiority,
    135–36; isolation and, 157–58;
    relationships, 219, 221, 223–24,
    225–26, 233, 252, 263–65; sex, 45,
    50, 72, 95–96, 139–40, 223–24,
    227, 238, 239–40, 242, 248,
    263–64, 266; trauma and loss,
    190–92, 196–98, 210, 211–12,
    260–61; *see also* early-life
    experience
adoption, 251
adulthood, 121; ego integrity vs.
    despair, 142–43; generativity vs.
    stagnation, 141–42; intimacy vs.
    isolation, 139–41; *see also* middle-
group men; older-group men;
    younger-group men
adversity, 160, 266, 298
African-American gay men, 16,
    24–26, 60, 100–102; AIDS/HIV
    and, 114; homosexual identity and,
    24–26; Uncle Tom role, 100
African-Americans, 60, 62, 67, 68,
    100, 186, 218; emancipation of,
    186; hate crimes, 62; interracial
    marriage, 218
aging, 6, 80, 170–71; ego integrity
    vs. despair, 142–43; middle-group
    men, 87–97; older-group men,
    80–87; younger-group men,
    97–117
AIDS/HIV, 5, 8–16, 35, 45, 64,
    73–74, 308*n15*, 310*n4*, 312*n15*,
    313*n26*; Condom Code legacy and,
    105–15, 140; death, 5–6, 9–16,
    65–68, 77, 80–87, 92, 98, 123,
    130, 134, 138, 140, 141, 142, 154,
    160, 170, 171, 175–77, 179, 187,
    188, 194, 200–205, 206, 288,
    291–95, 317*n15*, 326*n11*; discovery
    of HIV virus, 67, 75, 76; dystonic
    vs. syntonic experience of, 98–99;
    early epidemic, 6, 8–12, 30,
    65–68, 75–87, 105, 106, 107, 113,
    119, 130–34, 136, 138, 140–43,
    146, 151, 154, 159, 160, 165, 170,

AIDS/HIV (*cont.*)
171, 181, 197, 198, 199, 200–205, 206, 210, 287–88, 291–95, 323*n23*, 325*n11*; early treatment of, 98; ELISA HIV antibody test, 67, 187; failure and, 107–108, 124, 131; grief and guilt, 169, 171, 175–77, 179, 199–204; HAART treatment, 14, 16, 75, 76, 78, 89, 90, 103, 113, 164–65, 166, 182, 206, 314*n31*, 317*n15*, 326*n11*, 328*n20*; hopelessness and, 92–93, 107; isolation and, 159–68; late epidemic, 16, 75, 76, 103, 104, 107, 119, 130, 131, 136, 138, 140–41, 143, 146, 187, 197, 206; media on, 65–67, 77, 78, 88, 90; middle-group men, 87–97; monuments and memorials, 326*n11*; negotiated safety, 111–12; older-group men, 80–87, 99, 106, 141–43, 159, 165, 200–204; PrEP and, 105, 113–15, 206, 313*n27*, 316*n44*; prevention, 106–15, 117, 292; Reagan response to, 65–68, 90; receptive anal sex and, 78–79, 109, 132; recovery from trauma, 200–216; relations between positive and negative men, 8–12, 79, 82–87, 91, 98, 99, 102, 124–27, 294, 323*n23*; social marketing, 108–109; statistics, 9, 12, 14, 16, 65, 67, 68, 76, 80, 98, 114, 206; stigma and shame, 78–79, 82–87, 103, 104–17, 131–32, 160, 199–200, 201–202; survivor guilt, 134, 180–81; survivors, 15–16, 80, 134, 180–81, 199, 202, 205, 210, 311*n12*; testing, 76, 77, 93, 98, 107, 110, 187, 314*n31*; trauma, 6–7, 8–16, 65–68, 77, 80–87, 141, 187–88, 199–216; trust and, 130; younger-group men, 97–117, 160–65
AIDS Healthcare Foundation, Los Angeles, 115
Alaska, 257, 259, 260, 261, 262, 265, 267

alcohol, 93, 94, 169, 170, 171, 172, 176, 180, 182; addiction, 183–85
ambivalence, 173, 180, 182, 269
American Medical Association (AMA), 147–48
American Psychiatric Association (APA), 146, 318*n2*, 319*n5*
anal sex, 52–56, 98, 109–10, 202, 305*n15*, 311*n13*, 315*n34*; bottom identity, 53–54, 55, 56, 78–79; hemorrhoids and, 202; insertive, 52, 53, 54, 91, 313*n29*; receptive, 52–56, 78–79, 109, 132, 313*n29*, 327*n13*; top identity, 53–54, 56, 91, 210; versatile man, 54–56
anger, 9, 47, 131, 132, 143, 173, 177, 188, 231, 236, 238, 241, 259, 273, 282, 283
antidepressants, 64, 149–50, 189, 320*n9*, 321*nn9–10*
anxiety, 64–65, 68, 91, 92, 150, 158, 197, 322*n12*; separation, 133
Arizona, 100
Arkansas, 4, 5
arm wrestling, 55, 56, 235
asexuality, 241
assimilation, 19, 76, 104, 136, 160, 252, 255
Associated Press, 31
attraction, loss of, 245–49, 331*n9*
authenticity, 47–50, 59, 136, 189, 197, 207, 208, 213, 215, 225, 255, 257, 298, 302
autonomy, 139, 144, 237; shame and doubt vs., 130–32

balance, 237; in relationships, 237–38
Baltimore, David, 67
baseball, 42, 44
basic trust vs. basic mistrust, 128–30
baths, sex at, 69–72
bearing witness, 208
Bears, 162
Beethoven, Ludwig van, 178, 181
Berkeley, California, 7, 10, 169–70, 293, 294, 295

bestiality, 20
Bible, 55, 297
Bill of Rights, 74, 217, 302
biology, 17, 37, 56–59, 220, 236;
    gender roles and, 39; in utero
    split, 37
bipolar II diagnosis, 152–56, 322*n13*
birth control pill, 115
bisexuality, 62, 67, 112
body dysmorphia, 322*n16*
body image issues, 161–62
Bond, James, 307*n28*
bootstrap operations, 233
boredom, 242, 246, 331*n9*
"born gay," 17
bottoms, 39, 52, 53–54, 55, 78–79,
    237; identity, 53, 54, 55, 56, 78–79
brain, 39; cancer, 296–97; gender
    differences, 39
breakthrough behavior, 93–96, 97
breeding, 23, 107
Broadway, 274
Brown University, 222
bullying, school, 251
Byrd, James, Jr., 62


camping, 203
cancer, 4, 6, 21, 296–97; brain,
    296–97; pancreatic, 4, 82
Cape Cod, 268–70, 272, 294, 297
career, *see* employment
carriage, 55
cars, 192; accidents, 190–91; driving,
    201, 202, 205; ownership of, 108
Cartier-Bresson, Henri, 270
Casanova, 260, 264, 265
cathexis, 29–32, 305*nn17–18*
Catholicism, 24, 284
cats, 257, 258, 282
celebrity, 32, 90, 91, 274
Centers for Disease Control and
    Prevention (CDC), 16, 63, 98,
    308*n15*
central nervous system depressants,
    185
characteristic self, 121, 127

cheerfulness, 211, 215
Chekhov, Anton, 266
chemistry, in relationships, 245–46
childhood, 5, 6, 16–17, 77, 92, 94,
    120–35, 225–27, 237, 244, 255,
    302; abuse, 61–62, 258, 280–84;
    autonomy vs. shame and doubt,
    130–32; basic trust vs. basic
    mistrust, 128–30; bullying, 251;
    developmental gender split, 35–47;
    Eight Ages of Man, 119–45; end
    of, 137; grief and guilt, 177–79;
    hate crimes, 61–62; identity vs.
    role confusion, 137–38; industry
    vs. inferiority, 135–36; initiative
    vs. guilt, 132–34; isolation and,
    157–58; trauma, 5, 6, 11, 15,
    16–17, 61–62, 70–72, 77, 123–36,
    144, 153–56, 167–68, 171, 177–81,
    187, 190–92, 196–98, 210,
    211–12, 257–65, 276, 277,
    280–84; *see also* early-life
    experience; family
Christianity, 7, 55, 90, 259, 284, 297
circumcision, 163, 313*n29*
civil rights, 147, 185
Civil War, 218
Clinton, Bill, 74
clothing, 35, 52, 55–56, 61, 136;
    gender sensibility and, 55–56;
    unisex, 56
coercion, 108–109
coherence, and emotional sensibility,
    47–50
college, 263–68, 272, 289, 290, 291
Colorado, 82
coming out, 5, 21, 110, 208, 223, 277
communities, gay, 58, 75–117, 157,
    186, 203, 208, 209–10, 300–302;
    Condom Code legacy and, 104–17,
    140; emerging from trauma, loss,
    and isolation, 186–216; gay-on-gay
    shaming, 104–17; incoherent, 104;
    isolation, 157–68; marriage and,
    249–56; middle-group men, 77, 78,
    87–97; older-group men, 15, 58,
    76–77, 78, 80–87; reconnection,

communities, gay (*cont.*)
209–16; tripartite, 75–117; younger-group men, 77, 78, 97–117, 249–56
complementarity, 237
compulsion and addiction, distinction between, 183–84, 309*n23*
Condom Code, 89, 105–15, 140, 305*n15*, 311*n13*, 314*n31*
condoms, 89, 91, 101–102, 105–15, 305*n5*, 313*n30*, 315*n32*, 316*n44*; Condom Code legacy, 105–15, 140; middle-group men, and, 89–92; for oral sex, 107, 313*n30*; PrEP and, 113–15; younger-group men and, 115–15
conformity, 137–38
Congress, U.S., 62; hate crimes legislation, 62
consciousness, bringing painful memories to, 208–209
Constitution, U.S., 74, 115, 217, 302
constrictive defenses, 196–97, 198, 211
control, 13, 69, 238; lack of, 151, 165
cooking, 42, 100, 210–11, 212
Cordon Bleu College of Culinary Arts, San Francisco, 100
counterphobic behavior, 93, 96–97, 312*n17*
Cox, Spencer, 205
creativity, 135, 141
crying, 43, 125, 174–75, 177, 179, 191, 197, 211–12, 213, 214, 222, 264–65, 272, 280, 285, 286
Cubs, 162

death, 4–5, 34, 220, 249, 275–76, 288, 293, 297–98; AIDS/HIV, 5–6, 9–16, 65–68, 77, 80–87, 92, 98, 123, 130, 134, 138, 140, 141, 142, 154, 160, 170, 171, 175–77, 179, 187, 188, 194, 200–205, 206, 288, 291–95, 317*n15*, 326*n11*; ego integrity vs. despair, 142–43; grief and guilt, 168–85; hate crimes,

60–62; multiple, 179; of parents, 6, 178–79, 190–92, 197, 210, 211–12, 266–67; of siblings, 123, 190–92, 194, 197
D'Emilio, John, 21, 22, 23, 147–48
denial, 15, 40, 97, 109, 147, 159, 180, 181, 196, 236, 310*n4*
dependency, 37, 38, 214, 219, 237
depression, 63, 64–65, 68, 69, 149–50, 151–56, 158, 170, 178, 188, 189–90, 197, 246, 274, 286, 320*nn7–8*, 321*nn9–11*
despair vs. ego integrity, 142–43
developmental gender split, 35–47, 236
diabetes, 103, 322*n12*
diagnosis, 80, 98, 144, 146–57, 308*n15*, 318*nn2–4*, 319*n5*, 320*n7*, 321*n11*, 322*n11*; of addiction, 183, 184; bipolar II, 152–56, 322*n13*; culpability and, 150–51; as obstruction to self-discovery, 146–57; older-group men and, 80; psychiatric, 146–57
*Diagnostic and Statistical Manual of Mental Disorders* (DSM), 146, 147, 318*n2*, 319*n5*
diffusion of innovation, 314*n32*
diminished capacity, as legal defense, 36
*Dinner, The* (film), 272
disappointment, 141, 142
Discreet, 162
discrimination, 60–62, 63, 292; gender, 292; hate crimes, 60–62; HIV, 78–79, 292; job, 60, 63, 251, 292; stigma and shame, 60–74
diversity, 104, 138, 186, 217, 218, 254, 301
divorce, 133, 249, 252, 284
Doan, Long, 27
dogs, 192–94, 195, 325*n6*
dominance, 52
doubt, 5, 68–73, 138, 207, 219, 224–25; autonomy vs., 130–32; shame and, 68–73
dreams, 14, 208, 247

drug use, 63, 64, 65, 67, 74, 93;
    intravenous, and AIDS, 67
dystonic experience, 98–99

early-life experience, 5, 6, 11, 15–17,
    77, 118–45, 255; autonomy vs.
    shame and doubt, 130–32; basic
    trust vs. basic mistrust, 128–30;
    Eight Ages of Man, 119–45;
    identity vs. role confusion, 137–38;
    industry vs. inferiority, 135–36;
    initiative vs. guilt, 132–34;
    significance of, 118–45; trauma, 5,
    6, 11, 15, 16–17, 61–62, 70–72, 77,
    123–36, 144, 152–56, 167–68, 171,
    177–81, 187, 190–92, 196–98, 210,
    211–12, 257–65, 276, 277, 280–84;
    see also adolescence; childhood;
    family; parents
earrings, 265
Eastwood, Clint, 307n28
economics, 236
effeminacy, 35, 36, 38, 45, 46, 49, 50,
    52, 54, 56, 57, 72, 79, 154, 156,
    235, 239, 240, 247, 258, 260;
    terminology, 35
ego-dystonic homosexuality, 318n3,
    319n5
ego integrity vs. despair, 142–43
Eight Ages of Man, 119–45;
    autonomy vs. shame and doubt,
    130–32; basic trust vs. basic
    mistrust, 128–30; ego integrity vs.
    despair, 142–43; generativity vs.
    stagnation, 141–42; identity vs. role
    confusion, 137–38; industry vs.
    inferiority, 135–36; initiative vs.
    guilt, 132–34; intimacy vs.
    isolation, 139–41
ELISA HIV antibody test, 67, 187
Emancipation Proclamation, 186,
    218
emerging from isolation, 204–205
emotional sensibility, and coherence,
    47–50
empathy, 35, 38, 144

employment, 141, 154, 223, 226, 231;
    discrimination, 60, 63, 251, 292;
    early retirement, 141; gay rights
    and, 251, 292
England, 222
Enovid, 115
entertainment, 155, 203, 258
envy, 253
erectile dysfunction (ED), 150,
    322n12
erection, 239, 269
Erikson, Erik, 42, 50, 119–27, 204,
    316n2; Eight Ages of Man, 119–45;
    on genital combat, 50–51
escorts, 210
Europe, 114, 222
"evil impulse," 21–22
exercise, 161–62, 231
exhibitionism, 20
external and internal coherence,
    struggle between, 47–50
eye contact, 23, 60, 306n24

Facebook, 33
failure, 59, 156; AIDS/HIV and,
    107–108, 124, 131; relationship,
    223, 228, 229, 231, 241
family, 5, 6, 15, 17, 24–26, 39, 59, 60,
    77, 85, 98, 100, 112, 115, 143, 157,
    171, 186–87, 188, 208, 209, 302;
    basic trust vs. basic mistrust,
    128–30; of choice, 220;
    developmental gender split and,
    41–47; disapproval of gay son,
    61–62, 70–72, 94–95, 123–25,
    152–54, 155, 167, 186, 223, 226,
    227, 229, 257–65, 276, 280–84,
    289, 297–98; Eight Ages of Man,
    119–45; grief and guilt, 177–79;
    homosexual identity and, 24–26;
    trauma and loss, 189–98, 210,
    211–12; see also childhood;
    early-life experience; father;
    mother; parents; siblings
fantasy, 230–34; about relationships,
    230–34, 243

father, 10, 91–92, 100, 122–23, 124, 231–32, 330*nn*3–4; death of, 6, 266–67; developmental gender split and, 41–47; disapproval of gay son, 94–95, 152–54, 167, 186, 223, 226, 227, 229, 257–65, 276, 280–84, 288; divorce, 133; grief and guilt, 177–79; trauma and loss, 190–92, 210, 211–12

fatigue and fever, 150

fear, 9, 92, 94–97, 114, 115, 126, 150, 158, 212; relationships and, 225–30

Feldman, Gary, 64–65, 103

feminine sensibility, 35, 36, 38, 45, 46, 49, 50, 52, 54, 56, 57, 72, 79, 154, 156, 235, 239, 240, 247, 258, 260; receptive anal sex and, 53–56, 79

Fernandez, Gabriel, 61–62

fidelity, 253

Fineberg, Harvey V., 67

fishing, 41, 42

flexibility, 54–55

flowers, 10

flying, 263, 267–68, 270, 275, 277–80, 285, 292, 293–94, 295–96, 299–300

food, 42, 169, 170, 171, 172, 182, 203, 210, 211, 212, 247, 269, 270, 284

Food and Drug Administration (FDA), 114, 149

football, 235

formal rights, 26–30, 185; Indiana study, 26–30

Freud, Sigmund, 29, 119, 147, 236, 305*n*18

Friedlander, Lee, 270

Friedman, Michael, 324*n*23

frottage, 107, 305*n*15

fun, 243–44

gay (term), 30–32

Gay & Lesbian Alliance Against Defamation (GLAAD), 31

gaydar, 35–36, 306*n*24

Gay Liberation, 73, 77, 104, 131, 136, 159, 160, 164, 254, 274, 301

gay marriage, 26, 28, 58, 99, 186, 218, 221, 225, 249–56; husbands, 58; 2015 Supreme Court decision on, 26, 185, 218, 250, 251

gay men: autonomy vs. shame and doubt, 130–32; basic trust vs. basic mistrust, 128–30; developmental gender split, 35–47, 236; diagnosis, 146–57; early-life experience, 118–45; ego integrity vs. despair, 142–43; Eight Ages of Man and, 119–45; emerging from trauma, loss, and isolation, 186–216; generativity vs. stagnation, 141–42; grief and guilt, 168–85; hate crimes against, 60–62, 147; homosexual identity and, 19–59; identity vs. role confusion, 137–38; industry vs. inferiority, 135–36; initiative vs. guilt, 132–34; intimacy vs. isolation, 139–41; isolation, 157–68; life and times of Matthias Johnston, 257–98; marriage and, 249–56; middle-group men, 87–97; older-group men, 80–87; population statistics, 329*n*2; relationships, 217–56; stigma and shame, 60–74; tripartite communities, 75–117; younger-group men, 97–117, 249–56

gay-on-gay shaming, 104–17

gay pride, 73

gay sensibility, 20, 240, 252; developmental gender split, 35–47, 236; sex position and, 52–56, 78–79, 91, 109, 237; sexual expression of, 47–56; terminology, 20

gender, 35, 236; biology and, 39; developmental gender split, 35–47, 236; discrimination, 292; integration, 35; third, 35

generativity vs. stagnation, 141–42

genital combat, 51, 140

Google, 236
Grand Island, Nebraska, 262, 263, 293
grandparents, 95, 267, 268
Great Depression, 106
grief, 9, 10, 34, 144, 168–85, 280, 327n13, 328n22, 329n22; AIDS/ HIV and, 169, 171, 175–77, 179, 199–204; family and, 177–79; four stages of recovery, 200–216; guilt and, 168–85; as obstruction to self-discovery, 168–85; Stage Three: grieving and talking through, 207–209
Grindr, 79, 93, 101, 102, 162, 164, 312n16
group closet, 22
guilt, 132–34, 139–40, 168–85, 226, 228, 241, 327n13; AIDS/HIV and, 169, 171, 175–77, 179, 199–204; family and, 177–79; grief and, 168–85; initiative vs., 132–34; as obstruction to self-discovery, 168–85; survivor, 134, 180–81, 322n23, 323n23, 324n23
gym, 44, 231
Gym Bunnies, 162, 163

HAART treatment for AIDS, 14, 16, 75, 76, 78, 89, 90, 103, 113, 164–65, 166, 182, 206, 314n31, 317n15, 325n11, 328n20
Haley, Jay, 237, 331n7
Hank, 5, 8, 268, 270, 272, 274, 275, 285–98, 299–302
Harvard School of Public Health, 67
Hatami, Jonathan, 61
hate crimes, 60–62, 147, 307n2; Fernandez case, 61–62
health care, 60, 112, 160, 169; inequity for gay men, 60, 63, 292, 308n14; older-group men, 80–87; primary-care physicians, 64–65, 81
health insurance, 26, 169, 206, 322n11
Hefner, Hugh, 307n28

helplessness, 166, 167, 237
hemorrhoids, and anal sex, 202
Herman, Judith, 144, 159, 168, 182, 188, 197, 199, 204, 205, 208, 209, 216, 325nn9–11, 328n18, 329n23; Trauma and Recovery, 199
heterosexuals, 26, 30, 51, 57, 78, 107, 112, 129, 140, 143, 188, 205, 250, 252, 304n5, 305n16; adolescents, 137, 239; fear of anal sex, 78; gaydar, 35–36; hate crimes by, 60–74; male privilege, 188; male stereotypes, 29; marriage, 250, 252, 253, 254, 255; perspective on homosexuals, 19–20, 26–28; relationship models, 219, 220, 225, 235, 250
high-risk behavior, 63–64, 81, 92, 112, 113
Hippocrates, 321n11
HIV, see AIDS/HIV
holding hands, 26, 60
Hollywood, 72, 255, 258
Holocaust survivors, 324n23
homocathexis, 29–32
homophile movement, 147, 160
homophobia, 36, 78, 306n26
homosexuality, 6, 19–59, 220, 238, 240, 254, 308n15; code for, 31; definition of, 19–24, 30–32, 164; developmental gender split, 35–47; diagnosis of, 147–48; identity, 19–59; Indiana study, 26–30; "medicalization" of, 21–22, 23, 150; psychiatry and, 20–22; sexual expression of gay sensibility and, 47–56; stigmatization and, 24–26, 29; terminology, 19–24, 30–32, 304n5
"homosexual panic," as legal defense, 36
hope, and relationships, 218–21
hopelessness, 230, 249; AIDS/HIV and, 92–93, 107; relationships and, 221–25, 230, 231, 233, 249, 252
hormones, sex, 39
hospital visitations, 26

housing discrimination, 60, 63
hugging, 241
Hugo, Victor, 259, 263; *Les Misérables*, 259
Human Rights Campaign (HRC), 250, 251, 252, 331*n11*, 332*n12*
humiliation, 36, 37, 38, 44, 137
husbands, 58
hyperactivity, 150

IBS, 176, 322*n21*
Ibsen, Henrik, 266; *A Doll's House*, 272
Idaho, 210
identity, 136, 139, 160, 204, 224, 237, 265, 266; role confusion vs., 137–38
identity crisis (term), 119
identity vs. role confusion, 137–38
immigration, 74, 81, 82, 217
inborn traits, 120
independence, 125, 210, 212
Indiana University study on homosexuality, 26–30
industry vs. inferiority, 135–36
informal privileges, 26–30; Indiana study, 26–30
initiative vs. guilt, 132–34
insertive anal sex (IAI), 52, 53, 54, 91, 313*n29*
insomnia, 170
insurance benefits, 26, 169, 206, 322*n11*
integration, 216
internal and external coherence, struggle between, 47–50
International AIDS Conference (1996), 14
Internet, 5, 89, 101, 112, 129, 162–64; addiction, 183; dating, 163, 221; pornography, 239
intimacy, 37, 91, 109, 130, 204, 218, 219, 224, 238, 242; isolation vs., 139–41; objectification vs., 162
intravenous drug users (IVDUs), 67
in utero, life in, 37

iPrEx, 114
isolation, 81, 104, 116–17, 119, 130, 135, 144, 149, 157–68, 170, 184, 207, 224, 310*n5*; adolescent, 157–58; AIDS/HIV and, 159–68; alcohol abuse and, 183–85; emerging from, 186–216; four stages of recovery, 200–216; intimacy vs., 139–41; as obstruction to self-discovery, 157–68; older-group men, 158–59, 165–68; post-trauma, 204–205; technology and, 162–64; trauma and, 157–68; younger-group men and, 160–65

Janet, aunt, 270–71, 272, 275–76, 287
John, Elton, 90
Johnson, Magic, 91
Johnston, Matthias, life and times of, 5, 8, 256, 257–98, 299, 300, 301, 302
*Journal of Health Communication*, 108
Juilliard, 289, 290, 292
Justice Department, U.S., 62

Kaiser Family Foundation, 63, 112
Kennedy, Brett, 161, 163
Kennedy, John F., assassination of, 262
Kinsolving, Lester, 65–67
kissing, 26, 241; on the cheek, 26, 27, 28; French-, 26, 27; in public, 26, 27
Krafft-Ebing, Richard von, *Psychopathia Sexualis*, 20–21
Krellenstein, James, 113

Lacan, Jaques, 301
Laguna Beach, California, 200, 201, 203, 204, 206
Lambda Legal, 292
Laramie, Wyoming, 62
Latino Americans, 81–82, 83, 226–27

lawyers, 268, 270

legal rights, 16, 26, 58, 60, 147, 186, 292; gay marriage, 26, 28, 58, 99, 186, 218, 221, 225, 249–56

lesbians, 21, 27, 28, 62, 147; Indiana study, 27, 28

Let's Kick Ass, 311*n12*

Lexapro, 156

LGBTQ people, 30, 57–58, 112, 250, 292, 307*n2*; hate crimes, 60–62; marriage and, 249–56; terminology, 30–32

libido, 305*n18*

lipodystrophy, 83, 86–87, 311*n11*

Lifton, Robert Jay, 179, 196, 197

Lincoln, Abraham, 186

literature, psychological, 20–21, 35

Little Rock, Arkansas, 5

London, Jack, 261, 264

loneliness, 71, 95, 101, 104, 129, 170, 220, 230, 254, 273

Los Angeles, 61, 115, 161, 190, 295, 299

Los Angeles Philharmonic, 295

*Los Angeles Times*, 61

loss, 189–98, 226; of attraction, 245–49; death of parents, 6, 178–79, 190, 196, 197; emerging from, 186–216; four stages of recovery, 200–216; of relationships, 233–34; romance of, 234; trauma, 189–98; *see also* death

love, 34, 52, 218, 219; "being in," 27, 28; "blinded by," 99; cathexis, 29–32; inability to, 69; Indiana study, 26–30; unconditional, 233


male camaraderie, 235–36, 241, 242

"man's man" role, 38–39

marginalization, 188

marriage, 16, 99, 136, 218, 249–56; conventional models of, 250, 252, 253, 254, 255; declining rates, 249; equality, 99, 218, 225, 249–56; gay, 26, 28, 58, 99, 186, 218, 221, 225, 249–56; interracial, 218; unhappy, 133, 178, 231, 249, 252

Mason, 288–92, 295, 299

Massachusetts Institute of Technology, 67

masturbation, 81, 242

Mattachine Society, 254

media, 30–31, 77, 112; on AIDS, 65–67, 77, 78, 88, 90; on hate crimes, 61; LGBT, 112

"medicalization" of homosexuals, 21–22, 23, 150

Medius Institute for Gay Men's Health, 205

Meet Up, 203, 327*n15*

methamphetamine, 93

metrosexual, 56

Mexico, 82

middle-group men, 77, 78, 87–97, 104, 114, 140, 141, 160, 198, 312*n15*; AIDS/HIV and, 87–97; condom use, 89–92; sex lives of, 87–97

middle school, 197

Middletown, Connecticut, 265, 269

military, 136; gays in, 99; veterans, 188, 205, 326*n11*

mind, shared, 249

minority groups, 74, 148, 161, 254; shame and, 78–79

miscegenation, 218

Mr. Right, 230

money, 236, 241, 275

monogamy, 249, 253

Monopoly, 245, 247

mother, 10, 22, 24, 70, 91, 100, 122–23, 171, 211, 220, 226–29, 231–32, 330*nn3*–4; death of, 6, 10, 178–79, 190–92, 197, 210, 266–67; developmental gender split and, 41–147; disapproval of gay son, 61–62, 70–72, 94–95, 123–25, 152–54, 155, 167, 186, 223, 257–65, 276, 280–84, 288; divorce, 133; grief and guilt, 177–79, 181

movies, 89

MTV, 90
muscled aesthetic, 161–62
mushrooms, 210–11
music, 42, 44, 45–46, 69, 71, 72, 178, 192, 288, 289, 290

Nagarjuna, 266
Names Quilt, 325*n11*
narcissism, 307*n28*, 330*n5*
National Academy of Sciences, 1986 report on AIDS, 67
National AIDS Memorial Grove, 325*n11*
National Gay and Lesbian Task Force, 292
nature vs. nurture, 120
Nebraska, 89, 262, 263, 293
Nebraska University, 263
negotiated safety, 111–12, 315*nn35–36*
Neptune Society, 13
Netherlands, 22
New Hampshire, 154, 156
New Orleans, 85
New Testament, 297
New York, 8, 151, 154, 161, 177, 261, 262, 272, 273, 274, 289, 290, 291, 292, 299, 300; Chelsea, 23, 254, 255
*New Yorker, The*, 9
*New York Times, The*, 30, 31, 67, 287, 301
New York University, 274
nostalgia, 128, 129
numbing, psychic, 185, 191, 196–98, 200, 325*n6*
nurture vs. nature, 120

Oakland, California, 189, 227, 276
Obama, Barack, 62
obesity, 169, 246, 247, 282
objectification, 162–64, 246–47, 331*n9*
Ohio, 24
older-group men, 15, 58, 76–77, 78, 80–87, 99, 104, 106, 113, 116, 132, 138, 140, 141–42, 145, 198, 251, 255, 310*n5*, 312*n15*; AIDS/HIV and, 80–87, 99, 106, 141–43, 159, 165, 200–204; ego integrity vs. despair, 142–43; generativity vs. stagnation, 141–42; grief and guilt, 168–85; health care, 80–81; isolation and, 158–59, 165–68; sex lives of, 81–87
online dating, 163, 221
oral contraceptives, 115
oral sex, 107, 263, 305*n15*, 311*n13*, 313*n30*, 314*n30*; condoms and, 107, 313*n30*
orgasm, 238, 239
ornamentation, 55
*Out of Africa* (film), 7
outsiderness, 135–36, 160, 252, 253, 261, 266
Owen, Wilfred, 169
*Oxford English Dictionary*, 31, 32

pancreatic cancer, 4, 82
panic attacks, 176, 275
paradise lost, 129–30
parallel process, 232
parents, 77, 91–92, 136, 231–32, 330*nn3–4*; death of, 6, 178–79, 190–92, 196, 197, 210, 211–12, 266–67; developmental gender split and, 41–47; disapproval of gay son, 61–62, 70–72, 94–95, 124–25, 152–54, 155, 167, 186, 223, 226, 227, 229, 257–65, 276, 280–84, 286, 297–98; divorce, 133; Eight Ages of Man, 119–45; grief and guilt, 177–79; homosexual identity and, 24–26; neglect by, 123–26; *see also* family; father; mother
pathologizing of gay people, 147–48
pedophilia, 20
peers, 39, 112, 135, 143, 157, 187, 197, 208, 223, 258
Pence, Mike, 289

penis, 56, 113; circumcision, 163, 313*n29*; size, 163
PEP, 206
perfectionism, 69, 233
perversion, 20–21
pets, 192–94, 195, 257, 258
Pew Research Center, 249
pharmaceuticals, 16, 64, 103, 149–51, 206, 321*nn9–10*, 322*n12*; antidepressants, 64, 149–50, 189, 320*n9*, 321*nn9–10*; bipolar, 155; birth control pill, 115; culture of, 103, 150; HAART treatment, 14, 16, 75, 76, 78, 89, 90, 103, 113, 164–65, 166, 182, 206, 314*n31*, 317*n15*, 325*n11*, 328*n20*; industry, 150, 321*n9*, 322*n11*; PrEP, 105, 113–15, 206, 312*n27*, 316*n44*
philosophy, 266
phone apps, 79, 93, 101, 102, 162–64
photography, 270, 275
physical assault, 60–62
physical fitness, 161–62
physical types, 54–55, 245–46; attraction and, 245–47; sex and, 54–55
planes, 263, 267–68, 270, 275, 277–80, 285, 292, 293–94, 295–96, 299–300
plastic surgery, 162
play, sexual, 242–45, 331*n9*
pornography, 51, 239, 242
Portland, Maine, 268
post-traumatic stress disorder (PTSD), 146–47, 150, 158, 168, 318*nn2–4*
power, 237, 238, 331*n8*
pregnancy, 23, 107, 115, 259
PrEP, 105, 113–15, 206, 313*n27*, 316*n44*
prevention, HIV, 106–15, 117, 292; Condom Code legacy and, 105–15; negotiated safety, 111–12; PrEP, 105, 113–15, 206, 313*n27*, 316*n44*; social marketing approach, 108–109

primary-care physicians, 64–65, 81
productivity, 135–36, 141
projection, 24
promiscuity, 6, 29–30, 73, 131, 138, 140
prostitution, 67
Proust, Marcel, 263; *Remembrance of Things Past*, 260
Provincetown, Massachusetts, 268–70, 272, 294, 297
psychiatry, 20–22, 116, 146–47, 158, 186, 197, 203, 208, 236, 240, 316*n2*; diagnosis, 146–57; Eight Ages of Man, 119–45; stigmatization by, 147–49
psychic numbing, 185, 191, 196–98, 200, 325*n6*
*Psychopathia Sexualis* (Krafft-Ebing), 20–21
puberty, 137–38
public displays of affection (PDA), 26–30, 60; Indiana study, 26–30
public health, 108, 133; HIV prevention approaches, 106–109
pupillary dilation, 306*n24*

queer movement, 35, 56

race and racism, 74, 78, 100, 101, 102, 136, 137, 185, 217–18, 292; AIDS/HIV and, 78–79, 292; miscegenation, 218
rape, 60, 182
Reagan, Nancy, 74
Reagan, Ronald, 65–68; response to AIDS crisis, 65–68, 90
receptive anal sex (RAI), 52–56, 78–79, 313*n29*, 327*n13*; AIDS/HIV and, 78–79, 109, 132; shame and stigma, 78–79, 109, 132, 238
reconnection, 209–16
recovery, 186–216, 327*n13*; emerging from trauma, loss, and isolation, 186–216; four stages of, 199–216; paradigm, 199; Stage Four: working

recovery (*cont.*)
    through, 209–16; Stage One:
    emerging from isolation, 204–205;
    Stage Three: grieving and talking
    through, 207–209; Stage Two:
    safety, 205–207
reenactment, 125–27
reengagement, 121–22, 127
regression, 121–22, 125–26
regret, 9
rejection, 40, 57, 59, 84, 116, 137,
    226, 241
relationships, gay, 6, 26, 34, 72,
    217–56, 265–98, 299–302;
    adolescent, 219, 221, 223–24,
    225–26, 233, 252, 263–65;
    asexual, 241; balance in, 237–38;
    between positive and negative
    men, 8–12, 79, 82–87, 91, 98, 99,
    102, 124–27, 294, 323n23;
    Condom Code legacy and, 104–17,
    140; fantasy about, 230–34, 243;
    fear and, 225–30; and feelings of
    failure, 223, 228, 229, 231, 241;
    gay marriage, 249–56; grief and
    guilt, 168–85; heterosexual
    models, 219, 220, 225, 235, 250;
    hope and, 218–21; hopelessness,
    221–25, 230, 231, 233, 249, 252;
    inside-out process, 235; intimacy
    vs. isolation, 139–41; longevity,
    219–20; loss of, 233–34; loss of
    attraction, 245–49; middle-group
    men, 87–97; older-group men,
    80–87; reconnection, 209–16; sex
    and, 239–49; shared mind, 249;
    ways that work in, 235–38;
    younger-group men, 97–117,
    249–56
religion, 23, 55, 90, 259, 284
repression, 196, 197, 200
resilience, 157, 172, 188, 200, 243
retirement, early, 141
Robb, 5, 7–14, 15, 294–98, 299, 300,
    301, 302
Rofes, Eric, 117
role confusion vs. identity, 137–38

sadism, 20
safety, 60, 205–207; Condom Code
    legacy and, 105–15; hate crimes
    and, 60–62; HIV prevention,
    106–15; Stage Two in recovery
    process, 205–207
Salt Lake City, Utah, 210
San Antonio, Texas, 276, 278, 279,
    280–85
San Francisco, 17, 24, 64, 65, 70, 81,
    82, 89, 92, 100–102, 147, 151, 154,
    161, 170, 171, 175, 176, 178, 182,
    189, 190, 192–94, 200, 201, 202,
    206, 210, 211, 212, 222, 226, 261,
    262, 272, 273, 300; Castro, 23,
    101, 117, 161, 163, 254, 255
San Jose, California, 226
San Jose State University, 226
Schopenhauer, Arthur, 266, 325n5
Scruff, 162
secrecy, 69, 81, 255; older-group
    men, 81
self-acceptance, 5, 6, 17, 300–302
self-confidence, 37, 69, 243; lack of,
    68–73
self-discovery, 104–105, 146–85, 255,
    256; diagnosis as obstruction to,
    146–57; grief and guilt as
    obstruction to, 168–85; isolation as
    obstruction to, 157–68; life and
    times of Matthias Johnston,
    257–98
self-doubt, 5, 68–73, 138, 207,
    224–25, 226, 274; autonomy vs.,
    130–32; shame and, 68–73
self-esteem, 251
self-loathing, 5, 59
self-sufficiency, 212, 213
separation anxiety, 133
serotonin reuptake inhibitors (SSRIs),
    320n9
sex, 23, 50–56, 269, 277, 290
    305n15; ABC, 248; addiction, 69,
    70, 183; adolescent, 45, 50, 72,
    95–96, 139–40, 223–24, 227, 238,
    239–40, 242, 248, 263–64, 266;
    balance and, 237–38; at baths,

69–72; bottom identity, 53–54, 55, 56, 78–79; Condom Code legacy and, 105–17, 140; diminishing, 238–45, 331n8; frottage, 107, 305n15; gay-on-gay shaming and, 104–17; high-risk, 53–54, 81, 92, 112, 113; identity vs. role confusion, 137–38; importance of, 74; interest, 242–45; intimacy vs. isolation, 139–41; loss of attraction, 245–49; middle-group men, 87–97; novelty and, 238, 239, 242, 248; objectified, 162–64, 246–47, 331n9; older-group men, 81–87; phone apps, 162–64; physical type and, 54–55; play, 242–45, 331n9; position, 52–56, 78–79, 91, 109, 237, 313n29, 327n13; promiscuity, 29–30; reasoned, 74; relationships and, 238–49; "safer," 112; shame and 69–72, 73–74; societal construction of sensibility and, 57–59; split-off, 239, 247; sport, 51–52, 238–40, 242, 245, 247; talking about, 240–41; top identity, 53–54, 56, 91, 210; "unsafe," 107, 111, 115; versatility and, 54–56; younger-group men, 97–117; *see also* anal sex; oral sex

shame, 9, 21, 37, 60–74, 78–79, 88, 139–40, 151, 156, 158, 166, 167, 180, 207, 218, 241, 247, 251, 301, 302, 310n4, 327n13; AIDS/HIV and, 78–79, 82–87, 103, 104–17, 131–32, 160, 199–200, 201–202; autonomy vs., 130–32; Condom Code legacy and, 105–15, 140; definition of, 68–69; developmental gender split and, 38; gay-on-gay, 104–17; minority groups and, 78–79; PrEP, 113–15, 206; receptive anal sex and, 78–79, 109, 132, 238; self-doubt and, 68–73; sex and, 69–72, 73–74; sex at baths and, 69–72; social marketing and, 108–109

shared mind, 249
Shepard, Matthew, 62
Shepard Byrd Hate Crimes Prevention Act (2009), 62
shopping addiction, 183
siblings, 190, 258, 280–84; death of, 123, 190–92, 194, 197
"silence is death," 327n13
smartphones, addiction to, 183
Socarides, Charles, 147, 319n5
social marketing, 108–109, 314n32
social media, 33
society, 17–18, 22, 23, 30, 143, 147, 188, 207, 247, 255, 327n13; American, 255; construction of sex and sensibility, 57–59; erotophobic, 247–48; gay-on-gay shaming, 104–17; gay marriage and, 249–56; gay men's relationships in, 217–56; hate crimes, 60–62; intimacy vs. isolation, 139–41; reconnection, 209–16; role confusion vs. identity, 137–38; stigma and shame, 60–74
South Carolina, 17
Speakes, Larry, 65–67
speech, 52, 60; flatness of affect, 189, 191
Spitzer, Robert, 147, 319n5, 320n5
split-off sex, 239, 247
sports, 42, 44, 135, 190, 231, 235
sport sex, 51–52, 238–40, 242, 245, 247
Sport Sex Club, 51
stagnation vs. generativity, 141–42
Staley, Peter, 105
stereotypes, male-gender, 29
steroids, 161
stigmatization, 6, 15–17, 21, 50, 57, 60–74, 75, 77, 78–79, 103, 147, 187–88, 204, 209, 217–18, 251, 277, 304n5, 310n4; AIDS/HIV, 78–79, 82–87, 103, 104–17, 131–32, 160, 199–200, 201–202; consequences of, 63–65; Eight Ages of Man, 119–45; gay-on-gay, 104–17; hate crimes, 60–62; homosexual identity and, 24–26, 29;

stigmatization (*cont.*)
  minority groups and, 78–79;
  psychiatry and, 147–49; Reagan's
  response to AIDS crisis, 65–68;
  receptive anal sex and, 78–79,
  109, 132, 238; relationships and,
  225–30; self-, 64; shame and,
  68–74
Stonewall riots, 75, 80, 138, 159, 274
"straight-acting," 23–24
Strindberg, August, 266
submission, 52
substance abuse, 63, 64, 65, 68, 93,
  94, 144, 180, 183–85, 324*n26*,
  325*n26*; *see also* addiction; *specific*
  *substances*
success, 122, 219
suicide, 32, 63, 68, 151, 154, 195–96,
  222, 260–61, 308*n15*; alcohol
  abuse and, 184, 185
Supreme Court, U.S., 26, 115, 217–18;
  on gay marriage, 26, 185, 218, 250,
  251; on miscegenation, 218
survivor guilt, 134, 180–81, 322*n23*,
  323*n23*, 324*n23*
symmetry, 237
syntonic experience, 98, 99


TAG (Treatment Action Group), 132,
  292
talent, 135
talking through, 207–209, 329*n23*
teachers, 77, 260, 261, 262, 263,
  264
technology, 103, 104, 162–64; phone
  apps, 79, 93, 101, 102, 162–64
television, 88, 90
Tennessee, 254
testing, AIDS/HIV, 76, 77, 93, 98,
  107, 110, 187, 314*n31*
testosterone, 161
Texas, 62, 220, 257, 258, 259, 276,
  278, 279, 280–85
theater, 266, 272, 274, 285, 287
Thoreau, Henry David, 312*n25*
thoughtfulness, 230

tops, 39, 52, 53–54, 91, 163, 210,
  237; AIDS/HIV and, 91; identity,
  53–54, 56, 91
torture, 62
transgender people, 62
trauma, 5, 6, 15, 121, 127, 143–44,
  186–216, 325*n11*, 327*n13*, 328*n22*;
  AIDS/HIV, 6–7, 8–16, 65–68, 77,
  80–87, 141, 187–88, 199–216;
  constrictive defenses, 196–98, 211;
  definition of, 187–89; early-life, 5,
  6, 11, 15, 16–17, 61–62, 70–72, 77,
  123–36, 144, 152–56, 167–68,
  171, 177–81, 187, 190–92, 196–98,
  210, 211–12, 257–65, 276, 277,
  280–84; Eight Ages of Man,
  119–45; emerging from, 186–216;
  four stages of recovery, 199–216;
  grief and guilt, 168–85; hate
  crimes, 60–62, 147; isolation and,
  157–68; late-life, 6, 142–43, 144;
  loss and, 189–98; middle-group
  men, 87–97; older-group men,
  80–87; psychic numbing and,
  196–98, 200; Stage Four: working
  through, 209–16; Stage One:
  emerging from isolation, 204–205;
  Stage Three: grieving and talking
  through, 207–209; Stage Two:
  safety, 205–207; younger-group
  men, 97–117; *see also specific types*
  *of trauma*
tribes, gay, 162–63
tripartite communities, 75–117,
  310*nn3–4*; AIDS/HIV and, 75–78,
  82–117; Condom Code legacy and,
  105–15, 140; defined, 76–79;
  gay-on-gay shaming, 104–17;
  middle-group men, 77, 78, 87–97;
  older-group men, 15, 58, 76–77,
  78, 80–87; younger-group men, 77,
  78, 97–117, 249–56
Trojan horse, 301, 302
truck stop sex, 95–96
Trump, Donald, 103, 306*n28*, 307*n28*
trust, 121, 124, 144, 158, 165–66,
  208; AIDS/HIV and, 130; basic

trust vs. basic mistrust, 128–30; childhood and, 123–25, 128–30, 144; development of capacity to, 124, 128–30, 144; lack of, 123–26, 128–30, 144, 198
truthfulness, 253
Truvada, 105, 114, 206, 313n27, 316n44
Twain, Mark, 260
Twinks, 162

UCLA, 295
unconscious, 50, 53, 55, 97, 121, 208–209, 240, 246
unisex clothing, 56
University of Arizona, Tucson, 100
University of California, Berkeley, 81
University of California, San Francisco, 81
University of California, Santa Cruz, 190, 193
Utah, 210

vacations, 154
vaginal sex, 56, 78, 107, 140, 247
versatility, and sex, 54–56
veterans, combat, 188, 205, 326n11
Vietnam War, 205, 326n11
Voelcker, John, 205
vomiting, 317n15
vulnerability, 36, 37, 38, 46, 48–49, 52, 97, 119, 120, 124, 127, 198, 219, 226, 264, 266; younger-group men, 97–117

Walmart, 284
Watchtower, The, 68
Weinstein, Michael, 115
Wesleyan University, 263–68, 272
West Hollywood, 255
white supremacists, 62
wholeness, 47, 48, 52, 59, 172, 197, 208, 247
Wisconsin, 40
Wittgenstein, Ludwig, 266, 272
"womanly woman" role, 38–39
women, 35, 51, 53, 55, 57, 235–36, 239, 268, 276–77, 306n25; assertive, 57; birth control pill, 115; choice of partner, 55; developmental gender split, 35–39; gaydar, 35–36; unintelligible nature of, 236, 239
working through, 209–16, 329n23
World War II, 8
Wyoming, 62

Xanax, 176

younger-group men, 77, 78, 97–117, 119, 120, 138, 140, 145, 187, 237, 249–56, 312n15; AIDS/HIV and, 97–117, 160–65; Condom Code legacy, 105–15; gay-on-gay shaming, 104–17; isolation and, 160–65; marriage and, 249–56; phone apps and, 162–64; PrEP and, 113–15, 206; relationships, 97–117, 249–56; self-discovery, 104–105; sex lives of, 97–117